Multimodal Literacies in Young Emergent Bilinguals

NEW PERSPECTIVES ON LANGUAGE AND EDUCATION

Founding Editor: Viv Edwards, *University of Reading, UK*

Series Editors: Phan Le Ha, *University of Hawaii at Manoa, USA* and Joel Windle, *Monash University, Australia.*

Two decades of research and development in language and literacy education have yielded a broad, multidisciplinary focus. Yet education systems face constant economic and technological change, with attendant issues of identity and power, community and culture. What are the implications for language education of new 'semiotic economies' and communications technologies? Of complex blendings of cultural and linguistic diversity in communities and institutions? Of new cultural, regional and national identities and practices? The New Perspectives on Language and Education series will feature critical and interpretive, disciplinary and multidisciplinary perspectives on teaching and learning, language and literacy in new times. New proposals, particularly for edited volumes, are expected to acknowledge and include perspectives from the Global South. Contributions from scholars from the Global South will be particularly sought out and welcomed, as well as those from marginalised communities within the Global North.

All books in this series are externally peer-reviewed.

Full details of all the books in this series and of all our other publications can be found on http://www.multilingual-matters.com, or by writing to Multilingual Matters, St Nicholas House, 31–34 High Street, Bristol, BS1 2AW, UK.

NEW PERSPECTIVES ON LANGUAGE AND EDUCATION: 105

Multimodal Literacies in Young Emergent Bilinguals

Beyond Print-Centric Practices

Edited by
Sally Brown and Ling Hao

MULTILINGUAL MATTERS
Bristol • Jackson

DOI https://doi.org/10.21832/BROWN2354
Library of Congress Cataloging in Publication Data
A catalog record for this book is available from the Library of Congress.
Names: Brown, Sally Ann, editor. | Hao, Ling, editor.
Title: Multimodal Literacies in Young Emergent Bilinguals: Beyond Print-Centric Practices/Edited by Sally Brown and Ling Hao.
Description: Bristol, UK; Jackson, TN: Multilingual Matters, 2022. | Series: New Perspectives on Language and Education: 105 | Includes bibliographical references and index. | Summary: "This book presents research focused on young emergent bilingual children's multimodal meaning-making processes in diverse cultural and linguistic settings. Each chapter includes practical pedagogical recommendations, making it an essential resource for using multiple modes to teach literacy with diverse student populations"— Provided by publisher.
Identifiers: LCCN 2021060902 (print) | LCCN 2021060903 (ebook) | ISBN 9781800412347 (paperback) | ISBN 9781800412354 (hardback) | ISBN 9781800412378 (epub) | ISBN 9781800412361 (pdf)
Subjects: LCSH: Education, Bilingual. | Literacy—Study and teaching (Elementary) | Reading (Elementary)
Classification: LCC LC3725 .M86 2022 (print) | LCC LC3725 (ebook) | DDC 370.117/5—dc23/eng/20220223
LC record available at https://lccn.loc.gov/2021060902
LC ebook record available at https://lccn.loc.gov/2021060903

British Library Cataloguing in Publication Data
A catalogue entry for this book is available from the British Library.

ISBN-13: 978-1-80041-235-4 (hbk)
ISBN-13: 978-1-80041-234-7 (pbk)

Multilingual Matters
UK: St Nicholas House, 31–34 High Street, Bristol, BS1 2AW, UK.
USA: Ingram, Jackson, TN, USA.

Website: www.multilingual-matters.com
Twitter: Multi_Ling_Mat
Facebook: https://www.facebook.com/multilingualmatters
Blog: www.channelviewpublications.wordpress.com

The policy of Multilingual Matters/Channel View Publications is to use papers that are natural, renewable and recyclable products, made from wood grown in sustainable forests. In the manufacturing process of our books, and to further support our policy, preference is given to printers that have FSC and PEFC Chain of Custody certification. The FSC and/or PEFC logos will appear on those books where full certification has been granted to the printer concerned.

Typeset by Nova Techset Private Limited, Bengaluru and Chennai, India.

Contents

Contributors

Moneerah M. Al Jabr is a PhD candidate in Curriculum and Instruction, Early Childhood Education, at Southern Illinois University Carbondale. She is also a lecturer at King Faisal University in Saudi Arabia. She has taught pre-service early childhood teachers and supervised their student teaching. Moneerah co-founded an after-school program to teach Arabic to children aged 5–10 in Southern Illinois. Her research interests include early literacy, multimodality, translanguaging and integrating technology in literacy instruction.

Adriana Alvarez is Assistant Professor in the Culturally and Linguistically Diverse Education program in the School of Education and Human Development at the University of Colorado Denver. Her research interests center on biliteracy development and pedagogy, multimodality and project-based learning in bilingual settings, and family-school partnerships, all with a focus on equity-oriented and strength-based approaches in Latinx communities. Adriana was a bilingual teacher for 11 years in the border community of El Paso, Texas, prior to receiving her PhD in Educational Equity and Cultural Diversity from the University of Colorado Boulder.

Laura Ascenzi-Moreno is an Associate Professor and the bilingual program coordinator at Brooklyn College, City University of New York. Laura was a bilingual teacher, literacy coach and new teacher mentor in New York City public schools for over a decade. At Brooklyn College she works with pre-service and in-service teachers to support their development as critical practitioners. Her research is focused on the literacy development of emergent bilinguals, the literacy assessment of emergent bilinguals, the development of teacher knowledge, and how these intersect with equity.

Ysaaca Axelrod is an Associate Professor in the Department of Teacher Education and Curriculum Studies in the College of Education at the University of Massachusetts, Amherst. She works with pre-service early childhood and elementary education teachers. Ysaaca is a former kindergarten teacher. Her research interests are in early childhood language and literacy development, with a particular focus on emergent bilingual children and the intersections between language and identity development.

Heidi R. Bacon is an Associate Professor of Language, Literacies and Culture in the School of Education at Southern Illinois University Carbondale. A former high school teacher and K-12 reading specialist, she currently teaches courses in disciplinary literacies, literacy leadership, practitioner research and qualitative research methods. Heidi's research focuses on literacy identities, disciplinary literacies in STEM education, culturally responsive and sustaining pedagogies, and home, school and community engagement using narrative inquiry, discourse analysis and critical theories and methods.

Leslie C. Banes, PhD, is an Assistant Professor at California State University, Sacramento. She spent five years as a bilingual teacher in the US and Spain. Leslie's research features equity in mathematics education, the relationship between mathematics and language, bilingual education and teacher professional learning.

Kristin Bengtson Mendoza teaches literature, writing and language to newcomer English learners at Wilbur Cross High School in New Haven, CT. After spending time in Guatemala as a Fulbright Scholar, she began her teaching career in 2005 as a New York City Teaching Fellow in Brooklyn, and has since taught elementary, middle and high school in New Haven. In 2020 Kristin was named New Haven Teacher of the Year and a CT Teacher of the year semifinalist. She is passionate about immigrant rights, advocating for undocumented students and families, restorative practices and supporting new teachers.

Sally Brown is a Professor of Literacy Education at Georgia Southern University, where she teaches undergraduate and graduate students. She holds a PhD in Language and Literacy from the University of South Carolina and worked as a public school educator for over 13 years. Sally's research focuses on helping emergent bilingual students successfully navigate literacy learning in English-only classrooms. This involves the use of multimodal approaches including technology. She is the author of *Digital Initiatives for Literacy Development in Elementary Classrooms: Engaging Research and Opportunities* (IGI Global, 2017). In addition, her most recent publications can be found in *The Reading Teacher*, *Early Childhood Education Journal* and the *European Early Childhood Education Research Journal*.

Emily Brown Hoffman is an Assistant Professor in Early Childhood Education at National Louis University. She examines how early childhood educators can implement equitable curriculum and instruction in order to provide genuine learning that affirms children and all their identities. Emily is committed to investigating sustainable education and professional development ventures that support the positive, daily interactions between students and teachers that are fundamental to children's early development.

Min-Seok Choi is a PhD candidate in Teaching and Learning at The Ohio State University. His research interests include multilingual students' learning and use of literacy practices, identity construction and academic literacy development in and out of school contexts. Min-Seok's current research examines the roles of imagination in international students' second and academic language socialization.

Fernanda Coelho Liberali holds a PhD in Applied Linguistics and Language Studies from the Pontifical Catholic University of São Paulo (PUCSP) and is a teacher educator, researcher and professor at the same institution. Presently she works at the Department of Language Sciences and Philosophy, at the Department of Applied Linguistics and Language Studies and at the Department of Education. Fernanda is the leader of the Research Group Language in Activity in the School Context (CNPq), and of the Study Group on Bi/Multilingual Education (GEEB). She has a research productivity scholarship from CNPq and her main research interests are related to language education, bilingualism and Vygotskian theories.

Julianne M. Coleman is a Professor at The University of Alabama in the Department of Curriculum and Instruction. Her research interests are elementary literacy teacher education at Pk-6 level, visual literacy and comprehension of multimodal science texts.

Mayra Cruz has been the proud Principal of Oyster-Adams Bilingual School (a 2020 National Blue Ribbon school) since July 2014. Mayra has served the students of Washington, DC, since 2009. She began her career in DC Public Schools as a sixth grade English language arts teacher at Columbia Heights Education Campus (CHEC) where she helped develop the dual language program for the middle school. In 2012, she was awarded the Excellence in Teaching Award by DCPS and the DC Public Education Fund and in 2020 she was awarded the Terrel H. Bell Award by the US Department of Education for outstanding school leadership.

Aijuan Cun is an Assistant Professor of Literacy Education in the Department of Language, Literacy and Sociocultural Studies at the University of New Mexico. Her research interests focus on literacy practices of immigrant and refugee children and families, multimodality, family and community literacies, and makerspaces. Aijuan's research can be found in journals such as *Early Childhood Education Journal* and *Pedagogies: An International Journal.*

Chunhua Dai is a doctoral candidate in Language and Literacy Education in the School of Teaching and Learning at the University of Florida. She worked as a lecturer for three and a half years in a college in China before her journey to obtain a PhD degree. Chunhua's research interests include investigating young children's play and their literacy development, adults' play perception and its impact on their practice, children's multimodal languaging, emergent and multimodal writing and translanguaging theories.

Cecilia M. Espinosa is an Associate Professor at Lehman College/CUNY. Cecilia was first a teacher assistant in a preschool and later on a bilingual-multiage teacher and director of a dual language program in Phoenix, Arizona. She works with bilingual teachers, birth–sixth grade, and teaches courses on biliteracy, where she infuses descriptive processes and a critical perspective on children's literature. Cecilia's research focus is on bilingual children's writing and children's literature that affirms and nurtures children's multiple identities. She is a member of the NYCWP, a committee member of the NCTE's Charlotte Huck Award and an Associate Investigator of CUNY IIE.

Lorraine Falchi is an Early Childhood Coach at the New York Early Childhood Professional Development Institute. Her research examines multilingual children's participation in multimodal literacies within educational settings and professional development support for early childhood educators' culturally responsive practices. Lorraine was a bilingual teacher and director of a dual language bilingual preschool. She designs professional learning support for early childhood practitioner research and practice with a focus on play and language, literacy and fostering children's positive social identities.

Marisa Ferraro is an Assistant Professor of Languages, Literacies and Cultures in the Department of Curriculum and Learning at Southern Connecticut State University. Her teaching interests include inclusive and transformative pedagogies for emergent bilinguals, biliteracy and multimodal literacy practices. Her research also includes the analysis of instructional discourses that create and sustain highly engaged practices that reimagine learners' classroom identities for social and cultural participation. Marisa works closely with teachers and administrators to support the education of emergent bilingual students by problematizing the inequities and challenges of educational systems.

Ruth Flores Bañuelos is currently a bilingual kindergarten teacher. She received her bilingual credential and MA in Education from the University of California, Davis. As a native Spanish speaker in English-only schools, she was a frequent recipient of attempts intended to dissuade her from using Spanish and discourage her from valuing her bilingualism. Now, as a teacher in a dual language program, Ruth is passionate about exploring ways to support her students in fostering a positive view of their own bilingual identities.

Brittany Frieson is an Assistant Professor of Literacy and Anti-racist Education at the University of North Texas in Denton, TX. She is an interdisciplinary scholar whose work traverses applied linguistics, literacy and bilingual education. Her primary research interests center on exploring the language and literacy practices of young Black American children in dual language bilingual education programs from critical perspectives. Brittany currently teaches literacy courses on culturally and linguistically diverse youth from a critical approach in the undergraduate and graduate programs at UNT.

Ling Hao is a Graduate Assistant in the Teaching and Learning PhD program at the University of South Carolina-Columbia. In addition to being a full-time doctoral student, Ling teaches Chinese preschool and elementary level students in Columbia. She received her Master's degree from the University of Florida with a specialization in English/Reading Education. Ling's research focuses on exploring emergent bilingual children's multimodal meaning-making processes and promoting the literacy development of students with diverse cultural and linguistic backgrounds. She has presented research at the Literacy Research Association and the Whole Language Umbrella.

Sara Hawley works at the UCL (University College London) Knowledge Lab, teaching MA and BA Digital Media students. Her research covers literacy in the digital age, learner agency and digital divides, looking at new ways to theorize the debate about technology in schools so that it reflects issues of equity and social justice. Sara's PhD, 'The sociomateriality of literacy, a study of the relationship between institutions, identity and the internet in a primary classroom', analyzed the digital literacy practices of 8–9 year olds. Sara previously worked in an inner London primary school as a teacher and assistant headteacher.

Cláudia Hilsdorf Rocha is a Professor in the Applied Linguistics Department at the University of Campinas, Brazil. She holds a PhD in Applied Linguistics and her main fields of interest include translanguaging, critical language education, (new/multi) literacies and education technology. Cláudia leads the research group E-lang (CNPq) and her current research is on academic literacies and language learning in digital environments.

Tracey S. Hodges is an Assistant Professor at The University of Alabama in the Department of Curriculum and Instruction. Her research interests are writing instruction in the middle grades focusing on teacher beliefs, instructional practices and preservice teacher preparation. Tracey is also interested in reading instruction, focusing on the integration of discipline-specific content and perspective-taking into the reading curriculum.

Kyungjin Hwang is a doctoral candidate in Language and Literacy at the University of South Carolina. She is a former English teacher at middle and high schools in South Korea. She currently works as an executive assistant at the Bilingualism Matters Center @ UofSC, which supports research and events to promote awareness about bilingualism. She also serves as a Korean teacher for Korean-American children at a community language school, particularly making an effort to devise and implement methods to allow bilingual children to use their semiotic and linguistic resources for their creative and critical meaning-making. Kyungjin's primary research interests include ESOL/bilingual education, language ideology, translanguaging, multimodal literacy and teaching reading and writing for emergent bilinguals.

Jerae H. Kelly is a doctoral candidate in the Special Education program at the University of Maryland, College Park. Her research interests include exploring the role sociocognitive variables play in reading comprehension and building cultural competency in pre-service special education teachers. Before pursuing her doctorate, Jerae was a special education middle school teacher for three years in Baltimore City public schools.

Lisa Kervin is a Professor of Language and Literacy Education in the Faculty of the Arts, Social Sciences and Humanities at the University of Wollongong. Lisa co-leads the 'Educated Child' strand of a national Centre of Excellence for the Digital Child and leads the UOW node (which includes the Children's Technology Play Space, a living laboratory for the center). She is the director for Early Start Research at UOW. Her current research interests are focused on young children and how they engage with literate practices and she is currently involved in research projects funded by the Australian Research Council focused on adult and child interactions when using technology, young children and writing, and digital play.

Ted Kesler is Associate Professor and directs the pre-service graduate program in Elementary Education in the Elementary and Early Childhood Education Department of Queens College, CUNY. His research interests include reader response, multimodal literacy, critical literacy and children's non-fiction. Ted's most recent book is *The Reader Response Notebook: Teaching Towards Agency, Autonomy, and Accountability* (NCTE, 2018). You can find out more at www.tedsclassroom.com and @ tedsclassroom.

Susan Lutz Klauda is a faculty specialist in the Reading Engagement and Diversity (READ) Lab at the University of Maryland, College Park and an Adjunct Professor in the Education Department at The Catholic University of America, Washington, DC. Susan's research centers on the interplay of cognitive, affective and social processes in children's literacy development and classroom interventions that strengthen children's reading comprehension and engagement.

Josh Lawrence is a Professor in the Department of Education at the University of Oslo. He conducts research on child and adolescent language and literacy development. Josh teaches courses on quantitative research methods and reading interventions.

Alison Lehner-Quam is an Assistant Professor and the Education Librarian at Lehman College, New York. Previously, Alison served as director of the resource center and publications at Lincoln Center Institute. At Lehman College, Alison teaches information literacy sessions, creates research guides, develops and maintains children's and education book collections and provides individual research support for students. Her areas of research include explorations into the information literacy experiences of teacher education students as well as inquiry into the impact of culturally and linguistically relevant children's book experiences on children and teacher candidates.

Zhuo Li currently works as an English instructor in the Center for Language Education at the Southern University of Science and Technology, China. She obtained her PhD in ESOL/Bilingual Education from the University of Florida, USA. Zhuo's research interests include cross-cultural communication, multiliterate approaches to language learning, and applying educational technology to second language acquisition and foreign language learning with a focus on English language learning through computer games.

David E. Low is an Associate Professor at California State University, Fresno. A former high school English teacher and cartoonist in Tucson, AZ, his research explores how critical multimodal literacy practices are enacted in robustly pluralistic settings. David's recent work has appeared in *Written Communication*, *Research in the Teaching of English*, *Pedagogies*, *Gender and Education* and *The Critical Literacies Handbook*.

Mary B. McVee is a Professor of Literacy Education and Director of the Center for Literacy and Reading Instruction at the University of Buffalo, The State University of New York. Her research traverses: positioning theory, social and embodied learning; digital literacies and multimodality; narrative, disciplinary literacies in engineering for children; and diversities of language, literacy and culture. Mary is Chair of the Semiotics in Education SIG of the American Educational Research Association. Her most recent book, co-authored with Lisa Roof, is *The Experiences of Refugee Youth from Burma in an American High School: Countering Deficit-based Narratives through Student Voice* (Routledge, 2020).

Carmen Liliana Medina is Professor of Literacy, Culture, and Language Education at Indiana University, Bloomington. Her research examines literacy/biliteracy as decolonial, social and critical practices, performative pedagogies and Latinx children's literature. For the past 10 years, Carmen has returned to Puerto Rico, engaging with children and teachers in critical literacy work as emerging decolonial knowledge production at the intersection of local and transnational social issues. Her recent publications include two books: *Literacy, Play and Globalization: Converging Imaginaries in Children's Critical and Cultural Performances* (Routledge, 2014) and *Methodologies of Embodiment: Reinscribing Bodies in Qualitative Research* (Routledge, 2015).

Antonieta Megale holds a PhD in Applied Linguistics from Unicamp, completed a doctoral internship at the University of Viadrina (Germany) and has a Master's degree in Applied Linguistics from PUC/SP. Antonieta is currently the bilingual education graduate program coordinator at Instituto Singularidades, where she also works as a Professor of the undergraduate program in Education.

Jessica Zacher Pandya is Dean and Professor in the College of Education at California State University, Dominguez Hills. A former kindergarten teacher in the California Bay Area who received her PhD at UC Berkeley, Jessica's research focuses on children's literacy and identity work in diverse urban classrooms. Her latest book is the co-edited *Handbook of Critical Literacies* (Routledge, 2021).

Vivian Presiado is an Assistant Professor of Bilingual and Bicultural Education in the School of Teaching and Learning at Illinois State University. She was an early childhood teacher for 10 years, primarily in bilingual/ELL classrooms, which informed her research interests. Vivian's initial work focused on Mexican-American students and families, with research also being conducted in elementary schools in Mexico. Her research is focused on exploring family literacy, multimodal literacy and bilingual education from a critical perspective.

Pengtong Qu is a doctoral candidate in Literacy, Culture and Language Education at Indiana University, Bloomington. Her research interests are in biliteracy, family literacy and multicultural children's literature.

Laura Schall-Leckrone, an educational linguist, is an Associate Professor and Director of the TESOL and bilingual education program in the Graduate School of Education at Lesley University in Cambridge, MA. Laura worked as a bilingual educator and curriculum director in K-12 urban and suburban schools. She is currently engaged in a linguistic ethnography of a multilingual elementary school in a gateway community in the northeastern United States.

Jill Scott began her teaching career as a kindergarten teacher and a literacy coach. She is currently a doctoral candidate in Literacy, Culture and Language Education at Indiana University where she teaches preschool and early elementary literacy courses. Jill's research interests are in early literacies, multiliteracies and teacher education.

Qi Si is a PhD student at The University of Alabama in the Department of Curriculum and Instruction. She is a former K-12 foreign language teacher. Her research interests are elementary literacy education, bilingual education, multicultural education and multimodal literacies in educational practices.

Marjorie Siegel is Professor of Literacy Education in the Department of Curriculum & Teaching at Teachers College, Columbia University. Her current research examines multimodality in school spaces, with a focus on transmediation. In collaboration with Stavroula Kontovourki, Marjorie has developed an analytic lens, 'performative semiotics,' for tracing the entanglement of performing schooled literacy and multimodal sign-making. This work is presented in Kontovourki and Siegel (2021) '"B is for Bunny": Contested sign-making and the possibilities for performing school literacy differently', published in *Reading Research Quarterly*.

Ana Taboada Barber studies reading comprehension from a cognitive and motivational perspective. Her work focuses the influence of cognitive, linguistic and motivation variables on the literacy and language development of students of diverse language backgrounds. As a former ESL teacher, Ana's work in reading comprehension development is principally concentrated within the population of Emergent Bilinguals (EBs) within the United States, but recently she has included Chilean Spanish-English speaking bilingual children. Her attention has also turned to the possible roles of executive functions, as one component of a larger system of self-regulation, in the reading comprehension of EBs and bilingual students.

Buyi Wang is an Assistant Professor in the English Department, School of Foreign Languages and Literature of Beijing Normal University. She is interested in bilingualism and creativity, English writing instruction and

English education in EFL contexts. Buyi's dissertation is entitled 'Translanguaging practice, the creative mind of bilingual scholars'.

Colleen E. Whittingham is an Assistant Professor of Reading and Elementary Education at UNC Charlotte. Colleen completed her doctoral degree in Literacy, Language and Culture at the University of Illinois at Chicago, where she served as a research assistant at the UIC Center for Literacy and the UIC Reading Clinic. Colleen's research investigates literacy events that position students as agentive learners in early childhood classrooms, and the factors that mediate academic success and teacher-child interactions in such classrooms. She considers how meaning-making can be prioritized in present early literacy contexts.

Karen Wohlwend is Professor of Literacy, Culture and Language Education at Indiana University, Bloomington. Her research reconceptualizes young children's play as an embodied literacy that produces action texts made with moving bodies or animated avatars, whether in dramatic play centers, video games, digital animation apps or live-action filmmaking. Karen's recent publications include the research methods book, *Literacies that Move and Matter: Nexus Analysis for Contemporary Childhoods* (Routledge, 2021).

Junyi Yang is a doctoral student in the Department of Education at the University of Oslo. Her research focuses on the language and literacy development of bilingual children. Junyi is currently working on a longitudinal study of Chinese-Norwegian bilingual children's home literacy environment and language development.

Shih-Fen Yeh was a Principal of Natural Way Children's School in Taiwan. She established the ESL program in preschool and kindergarten for 10 years. She acquired her PhD in Literacy from the University of Florida, USA. Shih-Fen's research interests are in biliteracy education, children's emergent writing and reading, cultural identity and second language acquisition.

Xiaodi Zhou is an Assistant Professor of Literacy Studies at the University of Texas Rio Grande Valley. He received his PhD in English Education from the University of Georgia and has interests in translanguaging theory and practice with emergent bilinguals, as well as writing engagements with cultural and linguistic minorities, especially with Mexican American youths. Xiaodi is a believer in Bakhtin's dialogic theory as well as Bhabha's notion of cultural hybridity and Anzaldúa's bordered identity for conceiving of languages and cultures.

Foreword

Together, we recently edited a special issue of *English Teaching: Practice & Critique* which featured articles theorizing multimodality through children's and youths' perspectives. The work we presented was intended to serve as an antidote to social semiotics research that is too often (and too far) removed from the contexts in which multimodal literacies are most excitingly enacted, in spaces populated by children and youth. In our opening editorial, we remarked that:

> Each of us has our own children, and as we struggled to teach, write, and think during the pandemic, we also watched our own children and the multimodal literacies they demonstrated, and remembered that we were fundamentally interested in how children think, what they know, and what they might teach us about multimodality (instead of the other way around). (Low *et al.*, 2021: 127)

The book you are now reading, edited by Sally Brown and Ling Hao, has transported us directly back into that feeling and those questions.

The chapters that compose the volume do much, as a linked collection of essays, to teach us about multimodality by anchoring that teaching in what and how children think and know. From authors who explore translanguaging in preschool settings to those who focus on elementary or out-of-school contexts, the book's contributors steadfastly commit to honoring emergent bilingual children's sophisticated ways of making and representing meaning with-and-across an astounding array of semiotic registers. The progression of the chapters focusing on educational contexts from the early childhood years through to the primary grades reminds us of the critical role educators play in ensuring that our pedagogical practices are responsive to our learners. Taken as a whole, this book reads as a love letter to the communicative creativity and agency of young multilingual learners as they envision and narrate the world anew.

One of the more unique contributions of Brown and Hao's edited volume is that it features global perspectives on emergent multilingualism as an epistemological throughline. While principally concerned with children's multimodal literacy enactments, the book's editors and contributors make a strong case that age is but one of many intersecting factors that must be attended to by researchers of young people's multimodal literacies. Children's home languages, family backgrounds, national origins and cultural identities all play crucial interrelated roles in their practice of multimodal literacy, whether print-based, on screens or in physical/material spaces with sociopolitical implications. The complexity of the work of an educator has never been greater.

As is the case with many studies of emergent bilinguals, linguistic hegemony serves as an imposing backdrop throughout the book. Numerous authors actively remind readers of the persistent deficit ideologies that follow multilingual children into schools in the form of curricular policies that treat monolingualism, monomodal print texts and white suburban ways of knowing as inviolable gold standards – labeling all else as inferior. No ideology can show children love or respect when it tells them that their identities are incompatible with the business of learning, and asks them to muzzle their communicative preferences out of subservience to standardization. Some of this book's power, then, comes from speaking back to an oppressive power dynamic that willfully misconstrues linguistic diversity as a pathology to be diagnosed and remediated.

Coming from a shared asset-based approach, the authors of this volume unite to show the emancipatory possibilities of culturally sustaining pedagogical approaches that recognize children themselves – their interests, cultures, languages, legacies and communities – as the most vital ingredient of any curriculum. Only when children are allowed and encouraged to be their whole selves, to bask in the richness of their communicative traditions and multimodal inventions, can teachers design classroom spaces that truly honor the promise of diverse and equitable schooling. With *Multimodal Literacies in Young Emergent Bilinguals: Beyond Print-Centric Practices*, educators have been handed a compelling plan for attaining this promise. We give thanks to the editors, the chapter authors and, above all else, the children, for what they teach us about multimodality.

David E. Low, *California State University, Fresno*
Lisa K. Kervin, *University of Wollongong*
Jessica Zacher Pandya, *California State University*

Reference

Low, D.E., Pandya, J.Z. and Kervin, L.K. (2021) Guest editorial: Theorising multimodality through children and youths' perceptions and experiences. *English Teaching: Practice & Critique* 20 (2), 125–129. doi:10.1108/ETPC-06-2021-192

Introduction

Ling Hao and Sally Brown

In this digital age, children are exposed to different modalities at a young age. Literacy education should not be print-centric. This book draws upon multimodality and social semiotics to understand the ways in which multiple modes of learning are used to teach literacy in early childhood contexts. The chapters push for a change in view of what counts as literacy and what is valued, especially when working with diverse populations. Issues of access to learning opportunities and constraints on traditional assessments are highlighted.

The series of chapters showcases the changing natures of languages and literacies globally. A multimodal approach provides a framework for rethinking what it means to be literate in the 21st century. This book's uniqueness stems from the coupling of multimodal literacy and young emergent bilinguals. It expands traditional notions of literacy to include other ways of representing and learning. For example, the role of images becomes a central tool for meaning-making, especially for students who are working to learn English as a new language. Each chapter informs teachers, teacher leaders, literacy researchers and graduate students about ways to promote an expanded view of literacy development where student assets are built upon to promote positive literate identities and learning experiences. We provide culturally sustaining pedagogical possibilities for using multimodal approaches to teach literacy with early childhood students learning multiple languages, thus impacting the daily lives of diverse learners as they try to navigate challenging settings where oral and written language is prioritized.

For the purposes of this book, emergent bilinguals (EBs) are students who are learning their home language and an additional language (usually English) simultaneously at a young age. In 2009, García renamed English language learners (ELLs) as 'emergent bilinguals', in order to stress the importance of developing children's bilingualism and avoid categorizing ELLs as either limited English proficient or English proficient. Internationally, teachers often view EBs with a deficit view and focus on what they do not know rather than what they know, which limits children's bilingualism development.

The Purpose of This Book

This book presents research focused on young emergent bilingual children's multimodal meaning-making processes in diverse cultural and linguistic settings. It aims to extend what is known in the field of multimodal literacy.

In this book, we address the following questions:

- In what ways are emergent bilinguals using multiple modes and culture to make sense of literacy events?
- How are multimodal multicultural texts being used to support the literacy development of emergent bilinguals in a variety of contexts?
- How does a multimodal approach support the composing processes of diverse young emergent bilinguals?
- How are multiple languages and pictures used as mediational tools for cultural constructions of personal experiences and the use of imagination?
- What role does translanguaging play in multimodal learning activities?
- How are the cultures, languages and experiences of young learners utilized as assets in a multimodal curriculum?
- How are the identities of emergent bilinguals impacted by multimodal practices?
- What are the challenges of multimodal literacy teaching?
- What are the practical implications of multimodal authoring or composing for preschool–fourth grade?

The chapters in this volume were selected to offer a unique insight into one of the four contexts organizing the book: preschool, kindergarten, primary grades and out-of-school contexts. The purpose is to change the ways in which current teachers enact literacy practices with emergent bilingual students and to inform teacher candidates who are enrolled in teacher education programs across the world. This book may be used as a course textbook to provide readers with insights into diverse early childhood classrooms and to add to a knowledge base about teaching literacy with marginalized populations that often go unrecognized by school systems. The end goal is to make a difference in the lives of children as they engage in daily classroom literacy events.

An Overview of Chapters

The book opens with a synthesis of research regarding the impact of multimodal literacies on emergent bilingual students' literacy and cultural identities. Next, the book is organized into four parts based on children's age groups: Preschool (Chapters 2–7); Kindergarten (Chapters 8–10); Primary Grades (Chapters 11–19); and Out-of-School Contexts (Chapters 20–22).

The students featured in the chapters range in age from 3–10 and represent various language groups, including Black English, Spanish, Mandarin, Portuguese, Arabic, Norwegian and Korean languages. The chapters include perspectives from areas of the United States where students are relegated to English-only policies and practices, as well as studies from China, London, Brazil and Norway. Individual chapters specifically address pedagogical issues that connect back to theory and ultimately impact literacy instruction and the policies guiding what gets counted as literacy in diverse spaces.

In Chapter 1, a synthesis of literature on emergent bilingual children's multimodal literacy practices provides foundational knowledge about the field. The authors outline and analyze different studies on bilingual children's cultural awareness and identity shaping through multimodal practices in PK–6 contexts. The authors conclude that multimodal literacies are effective tools in supporting children's language development and identity construction and developing various competences in school and out-of-school contexts.

Part 1 presents six chapters about preschool children's multimodal practices. Chapter 2 features a four-year-old bilingual Korean child's classroom play and his use of multimodal resources with other children. Through nexus analysis, the authors argue that 'young bilinguals' play narratives and classroom participation are supported by a nexus of multimodal interactions with other children, toys, furniture, the physical environment, and teachers' provision of materials and time through routine and repetition' (pp. 17–18).

Chapter 3 presents a four-year-old Chinese-English speaking child's multimodal and multilingual home literacy practices. Grounded in translanguaging and superdiversity theories, the authors find that the girl creatively uses her linguistic resources, gestures and spatial resources in her biliteracy development process. This chapter provides insights into understanding young children's biliteracy development from a holistic perspective that includes 'learners' languages, dialect, gestures, intonations and knowledge of space and direction, as well as body language' (p. 44).

Chapter 4 highlights two Black four-year-olds' collaborative multimodal narrative composition with plastic animals and blocks in an urban Head Start classroom. Guided by multimodal meaning-making, linguistic authenticity, cultural knowledge and identity construction theories, the authors discuss the questions of 'What counts as narrative?' and 'Whose narratives count?' as they analyze the children's storytelling during play.

Chapter 5 examines emergent bilingual children's multimodal and multilingual practices in a Head Start classroom and a second-grade class and prioritizes the children's agency and complex language use. Situated within translanguaging and multimodality, the authors find that the children use their language repertoires and translanguaging based on their preference and for their aims. This chapter highlights the flexibility of children's translanguaging and multimodal practices as the children navigate diverse linguistic and cultural settings.

Chapter 6 explores different multimodal ways to teach Chinese preschool children in Beijing and Taiwan. Guided by new literacies and multimodality, the authors design various activities including dramas, stories, music and drawings for the children to understand solar terms and discuss the dialogic interaction of the modalities.

Chapter 7 introduces the Brazilian educational context and stresses the needs to challenge monolithic and monolingual ideologies in Brazilian education. The authors call for a politically engaged and socially, culturally and linguistically just language education through critical multimodal literacy. The authors showcase *going to bed* activities in a preschool English class in an underprivileged community in Brazil and explain how different modes like singing, dancing and playing enhance children's funds of *perezhivanie*. This chapter informs audiences how multimodality could be utilized to promote a socioculturally transformative and plurilingual education as well as to support emergent bilingual children's meaning-making process.

The three chapters in **Part 2** focus on children's multimodal practices at kindergarten levels. Chapter 8 depicts a multimodal storytelling activity in a bilingual kindergarten. During the storytelling activity, the Latinx children in the kindergarten utilize various communication modes available to them in their meaning-making and composing process. From a translanguaging perspective, this chapter demonstrates bilingual children's learning and engagement in the story genres through multiple modalities. The author suggests that the semiotic resources of oral and written languages, material objects, movement and drawing support emergent bilingual children's multiliteracy development.

Chapter 9 presents an integrated view of translanguaging and multimodality as an approach to teaching emergent bilingual children. Drawing upon data from two classroom vignettes in urban communities with Latinx students, this chapter depicts multimodal read-alouds with young bilingual children, and a community of teachers and researchers discussing ways of incorporating play into literacy instruction. The authors suggest a teaching plan for multimodal and multilingual experiences to enrich children's play and value children's linguistic repertoire.

Chapter 10 describes bilingual identity construction in a Spanish-English dual language program in a kindergarten. The authors develop and implement a three-phase multimodal pedagogical approach to help the children explore their bilingual identities. The authors conclude that multimodal resources like portraits, music and drawing help the children communicate their ideas about bilingualism and construct their bilingual identities.

In **Part 3**, nine chapters portray the meaning-making processes of children from primary grades (1–4) through multiple modes. Chapter 11 investigates how teachers use creative drawings and artifacts as ways to discover and integrate children's lives and experiences in the classroom. Drawing from a multimodal social semiotics lens, the author presents two studies on first-grade Spanish-English speaking bilingual children's drawings and family storybooks. The author argues that multimodal creations are a source for engaging emergent bilingual children's funds of knowledge. This chapter demonstrates that children's multimodal expressions can be used as a tool for promoting biliteracy development and understanding funds of knowledge.

Chapter 12 presents two bilingual Arabic-dominant 7-year-old children's retelling in multiple modes using an iPad app. The authors compare the children's oral retelling and digital retelling scores and find that digital tools provide opportunities for children to interpret stories while creating their own stories. They conclude that 'creating stories in multiple modalities enhanced Layla and Rosa's oral language, literacies and social interaction' (p. 169).

Chapter 13 exhibits the narrative composing process of second grade bilingual students. The author applies a multimodal approach to writing instruction and showcases a three-phase composing workshop. The results show that explicit teacher instruction about words, art and design is significant in transforming knowledge, developing children's semiotic landscapes and fostering their metalinguistic awareness.

Chapter 14 foregrounds a STEERS model of literacy as a new way to theorize literacy and integrated multimodal perspectives. A STEERS model of literacy 'highlights the importance of sponsors, tools, emotions, experiences, reflexivity and syncretism' (p. 187) and bridges the home and school literacy practices. The author presents third- and fourth-grade bilingual students' use of an online technology platform and investigates how the social and material become woven in sharing the students' literacy practices. The author calls for a STEERS model of literacy to tackle social injustice.

Chapter 15 portrays stories of refugee children from Burma. The authors examine three bilingual children's use of multiple semiotic resources to make sense and tell their family stories. Guided by positioning theory and the social semiotics multimodal perspective, the authors find that the children position themselves in different ways and present their family's culture, religion and educational backgrounds through their multimodal creations. This chapter empowers the voices of refugee children and their families through their multimodal artifacts.

Chapter 16 explores bilingual children's multimodal flexibility in a Spanish/English dual language program. Utilizing translanguaging and multimodal literacies as theoretical frameworks, the authors investigate how the multilingual children use multimodal resources to navigate their social worlds. This chapter presents two ethnographic case studies on elementary-aged African American children's use of translanguaging and multimodal resources in their language and literacy practices. The authors conclude that 'translanguaging, gestures, artifacts and visuals served as devices that facilitated learning and interaction for multilingual Black girls to navigate and explore their identities as literate and capable enactors of knowledge' (p. 221).

Chapter 17 delineates a missing piece of understanding EBs' comprehension of multimodal narrative texts. The authors build upon Theory of Mind to highlight emergent bilingual children's social awareness. This chapter shows how characteristics of multimodal texts can leverage bilingual children's Theory of Mind skills and facilitate their comprehension.

Chapter 18 shares an ethnographic case study about fourth-grade linguistic diverse bilingual learners' multimodal literacy practices. Drawing upon a literacy engagement framework, the authors present how bilingual learners engage with graphic text production and how these multimodal literacy practices promote the learners' identity construction and language development.

The last chapter in the primary grades section provides sociomaterial insights into a young African student's multimodal literacy experiences in an English-only school setting. The research applies the concept of learning stories to highlight the child's assets as a meaning-maker and storyteller. The implications provide insight into the ways teachers can document the learning growth of EBs.

In **Part 4**, the chapters focus on EBs' multimodal practices in out-of-school contexts. Chapter 20 exhibits a parent-reported survey of Chinese-Norwegian bilingual children's multimodal literacy resources and practices at home across age and language dominance. The multimodal resources available for children include print-based and screen-based resources. By analyzing the books and apps mentioned by parents, the authors conclude that children utilize multiple modalities to make meaning and learn languages at home.

Chapter 21 portrays how two emergent bilingual children use multiple modes to understand and produce multimodal texts. The author explores the EBs' multimodal activities based on the concepts of meaning functions, transmediation and synesthesia. This chapter sheds light on the multiple modes emergent bilingual children leverage as they make sense of the digital multimodal texts.

Chapter 22 showcases a bilingual family's multimodal interaction and meaning-making in a science museum. Built on multimodality, this chapter explains how the family creates learning opportunities by utilizing multimodal resources and interacting with the exhibits. The author focuses on a Korean first grade child and his family members' meaning-making as they read signage texts in the museum.

Early childhood professionals will find this book invaluable as a tool for expanding the way literacy is conceived and ultimately ensuring literacy success for diverse learners. Insights into various original research studies help readers understand the many avenues one can take as a practitioner. In other words, the chapters are filled with a plethora of practical suggestions and implications. The book is truly the ultimate resource on using multiple modes to teach literacy with diverse student populations.

Reference

García, O. (2009) Emergent bilinguals and TESOL: What's in a name? *TESOL Quarterly* 43 (2), 322–326.

1 A Synthesis of How Multimodal Literacies Impact Emergent Bilingual Students' Literacy and Cultural Identities

Qi Si, Tracey Hodges and Julianne Coleman

Multimodal literacies, also referred to as visual literacies, digital literacies and new literacies in different research contexts, are studied by literacy education scholars to investigate how students make meanings across the disciplines (Lapp *et al.*, 2012; McTigue & Flowers, 2011). Generally, multiliteracy scholars have shown that including various types of literacies increases students' comprehension and knowledge (Bernstein, 2017; Shin, 2014). Bilingual scholars have noted that including multimedia helps students learn in their first and second language (Brown, 2016; Chang & Martínez-Roldán, 2018). However, a gap in the studies is left unexplored regarding how multimodal literacies impact emergent bilingual students' literacy and cultural identities development.

Multimodal literacies include all types of formats that contain and convey information in both print-based and digital texts (Sanders & Albers, 2010). In recent decades of research studies, multimodal literacies have been widely used in various K-12 educational settings, such as classroom instruction in multiple subjects, programs held outside of school spaces and within bilingual family settings (McVee *et al.*, 2017; Zhao & Hewitt, 2020). With multimodal literacies, teachers can engage bilingual students in meaningful ways to develop their literacy and/or bilingual skills and help students to experience cultural differences (Lotherington & Jenson, 2011). Although plenty of research studies (e.g. Catalano *et al.*, 2020; Pacheco & Hamilton, 2020) focus on bilingual children's literacy abilities, fewer studies summarize and analyze the approaches of multimodal literacies in the facilitation of emergent bilinguals' development of literacy skills and cultural identity. Thus, the purpose of the current study is to provide a synthesis and analysis of multimodal literacy practices to support the development of bilingual children in PK-6 classrooms and other learning contexts. These findings would be beneficial to early childhood teachers, literacy and bilingual education field researchers and bilingual families. The current study aims to answer the following research questions:

(1) How can multimodal literacies effectively facilitate emergent bilinguals in literacy development?
(2) How can multimodal literacies support emergent bilinguals in cultural identity development?

Theoretical Framework

We draw upon three theoretical perspectives to inform the present study. The social semiotic theory (Jewitt, 2008; Kress, 2003, 2010) guides multimodal literacies studies in meaning-making modes, while the sociocultural theory and translanguaging theory help researchers to understand bilinguals' literacy and cultural identity development (García, 2009; Vygotsky, 1980).

Social semiotic theory suggests that meaning can be made through different modes – not just the written word (Jewitt, 2008). Central to this theory is that multiple literacies (New London Group, 1996) are supported through various modes such as sound, color, image, action and gesture. These modes are organized sets of semiotic resources for making meaning, with language-based modes being one (Jewitt, 2008; Kress, 2003). The linguistic modes can be used in concert with other modes (Kress, 2010), as opposed to being the primary mode of communication. Thus, in light of the social semiotic theory, communicative message composers make choices to use various modes that are shaped by sociocultural factors to contextualize communication. Additionally, multimodal messages can vary in content and thus vary in interpretations for different audiences beyond just linguistic meanings (Serafini, 2012). As such, the social semiotic theory affords more opportunities for message creation and thinking beyond the use of linguistic or language-based modes of communication.

Sociocultural theories are informed by the work of Vygotsky (1980), who explained that students learn from more knowledgeable others (MKOs). This is particularly important for emergent readers and writers who are beginning to learn the foundational skills of literacy from skilled readers and writers. Additionally, bilingual students are learning these foundational skills simultaneously in their native and second language, so having high-quality models to learn from is critical. Additionally, sociocultural theories are informed by students' Zone of Proximal Development (ZPD; Vygoktsky, 1980), which suggests that students can increase their knowledge by the amount of difference between them and the MKO.

When considering multiliteracies, teachers should think about students' literacy skills, their comfortableness with digital and visual texts and their linguistic skills in both the first (L1) and second language (L2). Finally, sociocultural theories encourage collaboration, developing efficacy and fostering positive social and cultural connections among students (Bandura, 1986; Perry, 2012; Prior, 2006). Particularly with the linguistic demands of bilingual learning, students need opportunities to practice, receive feedback and learn from others. Emergent bilinguals would benefit from collaborating with peers through their understanding of multimodal texts with a range of academic skills and abilities, as well as from opportunities to co-construct knowledge with the teachers.

The monolingual instruction orientation, which aims to use L2 only in class teaching and learning, is dominant in most K-12 bilingual education or L2 immersion programs (Cummins, 2019). However, translanguaging pedagogy encourages using L1 in L2 expression to represent comprehension and support meaning-making. García (2009) stated that translanguaging pedagogy allows communication across linguistic and cultural boundaries in our complex community. Built on this perspective, young learners employ all the linguistic resources they have acquired to produce multiple language meanings, which are commonly seen in oral expression and writing (Bauer *et al.*, 2017). Additionally, translanguaging is a 'culturally relevant, non-deficit additive approach that affirms and validates the hybrid language identities and practices' (Aquino-Sterling & Rodríguez-Valls, 2016: 74). Thus, translanguaging helps teachers scaffold instruction by combining students' L1 skills with their developing L2 language proficiency and cultural identities.

Methods

In this systematic literature review (Cooper, 2015), we analyzed the pool of research on multimodal literacies as tools to support emergent bilinguals from 2000 to 2020. In the following sections, we detail by literature search procedures, screening process and coding procedures.

Data collection

Initially, we conducted a search using academic databases to retrieve journal articles published between 1 January 2000 and 1 August 2020. Specifically, we located journal articles through EBSCO/ERIC and Web of Science. From our search, we retrieved 553 academic pieces and removed 370 duplicates, resulting in 183 pieces for title and abstract screening procedures. In order to locate as many articles as possible, we searched combinations of terms focused on multimodal literacies and emergent bilinguals in different keyword combinations, which resulted in eight searches (see Table 1.1).

Table 1.1 Search terms and record retrieved breakdown

Search terms	**EBSCO/ERIC**	**Web of Science**	**Total records retrieved**
'multimodal literacies' + 'emergent bilingual'	47	16	63
'digital literacies' + 'emergent bilingual'	27	9	36
'multimodal literacies' + 'ELL'	50	7	57
'digital literacies' + 'ELL'	172	15	187
'visual literacies' + 'emergent bilinguals'	39	9	48
'visual literacies' + 'ELL'	154	8	162
Total with duplicates	489	64	553
Duplicates	–	–	370
Total remaining	–	–	**183**

To determine the articles that best answered our research questions, we conducted two rounds of screening. We conducted the first round of screening the title and abstract with the retrieved 183 articles by using the following four inclusion criteria: (a) written in English; (b) published in peer-reviewed journals; (c) focused on teaching or learning with multimodal literacies; and (d) participants of research were emergent bilinguals (birth through sixth grade). In this round, 127 pieces were eliminated because: (a) not journal articles ($n = 56$); (b) research on special education ($n = 1$); (c) not having a clear research process ($n = 9$); and (d) not focusing on emergent bilinguals ($n = 61$). We conducted the second round of screening the full text with the 56 remaining articles. In this round, 26 articles were eliminated because: (a) focus was not on emergent bilingual children ($n = 11$); (b) focus was not on instructional practices ($n = 1$); (c) practical or review studies ($n = 5$); and (d) focus was not on literacy or cultural identity development ($n = 9$). Therefore, 30 articles remained for coding procedures. Figure 1.1 shows our whole screening process.

Data analysis

To synthesize the findings from the retrieved 30 articles, we developed a heuristic for coding the information from those articles. The template included focused field, multimodal tool, learning setting, location, language, age/grade level, research question, research purpose, theoretical/conceptual framework, the methodology of data collection and analysis, key findings and implications for education. Further, we answered seven secondary questions that expand from the research questions through this coding procedure: (a) Is this research focused on literacy education or cultural identity development? (b) If the research topic is literacy

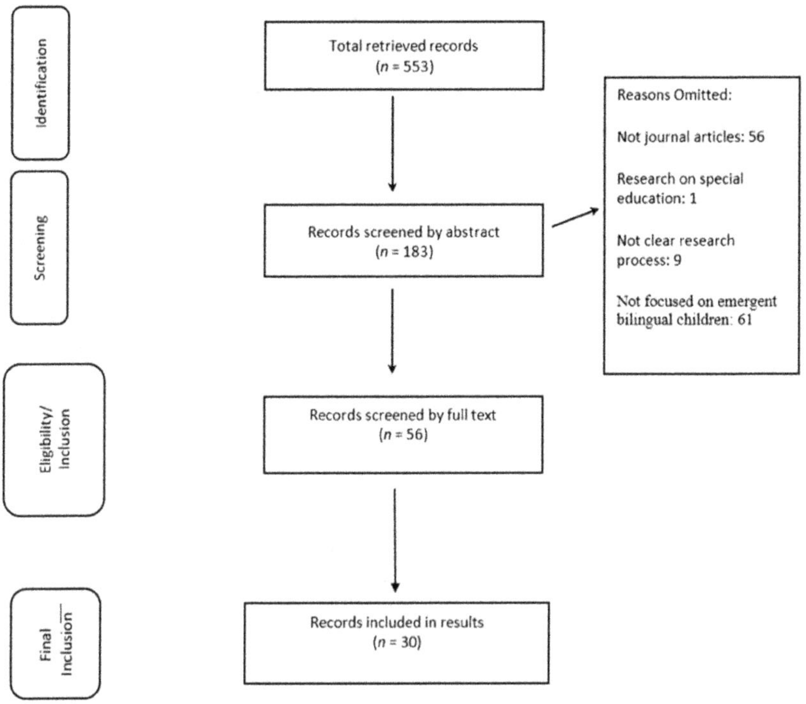

Figure 1.1 Study identification process

education, is this research focused on reading, writing or oral expression? (c) Is this research focused on single language or dual languages learning? (d) How does multimodal literacies support emergent bilinguals' development? and (e) What is the effectiveness of teaching and learning with the multimodal literacies? To answer these questions, we categorized the 30 articles into different groups and summarized the information about each in the findings of the current study.

Findings

In this section, we report our findings in two categories based on the coding of the 30 included articles: (a) descriptive characteristics of the studies; and (b) effectiveness of integrating multimodal literacies with bilingual children's literacy and cultural identity development.

Descriptive characteristics

The descriptive characteristics of the included articles present recent research trends about the learning practices of bilingual children with multimodal literacies. Specifically, we concentrated on the focusing areas,

Table 1.2 Descriptive characteristics of retrieved articles

Focusing areas	Learning contexts	Target languages	Classroom language choices	Type of multimodal literacies
Writing skills (n = 14) 46.7%	English monolingual classroom (n = 22) 73.3%	English literacy (n = 18) 60%	Target language only (n = 24) 80%	Digital texts (n = 20) 66.7%
Oral skills (n = 12) 40%	Dual language classroom (n = 5) 16.7%	Dual language (n = 5) 16.7%	Translanguaging (n = 6) 20%	Print-based texts (n = 4) 13.3%
Reading skills (n = 8) 26.7%	Outside school program (n = 4) 6.7%	First language other than English (n = 2) 6.7%		Both print-based and digital texts (n = 4) 13.3%
Cultural identity (n = 5) 16.7%	Bilingual family settings (n = 4) 13.3%			Body movements (n = 2) 6.7%

learning contexts, target languages, classroom language choices and type of multimodal literacies, as shown in Table 1.2.

The results may have overlaps because some studies fit into more than one subcategory. Overall, these findings indicate that multimodal literacies are more commonly used to support bilingual children's English literacy development, and teachers tend to use the target language only in class teaching. Also, digital literacies are more commonly used to support the development of emergent bilinguals.

Teaching and learning effectiveness with multimodal literacies

From the descriptive characteristics, multimodal literacies are being widely used within various bilingual teaching and learning contexts for multiple development.

English literacy development

Most of the retrieved articles that focused on literacy development investigated English literacy abilities in writing, reading and speaking. For example, Shin (2014) investigated a second-grade Spanish-speaking student who used a web-based blog to conduct English writing, which helped him engage more in schoolwork and increased his self-efficacy in English learning. Also, Martin-Beltrán and colleagues (2017) compared the students' reading achievement by using both digital and print-based English books. They found that K-5 students who read digital books became more engaged in text-based discussions, whereas students who read print books tended to generate more in-depth and longer responses. Moreover, Ntelioglou and colleagues (2014) investigated second- and third-grade classrooms where students practiced writing and speaking by adding audio narrations and pictures on PowerPoint files. In these studies, multimodal literacies provided opportunities for bilingual students to practice English literacy skills and helped them to gain confidence and motivation in the learning process.

Bilingual and home language development

Several retrieved articles focused on bilingual or home language instruction and practices. Sembiantea and colleagues (2020) observed two Spanish/English dual language program classrooms in a preschool, and discovered that teachers used sounds, images, gestures and other physical movements in a show-and-tell activity. The bilingual students are found to have effectively obtained linguistic consciousness orally in both languages through the activity. Additionally, in a third-grade after-school program, students who speak Chinese at home practiced their Chinese writing and speaking by using digital tools such as iPads and Wikispace. Students were observed practicing Chinese phonetic symbols, character strokes writing and science-oriented texts, writing on different digital tools. The digital literacies allowed them to check sound and character corrections on the app and encouraged them to interact with peers (Chang & Martínez-Roldán, 2018).

Cultural identity development

Five retrieved studies investigated educators using multimodal literacies to facilitate bilingual children's cultural identity development. In a third-grade English-only classroom, the Spanish-speaking students watched the Disney film *Cinderella* and expanded their connections beyond the film to issues of feminism, social justice and cultural comparisons (Ajayi, 2012). Ajayi (2012) found that some female students thought that women can be as powerful and independent as men and are not reliant upon men to support them, and some students compared the royal culture from the film to current US culture, specifically the role of democracy and equity. Also, Brown (2020) observed 12 second-grade students using a web-based platform to record their responses toward children's literature and engaged in dialogic interactions with peers. The students used informal language to interact with peers and compared their identities with the contents in the text. These studies indicate that bilingual students bring their linguistic resources and diversity into classroom activities and therefore affect their language learning and cultural identity development.

Discussion

The ability to articulate in more than one language to communicate and collaborate with others is essential for meeting the 21st century skills of students (Cruz, 2016). From the findings, various types of multimodal literacies were utilized in different kinds of literacy development, such as English literacy, bilingual literacy and home language learning. Compared to reading and speaking, writing needs more scaffolded and comprehensive skills. Specific to bilingual or L2 students, L2 writing requires bilingual students to use cross-linguistic skills in unison (Gort, 2006). Additionally, multicultural consciousness and cultural identity development are closely related to L2 learning (Stille, 2015). K-5 class instruction should consider extending language teaching to build cultural consciousness and identity development (Creese *et al.*, 2006). Our findings indicate that multimodal literacies are good tools to support language learning and identity shaping. The multimodal literacies used in classrooms and bilingual families expand bilingual children's cultural experiences and facilitate their sociocultural thinking (Park, 2018).

The traditional trend of language education tends to believe that using only the target language in class would be more helpful for students to learn and practice the language in an authentic context (Littlewood & Yu, 2011). However, translanguaging allows teachers and students to transfer meanings between languages. It provides more opportunities for bilingual children to demonstrate their comprehension and cultural consciousness, and brings educational equity to all students (Cummins, 2019; García, 2009). From the retrieved studies, multimodal literacies effectively facilitated bilingual children's learning in classroom and family settings. Dual language preschool teachers allowed students to interact in both English and Spanish to demonstrate their social consciousness and comprehension based on the information in a sociodramatic play; a Chinese immigrant family let their six- and eight-year-old children use multimodal texts, which included images, emoji stickers, voice messages and other visual formats on a social media app, to communicate with their Chinese speaking only family members (Bengochea *et al.*, 2018; Zhao & Hewitt, 2020).

From the findings of this study, the main types of multimodal literacies being used in bilingual education are digital literacies, such as videos, digital apps, online platforms, websites, web-based software and multimedia tools (Martinez-Alvarez, 2017; Rowe & Miller, 2016). The creative and practical modes of digital tools are more likely to attract young learners. These practices help emergent bilinguals establish literacy awareness and linguistic consciousness in both L1 and L2. Specifically, digital literacies can help younger children to develop their lingual awareness and build their emerging bilingual consciousness independently and socially (Harrison & McTavish, 2018). For older bilingual students, digital writing tools and drawing help to strengthen confidence toward writing and add more meaningful materials to express their thinking (Castañeda *et al.*, 2018; Chen *et al.*, 2017; Ntelioglou *et al.*, 2014). Bilingual students used multiple texts to show their comprehension of concepts, express their thinking, create bilingual meanings and engage in interactions with monolingual peers beyond English-only texts (Bengochea *et al.*, 2018; Rowe, 2018).

Although our findings indicate that digital modalities and digital literacies are most frequently used in various settings to support emergent bilingual children's development, other forms of multimodality such as visual, gestural, oral, textural and other modes can also effectively develop bilingual children's competences (e.g. Alvarez, 2018; Bengochea *et al.*, 2018; Sembiante *et al.*, 2020). Visual representations (e.g. drawing, pictures, graphs, tables, print-based texts, etc.) are found being used to support bilingual children in creating meaning. For example, some K-6 Sami-speaking students in Finland were observed in class practice creating a little six-page book with their drawings and written descriptions in English (Pietikainen & Pitkanen-Huhta, 2013). The Sami-speaking students practiced their English reading and writing skills during the book creation process. Also, visual representations such as scientific sketches and graphs can be integrated in content and language learning to scaffold bilingual children's visual thinking skills (Fernández-Fontechaa *et al.*, 2020). Beyond verbal and visual modes, actions and body movements can also serve as multimodal resources for bilingual preschoolers to engage in presentations through a classroom activity (Sembiante *et al.*, 2020). Therefore, emergent bilingual children can benefit from various multimodalities to improve comprehension and create meanings.

Implications

In bilingual education, multimodal literacies become effective tools to support teachers and parents to facilitate young bilingual children in various learning settings. From our findings, both digital and print-based texts are used to help emergent bilingual students develop literacy skills and cultural awareness. Thus, teachers are recommended to employ digital literacies as much as possible to scaffold content knowledge in different subjects and help bilingual students to improve comprehension and confidence in expressing their consciousness. Parents in bilingual families also can help their children to conduct L1 or L2 communication with family members on social media or using other digital apps to develop literacy skills in collaborative settings.

Furthermore, our search retrieved just over 500 articles that addressed this topic and only 30 that met our inclusion criteria. Therefore, the field is still emerging and limited, meaning that our findings should be taken in conjunction with future research to continue developing the field. Additionally, most retrieved studies employed qualitative research methods such as case studies, which reflect authentic learning settings and interactions and focus on highly specific samples or include small samples. However, they are not generalizable to indicate the effectiveness and outcomes of using multimodal literacies in teaching and learning to larger samples or education as a whole. Comparative data allow researchers to make comparisons and therefore to generalize to a larger population. Thus, we recommend that more comparative data should be brought into the field to understand how multimodal literacies can effectively facilitate bilingual children.

Limitations

Although detailed analysis has been provided from summarized scholarly works, the current study has limitations. First, the included articles in this study have been retrieved from EBSCO and Web of Science databases by using multiple terms, but we still could have missed articles that did not appear with the literature searches. This represents a publication bias that should be considered when reviewing our findings. Second, most of the included articles employed case study methods in their research, so the findings were positive but cannot be generalized. Case study is rigorous, time-intensive methodology that presents a focused lens on teaching and learning. While we can glean quite a bit from these studies, we do not have evidence that the findings would generalize across other classrooms, teachers or students. Therefore, using these studies as a model and starting point, and planning comparative quantitative studies that build on the findings, could enhance the field and continue to fill gaps in the research.

Conclusion

The current study contributes to the synthesis and analysis of the existing literature on the use of multimodal literacy practices on emergent bilingual children. Employing the systematic literature review as a methodological approach, this study suggests that multimodal literacies, especially digital literacies, have effectively helped bilingual children to develop their literacy skills and cultural identity in multiple ways, such as classroom instructions, practice tools and activity engagements. Multimodal literacies can be used as effective tools in class translanguaging practices that support emergent bilinguals in expression and comprehension. Finally, the current study concludes that multimodal literacies can facilitate young bilingual children in both school and family settings to develop various competences.

References

Aquino-Sterling, C.R. and Rodríguez-Valls, F. (2016) Developing teaching-specific Spanish competencies in bilingual teacher education: Toward a culturally, linguistically, and professionally relevant approach. *Multicultural Perspectives* 18 (2), 73–81.

Bandura, A. (1986) *Social Foundations of Thought and Action: A Social Cognitive Theory*. Upper Saddle River, NJ: Prentice-Hall.

Bauer, E.B., Presiado, V. and Colomer, S. (2017) Writing through partnership: Fostering translanguaging in children who are emergent bilinguals. *Journal of Literacy Research* 49 (1), 10–37.

Catalano, T., Kiramba, L.K. and Viesca, K. (2020) Transformative interviewing and the experiences of multilingual learners not labeled 'ELL' in US schools. *Bilingual Research Journal* 43 (2), 178–195.

Cooper, H. (2015) *Research Synthesis and Meta-Analysis: A Step-by-Step Approach*. Thousand Oaks, CA: Sage.

Creese, A., Bhatt, A., Bhojani, N. and Martin, P. (2006) Multicultural, heritage and learner identities in complementary schools. *Language and Education* 20 (1), 23–43.

Cruz, M. (2016) 21st century skills in the teaching of foreign languages at primary and secondary schools. *Turkish Online Journal of Educational Technology (Special Issue for IETC, ITEC, IDEC, ITICAM 2016)* July, 1–12.

Cummins, J. (2019) The emergence of translanguaging pedagogy: A dialogue between theory and practice. *Journal of Multilingual Education Research* 9 (13).

Fernández-Fontecha, A., O'Halloran, K.L., Wignell, P. and Tan, S. (2020) Scaffolding CLIL in the science classroom via visual thinking: A systemic functional multimodal approach. *Linguistics and Education* 55, 1–10.

García, O. (2009) *Bilingual Education in the 21st Century: A Global Perspective*. Malden, MA: Wiley.

Gort, M. (2006) Strategic codeswitching, interliteracy, and other phenomena of emergent bilingual writing: Lessons from first grade dual language classrooms. *Journal of Early Childhood Literacy* 6 (3), 323–354.

Jewitt, C. (2008) Multimodality and literacy in school classrooms. *Review of Research in Education* 32 (1), 241–267.

Kress, G.R. (2003) *Literacy in the New Media Age*. Hove: Psychology Press.

Kress, G.R. (2010) *Multimodality: A Social Semiotic Approach to Contemporary Communication*. Abingdon: Taylor & Francis.

Lapp, D., Moss, B. and Rowsell, J. (2012) Envisioning new literacies through a lens of teaching and learning. *The Reading Teacher* 65 (6), 367–377.

Littlewood, W. and Yu, B. (2011) First language and target language in the foreign language classroom. *Language Teaching* 44 (1), 64.

Lotherington, H. and Jenson, J. (2011) Teaching multimodal and digital literacy in L2 settings: New literacies, new basics, new pedagogies. *Annual Review of Applied Linguistics* 31, 226–246.

McTigue, E.M. and Flowers, A.C. (2011) Science visual literacy: Learners' perceptions and knowledge of diagrams. *The Reading Teacher* 64 (8), 578–589.

McVee, M., Silvestri, K., Shanahan, L. and English, K. (2017) Productive communication in an afterschool engineering club with girls who are English language learners. *Theory into Practice* 56 (4), 246–254.

New London Group (1996) A pedagogy of multiliteracies: Designing social futures. *Harvard Educational Review* 66 (1), 60–93. doi:10.17763/haer.66.1.17370n67v22j160u

Pacheco, M. and Hamilton, C. (2020) Bilanguaging love: Latina/o/x bilingual students' subjectivities and sensitivities in dual language immersion contexts. *TESOL Quarterly* 54 (3), 548–571.

Perry, K. (2012) What is literacy? A critical overview of sociocultural perspectives. *Journal of Language and Literacy Education* 8 (1), 50–71.

Pietikainen, S. and Pitkanen-Huhta, A. (2013) Multimodal literacy practices in the indigenous Sami classroom: Children navigating in a complex multilingual setting. *Journal of Language Identity and Education* 12 (4), 230–247.

Prior, P. (2006) A sociocultural theory of writing. In C.A. MacArthur, S. Graham and J. Fitzgerald (eds) *Handbook of Writing Research* (pp. 54–66). New York: Guilford Press.

Sanders, J. and Albers, P. (2010) Multimodal literacies: An introduction. In P. Albers and J. Sanders (eds) *Literacies, the Arts, and Multimodality* (pp. 1–26). Champaign, IL: NCTE.

Serafini, F. (2012) Expanding the four resources model: Reading visual and multi-modal texts. *Pedagogies: An International Journal* 7 (2), 150–164.

Vygotsky, L.S. (1980) *Mind in Society: The Development of Higher Psychological Processes*. Cambridge, MA: Harvard University Press.

Reviewed Studies

Ajayi, L. (2012) Video 'reading' and multimodality: A study of ESL/literacy pupils' interpretation of 'Cinderella' from their socio-historical perspective. *Urban Review: Issues and Ideas in Public Education* 44 (1), 60–89.

Alvarez, A. (2018) Drawn and written funds of knowledge: A window into emerging bilingual children's experiences and social interpretations through their written narratives and drawings. *Journal of Early Childhood Literacy* 18 (1), 97–128.

Bengochea, A., Sembiante, S.F. and Gort, M. (2018) An emergent bilingual child's multimodal choices in sociodramatic play. *Journal of Early Childhood Literacy* 18 (1), 38–70.

Bernstein, K.A. (2017) Writing their way into talk: Emergent bilinguals' emergent literacy practices as pathways to peer interaction and oral language growth. *Journal of Early Childhood Literacy* 17 (4), 485–521.

Brown, S. (2016) Young learners' transactions with interactive digital texts using E-readers. *Journal of Research in Childhood Education* 30 (1), 42–56.

Brown, S. (2020) Pushing against hegemonic practices: Emergent bilinguals respond to children's literature. *European Early Childhood Education Research Journal* 28 (2), 242–255.

Brown, S. and Allmond, A. (2020) Constructing my world: A case study examining emergent bilingual multimodal composing practices. *Early Childhood Education Journal* 49 (2), 209–221. doi:10.1007/s10643-020-01062-4

Castañeda, M.E., Shen, X. and Claros Berlioz, E.M. (2018) This is my story: Latinx learners create digital stories during a summer literacy camp. *TESOL Journal* 9 (4), 1–14.

Chang, S. and Martínez-Roldán, C.M. (2018) Multicultural lessons learned from a Chinese bilingual after-school program: Using technology to support ethnolinguistic children's cultural production. *Multicultural Education* 25 (2), 36–41.

Chen, Y., Carger, C.L. and Smith, T.J. (2017) Mobile-assisted narrative writing practice for young English language learners from a funds of knowledge approach. *Language Learning & Technology* 21 (1), 28–41.

Harrison, E. and McTavish, M. (2018) 'I'babies: Infants' and toddlers' emergent language and literacy in a digital culture of iDevices. *Journal of Early Childhood Literacy* 18 (2), 163–188.

Hasty, M.M. and Fain, J.G. (2014) Emergent understandings: Multilingual fourth grade students generating close readings and multimodal responses to global and informational texts. *Penn GSE Perspectives on Urban Education* 11 (2), 10–20.

Martin-Beltrán, M., Tigert, J.M., Peercy, M.M. and Silverman, R.D. (2017) Using digital texts vs. paper texts to read together: Insights into engagement and mediation of literacy practices among linguistically diverse students. *International Journal of Educational Research* 82, 135–146.

Martínez-Álvarez, P. (2017) Language multiplicity and dynamism: Emergent bilinguals taking ownership of language use in a hybrid curricular space. *International Multilingual Research Journal* 11 (4), 255–276.

McGlynn-Stewart, M., Murphy, S., Pinto, I., Mogyorodi, E. and Nguyen, T. (2019) Technology supported early literacy learning in a multilingual community preschool. *Education 3–13* 47 (6), 692–704.

Moses, L. (2013) Viewing as a cultural tool in the construction of meaning with expository texts for young bilinguals. *Journal of Language and Literacy Education* 9 (2), 72–93.

Ntelioglou, B.Y., Fannin, J., Montanera, M. and Cummins, J. (2014) A multilingual and multimodal approach to literacy teaching and learning in urban education: A collaborative inquiry project in an inner-city elementary school. *Frontier in Psychology* June.

Park, H. (2018) Influences of reading online texts in Korean English language learners' cultural identities. *Journal of Educational Research* 111 (4), 385–397.

Piller, B. and Skillings, M.J. (2005) English language teaching strategies used by primary teachers in one New Delhi, India school. *TESL-EJ* 9 (3).

Proctor, C.P., Dalton, B. and Grisham, D.L. (2007) Scaffolding English language learners and struggling readers in a universal literacy environment with embedded strategy instruction and vocabulary support. *Journal of Literacy Research* 39 (1), 71–93.

Rowe, D.W. and Miller, M.E. (2016) Designing for diverse classrooms: Using iPads and digital cameras to compose eBooks with emergent bilingual/biliterate four-year-olds. *Journal of Early Childhood Literacy* 16 (4), 425–472.

Rowe, L.W. (2018) Say it in your language: Supporting translanguaging in multilingual classes. *The Reading Teacher* 72 (1), 31–38.

Rowe, L.W. (2019) Constructing language ideologies in a multilingual, second-grade classroom: A case study of two emergent bilingual students' language-use during eBook composing. *Linguistics & Education* 52, 1–12.

Rowe, L.W. (2020) Emergent bilingual students' use of humour in digital composing: Academic and social work. *Journal of Early Childhood Literacy*. doi:10.1177/1468798420911143

Sembiantea, S.F., Bengochea, A. and Gort, M. (2020) 'Want me to show you?': Emergent bilingual preschoolers' multimodal resourcing in show-and-tell activity. *Linguistics and Education* 55, 100794.

Shin, D. (2014) Web 2.0 tools and academic literacy development in a US urban school: A case study of a second-grade English language learner. *Language and Education* 28, 68–85.

Skinner, E.N. and Hagood, M.C. (2008) Developing literate identities with English language learners through digital storytelling. *Reading Matrix: An International Online Journal* 8 (2), 12–38.

Stille, S. (2015) Identity as a site of difference: Toward a complex understanding of identity in multilingual, multicultural classrooms. *Intercultural Education* 26 (6), 483–496.

Toohey, K., Dagenais, D., Fodor, A., Hof, L., Nuñez, O., Singh, A. and Schulze, L. (2015) 'That sounds so cooool': Entanglements of children, digital tools, and literacy practices. *TESOL Quarterly* 49 (3), 461–485.

Zhao, S. and Hewitt, R. (2020) Young Chinese immigrant children's language and literacy practices on social media: A translanguaging perspective. *Language and Education* 34 (3), 267–285.

Part 1

Preschool

2 Multimodal Literacies at the Train Table: Supporting Young Emergent Bilinguals through Play

Karen Wohlwend, Pengtong Qu, Jill Allison Scott and Carmen Liliana Medina

Most preschool and elementary school teachers in the US are monolingual, in part due to their own educational histories as K-12 learners in English-only classrooms (Gándara & Escamilla, 2017). The result is that the growing number of children whose home language is not English are often taught through the medium of spoken English (AACTE, 2002). Krashen's (1981) widely accepted notion of a 'silent stage' in second language acquisition suggests that as young emergent language learners venture into schooling, they may initially enter into a period when they do not speak in their new setting. During this silent stage, young students are soaking up large amounts of linguistic input while being silent but listening. Sociocultural research on emergent bilingual children's unobservable language reveals that children are not only observing the world but learning how to fit into a multicultural and multilingual environment (Igoa, 1995). Although bilingual speakers do not produce much language in their silent period, they are not passive learners or spectators (Iddings & Jang, 2008). The silent stage is not so silent when examined through a lens of multimodal meaning-making.

This chapter takes a closer look at preschool children's multimodal literacies – active and collaborative use of multimodal meanings and resources – during an episode of classroom play to reveal the action-packed communication that happens during the silent stage. Following Bengochea *et al.* (2018), we argue that young bilinguals' play narratives and classroom participation are supported by a nexus of multimodal interactions with other children, toys, furniture, the physical environment and teachers' provision of materials and time through routine and repetition. This broader perspective on language and literacy focuses on making meaning through actions with objects, modes and spaces, further contradicting the characterization of emergent bilinguals as silent and isolated.

Theorizing Play, Action Texts and Multimodal Literacies

To understand how children communicate through nonverbal meanings during the silent stage, we consider play as a literacy that creates *action texts*, or pretend stories made with bodies and toys (Wohlwend, 2011). Action texts can range from snippets of unrecorded live-action play to dramatized videos to video games, or digital animations. When young children collaborate in play, they coordinate, dispute and negotiate the possible meanings for their physical actions, toys and material props until they agree upon what each player will do or say. When these material meanings are mutually understood by the children, they 'go without saying' and children can easily communicate their intended meanings and create joint action texts without much need for discussion or elaboration. That is, children are reading and accessing their shared understanding of the embedded narratives in a toy's or other physical object's material text.

Scollon's (2001) nexus theory explains how pretend stories can be created so easily without words. Classrooms, like all cultural spaces, bring together a nexus of expected social practices, ways of belonging and cooperating through normalized practices that everyone seems to 'just know how to do.' In schools, these embodied understandings are often expressed in routines as the everyday ways of doing school. As children play together over time, certain ways of playing with a toy become part of a familiar routine that shapes who can play or how toys should be used. These shared meanings for toys help children create cohesive narratives that are quickly and mutually understood by all players without verbal explanations.

When creating action texts, children use nonverbal modes – gestures, posture, facial expression, sound effects – that make their intentions clear and allow them to quickly agree on who should hold which toy or who

Table 2.1 Examples of modal resources: Embodied and environmental

Modal category	Embodied modes	Environmental modes
Visual	Gaze	Color, light
Auditory	Speech, singing, laughter	Sound, sound effect
Spatial	Movement	Layout
Gestural	Posture, gesture	Proxemics
Tactile	Haptic	Texture, shape

Source: Adapted from Wohlwend (2021).

should lead and who should follow (Wohlwend, 2011). The sensory properties and the shared cultural meanings of objects and spaces in the physical environment make up modal resources (Table 2.1). For example, a large wooden table in the classroom provides a smooth, hard, flat surface; the texture and shape environmental modes that describe the sensory aspects of this surface afford multiple actions: scribbling in a coloring book, stacking blocks or racing toy cars. These become resources for making stories with multimodal literacies such as play.

Multimodal literacy pedagogies and bilingual children

Literacy pedagogies are subtractive and limiting when they take away a language that a bilingual child owns or restrict bilingual speakers to a specific literacy repertoire (de Jong, 2013; Igoa, 1995; Ruiz, 1984; Wiley & Lukes, 1996). Literacy pedagogies are expansive and supportive when they enable all students' full capacity to learn together, to co-construct narratives and to use available resources to mediate linguistic constraints (Edwards, 2004; New London Group, 1996). Emergent bilinguals, including learners who do not produce much oral language, can be actively engaged in classroom literacies when teachers mediate their learning. Bligh (2012) found that teachers who mediate linguistic challenges in English-dominant classrooms through modelled observable practices allow emergent bilinguals to gain new ways of learning. As a result, emergent bilinguals make connections between what they know (e.g. mother tongues, symbols, facial expressions, etc.) and are capable of understanding so that they can gradually participate in classroom practices.

Expansive literacy pedagogies take a scaffolded approach to language; they model and encourage multiple modes of communication as students become immersed in the classroom routines and language. Multimodal literacy pedagogies do not rely solely on print and spoken language in classroom routines and activities. For example, before having children choose an activity center, language differences are mediated by photos of centers paired with printed descriptions. Teachers physically model each activity center and then allow children to point to pictures of a chosen activity rather than requiring students to speak before they are ready, thus broadening participation for all children.

Multimodal literacy pedagogies recognize language beyond speech and texts beyond print. Children develop deeper understandings of the possible meanings of actions and objects through opportunities to negotiate and improvise stories and collaborate with peers in dramatic play performances (Medina & Wohlwend, 2014). Play also opens access to multimodal resources that connect bilingual learners' inside worlds to their outside audience (Igoa, 1995). In a case study of a four-year-old Spanish-speaking boy playing in a preschool classroom, Bengochea *et al.* (2018) found that emergent bilingual children are not only observing the world, they are communicating and collaborating through modal resources made available by recognizing the broader range of literacies and texts that occurs through varied modes. The authors argued that classrooms with diverse modal resources support emergent bilingual children by providing additional ways of negotiating and expressing meanings. Multimodal resources open access for young bilinguals to shared knowledge and valued ways of participating in classroom communities, particularly evident during play:

> Working collaboratively among bilinguals of varying bilingual proficiency in sociodramatic play – a unique community of practice – necessitated shared understandings by all play participants of when, how and why they engage particular modes. Under a variety of circumstances and following different objectives, [an emergent bilingual child] patterned deployment of different modalities to make meaning supported and reified in the community of practice in this translanguaging space. (Bengochea *et al.*, 2018: 62–63)

In this study, we looked beyond verbal translanguaging to reveal the nonverbal, modally rich narratives that emergent bilingual children create and negotiate with multimodal literacies such as play. Specifically, we sought to answer the following research questions:

- *How do children's multimodal literacies support collaborative play and emergent bilinguals' participation?*
- *How does teachers' intentional design for multimodal literacies affect collaboration and participation among emergent bilinguals as well as young children in general?*

Analyzing Actions and Modes in Preschool Play

The featured play episode at the train table is excerpted from a yearlong ethnographic study in a US preschool classroom to understand how play-based pedagogy in a modally rich environment affects diverse learners' developing literacies and classroom participation. The preschool class included 23 three-year-old to five-year-old children (13 boys and 10 girls), two teachers and one paraprofessional in a preschool in a midwestern university community in the United States. There were seven children with emerging bilingual abilities whose home languages included Chinese (3), Korean (2) and Arabic (2). The excerpted instance of data features nonverbal collaborative play by a four-year-old boy who spoke primarily Korean in the classroom and a four-year-old girl who spoke only English.

In weekly visits during two-hour play periods in this preschool classroom over the course of one academic year, Karen video-recorded instances of play interactions with two or more children. Nexus analysis of instances where children played with toys examined how they negotiated (1) their shared action texts; and (2) their social relationships in play groups. Nexus analysis (Wohlwend, 2021) systematically searches through the buzz of classroom activity to determine how moments of children's mediated actions with materials support shared meanings and social participation. Multimodal interactional analysis (Norris, 2004) focuses on how individuals manage the complex mix of modes and meanings as they shift their attention among people, things and spaces. For example, even very young children coordinate gestures, gaze, posture, scribbled images and speech to craft messages that mean more than they can communicate through verbal dictation (Rowe, 2018). This analysis of interaction closely examines a moment of activity to identify ways of communicating and collaborating.

Using the filtering process in nexus analysis, we identified instances where a group of children that included an emergent bilingual shared a common set of toys and played together. After locating complete play episodes with primarily nonverbal communication, we used multimodal analysis to examine children's actions with toys and interactions with one another. Looking closely at actions revealed modes such as gaze, postures, facial expressions and movement that allowed players to nonverbally cooperate in producing action texts such as driving a train along a track. Changes in modes such as shifts in posture, movement and children's proximity to one another reveal nonverbal collaboration and coordination of the story being co-constructed. We then located and analyzed the multimodal supports in teachers' design of the classroom environment that made this kind of collaborative storytelling possible.

Children's multimodal literacies

In this multi-age class, each fall a new group of three-year-olds joined the class as five-year-olds left for kindergarten. Children's play groups developed over the years, usually among older children. Younger children and emergent bilinguals often played alone or near playgroups, silently watching on the edge of the action. Three four-year-old emergent bilingual boys (two Korean speakers, one Chinese speaker) frequently played with miniature vehicles, including a plastic train set, the toy that is the focus of this chapter. Space for the train set was designated by the teachers on a large eight-foot wooden table that had two cutouts that enabled children to stand inside the table as well as walk around the perimeter of the table.

We focus here on one emergent bilingual (Korean/English) four-year-old boy, Minjoon (pseudonym), to see how his play interactions with another child, a monolingual (English) four-year-old girl, Kayli (pseudonym), relied on their shared understanding of multimodal meanings of toys in the classroom environment. In this instance, there was almost no spoken language but play roles and rules were fluidly negotiated nonverbally. The children shared a joint understanding of how the train toys should be used as they followed one another around the wooden train table. Finally, we examine the intentional use of embodied and environmental modal resources in teachers' design of activities and classroom environment and implications for early childhood teachers.

Examination of situated activity at the train table center in the preschool classroom showed that repeated play themes with familiar toys and player roles created ingrained expectations for actions (i.e. nexus of practice) which enabled children to coordinate their use of embodied and environmental modes such as of gaze, sound effects, proximity and furniture layout.

In the action transcript in Table 2.2, the communication builds slowly as the players negotiate who will lead and who will follow in this impromptu 'Follow the Leader' game. After initially watching Minjoon driving a Lego train around the rectangular perimeter, Kayli begins

Table 2.2 Transcript of actions and modes in shared meaning-making and play collaboration

Action and modes used	Action in instance	Shared meaning and play collaboration
Sequence 1 0:00 Meet up: gaze, laughing *Sequence 2* 0:33 Kayli follows Minjoon's train around perimeter. Minjoon's train suddenly falls off table as it's circling. Minjoon looks at Kayli in surprise and both laugh.		***Solitary play*** Kayli bids to join play: Kayli follows **movement* of** Minjoon's train. Kayli laughs loudly (**sound**) when Minjoon's train falls to floor, delighted at the joke. Kayli 's **gaze** follows Minjoon as he climbs on table.
Sequence 3 0:42 Minjoon & Kayli pick up Minjoon's train; watching and mirroring of picking up train cars; Minjoon sings ABC song.		***Collaborative play begins*** Kayli mirrors Minjoon: Copied **movements** and coordinated **layout** of train cars on table, shared **gaze**. Cooperative repair of M's broken train. **Layout** of play scene, working together; close **proximity.**
Sequence 4 1:35 Minjoon alone; still singing and moving train around table. Kayli leaves train table to get mini cars.		***Collaborative play breaks down*** Individual play with materials. Distant **proximity** from one another.

*Note: Bolded words in the third column indicate modes. Faces in the photos have been intentionally blurred to maintain confidentiality while preserving indicators of modes such as gaze and facial expression. Sequences 11-13 consisted of similar play actions and are not included in the tables.

mirroring modes of **movement** around the table edge (Sequences 1–2), and **proximity** as she stands near him as collaborative play begins and they recreate the **layout** of his train cars on the table.

Collaborative play resumes and becomes modally rich as the children coordinate their actions, meanings and modes. Kayli continues following Minjoon's train, adding train whistle sound effects and staying in close proximity to him (Sequence 5, Table 2.3), watching and mirroring his stops and starts, waiting for him to rebuild his train (Sequence 6), copying his posture and positioning inside the table's two openings (Sequence 7). They laugh together when Minjoon's train drops unexpectedly through the hole in the table (Sequence 8). Kayli continues the train play when Minjoon leaves for a short break in a nearby chair where he sings softly to himself (Sequences 9–10).

As the play continued, the rules and roles of train play were negotiated through players' wielding of unspoken modal resources. For instance, when Kayli first crashed into Minjoon's train (Sequence 14, Table 2.4), Minjoon indicated that Kayli's train must stay back by slowing his train speed until his train pushed her train backward. When she crashed a minute later, Minjoon physically grabbed Kayli's train car and pushed it back himself to reinforce the rules of the Follow the Leader play and his role as leader. Minjoon used gaze, sound effects, proximity and movement in place of language to negotiate and re-establish the rules of play and his role as the leader of the train play.

When Minjoon stopped to add cars to his train (Sequence 15), Kayli mirrored and stopped to wait for him. When they restarted, Kayli stopped to add cars to make her train longer, but Minjoon kept going, circling until his train reached Kayli. Kayli looked up, saw Minjoon's train waiting, and laughed; she allowed him to physically pass her train and continue as leader of their game. Their shared understanding of the roles of the two players was made clear through modes of their relative proximity, their facial expression and sounds, and their stops and starts in movement: Minjoon was leading while Kayli was following.

Finally, two more children noticed the play at the train table, joining quickly and staying briefly (Sequence 16). At 8:19, a boy named Graham came to the table with a train in hand, then circled the table following Minjoon and Kayli. A minute later, Isabelle joined the game holding a small block in her hand. Minjoon continued to lead the game with Kayli and Graham now following him. The two children who joined in the game easily recognized and followed the rules that had been negotiated by Minjoon and Kayli.

It is crucial to recognize how Minjoon was accessing modal resources to actively lead the game and co-construct rules with the other children throughout the episode. Following and copying other players in new situations can be more typical for young children. Bligh (2012) found it can be particularly challenging for emergent bilinguals to make connections

Table 2.3 Transcript of actions and modes in shared meaning-making and play collaboration

Action and modes used	Action in instance	Shared meaning and play collaboration
Sequence 5 2:01 Minjoon drives train around circle. Kayli returns to table. Kayli narrates train movement with train whistle sound (Wohaaa).		***Collaborative play resumes*** Kayli makes train whistle **sound effect.** Kayli follows Minjoon's **movement** of train around train table **layout**; maintains close **proximity.**
Sequence 6 2:07 Kayli watches Minjoon steer train around table. Minjoon sings ABC song; Kayli waits for him to start a train or for train to be completed.		***Collaborative play continues*** Shared **gaze** on Minjoon's moving train; close **proximity.**
Sequence 7 2:17 Kayli mirrors Minjoon's position inside train table opening.		***Collaborative play continues*** Mirrored facing **posture** inside table openings; close **proximity.**
Sequence 8 2:36 Minjoon drives around circle opening and train drops into circle. Both laugh at the unauthorized use of the toy.		***Collaborative play continues*** Mirrored **posture** inside table openings; close **proximity;** shared laughter (**sound**).
Sequence 9 2:40 Minjoon leaves. Kayli drives train around circle with sound effects.		***Collaborative play breaks down*** Distant **proximity.**
Sequence 10 2:46 Minjoon alone, sitting on chair singing ABC song. Kayli drives train along circle, repeating Minjoon's earlier action with sound effects.		***Solitary play*** Minjoon and Kayli in distant **proximity.** RePlay: Kayli replays Minjoon's **posture**, train **movement** and **layout** patterns.

Table 2.4 Transcript of actions and modes in shared meaning-making and play collaboration

Action and modes used	Action in instance	Shared meaning and play collaboration
Sequence 14 6:00 Kayli crashes her train into Minjoon's train. Minjoon looks, laughs and fixes his train then begins again. Kayli crashes again and laughs. Minjoon goes very slowly and Kayli mirrors his slow speed. Then Minjoon speeds up and Kayli speeds up. They circle until Kayli crashes into Minjoon's train a third time and he moves her train back.		***Collaborative play negotiation*** During this play period, the rules are negotiated and reinforced through shared **gaze** on one another's trains, mirrored **movement** and **proximity** that must be monitored and coordinated to sustain circling action and prevent crashes.
Sequence 15 8:52 Minjoon stops. He was distracted by a piece of block on the floor. Kayli stops and picks up the piece while Minjoon waits. Next, Minjoon keeps circling. Kayli moves 2 steps then picks up two more blocks from the floor and makes her train longer. Minjoon circles then reaches Kayli and wants to pass Kayli's train.		***Collaborative play negotiation*** Minjoon and Kayli negotiated rules: Kayli circles when Minjoon is temporarily absent. Kayli then attempts to lead; Minjoon re-establishes role as leader. Both used **movement, proximity, gaze** and **facial expression** to negotiate Minjoon's role as leader of the game.
Sequence 16 8:19 Graham joins the game. At first, Graham was in front of Minjoon. When Graham catches up with Kayli at the end of the line, they both wait for Minjoon to move forward again. 9:48 Isabelle comes to the table with a block in hand, circling outside the table. Minjoon is still leading the game and Kayli and Isabelle follow him.		***Collaborative play*** More players arrive. Two children (Graham and Isabelle) join the game for a short time. They follow the unspoken rules of this game through **proximity** and **movement.**

between their existing knowledge repertoire and unfamiliar linguistic cues when playing independently with other children without active adult assistance. In Bligh's study, a young emergent bilingual child copied his peers, laughing when others laughed while children watched cartoons, trying to learn and following his peers' reactions.

In this play episode, densely multimodal and repetitive play supported young children in their language and literacy development in ways that opened up pathways for participating fully in the classroom. Bengochea *et al.* (2018) found that during play, children who are emergent bilinguals use their language and cultural resources to elaborate on the meanings of their ways with things in play events, to negotiate roles and rules of play and to develop social identities through play. Our findings build upon this research to suggest that even without spoken language, children quickly and easily negotiated play rules, roles, plans and identities to maintain their shared action text.

Teachers' Intentional Design for Multimodal Literacies and Supportive Spaces

Each day, the preschool teachers in this classroom set out new materials to encourage a variety of multimodal experiences. Examples include:

- Literacy activities included paging through new picture books on the small sofa or tracing letters with glitter glue at the art table.
- Sensory activities included water and sand tables, fingerpainting, or playdough sculpture at the art table.
- Math activities included block construction with small manipulatives to oversized wooden blocks in the block center or measuring objects around the classroom.
- Science activities included sorting stones and shells and filling containers at the water table and other activities often found in progressive play-based preschool education.

The changing daily activities attracted children to new materials for as long as their interest in the materials held, but when their interest faded, the children often returned to play with their favorite toys, friends and preferred play themes. The rich multimodal environment in this classroom supported interaction through open access to familiar materials and daily routines, including many dramatic play centers, such as the train table. Moreover, the day was arranged to allow ample time for participation in play. These intentional decisions by the teachers allowed bilingual children to get involved, socialize, lead play and communicate with peers.

The entry points for participation were multiplied to make space for all children, including learners who may not yet be speaking much in a new language. In play centers the language learners were able to flexibly use other ways of communicating that included gestures, actions, gaze, sound effects, movements and positioning of artifacts to convey their messages (Bengochea *et al.*, 2018; Jewitt, 2008; Kress, 2003). By creating regular and frequent opportunities for play with familiar toys such as Lego trains and miniature cars, the preschool teachers increased children's access to a common set of shared meanings. In this way, the teachers designed a more multimodal and equitable classroom environment. This was evidenced when Minjoon and Kayli shared in the humor of the train falling into the hole in the train table (Sequence 8, Table 3). As soon as the train fell, the children burst into laughter. This shared laughter at the unexpected and unauthorized use of the train makes clear that there is a shared expectation for trains to run in an orderly way on the table, not tumble off of it. In that moment, differences across language didn't matter; the shared meanings around train play permitted a shared moment of bonding, humor and understanding. Within this expanded literacies pedagogy, play becomes a unifying and inclusive literacy that values multimodal meaning-making as a legitimate way to communicate.

Implications

Young children's development of literacy understandings varies widely; therefore, the developmentally appropriate nature of multimodality-resourced pedagogy (as described in this chapter) is not only beneficial for emergent bilinguals, it supports all students. Verbally dominant teacher-directed activities often privilege students who are already using print or spoken language. Such didactic teaching methods can marginalize children who are newly emergent readers, writers and speakers, overlooking their linguistic and multimodal resources, positioning them as behind, and preventing them from fully participating in classroom communities. It is essential that we balance the early childhood curriculum with child-centered play that enables children with diverse abilities and resources to fully participate using nonverbal and nonprint modalities. This will help ensure that all children have a sense of belonging and connection.

Play is a developmentally appropriate child-centered literacy that offers the chance for equitable participation, social emotional well-being and a sense of belonging, which contribute to a child's happiness and feelings of success. Play is a source of collaborative meaning-making, which is at the heart of literacy. As children play together, they create new shared scripts and stories which are enacted in action texts and then replayed as familiar stories. Knowing this, teachers will want to consider the whole context of play activities and make space for inclusive playscapes that inspire communal play, spark negotiations in play and deepen multimodal meaning-making.

The role of the teacher is critical (Igoa, 1995) and must be a consideration when building a supportive environment for bilingual children. A warm and welcoming teacher who actively mediates language differences is key to helping the student feel at ease in their new surroundings. We also know that part of creating a warm and welcoming classroom involves engaging young bilingual children in learning that builds on their known culture, language and funds of knowledge (Moll *et al.*, 1992). Providing opportunities for children to bring their favorite familiar artifacts to school and providing ample time for play opportunities with popular culture toys that have well-known narratives will also open more possibilities for multimodal interactions that leverage and create shared meanings, and open opportunities for more equitable participation.

References

AACTE (2002) *Educators' Preparation for Cultural and Linguistic Diversity: A Call to Action*. Washington, DC: Committee on Multicultural Education, American Association for Colleges of Teacher Education.

Bengochea, A., Sembiante, S.F. and Gort, M. (2018) An emergent bilingual child's multimodal choices in sociodramatic play. *Journal of Early Childhood Literacy* 18 (1), 38–70. doi:10.1177/1468798417739081

Bligh, C.A. (2012) Sociocultural understandings of the silent period: Young bilingual learners in early years settings. Paper presented at Developing Early Years Practice: Reflecting on Developments in Practice and Research Conference, Birmingham. See http://eprints.leedsbeckett.ac.uk/755/

de Jong, E.J. (2013) Policy discourses and U.S. language in education policies. *Peabody Journal of Education* 88 (1), 98–111. doi:10.1080/0161956X.2013.752310

Edwards, P.A. (2004) *Children's Literacy Development: Making it Happen through School, Family, and Community Involvement*. Boston, MA: Allyn & Bacon.

Gándara, P. and Escamilla, K. (2017) Bilingual education in the United States. In O. García, A. Lin and S. May (eds) *Bilingual and Multilingual Education* (3rd edn, pp. 439–452). Cham: Springer. doi:10.1007/978-3-319-02258-1_33

Iddings, A.C.D. and Jang, E.Y. (2008) The mediational role of classroom practices during the silent period: A new-immigrant student learning the English language in a mainstream classroom. *TESOL Quarterly* 42 (4), 567–590. doi:10.1002/j.1545-7249.2008.tb00149.x

Igoa, C. (1995) *The Inner World of the Immigrant Child*. Mahwah, NJ: Lawrence Erlbaum.

Jewitt, C. (2008) Multimodality and literacy in school classrooms. *Review of Research in Education* 32 (1), 241–267. doi:10.3102/0091732X07310586

Krashen, S.D. (1981) *Second Language Acquisition and Second Language Learning*. London: Pergamon.

Kress, G. (2003) *Literacy in the New Media Age*. Abingdon: Routledge.

Medina, C.L. and Wohlwend, K.E. (2014) *Literacy, Play, and Globalization: Converging Imaginaries in Children's Critical and Cultural Performances*. New York: Routledge.

Moll, L.C., Amanti, C., Neff, D. and Gonzalez, N. (1992) Funds of knowledge for teaching: Using a qualitative approach to connect homes and classrooms. *Theory into Practice* 31 (2), 132–141.

New London Group (1996) A pedagogy of multiliteracies: Designing social futures. *Harvard Educational Review* 66 (1), 60–93. doi:10.17763/haer.66.1.17370n67v22j160u

Norris, S. (2004) *Analyzing Multimodal Interaction: A Methodological Framework*. London: Routledge.

Rowe, D.W. (2018) Pointing with a pen: The role of gesture in early childhood writing. *Reading Research Quarterly* 54 (1), 13–39. https://doi.org/10.1002/rrq.215

Ruiz, R. (1984) Orientations in language planning. *NABE: National Association for Bilingual Education* 8 (2), 15–34.

Scollon, R. (2001) *Mediated Discourse: The Nexus of Practice*. London: Routledge.

Wiley, T.G. and Lukes, M. (1996) English-only and standard English ideologies in the US. *TESOL Quarterly* 30 (3), 511–535. doi:10.2307/3587696

Wohlwend, K.E. (2011) *Playing Their Way into Literacies: Reading, Writing, and Belonging in the Early Childhood Classroom*. New York: Teachers College Press.

Wohlwend, K.E. (2021) *Literacies that Move and Matter: Nexus Analysis for Contemporary Childhoods*. New York: Routledge.

3 'Can I "*Mai*" that "*Bao*"?': An Emergent Bilingual's Multimodal Meaning-Making Practice

Buyi Wang and Chunhua Dai

Introduction

The mixed-language title is borrowed from Duo, a then four-year-old girl and our focal research participant. Duo was born in America and is growing up in both the US and China. Her experiences of growing up in the two countries enable her flexible deployment of semiotic modes as effective meaning-making tools, which is found to be ubiquitous during the authors' one-year study with Duo and her family. This chapter looks at Duo's orchestration of communication resources, both multilingual and multimodal, as she develops emergent biliteracy in English and Chinese. Emergent biliteracy is defined as the 'ongoing, dynamic development of concepts and expertise for thinking, listening, speaking, reading, and writing in two languages' (Gort, 2019: 233).

Informed by superdiversity (Creese & Blackledge, 2018; Vertovec, 2007) and a translanguaging literacies framework (García & Kleifgen, 2020), the authors report findings from a case study that examines an emergent bilingual's (EB's) multilingual and multimodal home literacy practice from 2019 to 2020. Findings suggest that Duo's skillful deployment of language(s) and nonlinguistic modes enables her to actively engage with her material and sociocultural environment, promoting biliteracy development. Taking a holistic perspective on a bilingual child's home literacy practice, the authors maintain that EBs' meaning-making process through both languages and nonlinguistic modes is complex and creative. Such practice can be a valuable resource in promoting children's biliteracy development.

Background

The US is becoming increasingly multilingual. A US Census report (Dietrich & Bauman, 2019) shows that in 2010, 59.5 million people spoke a language other than English at home – a 159% increase compared to the 23.1 million in 1980. Additionally, over 300 languages are listed as languages spoken in American homes. Among these languages, Chinese is the third-largest home language after English and Spanish, with 2.9 million people speaking Chinese at home in 2011 (Ryan, 2013). From 1980 to 2010, the number of Chinese/English bilinguals aged five and above increased by 345.3%, with a continuing trend of population growth. Meanwhile, with China's increasing economic and political power, Mandarin is gaining popularity as a second/third/foreign language in various educational settings such as public and private schools, bilingual programs, heritage community schools and adult language classes (ACTFL, 2010). For example, Chinese-English and Spanish-English were the two most popular language pairs in dual language education programs during the 2012–2013 school year (Boyle *et al.*, 2015).

Unlike Spanish/English bilingual students, with whom researchers have conducted numerous empirical studies to understand their meaning-making practices across educational contexts, the rising Chinese/English bilingual population has been understudied in the field of education. As English and Chinese are two languages with distinct orthographical systems and cultural traditions, biliteracy development in these two languages can be drastically different from that of Spanish/English bilinguals. Also, Chinese is an encompassing term for hundreds of languages, dialects and language variations, with Mandarin and Cantonese being just two common examples. The seemingly simple term of Chinese/English bilingualism encompasses a wide range of language varieties, cultural backgrounds, educational experience, migration status, etc. (Fan, 2014; Xiao, 2016). Thus, there is a practical and urgent need for educators and researchers to better understand the bilingual and biliterate experiences of this increasing Chinese/English bilingual population with diverse linguistic and migration experience (Li, 2006; Yaden & Tsai, 2012).

Literature Review

This chapter explores how languages and dialects, body languages and gestures, toys and books are utilized by a Chinese/English EB and her caregivers to make meanings, to communicate and to develop emergent biliteracy. This section first reviews superdiversity theory, and then discusses how a translanguaging literacies framework brings together translanguaging theory on bilingualism and a multiliteracies perspective on literacy learning.

Superdiversity and language education

Globalization and technological advancements have diversified the media and channels of human communication. Li (2018: 15) points out that 'boundaries among nation-state languages, between language and other communicative means, and the connection between language and the nation-state are constantly being broken, crossed, reassessed and redefined.' Nonprint modes like image and sound play an increasingly important role in conveying meaning. The internet and computer also shift the ways we read and write (Kress, 2003). The multiplicity and interconnectedness of human semiotic work means that our children need to be able to interact with 'multiple languages, multiple Englishes, and communication patterns that more frequently cross cultural, community and national boundaries' (New London Group, 1996: 64).

Superdiversity was originally proposed as a term to capture the rapid demographic change as people of different cultural and linguistic backgrounds, legal status and migration itineraries come into regular contact with each other in expanding cities (Vertovec, 2007, 2015). When it comes to the education of and research into bilingual children, superdiversity is in direct contrast with the idea that there is only one correct way of meaning-making (Blommaert & Rampton, 2012). Print-centeredness, mere literacy (New London Group, 1996) or monolingual ideologies (Blackledge, 2000) are far from desirable for the benefit of bilingual children's well-being. To better prepare our 21st century global citizens for the increasingly diversified world, parents, educators and researchers need to consider ways in which differences can be turned into resources for learning and development. In the next section, the authors review how theories of translanguaging and multiliteracies can bring insights to this endeavor.

A translanguaging literacies framework

García and Kleifgen (2020) propose a translanguaging literacies framework by connecting translanguaging theory (García & Li, 2014), biliteracy research (Cummins, 2000; Hornberger & Skilton-Sylvester, 2000) and multiliteracies (New London Group, 1996). Biliteracy is defined as 'any and all instances in which communication occurs in two (or more) languages in or around writing' (Hornberger, 2002: 213). A translanguaging literacies framework foregrounds bilinguals doing language and literacy in their lives. It emphasizes day-to-day literacy practice. Languages and nonlinguistic modes are all semiotic resources utilized by bilingual children to engage with their world in practice. All semiotic modes can be utilized to form one's intellectual toolkit with the aim of solving real-life problems (Kress, 2003).

The New London Group (1996) note that the changing realities of working, public and private lives have brought new challenges to literacy education. They emphasize nonlinguistic modes of image, sounds and gestures as equally valuable meaning-making tools in teaching and learning. Humans are designers of meaning. The six design elements in a meaning-making process are: 'linguistic meaning, visual meaning, audio meaning, gestural meaning, spatial meaning and the multimodal patterns of meaning, the last being the relationship between the first five modes of meaning to each other' (New London Group, 1996: 65). They argue that 'all meaning-making is multimodal' (New London Group, 1996: 81). Even punctuation marks are a semiotic combination of visual, spatial and linguistic modes that express meanings (Kress, 2003). Multiliteracies pedagogy underscores individual agency in creating new meaning. It also acknowledges that meaning is constantly redesigned, in contingency with social conventions, cultural rules, registries, styles and genres.

Based on a dynamic view of bilingualism, translanguaging is defined as 'multiple discursive practices in which bilinguals engage in order to make sense of their bilingual world' (García, 2009: 45). Translanguaging theory on bilingualism argues that bilinguals have one unified language system with linguistic features from different languages (García & Li, 2014). The system is dynamic, fluid, and constantly evolving as bilinguals continue to deploy their whole linguistic repertoire to engage with their world.

Taking a translanguaging literacies perspective on young children's biliteracy development draws our attention to bilingual children's use of and experience with their language and nonprint modes in developing emergent biliteracy.

Methodology

This study is framed as a case study, to 'focus in-depth on a "case" and to retain a holistic and real-world perspective' (Yin, 2018: 18). A case study involves 'studying a person, program, policy, or any other phenomenon that is intrinsically bounded by the interest of the researcher' (Bhattacharya, 2017: 26). Because of the case study's empirical nature, it does not aim to distill 'correct' or 'true' interpretations (Bromley, 1986). Instead, researchers interested in case studies are more inclined to describe, understand and interpret their case more inductively (Merriam, 1998). Therefore, using a qualitative case study in this research allows the researchers to delineate the EB's biliteracy development in real-life settings, thus offering insights on how to support biliteracy development in practice.

Research context

This study is contextualized in a multilingual family in which three members (a four-year-child Duo, her mother Flora and her grandmother Lan) speak multiple languages in a southern state in the US. The study mainly focuses on Duo's multilingual and multimodal literacy experience at home.

Family migration itineraries

The key participant, Duo, was born in the US and spent her time equally in the US and China. Her mother, Flora, was enrolled in a PhD program at a large public university in the southeastern United States. With Duo's father working in China, the mother and daughter frequently commuted back and forth between the two countries. Lan often accompanied her daughter and granddaughter to the US to take care of them.

According to the family's plan, Duo would finish her primary and secondary education in China before returning to the US to pursue higher degrees. However, the parents hoped that Duo would maintain her cultural ties with the US by spending her winter and summer breaks in the States, attending activities such as summer camps. They hoped that Duo would become multilingual and biliterate when she grew up. It was worth acknowledging that the socioeconomic status of the family provided material resources for the transnational and rich linguistic life experiences that were needed for Duo's biliteracy development.

Family language environment

Duo spoke English, Chinese Mandarin and Suzhou dialect, a language spoken in a southern region where the family originated. Flora grew up speaking the two Chinese languages. She was also fluent in English. Lan only spoke Suzhou dialect and a little Mandarin. The multilingual family members frequently switch among languages, mixing linguistic features from different sources in their daily communication.

Duo's caregivers created a supportive language environment so that Duo could develop literacy in both English and Chinese, meanwhile maintaining her Suzhou dialect. To achieve this goal, Flora intentionally encouraged the use of the non-dominant language in their immediate environment, ensuring Duo's continuous exposure to rich language and literacy resources in both English and Chinese. In China, Flora mostly spoke English to Duo in their daily communication. In the US, Duo attended a preschool where English was the only language. Thus, Flora switched to mostly Mandarin and Suzhou dialect while conversing with Duo and encouraged Duo to do the same. Most of the time, Lan kept communicating in Suzhou dialect with Duo and Flora. Unlike many bilingual families, this household did not have a rigid one parent/caregiver one-language policy. Rather, Flora and Lan gave Duo the freedom to communicate and express herself in whichever language she was comfortable with.

Research Method

Data were collected from August 2019 to August 2020, during which time Duo, Flora and Lan stayed in the US. Weekly participatory observations of Duo's multilingual and multimodal practice at home were audio- and video-recorded. Interviews with Duo's caregivers were also conducted.

Data sets include audio and video transcriptions of Duo's language behaviors, facial expressions and body language, interview transcripts, field notes and researchers' reflective notes, as well as artifacts of Duo's toys, drawings, children's literature books and so on.

Data analysis was based upon Tracy's (2020: 369) phronetic iterative analysis approach, which 'result in rich exemplars, artistic representations, conceptual models, and textual analyses'. This process included organizing and preparing the data (reading and re-reading the data, recording analytical reflections, transcribing, revisiting the transcripts), primary-cycle (developing descriptive codes) and secondary-cycle (developing analytic codes) coding, synthesizing activities such as documenting analytic memos to figure out the outstanding stories in the data, and generating a loose analysis outline. This data analysis was a not linear process; on the contrary, it happened by 'moving recurrently back and forth between considering emergent data … [and] reviewing existing theories, literatures, and research interests' (Tracy, 2020: 407).

Findings

During our one-year study, Duo demonstrated her creative orchestration of communication resources, both multilingual and multimodal, as she developed emergent biliteracy in English and Chinese. Specifically, we found that in the supportive home environment created by Flora and Lan, Duo actively deployed all her linguistic and nonlinguistic modes to achieve successful communication, as well as to approximate English and Chinese biliteracy.

Supportive home environment

As mentioned above, Flora and Lan strived to provide an environment in which Duo could express herself freely with whichever language and language features as she saw fit. They made sure that Duo had ample opportunities to engage in various kinds of literacy activities around the house. Figure 3.1 shows a wall that was decorated by Duo and Lan with Chinese characters and artifacts.

Reading stories was a favorite literacy activity in the family. Classic European fairy tales and high-quality contemporary children's literature titles were carefully selected by Flora and read to Duo. Among their favorite books were *San Zhi Xiao Zhu [The Three Little Piggies], Xiao Hong Mao De Gu Shi [Little Red Riding Hood], Jie Ke Yu Mo Dou [Jack and the Beanstalk], Lilly's Purple Plastic Purse, The Tale of Jemima Puddle-duck* and *Madeline in London*. During reading time, Flora did not stick with one particular language. Rather, she frequently translated words in one language to another, making connections between and among languages. As a result, Duo developed an interest in books and stories,

Figure 3.1 A bedroom wall decorated with Chinese characters and artifacts

demonstrating signs of emergent literacy. For example, although Duo could not read, she would hold a book upright and pretended to 'read' it. Duo also was fond of creating her own stories with her toys such as Lego figures, which will be further illustrated later in the chapter.

Deploying communication resources in daily communication

As previously reported, Duo's linguistic repertoire consisted of English, Chinese Mandarin and Suzhou dialect. At the early age of three, she showed an ability to distinguish language and language varieties when talking with others. Duo was sensitive to her interlocutors' language preferences and would adjust her linguistic choices accordingly. Such awareness was also found in situations when languages and language varieties were mixed. Duo only selected elements from the languages that she knew her interlocutor could understand. For example, when communicating with her trilingual mother, Duo selected linguistic features from all three languages. Knowing that Lan did not speak English, Duo limited her language choice to mostly Suzhou dialect, with some Mandarin. Here is an example of Duo's use of mixing language to achieve successful communication.

> Today Duo and I went shopping at Belk, and we saw a unicorn-shaped girl's handbag. Duo liked the bag so much and she was so eager to get it, but she forgot how to say the English word 'bag' and 'buy.' But she wanted the bag so much, she said 'Can I *mai* that *bao*?' The syntax was mixed but the whole question was said with a rising intonation as if this were an English-only question. I was so amused, also impressed. And I bought the bag for her.

> This looked like an example of translanguaging practice. Duo's purpose was to communicate. She wanted me to buy the bag. So, she used whatever that was available to achieve this purpose. She was not constrained by named languages of English or Chinese. This is not 'correct' English or Chinese, but her communicative purpose was achieved.
>
> (Researcher's field notes, 3 January 2020)

In this example, the authors found Duo's language mixing strategic. 'Mai' and 'bao' are two Chinese characters meaning 'buy' and 'handbag,' respectively. 'Mai' as the main verb and 'Bao' as a countable noun are combined with English words of 'can' and 'that,' forming a grammatically appropriate question in English. Also, her interlocutor valued such creative and flexible language mixing in aid of communicative purpose.

In the excerpt shown in Table 3.1, we found that even when Duo appeared to be speaking only one language, her knowledge of other languages was still present and active, helping her to fulfil communicative purposes.

In this exchange among Lan, Duo and the researcher, Duo appeared to be speaking monolingually and conversing only with the researcher in English, as she did not directly respond to Lan's comment in Suzhou dialect. However, a closer examination of meaning exchange showed that Duo's Suzhou dialect and Mandarin were still actively supporting her meaning-making practice. Duo understood Lan's and the researcher's words, but did not respond directly. Her choice of using the comparative adjective 'prettier' showed that she understood the Chinese word 'beautiful.' Otherwise, she would have said 'to make the carpet look pretty.' This example indicated that even when Duo appeared to be under a monolingual mode (Grosjean, 2008), her whole linguistic repertoire still actively and implicitly supported her understanding and communication with others.

Table 3.1 Duo's translanguaging daily conversation

Duo and I were sitting at a table, facing each other. Duo was decorating a Lego house with cartoon stickers as Lan walked to the table, looking at us, and commented:

Lan:	搭得忒漂亮了! [a]
Researcher:	真漂亮! [b]
Duo:	Can I put those [stickers] on the rag to [make it] look prettier? Can I have those stickers?

The researcher handed the sticker to Duo. She took it, peeled a flower-shaped sticker off and adhered it to the carpet of the Lego house.

Duo:	Do you know why I'm doing this?
Researcher:	I'm wondering.
Duo:	Because I'm decorating!

Notes: [a]*Spoken* in Suzhou dialect. 'You did a beautiful job!' in English. [b]*Spoken* in Chinese Mandarin. 'Indeed!' in English.
Source: Researcher's field notes, 6 November 2020.

A multiliteracies perspective in this instance revealed yet another layer of this short episode of meaning exchange. Duo used her spatial knowledge (these vs. those stickers), body language (taking the sticker, peeling, adhering and decorating) and intonation (excitement in declaring her purpose), to respond to Lan. These nonlinguistic modes showed her excitement and acknowledgement upon others' compliments, as if she were saying: 'Thank you! Look, I am making it even more beautiful.' Duo's deployment of spatial, gestural and sound modes to convey meaning helped her to smoothly and successfully communicate with others.

Developing emergent biliteracy

Duo's multimodal engagement with her material world and family members was also found to be related to her emergent biliteracy. One day, Duo demonstrated her understanding of how to use a calendar (see Figure 3.2 and Table 3.2) to indicate date and month.

Figure 3.2 shows the bilingual calendar with English and Chinese characters, as well as numbers arranged in a seven-column table. Two significant issues emerged here. First, on Duo's second try, she successfully answered the researcher's question of 'When are you going back to China?' Duo's answers were multilingual and multimodal. Rather than saying out loud her leaving date and month, Duo used the actions of pointing at the

Figure 3.2 A Chinese/English calendar on a living room wall

Table 3.2 Researcher's field notes, 5 November 2020

Verbal communication	English transcription	Body language and proximity
Researcher: 你什么时候回中国呀? Do you know? **Duo:** 嗯 …	**Researcher:** When are you going back to China? Do you know? **Duo:** Mhm …	Turned away from Lan and the researcher. Ran toward the calendar hanging on the living room wall. Stood in front of the calendar.
Duo: 这上面有, 我都在这上面看(日期). **Researcher:** 哪一天? *Which date?*	**Duo:** We have it here. I always check [my dates] on here. **Researcher:** Which day? Which date? (Reiterate in English)	The researcher followed Duo. Stopped at Duo's left side, facing the calendar.
Duo: 我觉得在这! **Researcher:** 那不是很快了吗?	**Duo:** I think it's here! **Researcher:** It's fast approaching!	Duo pointed at November 4th with her first finger. Hesitated, and took her hand back.
Duo: 或者 … (翻页) … 这	**Duo:** Or … here.	Duo stood on her tiptoe and flipped the calendar to the next month (December). Right first finger moved on the page and stopped at December 2nd. Lan approached the calendar
Researcher: 这是几号啊? 这是哪个月份? 十二月对不对? **Lan:** 十二月份. **Researcher:** December.	**Researcher:** Which date it is? Which month? Is it December? **Lan:** [we are leaving in] December. **Researcher:** December.	Researcher pointing at the dates on December page of the calendar.
Duo: 诶呀! 我说不出来啦!	**Duo:** Oh! I don't know how to say it!	Duo ran away from the calendar, returning to her toys.

correct date on the calendar page. She relied on speech, body language, Chinese print, number and space approximation to achieve successful communication. This example indicated that Duo's meaning-making and communication took on complex forms, involving not only multiple languages but also different modes. If Duo had only been allowed to answer the question with language, or if she could only answer the question in one language, she might not have been able to demonstrate her knowledge to the researcher.

Second, this example showed Duo's emergent understanding of reading. She showed knowledge of using a calendar to perform a series of literacy activities, such as planning future events and indicating dates. When she was asked about her future travel plans, she immediately 'ran toward the calendar' to show the dates to the researcher and 'flipped the calendar to the next page/month' when she realized she was on the wrong page. It was worth mentioning that Duo's 'reading' of the calendar was not reading in the conventional sense. She did not start to read the numbers and characters one by one, following the left-right, top-down sequence of text reading. Rather, she approached the calendar pages as a whole and extracted the information she needed.

Duo's multimodal literacy practice could also be found during her play time. The following storytelling happened after Duo and the first author built a Lego house together. The Lego set was based on the Disney movies *Frozen* and *Frozen II*. Duo liked the movies and was familiar with the story. Four minifigures of Elsa, Anna, Kristoff and Olaf as well as some cartoon stickers were included in the Lego box. After finishing building her Lego Frozen castle, Duo began to arrange the stickers, moved the minifigures around and began to recreate her own Frozen story with speech, movement, gesture and intonation. Table 3.3 illustrates Duo's spontaneous storymaking.

The story was about the two princesses' life in the castle. It began on one winter day. Duo fantasized a snowy day, probably because the snow was an important element in the original *Frozen* story. Duo put on a stair sticker so the two princesses could take the stairs to the second floor to appreciate the snow. The story continued with Elsa's and Anna's daily activities in the castle, as Duo chose the stickers and objects such as a piano, book and carpet, based on which Duo came up with the activities of reading, dancing, and piano and singing lessons. When it was 12 o'clock, Duo carefully selected places to rest for the princesses, the prince and the snowman, Olaf.

The above vignette indicates Duo's talent in combining linguistic and literary elements to create an original and interesting story. She used poetic language ('the snow falling quietly outside'), interesting details ('dirty socks left on the carpet') and creative thoughts ('Turning the A/C so low that the snowman won't melt') to compose a complete story with main characters, scenes, time, events and an ending. While the researcher played a supporting role in constructing this story, Duo took the initiative and led this storytelling activity. This vignette further legitimized the important role supportive adults play in creating an environment to facilitate bilingual/trilingual or even multilingual children's optimal development of multiple literacies (Bauer & Mkhize, 2012).

A closer look at Duo's storytelling process revealed its multimodal nature. Words, body language, gestures and intonations and objects (Lego and stickers) were all at Duo's disposal in creating this creative and interesting story. The three-dimensional and multimodal storytelling created rich meaning and vivid details that were otherwise missed if examined through a language-only lens.

Conclusion

The findings above show that with the support of her caregivers, Duo actively engaged in her material and sociocultural world, selecting

Table 3.3 Duo's multimodal storytelling

Still image	Movement, gesture, intonation	Verbal comments	Story plot being constructed
	Duo adheres a stair sticker so it connects the first and second floor. She puts the snowflake stickers on the window.	**Duo:** They need to go … This is when they go up. They continue walking up and up and up. And this is the snow, which is falling quietly outside.	Elsa and Anna live in a castle. On a snowy day, they take the stair and walk to the second floor to appreciate the snow in their garden.
	Duo holds the Elsa and Anna, places them on each side of the second floor, facing the garden.		
	Duo moves the minifigures on to their beds.	**Duo:** When it is twelve o'clock, they have to go to bed.	Elsa and Anna go to sleep at 12 o'clock.

<table>
<tr><td></td><td>Duo places the storybook sticker on the carpet.

She moves Elsa and Anna toward the piano.

She nods at researcher to show agreement for the two characters to dance.</td><td>Duo: Anna can also read the story books.
Researcher: They got lots of things to do in the castle. They can eat, play piano, sleep and dance. Can they dance? Is there a place to dance?
Duo: And then they can have their singing lesson. This is also a piano lesson.
Researcher: Elsa plays piano and Anna can sing.</td><td>Every day, Elsa and Anna sing, dance and read. They have singing and piano lessons.

When Elsa plays the piano, Anna sings.</td></tr>
<tr><td></td><td>Duo raises her voice in excitement and points at the white dots printed on the purple carpet.</td><td>Duo: Here's some dirty socks on the rug!
Researcher: Really?
Duo: Those white things are dirty stinky socks on the rug!</td><td>One day, someone left her dirty socks on the carpet! That is really bad!</td></tr>
</table>

(continued)

Table 3.3 Duo's multimodal storytelling (*Continued*)

Still image	Movement, gesture, intonation	Verbal comments	Story plot being constructed
	Duo moves minifigures around the castle.	**Duo:** Now they are tired. Can I put her here and where should Anna sleep? Maybe she can sleep on her mat. Where does Kristoff sleep? **Researcher:** Boys should sleep in a separate place. **Duo:** Where? **Researcher:** Maybe in the sled?	At night, everybody has a place to sleep. Elsa sleeps on her bed. Anna sleeps on the carpet. Kristoff sleeps in his sled. They turn the A/C really low, so Olaf can sleep inside the castle and won't melt.
	Duo picks up the Olaf minifigure and looks at it. She laughs at the idea of turning A/C down.	**Duo:** Olaf, he can sleep in the garden in the snow. Because he will not melt in the snow. **Researcher:** Otherwise if he sleeps in the castle, it's warm and he will melt. **Duo:** But they turn the A/C so so so so cold… **Researcher:** So he won't melt!	

features from languages, dialects, nonprint modes such as body language, gestures and spatial resources to communicate and to develop emergent biliteracy. A translanguaging literacies lens highlighted the rich meaning and creative design that characterized Duo's home literacy practice.

In Duo's specific case, the binary distinction between EBs' first and second language, home and school language and stronger vs. weaker language fall short in conceptualizing Duo's language and literacy development trajectory. Both English and Chinese are Duo's home language and mother tongue; both continued to develop as Duo grew. In her daily communication and literacy practices, we found that Duo skillfully mobilized semiotic resources for her own advantage to achieve successful communication, developed emergent biliteracy and created her own multimodal stories. This finding reminds parents and educators of bilingual children to think beyond perceived boundaries of nation-state languages, and between languages and other communicative modes.

A translanguaging literacies perspective foregrounds multilinguals doing language and literacy with their whole meaning-making repertoire. A holistic perspective on bilingual meaning-making practices calls for a comprehensive examination of learners' languages, dialect, gestures, intonations and knowledge of space and direction, as well as body language. To prepare children for today's increasingly diversified world, parents and educators can turn bilingual children's linguistic and cultural differences into advantages by highlighting, embracing and cultivating their creative use of communicative resources in everyday life.

References

ACTFL (American Council on the Teaching of Foreign Languages) (2010) *Foreign Language Enrollments in K-12 Public Schools: Are Students Prepared for a Global Society?* See https://www.ced.org/pdf/actfl-k12-foreign-language-for-global-society.pdf (accessed March 2021).

Bauer, E.B. and Gort, M. (eds) (2012) *Early Biliteracy Development: Exploring Young Learners' Use of Their Linguistic Resources*. Abingdon: Routledge.

Bauer, E.B. and Mkhize, D. (2012) Supporting the early development of biliteracy: The role of parents and caregivers. In E.B. Bauer and M. Gort (eds) *Early Biliteracy Development: Exploring Young Learners' Use of their Linguistic Resources* (pp. 14–33). Abingdon: Routledge.

Bhattacharya, K. (2017) *Fundamentals of Qualitative Research: A Practical Guide*. Abingdon: Taylor & Francis.

Blackledge, A. (2000) Monolingual ideologies in multilingual states: Language, hegemony and social justice in Western liberal democracies. *Sociolinguistic Studies* 1 (2), 25–45.

Blommaert, J. and Rampton, B. (2012) Language and superdiversity. MMG Working Paper No. 12-09.

Boyle, A., August, D., Tabaku, L., Cole, S. and Simpson-Baird, A. (2015) *Dual Language Education Programs: Current State Policies and Practices*. See https://ncela.ed.gov/files/rcd/TO20_DualLanguageRpt_508.pdf (accessed March 2021).

Bromley, D.B. (1986) *The Case-study Method in Psychology and Related Disciplines*. Hoboken, NJ: John Wiley.

Creese, A. and Blackledge, A. (eds) (2018) *The Routledge Handbook of Language and Superdiversity*. New York: Routledge.

Cummins, J. (2000) *Language, Power and Pedagogy: Bilingual Children in the Crossfire*. Clevedon: Multilingual Matters.

Dietrich, S. and Bauman, K. (2019) The association between household and community characteristics and children's acculturation. Working Paper No. SEHSD-WP2019-16. *US Census Bureau*, 9 April. See https://www.census.gov/library/working-papers/2019/demo/SEHSD-WP2019-16.html (accessed March 2021).

Fan, L. (2014) Understanding home language use in Chinese families who are living in the United States. Unpublished MA thesis, Iowa State University.

García, O. (2009) *Bilingual Education in the 21st Century: A Global Perspective*. Hoboken, NJ: John Wiley.

García, O. and Kleifgen, J.A. (2020) Translanguaging and literacies. *Reading Research Quarterly* 55 (4), 553–571.

García, O. and Li, W. (2014) *Translanguaging: Language, Bilingualism and Education*. London: Palgrave Macmillan.

Gort, M. (2019) Developing bilingualism and biliteracy in early and middle childhood. *Language Arts* 96 (4), 229–243.

Grosjean, F. (1989) Neurolinguists, beware! The bilingual is not two monolinguals in one person. *Brain and Language* 36 (1), 3–15.

Grosjean, F. (2008) *Studying Bilinguals*. New York: Oxford University Press.

Hornberger, N.H. (2002) Multilingual language policies and the continua of biliteracy: An ecological approach. *Language Policy* 1 (1), 27–51.

Hornberger, N.H. and Skilton-Sylvester, E. (2000) Revisiting the continua of biliteracy: International and critical perspectives. *Language and Education* 14 (2), 96–122.

Kress, G. (2003) *Literacy in the New Media Age*. Hove: Psychology Press.

Kress, G. (2009) *Multimodality: A Social Semiotic Approach to Contemporary Communication*. New York: Routledge.

Leopold, W. (1949) *Speech Development of a Bilingual Child: A Linguist's Record. Diary from Age 2*. Evanston, IL: Northwestern University Press.

Li, G. (2006) Biliteracy and trilingual practices in the home context: Case studies of Chinese-Canadian children. *Journal of Early Childhood Literacy* 6 (3), 355–381.

Li, W. (2018) Translanguaging as a practical theory of language. *Applied Linguistics* 39 (1), 9–30.

Merriam, S.B. (1998) *Qualitative Research and Case Study Applications in Education* (Revised and expanded from *Case Study Research in Education*). Hoboken, NJ: Jossey-Bass.

New London Group (1996) A pedagogy of multiliteracies: Designing social futures. *Harvard Educational Review* 66 (1), 60–93. doi:10.17763/haer.66.1.17370n67v22j160u

Ryan, C.L. (2013) *Language Use in the United States: 2011*. See https://www2.census.gov/library/publications/2013/acs/acs-22/acs-22.pdf (accessed March 2021).

Tracy, S.J. (2020) *Qualitative Research Methods: Collecting Evidence, Crafting Analysis, Communicating Impact* (2nd edn). Hoboken, NJ: Wiley-Blackwell.

Vertovec, S. (2007) Super-diversity and its implications. *Ethnic and Racial Studies* 30 (6), 1024–1054.

Vertovec, S. (ed.) (2015) *Diversities Old and New: Migration and Socio-Spatial Patterns in New York, Singapore and Johannesburg*. New York: Springer.

Xiao, Y. (2016) Chinese education in the United States: Players and challenges. *Global Chinese* 2 (1), 23–50.

Yaden Jr, D. and Tsai, T. (2012) Learning how to write in English and Chinese: Young bilingual kindergarten and first grade children explore the similarities and differences between writing systems. In E.B. Bauer and M. Gort (eds) *Early Biliteracy Development: Exploring Young Learners' Use of Their Linguistic Resources* (pp. 55–84). Abingdon: Routledge.

Yin, R.K. (2018) *Case Study Research and Application: Design and Methods* (6th edn). Thousand Oaks, CA: Sage.

4 Multimodal Narrative Composition in Urban Preschool(ed) Places: What Counts as Narrative and Whose Narrative Counts?

Colleen E. Whittingham and Emily Brown Hoffman

By infusing situatedness, playfulness, oral narrative and culture into the ways preschool teachers observe and make sense of children's storytelling, teachers normalize a range of possible 'pathways to literacy' (Dyson, 1993) for young children. This chapter serves as a springboard for necessary conversations regarding multimodal composition and culturally sustaining pedagogies as elements of early writing development, particularly relevant at a time when the preschool population is more diverse than ever before (Friedman-Krauss *et al.*, 2021).

Grounded in sociocultural theories, emergent writing challenges the idea that writing is an individual act, and instead purports that writing occurs 'between people, as they negotiate authoring processes, meaning, and textual forms as part of their everyday activities' (Rowe, 2008: 390). From this sociocultural perspective, learning to write involves not only the multifaceted skill of encoding print, but also learning ways of talking about text, what genres are valued and how they are taken up in various social settings, and appropriate ways of handling the material tools of 'writing' (Rowe, 2008). Kress (2000) further expands this sociocultural perspective on early writing to encompass the multimodal, including 'made objects' and the processes of making and materiality as equally valid and necessary forms of communication. The ideas, concepts, relations and affective states represented in multimodal making are no less cognitively demanding nor less effective than those represented through written language.

While teachers and children construct many social understandings about the nature and purpose of writing, this chapter focuses on the multimodal narrative composition of two Black four-year-old males in a Head Start classroom with plastic animals and Magna-Tiles, and how their play produced a sustained narrative that evolved over multiple weeks. The composing of the sustained narrative occurred most often during daily small-group center time, which lasted on average for 40–45 minutes each day. During this time, the two children of focus regularly elaborated on the multimodal narrative they were collaboratively composing, using talk, movement, gesture and physical objects to contribute to their storymaking. These sustained conversations served as rich sources of data, documenting patterns in both students' interactions around meaning-making. Observation of these literacy practices generated two research questions of interest: What counts as narrative? And whose narrative counts?

Literature Review and Theoretical Framing

Our operational definition of *narrative* is a simple one – narrative is, essentially, a story. In the case presented here, we refer to stories told by two preschool children through spoken word and toys. The existing body of research demonstrates strong potential in leveraging multimodality in oral storytelling to help learners in their vocabulary development, story retelling and reading comprehension (Huang, 2006; Isbell *et al.*, 2004). Lwin and Teo (2015) extend this body of knowledge by exploring the potential of oral storytelling to help learners develop a multimodal understanding of the composing process, with promising impacts on students' traditional writing.

Curriculum is reflective of the beliefs of those with the power to write, adopt and enact it (Apple, 1992, 2004). Curriculum in schools equates whiteness with normalcy through centering monolithic, Eurocentric perspectives and erasing the rich funds of knowledge (Moll *et al.*, 1992) and cultural wealth (Yosso, 2005) of Black, Indigenous and People of Color (BIPOC) children and their families. Early childhood contexts often enact this centering of whiteness and perpetuation of white supremacy through color-evasive discourse, assuming and perpetuating whiteness in curriculum habitually and without compromise (Butler *et al.*, 2019). For example, the writing curricula used ubiquitously in classrooms perpetuate 'standardized English' as correct and marginalize other Englishes by not including diverse English varieties as legitimate content (Falter *et al.*, 2020). Oral storytelling traditions are critical features of African American culture (Banks-Wallace, 2002), and are often ignored in writing curricula throughout the US. Boutte and Bryan (2021) describe curricular and pedagogical anti-Black violence in early childhood settings through the teaching of texts, materials and standards that have Eurocentric notions of existing in the world. The emphasis on code-based instruction caused by the 'perceived academic and social prestige' associated with the printed word has caused an emphasis on code-based instruction at the expense of 'the unique resources that the spoken word and other modes of meaning making can offer' (Lwin & Teo, 2015: 239), and is just one example of how white ways of being are centered even in children's earliest encounters with school. In an effort to expand notions of narrative, we present the theoretical underpinnings of our work as informed by the current research literature.

What counts as narrative?

Backgrounding the current verbo-centric focus of our educational system and instead turning our attention to multiple semiotic modes increases opportunities for intersubjectivity by attending to multimodality and embodied meaning in ways that written language cannot. When considering what counts as narrative, this includes allowing, advocating for and celebrating *multimodal meaning-making* and *linguistic authenticity* when oral language is one of those modes.

Multimodal meaning-making

We must shift our text-centered focus to attend instead to *meaning-making* as the ultimate goal, undergirded by linguistic development. All modes enable cognition, and cognition is possible in all modes, but in different ways. Cognition can therefore be seen as transformative, allowing people to arrive at similar places of meaning-making but through different paths. 'Written language enables one form of cognition, drawing another, colour as a medium another, the production of physical objects and their interactive use yet others' (Kress, 2000: 43). Students' potential for knowledge construction, and the demonstration of such cognition, depend very much on how schools react to students' attempts to employ these diverse frameworks for meaning-making (O'Loughlin, 1992: 5). We can encourage a multimodal focus on meaning-making by equally privileging the use of all available modes, including linguistic diversity.

Linguistic authenticity

So-called 'achievement gaps' between minoritized populations and their white peers are a part of the fabric of the US education system that has been attributed in part to the 'cultural incongruence between students and their teachers' (Howard, 2001: 181). Teachers largely believe Black students to have less academic potential than their white peers (Irvine, 1990), too often making judgments about students that have 'nothing to do with their intellectual ability, and everything to do with stereotypes, assumptions, and fear' (Love, 2013: 3). Additional often-offered explanations for such gaps are language differences and language proficiency because many African American children are bi/multidialectal (Terry *et al.*, 2018).

Morgan (2009) critiques the social construction of an 'African American speech community,' noting that the presumptions created by documenting, naming and otherwise essentializing 'African American English' perpetuate dominant ideologies that language is objective and neutral, and is therefore unable to 'do good' for marginalized groups of people. Despite these tensions, bidialectalism is not a 'risk' to be remedied, but rather evidence of unique language experiences with different implications for different children's English language knowledge. Beyond that, evidence demonstrates that 'when provided with rich and robust language interactions, bidialectalism and bilingualism can be leveraged as strengths to support literacy learning' (Terry *et al.*, 2018: 50).

Whose narrative counts?

Because literacy, language and meaning-making are social, preschool children rely on various communicative modes to compose and co-author, with peer interactions becoming increasingly complex as students learn to engage and respond to each other via modal resources (Bengochea *et al.*, 2020). These forms of collaboration are often met with resistance in a school system that values writing above speech, and therefore monologic forms of meaning-making above dialogic ones (Kress, 2003). Curriculum and instruction must privilege the knowledge in the community and of the students. When considering whose narrative counts, this includes allowing, advocating for and celebrating students' *cultural knowledge* and *identity construction* in school.

Cultural knowledge

Grounded in the work of Ladson-Billings (2014), culturally sustaining pedagogies acknowledge that each student 'possesses multiple frames of reference with which to construct knowledge by virtue of their ethnic background, race, class, gender, language usage, religious, cultural, and political identities' (O'Loughlin, 1992: 5). Abundant literature demonstrates how children with racial and linguistic backgrounds marginalized in schools engage in complex and sophisticated language and interactional practices at home (e.g. Au & Mason, 1981; Delpit, 2006; Heath, 1983). 'However, too few schools make use of early school-based practices that resonate with these language practices and build on them, therefore failing to build the initial strong sense of affiliation with school that often occurs for other children' (Gee, 2008: 102). As a result, Black children in particular are not faring well in early childhood settings (Boutte & Bryan, 2021). And yet, teachers can structure their classrooms in ways that encourage children to be active navigators of their own 'pathways to literacy' (Dyson, 2013). Particularly in early childhood settings, teachers can orchestrate a physical space and social structure that communicates to students their autonomy, their value and their responsibility to themselves and others. The environment is 'a motivating and animating force in creating spaces for relations, options and emotional and cognitive situations that produce a sense of well-being and security' (Malaguzzi, 1996: 40). By validating and elevating students' identities as learners, and the narratives they bring to the classroom, teachers are creating a culturally sustaining environment.

Identity construction

Culturally sustaining environments also simultaneously encourage the expression of individual identities, recognizing that shared racial and linguistic characteristics do not represent a homogenized community. Particularly in early childhood settings, exposure to a wide variety of narrative forms enriches students' understanding of their own and others' identities. As Bishop describes:

> Books are sometimes windows, offering views of worlds that may be real or imagined, familiar or strange. These windows are also sliding glass doors, and readers have only to walk through in imagination to become part of whatever world has been created or recreated by the author. When lighting conditions are just right, however, a window can also be a mirror. Literature transforms human experience and reflects it back to us. (Bishop, 1990: ix)

Bishop's words hold true even as the notion of text has expanded beyond the book or printed word to include additional semiotic tools. For example, Wohlwend (2009) examined kindergarteners' play with Disney Princess dolls to discover how young girls read and respond to constraining story lines attached to toys. When engaging in multimodal narrative construction, children drew upon their media knowledge as well as valued school literacy practices (Street, 1995, cited in Wohlwend, 2009). The opportunities for children to live in-character through narrative play, drawing upon and representing their cultural knowledge with toys, endorses the idea that teachers must become educated about popular culture of interest to our students and be self-critical when examining our own assumptions about media (Brownell, 2018; Wohlwend, 2009).

Study Design and Methodology

The data were generated during an eight-week case study (Dyson & Genishi, 2005) of one preschool classroom located in a community center on the south side of a large city in the midwestern United States. Situated within a broader research study, qualitative data collection informing the research questions discussed in this chapter includes observational field notes collected during literacy instruction, complemented by video-based field work (Jewitt, 2012) collected via two stationary camcorders outfitted with external microphones to capture teacher-child interactions and small-group settings. The Triangle classroom was led by Miss Zachmann, Ms O'Neal and Mr Pearson and served 17 African American four- and five-year-old children.

Edward and Richard were four-year-old members of the preschool classroom. Richard's mother and stepfather were security guards at a local office building, and as part of their regular interactions Edward and Richard 'took up' this narrative, often reenacting cops-and-robbers scenarios during dramatic play. Edward's primary caretakers were his grandparents. His teachers described him as 'emotionally intelligent,' often 'checking in' on students who appeared sad or upset. Narratives constructed by Edward and Richard became of interest during constant-comparative coding (Saldaña, 2015) of video data generated during daily center time. In reviewing the video data, then returning to field notes of the same events, and cross-referencing an interview with the classroom teacher, it became evident that Edward and Richard's engagement in multimodal narrative composition sustained over time demanded further attention. When asked about Edward and Richard's persistent gravitation toward certain materials used for the same purposes repeatedly during daily center time (which afforded many choices, most of which the other preschoolers migrated through regularly), lead teacher Miss Zachmann replied:

> I can see their play starting to get more and more complex, and I see them learning the concepts ... in terms of social, emotional and self-regulation; problem solving when things occur like when they both want the same animal, and they are getting those things out of that toy. They are also building more and more complex things and having more and more complicated storylines and plots with what they are doing. I can pop in every once in a while, and see what they are doing and just push the level higher and then step back and see them do it themselves. So, I am confident that they are getting what they need out of their day.

In an effort to further explore the complexities of Edward and Richard's play, we first identified all instances of collaboration between the two boys as documented during center time. These data curated 22 video clips spanning three weeks of instruction. Edward and Richard engaged in collaborative play using Magna-Tiles and plastic animals on eight of the 12 days observed during these three weeks. Once the data were cataloged, we engaged in two cycles of qualitative coding. Identifying themes to answer *what counts as narrative?* was a deductive process, with *a priori* codes loosely defined by the commonly agreed-upon features of narrative composition. Identifying themes to answer *whose narrative counts?* was an inductive process, with codes emerging more organically. Codes were collapsed into broader themes, and these themes are representative of the full data set. Regarding what counts as narrative, we found the multimodal play contained evidence of narrative story arcs, improvisation in the form of revisions to their work, and attention to audience as they collaborated. In terms of whose narrative counts, we found evidence of popular culture references, Rudine Sims Bishop's mirrors, windows and sliding glass doors, as well as evidence of collaborative composition.

Findings

While the physical context of the collaborative multimodal narrative composition observed between Edward and Richard remained constant (always including Magna-Tiles and plastic animals, always seated at a tabletop), the imagined worlds created through their play were fluid. The physical tools, the verbal discourse and the shared imagination transformed quickly, set on a rocket ship, at a pool or in the jungle. Edward and Richard's creations built an underwater world and a killing machine, improvisationally taking on the personas of Lion Guard or Teenage Mutant Ninja Turtle characters. The transcript excerpts shared here are representative of the larger data set, in that regardless of the setting and characters in play, Edward and Richard consistently composed narratives reflective of their own lived and projected experiences through collaborative multimodal engagement with one another.

What counts as narrative?

While traditional writing (with a paper and pencil) is an important skill and should not be dismissed, much teaching, learning and assessment in early childhood writing curricula discounts both collaborative multimodal composition and oral storytelling as worthy of being both the process and the final product. In the following example, Edward and Richard displayed many components included in traditional narrative writing curricula (e.g. Calkins & Marron, 2013). Their story showed organization, elaboration, crafting of details and recursive editing and revisions. Their *Deep Sea* narrative involved a complex plot full of conflict and characters that engaged in a story arc. The following transcript of 2 minutes and 30 seconds offers a glimpse of their 45 minutes of narrative writing that day, presented in 30-second intervals.

Edward and Richard are at the table playing with Magna-Tiles and plastic animals. In what follows, Richard introduces, and Edward picks up, the deep sea setting. The children lay the Magna-Tiles flat to create a deep sea. Then, Edward begins identifying two main characters out of animal figurines and Richard elaborates on these characters' identities and limits.

E: This our water. I'm swimming in the water.
R: And this the deep sea.
E: Yea, that's the deep deep sea.
R: I'm gonna go in the deep sea. Let's go – lets go catch some food. We need put all these things, put everything within the water.
E: But not these two.
R: Yea because they gonna they gonna spread the water all the way down and things cannot breathe and we cannot walk in and then we cannot open up our mouth.

Edward introduces another main character (the baby) and Richard revises character limits before introducing the plot of a party in the deep sea.

E: No no because because cause we have a baby. SEE?
R: Yea uh only put every kinda under ... let's think if all these things is underwater creatures. Oh we gonna have a party!
E: Let me – let me – let me Richard. Then I'll let you.

Edward picks up on the party plot and both children engage the characters in partying through use of onomatopoeia and making their animals dance on the Magna-Tiles.

R: Oooh, ooh, ooh, YEA.
E: Yea we gonna have a party here. A party.
R: An underwater sea – BOOM. Waaaaaaa. Boom
E: Gonna have a party here. Yea, we're gonna have a party here.

Edward introduces a conflict and new characters; sharks may interfere with the party! Richard suggests putting all the sharks in a Magna-Tile cage so they will not interfere and then both children negotiate and engage in revision regarding what to do with the shark problem through moving Magna-Tiles and animal figurines around.

E: Now we're gonna be ready. Very. There gonna be a lot of sharks here right buddy? There gonna be a lot of sharks.
R: Guess what? We gonna put all of them in here so we can have a real party!
E: Yea, a real party and then and then we can sharpen them and then hang them all up.
R: No, no, no, lets like make like all these is, our is, our is, our ...

Richard introduces dialogue from one of the main characters identified in the first 30 seconds and introduces another conflict, the deep sea becoming too deep for his character. In the final seconds, Richard describes their narrative writing in response to a teacher's question.

R: I mean, so I can swim with em and eat em
E: Yea, yea, yea.
R: 'Come on, son, let's go in here that's a good place.' 'Oh yea it's my bed time so I can eat y'all.' 'AH! Get down, it's too deep.'
Teacher: What's goin on over here at the animal table? What are you building?
R: We building this, a underwater scene, and this uh and this uh our water and this our under water sea.

As seen in other studies regarding preschool multimodal composition (Bengochea *et al.*, 2020), children can use strategic thinking to combine modes in unique ways to maximize goals and effectively communicate a narrative. Similarly, Edward and Richard used magnetic tiles, animal figurines and oral storytelling to collaboratively compose. The children's use of gestures and toy movement in coordination with their talk enhanced their ability to create and share meaning (Flewitt *et al.*, 2014; Goffman, 1981). In this short example, there is evidence of: *organization* through creating a steady setting and the construction of complex plots involving conflict, resolution and multiple characters as well as being able to summarize their narrative for an audience; *elaboration* through collaborative composing and character dialogue; *crafting of details* through creating character identities and relationships; and *recursive editing and revision* through physical manipulation of the animal figurines and Magna-Tiles and changing character limitations and negotiating story resolutions. Understanding that this short Deep Sea transcript represents a story that evolved not only throughout center time that day but was subsequently developed on the days prior to and later that day, Edward and Richard engaged in extensive collaboration through use of multiple modes to engage in a sustained and detailed narrative.

Whose narrative counts?

While in many early childhood education settings popular culture references may be discounted when considering children's narrative composition, the presence of familiar characters or settings is actually evidence of students' incorporation of out-of-school literacies in school(ed) spaces (Brownell, 2018). In their following narrative example, Edward and Richard use a popular children's animated Disney television show where the heroes make up the 'Lion Guard.' The use of the *Lion Guard* show does not invalidate the narrative as uniquely created by Edward and Richard. Rather, the use of the show allowed the children to 'try on' the roles and story structures that reflect their own lived experiences, their ideal lived experiences or the lived experiences of others. Much like literature can serve as a mirror, window or sliding glass door for the reader (Bishop, 1990), so can the act of multimodal composition serve as these for the author. In the following *Lion Guard* example, Richard and Edward 'try on' and share their linguistic and cultural repertoires. The following transcript of 2 minutes and 30 seconds offers a glimpse of their 45 minutes of narrative writing that day, presented in 30-second intervals.

Edward and Richard are at the table, playing with Magna-Tiles and plastic animals. The Magna-Tiles are flat on the ground and the animals are positioned on top of them. In what follows, Richard introduces the narrative of the Lion Guard. Edward elaborates on this idea through finding an owl and adding it as a character to the story. The owl is a hero in both the Lion Guard television show and Edward and Richard's narrative.

R: Hey can you put? Listen, let's put all the Lion Guards. All these people right here is the Lion Guard.
R: Now let me see. Where's the other owl buddy?
E: Ummm, hoo hoo!
R: Hoo, hoo, hoo, hoo!
E: That's how he talks ... all the owls.

The children begin building a large tower out of Magna-Tiles to form a 'killing machine' for the Lion Guard to put the villains in as they discuss which animals will be part of the hero group (the Lion Guard) and the villain group (to go into the killing machine). They then begin switching roles as they move the animals around, changing who is playing the villains and who is playing the heroes.

R: Hoo, hoo!
E: Who's that?
R: It's some bees. Let's build a killing machine
E: And who's this?
R: Huh?
E: Who's this?
R: Uh this this one a lion guard.
E: And who this right over here?
R: Oh, watch out because ...
E: Ahhhhhh! Okay, now you can be the lion guard and I'll follow you okay.
R: You can always talk to him.
E: I know. Hi. Reeeeeerereree (animal noises).

As the children take on roles, Richard contributes dialogue in the form of the Lion Guard while Edward contributes the villain's dialogue.

E: Reeeeer, reeeer (animal noises).
R: 'Watch out that's my buddy okay.' You can take him off if you want to.
E: 'Heeeey! Take a bath! Hey! Hey! Hey! Yea!'
R: 'Doing!'
E: 'Ooh! Ow! Ow! Hey watch it!'

The children play by hitting the toy animals together and making loud onomatopoeia fighting noises. Richard edits Edward's contribution through describing how some villains are only mean in certain circumstances.

E: 'Ooh! I'm bouncing! Ooh!'
R: He don't be mean. He only be mean to, to the, uh, to the people who try, who try to do this. [collides Edward's animal with a different animal]

The children spend more time enacting a fight scene with the animals. Richard and Edward re-engage with the owl presented in the first 30 seconds of the transcript. Then Richard notices that the Magna Tile 'killing machine' is not finished and Edward says he will help Richard finish it.

R: Wait a minute. This sound like the, this sound like the ... uh thing that uh 'hoo hoo hoo'
E: 'Hoo, hoo, hoo.'
R: What! Not done yet!
E: Gonna help you make this.

Edward and Richard negotiated shared authorship of their multimodal narrative composition by using a popular children's television show to 'try on' different roles and story structures. In this short excerpt from their sustained composition, Edward and Richard reflect: (1) *their own lived experiences* through bringing a television show they are both very familiar with into their school while adding ideas that make sense to them regarding what characters should act like, say and do; and (2) *their ideal lived experiences* and *the lived experiences of others* through a narrative where heroes are victorious over villains. Edward and Richard could embody heroes and villains to create a story where good triumphs over evil and justice prevails as well as recreate the experiences of the characters in the television show through their unique words, toys and actions. Moreover, Edward and Richard use Black Language to enact their powerful narrative, even though the preschool curriculum normalizes whiteness. Through using Black Language to expand their storytelling, and not the white standardized English perpetuated within US classrooms, Edward and Richard are bringing their funds of knowledge and cultural wealth into the classroom in authentic, joyful practice.

Throughout the 45-minute composition on this day, as well as subsequent days, Edward and Richard continued to build and expand on their Lion Guard narrative, continuing their collaboration through integrating unique ideas into the story's premise and characters.

Limitations

It is necessary to identify a few limitations of this work, both to increase the transparency with which the findings are interpreted, and to inform similar future work that may be taken up by others. First, as observers of the preschool classroom during the spring term, we do not know the origins of the storymaking, as we joined the narrative construction already in process. We do not know how Edward and Richard found each other as compatible co-authors, nor the catalyst for their interest in the specific toys used. The importance of relationship building through collaborative making cannot go unnoticed, and yet we cannot trace the beginnings of the relationship described here.

Second, there are no concrete artifacts documenting the compositions constructed each day. Interest in Edward and Richard's narrative play began during data analysis, not data collection, and the value of documenting their daily creations was not foreseen. While such photos could inform future research, we believe the artifacts constructed through multimodal composition are fluid in nature, never truly complete, and our primary interest remains in the process more so than in the product.

Finally, it is somewhat impossible to separate the constructs of *what counts as narrative* from *whose narrative counts*. As such, the theoretical constructs and bodies of literature we applied to each analysis are not cleanly delineated, but rather informed by one another. Findings regarding what counts as narrative reference scholars who influenced our thinking about whose narrative counts, and vice versa. We present this tension in the name of transparency, but simultaneously believe it is such tensions that reflect the complex and interconnected nature of this work.

Discussion

With these findings and limitations in mind, we turn our attention to the broader conversation about multimodal teaching and learning, referencing our own reflections on this work to: (1) describe the positive implications of prioritizing such multimodal composing in early childhood spaces; (2) describe some of the challenges of multimodal literacy teaching that became evident in this preschool(ed) space; and (3) share insights from the observed teacher practices as suggested ways to facilitate multimodal narrative composition in classrooms.

Positive implications

Curriculum in US schools, even unwritten and preschool curriculum, overwhelmingly favors white, affluent students and harms Black students (Boutte & Bryan, 2021). However, when curriculum is expanded, students are provided with the space needed 'to name and critique injustice to help them ultimately develop the agency to build a better world' (Muhammad, 2020: 12). Pedagogical approaches that intentionally center the linguistic needs of Black students are needed to dismantle the white linguistic supremacy that perpetuates within schools (Baker-Bell, 2020). Tolentino (2013) found that teachers create a culturally sustaining environment when they embrace a pedagogy of listening to students. When writing instruction centers the teacher as a listener, preschool students feel empowered to act and speak in ways that define themselves through composition. Through privileging listening to and observing children enacting their out-of-school literacies in a school(ed) space, the curriculum can change to one that includes sustained, collaborative and authentic ways of learning. The lack of teacher presence in the transcripts presented here is representative of the full data set, as none of the three classroom teachers was immediately instrumental to the composition. Teachers did not often interrupt the children's play and no teacher ever questioned or shut down 'the killing machine' as inappropriate in a school setting. In this classroom, the teacher served as an audience (or listener) to students' ideas, never correcting language, grammar, genre or topic. Teachers did not try to 'remedy' children's language experiences but rather leveraged authentic language interactions as strengths. Similarly, popular culture references were present in the multimodal composition in a way that was never about teachers appropriating students' out-of-school literacies, but was instead about allowing children to navigate these identities free of judgment or censorship. Curriculum including multimodal narrative composition can offer such opportunities for children, providing a space for creating, imagining and sharing lived experiences in early childhood classrooms.

Challenges in preschool(ed) spaces

Deep-seeded beliefs about the separation of school and home experiences threaten the spirit of multimodal narrative composition. Not all teachers are capable of (or supported by administration in) enacting a culturally sustaining environment focused on a pedagogy of listening. When teachers experience discomfort, the possible prioritization of their own comfort is a direct threat to students' voices. External accountability pressures coupled with teachers' various cultural ways of knowing are existing challenges, or potential threats, to multimodal literacy teaching. If a preschool or kindergarten rubric contends that writing a short story with a beginning, middle and end with drawn pictures is excellent work, then enacting a continuous 45 minutes of multimodal composition with peers is (or should be) astounding. And yet, traditional measures of success prioritize monolithic written products over dialogic oral processes in an attempt to quantify student learning for external accountability purposes. When teachers' cultural ways of knowing align with (or are influenced by) these external measures of success, it is unlikely that students will experience opportunities to engage in multimodal making in a way that 'counts.' However, when teachers adopt a both/and mentality rather than an either/or approach to documenting student learning (Whittingham & Hoffman, 2020), they prioritize space in the curriculum for students to engage in multimodal meaning-making while simultaneously learning the code.

Insights for classroom practice

When thinking about the specific features of the Triangle classroom that made this composition possible, we determined that, in this space, multimodal composition was facilitated by the physical environment, the teachers' tendencies to encourage and value multimodal narrative composition and the teachers' ability to plan opportunities for multimodal narrative composition. First, *materials for making* were always present and known, while *making spaces* were always identified, available, visible and accessible. The table tops were always available during center time for student use, never cluttered, and a clear path from the carpet, the library and the dramatic play area were always present for optimal student accessibility. Second, the three Triangle teachers engaged in reflective decision making, often rotating the table toy choices to remove those of lesser interest and to introduce something new. Based on their observations of student use, the Magna-Tiles and the plastic animals were never taken out of rotation. Finally, Triangle teachers created the space and time to allow narrative composing to happen. They played the role of audience not author (i.e. students often determined the teacher's role – when they invited her into their play, she obliged), serving as hummingbird not helicopter (i.e. the teacher refrained from evaluation or critique, instead validating student play, asking an elevating question and walking away).

Conclusion

In an incredibly multimodal world, we must 'broaden and layer the canvas on which stories are told. Educators need to respond by engaging with these multimodal resources to help students recognize and utilize them in such a way as to express more nuanced and complex rhetorical intents to meet the needs of their increasingly sophisticated audiences' (Lwin & Teo, 2015: 239). These educational imperatives become even more crucial when viewed through an equity lens, centering the systemic bias and perpetually disenfranchised lived experiences of Black students in school(ed) spaces. 'Two children have not had the same opportunity to learn if, however unconsciously, schooling or assessment ignores, dismisses, or demeans the one child's home- and community-based self and ways with words, deeds, and interactions' (Gee, 2008: 103). Our instructional focus then is not on appropriating student learning, but centered around students learning who they are and what story they wish to tell, and having time to navigate such imagination and discovery. Opportunities to compose narratively, multimodally, and collaboratively afford the lived experiences that become fodder for student reading and writing.

References

Apple, M. (1992) The text and cultural politics. *Educational Researcher* 21 (7), 4–19.

Apple, M. (2004) *Ideology and Curriculum* (3rd edn). New York: Routledge.

Au, K.H. and Mason, J.M. (1981) Social organizational factors in learning to read: The balance of rights hypothesis. *Reading Research Quarterly* 17 (1), 115–152.

Baker-Bell, A. (2020) Dismantling anti-black linguistic racism in English language arts classrooms: Toward an anti-racist black language pedagogy. *Theory into Practice* 59 (1), 8–21.

Banks-Wallace, J. (2002) Talk that talk: Storytelling and analysis rooted in African American oral tradition. *Qualitative Health Research* 12 (3), 410–426.

Bengochea, A., Sembiante, S.F. and Gort, M. (2020) Attracting and responding to an audience: Preschoolers' multimodal composing in show-and-tell activity. *Language Arts* 97 (3), 135–145.

Bishop, R.S. (1990) Mirrors, windows, and sliding glass doors. *Perspectives* 1 (3), ix–xi.

Boutte, G. and Bryan, N. (2021) When will Black children be well? Interrupting anti-Black violence in early childhood classrooms and schools. *Contemporary Issues in Early Childhood* 22 (3), 232–243.

Brownell, C.J. (2018) Creative language play(giarism) in the elementary English language arts classroom. *Language Arts* 95 (4), 218–228.

Butler, A., Teasley, C. and Sánchez-Blanco, C. (2019) A decolonial, intersectional approach to disrupting whiteness, neoliberalism, and patriarchy in Western early childhood education and care. In P.P. Trifonas (ed.) *Handbook of Theory and Research in Cultural Studies and Education* (pp. 1–18). New York: Springer.
Calkins, L. and Marron, A. (2013) *Narrative Craft*. Portsmouth, NH: Firsthand.
Delpit, L.D. (2006) *Other People's Children: Cultural Conflict in the Classroom*. New York: The New Press.
Dyson, A.H. (1993) From invention to social action in early childhood literacy: A reconceptualization through dialogue about difference. *Early Childhood Research Quarterly* 8, 409–425.
Dyson, A.H. (2013) *Rewriting the Basics: Literacy Learning in Children's Cultures*. New York: Teachers College Press.
Dyson, A.H. and Genishi, C. (2005) *On the Case*. New York: Teachers College Press.
Falter, M.M., Alston, C.A. and Lee, C.C. (2020) Becoming anti-racist ELA teachers. White Paper, North Carolina State University College of Education.
Flewitt, R., Hampel, R., Hauck, M. and Lancaster, L. (2014) What are multimodal data and transcription? In C. Jewitt (ed.) *The Routledge Handbook of Multimodal Analysis* (pp. 40–53). London: Routledge.
Friedman-Krauss, A.H., Barnett, W.S., Garver, K.A., Hodges, K.S., Weisenfeld, G.G. and Gardiner, B.A. (2021) 'The State of Preschool 2020: State Preschool Yearbook.' National Institute for Early Education Research.
Gee, J.P. (2008) A sociocultural perspective on opportunity to learn. In P.A. Moss, D.C. Pullin, J.P. Gee, E.H. Haertel and L.J. Young (eds) *Assessment, Equity, and Opportunity to Learn* (pp. 76–108). Cambridge: Cambridge University Press.
Goffman, E. (1981) *Forms of Talk*. Philadelphia, PA: University of Pennsylvania Press.
Heath, S.B. (1983) *Ways with Words: Language, Life and Work in Communities and Classrooms*. Cambridge, MA: Cambridge University Press.
Howard, T.C. (2001) Powerful pedagogy for African American students: A case of four teachers. *Urban Education* 36, 179–202.
Huang, H. (2006) The effect of storytelling on EFL young learners' reading comprehension and word recall. *English Teaching & Learning* 30 (3), 51–74.
Irvine, J.J. (1990) *Black Students and School Failure*. New York: Greenwood Press.
Isbell, R., Sobol, J., Lindauer, L. and Lowrance, L. (2004) The effects of storytelling and story reading on the oral language complexity and story comprehension of young children. *Early Childhood Education Journal* 32 (3), 157–163.
Jewitt, C. (2012) An introduction to using video for research. NCRM Working Paper No. 312, National Centre for Research Methods.
Kress, G. (2000) *Before Writing: Rethinking the Paths to Literacy*. London: Routledge.
Kress, G. (2003) *Literacy in the New Media Age*. London: Routledge.
Ladson-Billings, G. (2014) Culturally relevant pedagogy 2.0: Aka the remix. *Harvard Educational Review* 84 (1), 74–84.
Love, B.L. (2013) 'I see Trayvon Martin': What teachers can learn from the tragic death of a young black male. *The Urban Review* 45 (3), 1–15.
Lwin, S.M. and Teo, P. (2015) Crossing borders: A multimodal perspective on storytelling. *Storytelling, Self, Society* 11 (2), 211–245.
Malaguzzi, L. (1996) *The Hundred Languages of Children: Narrative of the Possible*. Reggio Emilia: Reggio Children.
Moll, L.C., Amanti, C., Neff, D. and González, N. (1992) Funds of knowledge for teaching: Using a qualitative approach to connect homes and classrooms. *Theory into Practice* 31 (2), 132–141.
Morgan, M. (2009) The African-American speech community: Reality and sociolinguists. In A. Duranti (ed.) *Linguistic Anthropology: A Reader* (2nd edn, pp. 74–92). Walden, MA: Wiley-Blackwell.

Muhammad, G. (2020) *Cultivating Genius: An Equity Framework for Culturally and Historically Responsive Literacy*. New York: Scholastic.

O'Loughlin, M. (1992) Appropriate for whom? A critique of the culture and class bias underlying developmentally appropriate practice in early childhood education. Unpublished conference paper, Conference on Reconceptualizing Early Childhood Education: Research, Theory, and Practice.

Rowe, D.W. (2008) Social contracts for writing: Negotiating shared understandings about text in the preschool years. *Reading Research Quarterly* 43 (1), 66–95.

Saldaña, J. (2015) *The Coding Manual for Qualitative Researchers*. New York: Sage.

Street, B.V. (1995) *Social Literacies: Critical Approaches to Literacy in Development, Ethnography, and Education*. New York: Longman.

Terry, N.P., Gatlin, B. and Johnson, L. (2018) Same or different: How bilingual readers can help us understand bidialectal readers. *Topics in Language Disorders* 38 (1), 50–65.

Tolentino, E.P. (2013) 'Put an explanation point to make it louder': Uncovering emergent writing revelations through talk. *Language Arts* 91 (1), 10–22.

Whittingham, C.E. and Hoffman, E.B. (2020) A teaching and learning tightrope: Navigating accountability mandates while maintaining sound pedagogical practices. *National Head Start Association (NHSA) Dialog* 23 (2), 51–71.

Wohlwend, K.E. (2009) Damsels in discourse: Girls consuming and producing identity texts through Disney princess play. *Reading Research Quarterly* 44 (1), 57–83.

Yosso, T. (2005) Whose culture has capital? A critical race theory discussion of community cultural wealth. *Race, Ethnicity, and Education* 8 (1), 69–91.

5 Learning from Emergent Bilinguals: Mobilizing Translanguaging and Multimodality to Reimagine School Literacy Curricular Spaces

Ysaaca Axelrod, Lorraine Falchi and Marjorie Siegel

In this chapter, we share vignettes from two longitudinal research projects that studied the language and literacy practices of young emergent bilinguals (Axelrod, 2014; Falchi *et al.*, 2014). The focus is on young children who navigated diverse linguistic and cultural settings with flexible, playful and unpredictable use of semiotic resources. We intentionally reflect on how they built on practices from their peers, families and communities, while interacting within programs that primarily serve immigrant families.

One vignette takes place in a four-year-olds' Head Start classroom, where Estrella and Peter (all names of participants are pseudonyms) are painting together at an easel and discussing their emerging composition. The other is in a second-grade classroom as a group of friends employ signs and covert communicative practices during a standardized test of English proficiency. We juxtapose these *literacy-as-events* (Burnett & Merchant, 2018) to analyze how children's interactions pulsated with possibilities affected by the sensory life of classrooms, children's agency and their complex language and literacy practices. We shine a light on how, when children's multimodal and multilingual assets are placed at the center of the curriculum, learners can access and mobilize them in purposeful ways to relate with peers, create, and engage in complex problem solving. Like many early childhood educators, we recognize the challenges presented by a narrowing of curricula, standards-based education and accountability with high-stakes testing, and policies that marginalize emergent bilinguals, casting many immigrant children as 'behind', especially when dominant curricular models exclude the local knowledge of children, families and teachers (Souto-Manning & Martell, 2016). We conclude with implications for supporting children's diverse learning pathways and teaching possibilities.

Theoretical Framework

At a time when monocultural, monolingual and monomodal conceptions of literacy and literacy pedagogy continue to be inscribed in policies, standards and curricula and reinforced by standardized accountability measures, educators have begun to expand what counts as literacy to include multimodality and translanguaging. Literacy educators have shown tremendous interest in multimodality (Kontovourki & Siegel, 2021; Siegel & Panofsky, 2009), yet, within the field of literacy education, 'The multilingual was largely excluded from the multimodal' (Kleifgen, 2013, cited in García & Kleifgen, 2020: 553). In what follows, we define translanguaging and multimodality and then draw on Burnett and Merchant's (2018) revision of Heath's (1983) 'literacy event' as 'literacy-as-event', which calls attention to relationality, materiality, affect and emergence to foreground 'the liveliness of literacy practices ... what happens as people and things come *into relation* rather than as separate, pre-existing entities' (Burnett & Merchant, 2018: 2).

Translanguaging as a verb 'shifts the emphasis to the actions of multilinguals and their spontaneous performances, always emergent, as they engage in assemblages of the forms of semiosis that are made available' (García & Kleifgen, 2020: 557). In other words, translanguaging captures the language in action of a multilingual child who selects and combines resources from their semiotic repertoire to accomplish a social act. We understand translanguaging as referring to the language practices of bilinguals and to pedagogies that transform learning interactions, relationships and curriculum through opportunities for inquiry into language.

Translanguaging pedagogy (García & Kleifgen, 2010; Pontier & Gort, 2016) attends to creative and fluid language practices used in children's homes and communities and carves out space for children to draw on their entire semiotic repertoires. This translanguaging stance disrupts and critiques notions of separation among languages, pushing against ideas of 'fixed language identities constrained by nation-states' (García & Li, 2014: 21), and instead shifts toward flexible dynamic bilingualism. Pedagogical practices that make use of translanguaging serve to decolonize bilingualism by challenging monoglossic ideologies that assume duality, the possession of two stable, bounded languages hierarchically positioned to reflect the language of power in nation-states and schools.

Multimodality is often traced to the New London Group's (1996) manifesto, 'A Pedagogy of Multiliteracies', yet the turn to multimodality in literacy studies can be traced back to the early 1980s when conventional theories of literacy and literacy learning were being uprooted by semiotic and sociocultural theories (see, for example, Dyson, 1990, 2003; Harste *et al.*, 1984; Siegel, 2006). Definitions of multimodality are grounded in a semiotic perspective on meaning-making which assumes that meanings are made through multiple sign systems by juxtaposing and combining signs to generate meanings that would not be possible if language were the only sign system available. Over the last 40 years, research on multimodality in literacy education has shown the limits of verbo-centric literacy curricula. In contrast, adopting a semiotic perspective on literacy, in which 'the orchestration of all signifying structures from all available communication systems in the event have a part' (Harste *et al.*, 1984: 208), has expanded what counts as literacy and who counts as literate. Themes prominent in the literature on multimodality and literacy include: children's knowledge of how different sign systems work; children's invention of signs and metaphors to generate their own meanings; and how children's literacies become visible and recognized when multiple sign systems are treated as basic, not peripheral, to literacy learning (Siegel, 2006).

There are important parallels between translanguaging and multimodality. Whether children are moving across and combining resources from their unitary language repertoire or moving across and combining multiple sign systems, both are instances of symbol making and symbol weaving (Dyson, 1990). To explore the significance of translanguaging and multimodality, we take up Heath's notion of a *literacy event* to examine the actions and interactions of the children in the vignettes presented below and to foreground the fluid way the children wove together multimodality and translanguaging to participate in school literacy. However, in our efforts to trace children's meaning-making in the literacy events we selected, we drew on Burnett and Merchant's (2018) notion of *literacy-as-event* to attend to not only children's translanguaging, but also to their multimodal sign-making (e.g. painting, gesturing), and their relations with humans and the 'stuff' of classrooms (e.g. the materials, objects, places), all the while noticing the emergence and in-betweenness of meanings. As Burnett and Merchant (2018) argue:

> This perspective invites literacy research to focus more on the relations mediated through the process of making meaning: the new collaborations, stories, conceptualizations, directions, intentions and so on that emerge as people engage in making meanings, all of which can and often do turn out in unexpected ways. (Burnett & Merchant, 2018: 8)

Still, in highlighting the relations mediated through the process of making meaning, we do not ignore classroom expectations, monitoring systems and district and national standards that regulate classroom life and meaning-making from afar in these neoliberal times, whether this involves displaying control of specific skills, strategies and languages, and/or compliance with social and instructional routines. Finally, the emphasis on relationality in the notion of *literacy-as-event* allows us to show the fluidity and generativity of children's translanguaging and multimodal sign-making.

Stories from bilingual classrooms

The two early childhood programs were located in a gentrifying neighborhood of New York City. Both sites serve children who are predominantly immigrant families from Mexico, including many who identified as Mixtec and spoke Mixteco and Spanish at home, as well as first- and second-generation immigrants from the Dominican Republic and third-generation migrants from Puerto Rico. The bilingual Head Start program served children aged three to five using a play-based curriculum that sought to create continuity and connection in using a strengths-based relational approach with teachers, children and families. In this classroom, children chose from language repertoires depending on preference, translanguaging as bilingual communities do, with support and modeling by teachers. In contrast, at a nearby elementary school within the dual language bilingual program, children participated in a second-grade curriculum that alternated daily between Spanish and English instruction. The bilingual program model aimed for bilingualism, biliteracy and academic achievement in two languages, and required teachers to instruct, interact and encourage children to use the language of the day and did not allow translanguaging.

Our findings highlight the fluidity of children's translanguaging and multimodal practices, capturing the emergent and relational nature of interactions among children and materials. In juxtaposing these events, we examine how children tap into their broad repertoires of multimodal literacies to achieve different aims in response to the sociopolitical space of their classrooms. In the Head Start classroom, with a flexible approach to language and literacy, collaboration was encouraged; children often co-constructed artifacts, navigating across languages and 'misunderstandings' to achieve social goals of working with friends in multimodal play. In the second-grade classroom, children taking a language proficiency test in English recognized the significance of proving they had gained the English skills required to pass and took joint social action by making liminal spaces for communication and collaboration, resisting the rules of standardized testing and 'language policing' that happens in classrooms.

'It's a chocolate rainbow'

This event took place in a four-year-olds' Head Start classroom where Ysaaca conducted her research. Estrella, a three-year-old Mixtec and Spanish speaker, and Peter, a four-year-old, the only Black child in the class and the only monolingual English speaker, went to the easel and started painting together. While there were two sides to the easel, the children often chose to paint together, sharing a paper. They were both very social and chatty children. At this point in the year, Estrella seemed to understand directions in English; however, she only responded in Spanish. Peter spoke primarily English, although he was enthusiastic about singing in Spanish and his use of a few phrases in Spanish drew attention and approval from the classroom teachers. The children often spoke to him in Spanish and, while he responded in English, he appeared to understand what they said.

[Researcher note/RN: Estrella and Peter were painting together, dipping the brushes into the pots of paint and making large movements across paper.]

Estrella: Yo veo Dora, ¿tu ves Dora? [I watch Dora, do you watch Dora?]

[RN: I was sitting next to easel and translated the sentence for Peter. He nodded in response and then stepped back from easel and responded to Estrella.]

Peter: I watch Dora, then Diego, girls don't watch Diego.

[RN: Estrella motioned to Peter to return to painting, waving the brush and motioning to the easel.]

Estrella: Ven [come]

[RN: Both children went back to painting. They were painting abstractly, putting brushes in different color paints and just painting over and on top of the same areas. Eventually the page was covered in paint, layers of paint, and mostly brownish from all the colors mixing together.]

Peter: Chocolate.

[RN: Estrella looked at painting, shook her head no.]

Estrella: No.

Peter: Chocolate with hotdog.

Estrella: Noooooo … Es un rainbow [no, it's a rainbow]

[RN: Estrella gestured at painting, with a swooping motion.]

Estrella: Mira ese rainbow [Look at this rainbow].

[RN: Peter looked at the painting again, and pointed at a spot where there appeared to be a swirl.]

Peter: Look, look, a yo-yo.

[RN: Estrella gave a puzzled look.]

Estrella: ¿Llovió? No llovió, un rainbow [Rained? No, not rained, a rainbow].

[RN: Peter looked at painting and swept his arm like an arch/rainbow.]

Peter: Yeah, it's a chocolate rainbow.

The children returned to painting for a few more seconds, adding more layers of paint, although even the paint in the containers was brown from all the mixing. The teacher called to clean up, and the children put the brushes into paint containers and joined their classmates in the line to wash their hands for snack. Estrella and Peter did not start painting with an image or drawing they wanted to create. As they painted, layering color after color, the story evolved, based on their interpretations of the shapes and colors of the paint on the page. Dyson (1990: 52) writes, 'art and play have critical roles in children's growth as symbol makers', and through these playful explorations, and interactions with peers, children develop composing practices. In this vignette, we see Estrella and Peter playing together with their painting to co-create an artifact that they read as a 'chocolate rainbow'. Similar to their play with images, we see them navigate across their linguistic differences, by drawing on their full linguistic repertoires, including gestures, such as Estrella's hand gesture to 'come' back to painting and sweeping arches that mimic the shape of a rainbow. Through translanguaging, the children were able to discuss their painting, including their disagreements about the image in front of them and move to a place of mutual understanding.

In the end, the painting was a blending of Estrella's desire to name a rainbow and Peter's desire to name the color 'chocolate'. Studies have demonstrated the complex ways that emergent bilinguals employ their linguistic repertoires, including translanguaging, to achieve their goals during play with peers (Orellana, 1994; Yun, 2008). Bengochea *et al.* (2018: 42) use the term *transmodal communication* to frame children's 'translanguaging as part of bilingual children's expansive transmodal repertoire'. Estrella and Peter's conversation, interactions and collaborative creation demonstrate the ways in which they seamlessly wove together multimodal resources in their symbolic play. Drawing on the notion of semiotic resources and using a *literacy-as-event* (Burnett & Merchant, 2018) lens allows us to situate this event within the larger classroom context and across time, providing greater insight into the children's language practices, their choices and how this interaction among two children and the painting highlights their language and literacy development within the context of this classroom. The word 'rainbow' as well as the use of the word 'chocolate' to describe the color brown can be seen as evidence of their sign-making, which fit into larger discourses within the classroom and are part of the children's shared experiences in the classroom.

Rainbows were a favorite in the classroom. Estrella frequently painted with Soraya, who played around with variations of the word 'rainbow', such as 'rainbowli' and said 'rainbow it up' to talk about adding more to a painting (Axelrod, 2014). It was not surprising that Estrella was familiar with and used the word 'rainbow' in English to describe her painting instead of the word 'arcoiris' in Spanish (which she knew and used in other contexts). Given the diversity of speakers of Spanish in the classroom (including the teachers who were from Argentina, the Dominican Republic and Puerto Rico), the teachers often discussed the various ways that objects are called, depending on the country of origin of the speakers (or their families). Additionally, they discussed cognates, words that are similar or the same in English and Spanish, as part of their classroom practices. The word 'brown' in English can be said in various ways in Spanish, 'marrón', 'café' and 'pardo', among others, although these were the ones that were used in the classroom. To bridge these differences, the teachers would often use the word 'chocolate' to describe the color 'brown', particularly as 'chocolate' is a cognate in English and Spanish. For example, in another conversation a teacher said, 'I love Estrella's hair, es como el color de chocolate,' using a description of the color to describe the child's hair color. The teachers in the classroom also frequently engaged in translanguaging to support their emergent bilingual students, and these practices were part of the classroom discourse.

A *literacy-as-event* lens provides an opportunity to think beyond this particular event, to better understand Estrella and Peter, their semiotic resources and sign-making, and to think about them over time and in connection to each other and the classroom community. Reflecting on pedagogical possibilities, we wondered: What if teachers drew on this lens to support classroom inquiry into children's language and literacy development within vibrant communities of transmodal practices? What could teachers learn about Estrella and Peter through observing this interaction, and how might that shape their curricular practices?

Friends and fists up: Translanguaging during standardized testing

In this second *literacy-as-event*, Lori observed as Mia and two of her second-grade friends completed the first day of their test of English proficiency by sharing answers. This is what some would call cheating. Yet the children's interactions and use of sign gestures to accomplish their collective agenda raise questions of how and why the children are negotiating these powerful high-stakes standardized testing pressures in our schools.

[Researcher note/RN: Mia and her group of friends often used gaze, gestures and facial expressions to communicate under the radar in their classrooms. One spring morning, Ms Fabiana, the second-grade Spanish component teacher, informed her class that they would begin their English proficiency testing with the listening portion. She explained the rules of the test for it to count and played a recording in English for children to listen to at their tables.

Mia looked at Xiomara and formed an 'A' sign with her hand, pointing to her, and nodded her head 'yes.' The children listened to prerecorded directions and filled in letter bubbles, coding their first and last names on scantron sheets.]

Ms Fabiana: There is no talking. I cannot answer questions because this is a test. You will listen to a story after listening to instructions about a nonfiction passage.

[RN: Mia raised and lowered her fist with an excited expression. Children listened to a question followed by multiple choice answers, a short passage, and the same question and choices again. Mia and Rebeca pursed their mouths in dismay.]

Ms Fabiana: You must choose one of the answers.

[RN: Mia looked at Xiomara and nodded her head as they heard the question. Mia and Xiomara exchanged glances. Mia formed the shape of an 'A' with her fingers twice. After the next question, Kelly looked at Mia and formed the shape of a 'C' with her hand. Mia looked at Xiomara and then formed the 'C' to which Xiomara nodded. When the correct sample answer 'A' was announced, Mia raised a fist up with a silent cheer. Kelly continued gesturing to Mia and Mia pivoted to sign the same answer to Xiomara several times.]

Ms Fabiana: This concludes the listening section. Tomorrow we will continue with the reading part.

[RN: Mia looked at Rebeca, pointed to herself and Xiomara and Kelly and then made a thumbs up. Then the children left and Lori approached Ms Fabiana.]

Lori: There was some sharing going on. Hand gestures with Mia and Xiomara and Kelly – a little sharing.

[RN: Ms Fabiana laughed and they laughed together.]

The teachers were under pressure and eager for the children to pass this English language proficiency test, while the children, who were categorized as English language learners, transformed the activity by sign making. As children worked individually and in silence – gesturing covertly while bubbling in the answers – they used available semiotic resources suitable to the circumstances. The children's translanguaging practices transformed language proficiency testing into a game of symbol making.

Mia's second-grade teachers negotiated the testing pressures and grappled with the tensions of a balanced literacy curriculum that focused on the processes of 'good readers' and 'good writers' that they were mandated to follow. Ms Fabiana prioritized getting to know her children as learners in order to build on their background knowledge, often using dialogic reading to engage and promote children's language development with sophisticated vocabulary, varied sentence structure and comprehension of texts of different genres. On occasion, teachers intentionally used translanguaging to support children's comprehension and co-construction of meaning during read-alouds. This strategy was important support for emergent bilinguals' access to literature, but it required that teachers depart from the curricular norm of monolingualism to scaffold language. Restricted from changing the balanced literacy curriculum to allow for more curricular flexibility and responsiveness to children's strengths, the teachers and children negotiated a dominant curricular model that devalued children's multimodal literacies, testing pressures and inflexible policies based on monolingual ideologies that marginalize emergent bilinguals' language practices. Yearly school progress monitoring meant that children and cohorts were labeled as inadequate, and these perceived deficits resulted in an increase in direct instruction. Expansive multimodal literacy approaches that they had sometimes used, like producing a play, were abandoned to focus on academics and tightly regulated interactions.

Mia routinely participated in school literacy curricula, yet she broke out of the expected when she began signing with friends. She refused to individually progress forward, instead collectively mobilizing semiotic resources from a set of social practices. Mia repositioned herself and friends as innovators enacting multimodal translanguaging practices, making liminal spaces for communication and collaboration. Despite the pressures of policies to promote 'academic skills', children negotiated and resisted the policy of language separation and a narrowed version of school literacy learning in their creative departures from dominant norms.

Learning from Emergent Bilinguals

Translanguaging, the norm among bilingual communities (García & Li, 2014), is not the norm in schools. And school literacy curricula remain verbo-centric and print-centric. In the second-grade classroom, we see the strict separation of languages: each teacher taught in a separate language, and the expectation was that children only used the language that was assigned to that part of their school day. In the Head Start classroom, while all members of the classroom community translanguaged, and the children were given time and space to play, the teachers were not always attending to or documenting the children's linguistic practices or multimodal meaning-making.

In looking at the two vignettes, we see the ways in which the children in the second-grade classroom resisted the strict separation of languages, particularly on the standardized assessment, by creating their own sign system in order to be able to collaboratively participate in the exam. In the Head Start classroom, Estrella and Peter relied on translanguaging to communicate with each other, and to draw on classroom community practices around language, such as rainbow and chocolate. While the teachers in the Head Start classroom did engage in some discussions around language, such as differences in vocabulary and cognates, these were usually teacher directed and drew on the ways that the teachers used language, rather than the children. We wondered, had a teacher watched the interaction among the children and the painting, what might they have learned? And, how might they revisit this painting and story, to continue to build the children's control of language and literacies? In the second-grade classroom, what might have happened if the teacher had noticed the interactions among the girls, recognized it as a form of resistance, and used it as a way to build students' criticality (Muhammad, 2020)?

Teachers play a crucial role in supporting translanguaging and multimodal meaning-making, to push against monoglossic ideologies of bilingualism (Gort & Sembiante, 2015) and print-centric practices. Teachers who intentionally transgress and resist inflexible language policy, with their children in mind, work toward transforming it. As we see in these two classrooms, emergent bilingual children already engage in these practices; however, they are not always affirmed, recognized or valued within classroom spaces. Instead, we advocate for practices that notice and start with what children are doing, documenting children's compositions, including those created collaboratively, to see the ways that children draw on their community resources, including those within the classroom community, to play with and compose. How might we then engage children in conversations about their work and their choices, and how could these conversations be an important component of the curricular practices of learning from children?

In the second-grade classroom, the teachers felt pressure to abide by district mandates and fluctuated between strictly enforcing norms, such as separation of languages and compliance with test-taking norms, while also empathizing with children's collaborations to resist. The teachers used multimodal composing, such as the creation of elaborate character maps and puppets; however, these were scaffolding to the 'real work' of writing, as is evident, for example, in teachers stapling children's puppets to bulletin board displays. Teachers encouraged children to use the puppets to compose stories but saw them as tangential to composing written products. How might documentation of children's transmodal composing processes and use of language and collaboration with peers change storytelling? We suggest teachers moving from linear, verbo-centric composing practices of children and embracing diverse language and literacy practices as foundational. We recognize and value translanguaging and transmodal practices on their own, and not just as pedagogical scaffolds. As Dyson (1990) writes:

> we should not assume that the developmental path is from child drawer to adult artists or from child story writer to adult novelist .... Stories, pictures, drama – these are children's ways of giving shape to their experiences, of figuring out who they are in relationship to the world and to each other. These are also children's ways of making their own tools that will serve them throughout their lives. (Dyson, 1990: 56)

This highlights how teachers might notice children's creative intelligence and how it offers us windows into the relationship between the child, their sign-making and symbol weaving in stories, and their social and cultural contexts of participation.

Lastly, we urge teachers and researchers to engage in culture-centered practices (Gay, 2000; Ladson-Billings, 2014; Paris, 2012) that build on children's cultural and linguistic practices, drawing on their resources and strengths in ways that foster and sustain, as well as transform toward more equitable schooling. Muhammad (2020) offers four pursuits as a way to examine instruction and curriculum, and one of these is *criticality*. She writes, 'criticality helps teachers understand and explain inequalities in education and is a step toward teaching anti-oppression' (Muhammad, 2020: 117). Mia and her friends used their shared repertoire of nonverbal gestures and facial expressions to fly under the radar at the circle time or during silent, seated work time and, in the example shared here, to refuse to comply with the constraints of the mandated, monoglossic and verbo-centric modes of communication. How might the teacher recognize the children's resistance and engage in conversations that allowed children to build criticality around standardized testing, artificial language separation and print-centric practices that did not draw on their semiotic repertoire?

We draw on these two different events to highlight the means by which children engage in multimodal meaning-making and translanguaging in ways that complement each other to accomplish their goals: in the first, two friends paint together; in the second, friends co-conspire to push against standardized testing. We examined children's everyday social interactions to consider how local curricular, language and literacy practices affect participation, perception and power dynamics (García & Kleyn, 2016) in the social spaces of schooling. In spite of the differences, our goal in sharing these two *literacy-as-events* is to bring together translanguaging and multimodality to reimagine teaching and curricula as inclusive, building on children's and communities' diverse literacy practices. Using a strength-based approach (Souto-Manning & Martell, 2016), we illustrate the overlapping, interconnected ways that emergent bilinguals engage in translanguaging and multimodality. We highlight how to read children's language and literacy practices through the dual lens proposed, and mobilize teachers to take up more expansive views of emergent bilingual children's language and literacy learning.

References

Axelrod, Y. (2014) 'Ganchulinas' and 'rainbowli' colors: Young multilingual children play with language in Head Start classroom. *Early Childhood Education Journal* 1 (45), 103–110.

Bengochea, A., Sembiante, S.F. and Gort, M. (2018) An emergent bilingual child's multimodal choices in sociodramatic play. *Journal of Early Childhood Literacy* 18 (1), 38–70.

Burnett, C. and Merchant, G. (2018) Literacy-as-event: Accounting for relationality in literacy research. *Discourse: Studies in the Cultural Politics of Education* 41 (1), 45–56.

Dyson, A.H. (1990) Research in review. Symbol makers, symbol weavers: How children link play, pictures and print. *Young Children* 45 (2), 50–57.

Dyson, A.H. (2003) *The Brothers and Sisters Learn to Write: Popular Literacies in Childhood and School Culture.* New York: Teachers College Press.

Falchi, L., Axelrod, Y. and Genishi, C. (2014) 'Miguel es un artista' – and Luisa is an excellent student: Seeking time and space for children's multimodal practices. *Journal of Early Childhood Literacy* 14 (3), 345–366.

García, O. and Kleifgen, J.A. (2010) *Educating Emergent Bilinguals: Policies, Programs, and Practices for English Language Learners.* New York: Teachers College Press.

García, O. and Kleifgen, J.A. (2020) Translanguaging and literacies. *Reading Research Quarterly* 55 (4), 553–571.

García, O. and Kleyn, T. (eds) (2016) *Translanguaging with Multilingual Students: Learning from Classroom Moments.* New York: Routledge.

García, O. and Li, W. (2014) *Translanguaging: Language, Bilingualism and Education.* London: Palgrave MacMillan.

Gay, G. (2000) *Culturally Responsive Teaching: Theory and Practice.* New York: Teachers College Press.

Gort, M. and Sembiante, S. (2015) Navigating hybridized language learning spaces through translanguaging pedagogy: Dual language preschool teachers' languaging practices in support of emergent bilingual children's performance of academic discourse. *International Multilingual Research Journal* 9 (1), 7–25.

Harste, J., Woodward, V. and Burke, C. (1984) *Language Stories and Literacy Lessons.* Portsmouth, NH: Heinemann.

Heath, S.B. (1983) *Ways with Words.* Cambridge: Cambridge University Press.

Kontovourki, S. and Siegel, M. (2021) 'B is for bunny': Contested sign-making and the possibilities for performing school literacy differently. *Reading Research Quarterly.* doi:10.1002/rrq.376

Ladson-Billings, G. (2014) Culturally relevant pedagogy 2.0: Aka the remix. *Harvard Educational Review* 84 (1), 74–84.

Muhammad, G. (2020) *Cultivating Genius: An Equity Framework for Culturally and Historically Responsive Literacy.* New York: Scholastic.

New London Group (1996) A pedagogy of multiliteracies: Designing social futures. *Harvard Educational Review* 66 (1), 60–93. doi:10.17763/haer.66.1.17370n67v22j160u

Orellana, M.F. (1994) Appropriating the voice of the superheroes: Three preschoolers' bilingual language uses in play. *Early Childhood Research Quarterly* 9 (2), 171–193.

Paris, D. (2012) Culturally sustaining pedagogy: A needed change in stance, terminology, and practice. *Educational Researcher* 41 (3), 93–97.

Pontier, R. and Gort, M. (2016) Coordinated translanguaging pedagogy as distributed cognition: A case study of two dual language bilingual education preschool coteachers' languaging practices during shared book readings. *International Multilingual Research Journal* 10 (2), 89–106.

Siegel, M. (2006) Rereading the signs: Multimodal transformations in the field of literacy education. *Language Arts* 84 (1), 65–77.

Siegel, M. and Panofsky, C.P. (2009) Designs for multimodality in literacy studies: Explorations in analysis. In *58th Yearbook of the National Reading Conference* (pp. 99–111). Oak Creek, WI: National Reading Conference.

Souto-Manning, M. and Martell, J. (2016) *Reading, Writing, and Talk: Inclusive Teaching Strategies for Diverse Learners, K-2.* New York: Teachers College Press.

Yun, S. (2008) Role-play and language socialization among bilingual Korean children in the United States. *Simulation & Gaming* 39 (2), 240–252.

6 Teaching English and Solar Terms through a Multimodal Approach to Young Chinese Children

Xiaodi Zhou, Zhuo Li and Shih-Fen Yeh

In this chapter, we explore the different multimodal ways Chinese preschoolers in Beijing and Taiwan learn English in their study of the 24 solar terms used to denote Chinese agricultural seasons spaced throughout the year (Schatten, 2005). The concept of these 'solar terms' relates to how each month is associated with two specific terms that describe the time of year. The students engage in hands-on activities, dramas and stories, while also singing, dancing and drawing to reinforce their understanding of these terms as well as the specific time of year to further embellish their learning. Their education is abetted by multimodal input and representation in their minds, as diverse strands of knowledge and experience join to create lasting learning.

Solar Terms in Chinese Culture

The solar terms represent a naturalistic approach to the changing seasons, categorizing the yearly calendar into 24 distinct periods in accordance with the Earth's position around the Sun (http://newyork.china-consulate.org/eng/whsw/cci/t1423968.htm). The terms guide agricultural activities with indicators of varying sunshine, precipitation and temperature by marking certain astronomical phenomena like the winter solstice and the vernal equinox. Chinese people have long used these markers to pace their agricultural activities, such as sowing, planting and harvesting certain crops. As such, these temporal indicators have profoundly influenced how Chinese people behave and their deep-seeded beliefs about the world. These terms have now become a philosophy toward the natural world and toward life in general.

Thus, these solar terms not only display the optimal times for agricultural activities, but also when to eat certain foods as well as implying the commencement of other activities. The Chinese people have also consulted this calendar for planning certain important dates, like weddings and funerals (Hung & Yeh, 2013). As such, these terms not only hold a place in agricultural life, but in social and civil life as well, becoming ingrained in the Chinese psyche to mark the cyclical tide of the change and growth of the natural world.

These solar terms have been part of the Chinese curriculum for the social and physical sciences since the Tang Dynasty in around 600 CE (Hung & Yeh, 2013). A calendar based on these terms had been in use since the Xia Dynasty in the 17th century BCE. These solar terms have been specifically employed to educate children about science and nutrition (Xue, 2012). From the framework of these solar units, children take an active stance on the exploration of the calendar and its relation to the four natural seasons. Teaching these terms to children to bolster their English acumen can be accomplished effectively via multimodal instruction.

Theoretical Framework: New Literacy and Multimodality

Children learn best through different means, via different modes that target their specific strengths (Yelland, 2018). Scholars (e.g. Mavers, 2003) have specifically investigated young children's learning as a multimodal process. For instance, Pahl's (2003) study brings us into the world of a child who played on the carpet of his bedroom floor with small figurines, including some models of Pokémon, a 'Woody' character from the film *Toy Story*, assorted trucks and miniature animals. She used photographs to record how the child expressed his meaning across different modes and explored a complex pattern of communicative practices in the world beyond merely linguistics.

According to the New London Group (1996), all meaning-making is multimodal. Both new literacies and traditional forms of literacy demand a new view of what comprehending multimodal texts signifies. Kress (2003) takes up the need in *Literacy in the New Media Age* to analyze literacy with a focus on modes. A mode is referred to as 'a regularized, organized set of resources for meaning-making, including, image, gaze, gesture, movement, music, speech and sound-effect' (Jewitt & Kress, 2003: 1).

Multimodal learning has also been shown to be effective in teaching languages (Lems, 2018). For instance, Lem found music to activate the brain's limbic centers and to provide a natural medium for language input, as we 'are required to produce and employ a repertoire of specific sounds, learn new patterns and rules, and master the "syntax" of songs and compositions' (Lems, 2018: 15). Using movement and music has been shown to be a great developmental approach to second language learning, as body coordination can be synchronized with rhythm and melody.

Listening to read-alouds can also be a great multimodal way for young children to learn (Frejd, 2021). In a study of a Swedish preschool, Frejd found that biological content was learned in addition to literary know-how. Students learned through studying the images as another layer of semiotic representation, as well as interpreting the words, both written and spoken. They gained disciplinary biological knowledge as well.

In studying 72 participants across primary schools in Taiwan, Chou (2014) found that young students demonstrated improved English vocabulary acumen and motivation for learning through a curriculum that consisted of games, stories and songs. In a mixed design consisting of pre- and post-tests, as well as classroom observations and interviews, results showed improvement in retention of new words and their meanings, as well as enthusiasm for learning.

Finally, body movement and play can also be essential conduits of a foreign language. For instance, Shin (2017) studied how young learners in particular benefit from dance and movement in their learning of a foreign language. Specifically, using 'songs and movement is one of the best ways to ensure that second- and foreign-language classrooms demonstrate' instructional efficacy (Shin, 2017: 14). The rhythm, cadence and meaning of language is bolstered through such kinesthetic learning. Furthermore, the cultural richness of children's songs lends itself nicely to teaching about other cultures and traditions.

Studies such as the aforementioned legitimize the instruction of a foreign language using multimodal means.

Research Methods

This study involved qualitative case studies (Dyson & Genishi, 2005) in two preschool settings in The Natural Way School in Central Taiwan and Peide School in Beijing, China. We chose such a design because of our 'interest in the *local particulars* of some abstract social phenomenon' (Dyson & Genishi, 2005: 2–3), in studying the multimodal learning of these young emergent bilinguals conducted in these specific contexts. The design of the year-long curriculum in the two preschool settings was with units divided into the months of the year, which included multimodal activities targeting the themes of the months, tasks related to the season or time of year, and specific activities pertaining to the solar terms.

By studying two contexts, we conducted a multiple case study approach (Stake, 2006) linking two preschool programs in two specific settings. As such, we use specific cases 'in [their] contexts and [their] particular situations ... to study the experiences of real cases operating in real situations' (Stake, 2006: 3). In particular, we were focusing on the learning of English as a foreign language for these young Chinese speakers through multimodal means. This study relied primarily on classroom observation data with other secondary documentary data such as schools' curricula and teachers' lesson plans, student work samples, both written and drawn, as well as kinesthetic manifestations of learning. These data were utilized to provide insights/rationale for our observations. The picture books were selected because they depicted daily life and also taught important cultural knowledge. We came to an agreement about which activities and which types of narratives to include, and also whether they were at the comprehension levels of our students. Since these texts were read aloud by teachers, they might be beyond students' independent reading abilities.

Participants

Our participant pool consisted of three groups of students in the bilingual pre-K program in each of the two settings. Students were categorized into the three- to four-year-old group, the four- to five-year-old group and the five- to six-year-old group, totaling around 120 students in all. We focused on the four- to five-year-old group, as well as the two lead teachers teaching the solar terms unit in English. In the study, there were 20 emergent bilingual students in The Natural Way School and 16 emergent bilingual students in Peide School. Additionally, we interviewed the two Chinese lead teachers, as well as one English instructor who taught at The Natural Way.

Data collection and analysis

In 2019, the third author spent two semesters in each of these classrooms, along with the two classroom teachers. She collected different qualitative data from observing students and teachers in both settings. She took classroom observation notes, conducted hour-long semi-structured interviews with the teachers (Longhurst, 2003) and collected student work samples. Additional interviews were conducted via Zoom and student work samples were digitally shared.

We utilized domain analysis (Glaser, 1992; Strauss, 1987) in the transcription and coding of data, meaning that we used relationships between symbols and their referents to decide on a specific domain in answering the research questions. All data were color coded digitally for themes, which included the different modalities of oral vocabulary building, singing songs related to the time of year and read-alouds of relevant picture books. The modes also included experiential activities related to the themes of the solar term, such as making a moon out of clay for September's solar term Autumn Equinox, and specific solar term activities such as putting on rain boots to play in the rain for February's themes of 'Start of Spring' and 'Rainwater.'

Via intensive coding, all data of a particular modality were sorted and categorized. We iteratively and collaboratively analyzed our data. Finally, we were able to sort the data into four distinct broader modalities: Songs, Stories, Hands-on Activities and Solar Term Related Activities. Via different types of learning, students engaged with the notions of solar terms and their heritage culture, as well as the English language and Western culture.

Research Results

In the following, we present the findings organized thematically into the curriculum's different learning modalities. Due to the distinct climates of our two settings, students engaged in different activities due to seasonal disparities.

Learning through song

The first aspect of these lessons involved singing, engaging students in musical learning. For instance, for the month of January, students sang 'Purple Polar Bear' and the song 'Snowman' to the melody of 'I'm a Little Teapot.' Students also sang a snowflakes song to the melody of 'Raindrops Are Falling on My Head.' Teachers selected those English songs most relevant to the meaning and atmosphere of specific Chinese solar terms. Students could participate in singing songs and experience the current climate and the sights of other climates.

These students learned conceptual knowledge of the presence of snow during this month, as well as English expressions from the lyrics and famous melody of a classic English song. By singing these songs, students were not only learning different notes, but also pronunciation of words. The lyrics of several of these songs, such as the Hibernation Song, taught children the phenomenon of hibernation. Four different animals' hibernation habits were depicted. In this way, students learned scientific information about how specific animal species hibernate.

Learning language through singing is a great way to develop vocabulary building and pronunciation, and to provide motivation (Chou, 2014). Children are familiar with singing songs, which accesses their experiential memories with music in their lives. The activity engaged the entire class in singing songs, learning together and building a sense of community.

Learning through reading picture books

The second component of this course involved reading picture books. Students learned about the times of the year through narratives pertaining to the seasons. For instance, for the month of June, titles like *The Rainbow Fish* by Marcus Pfister, Eric Carle's *Mister Seahorse* and *Just Me and My Dad* by Mercer Mayer were part of the curriculum. These books are authentic texts with beautiful illustrations. Therefore, not only were the children gaining literacy skills like word recognition and phonemic and alphabetic awareness, but they are also exposed to vibrant artwork.

When picture books were read aloud to students, they engaged in a vivid experience with the texts (Frejd, 2021). Being read to, the students heard not only the pronunciation, but also the prosody, cadence and emphasis that certain fonts or punctuations compel. They heard the different voices of the different characters and experienced their emotions. This activity taught literacy, while the theme of the month was reinforced.

Additionally, June is a time for going to the beach and seeing or thinking about sea creatures (in the differentiated instructional context accommodated for children in Taiwan). Father's Day also falls during this month, so Mayer's *Just Me and My Dad* provided a great opportunity to teach about this US holiday, which is not officially recognized in Taiwan or Mainland China. Thus, through these quality works of children's literature, students learned about another culture's traditions.

Learning through experiential activities

In this unit, students participated in learning by doing, as they engaged with their world in hands-on tasks. For instance, for the month of October, with the theme 'The Colorful Days of Autumn,' the children collected leaves, comparing and empirically studying their various qualities (in the differentiated instructional context accommodated for children in Beijing). They also decorated an Autumn glass vase and mimed different weather conditions like thunder and rain. Students acted out the story of 'Goldilocks and the Three Bears' by cooking different sized bowls of porridge, a common fall meal in Beijing. Thus, their scientific learning coincided with artistic, literary, culinary and mathematical concepts in this one lesson. The children in Taiwan went into the yard to observe the sponge gourds. The teacher picked one sponge gourd and invited students to have a taste. Everyone said that it tasted awful and that it was too hard to chew. The teacher asked the children what they should do with the gourd. Should they just simply throw it away? The children had no idea, so the teacher suggested they should leave the gourd outdoors. After one week, the teacher took the gourd back into the classroom. Seeing the teacher break open the gourd, the children were excited to find the black seeds bursting out and had a conversation as follows:

Child 1: They look like cucumbers.
Teacher: Do you smell anything?
Children: Yes, it smells good.
Child 2: The young fruit is eaten as vegetable and it is delicious.
Teacher: Do you like it?
Children: Yes! Yummy!
Teacher: There are many seeds inside. What color are they?
Children: Black.
Child 3: Can we eat the seeds?
Teacher: No, we don't eat the seeds.

Teacher: Look! The fully ripened fruit has many fibers. [The teacher showed the fibers]
Children: They look like sponges.
Teacher: Yes. What do we do with them?
Child 4: For bath?
Teacher: Try them!
Child 4: Oh, it hurts.
Teacher: That's why we use them to clean up dishes.
Child 5: How about the seeds?
Child 6: We can plant them again.
Teacher: Yes. Maybe next year, we can eat the gourds again.

The conversation about the gourd occurred while the children were experiencing different senses of sight, smell, touch and taste. Language use through the senses and life experience became meaningful.

In these experiential activities, students were able to work individually or collectively, collaborating on constructing and representing their learning (Shin, 2017). They were encouraged to act creatively, engaging their artistic inclinations as they constructed representations of their learning. These activities also engaged different types of learning simultaneously. For example, students conducted kinesthetic learning by miming various weather types, such as rain, lightening and wind. Students also engaged in cooking the porridge, where they used math to measure the ingredients and used science for figuring out the cooking temperature and time, while using literacy skills to comprehend the story. These tasks engaged students in multimodal disciplinary learning, reinforcing the Chinese solar terms while also targeting language.

By including this kinesthetic modality, the students were specifically encouraged to collaborate with peers, working through problems like how to make a kite and fly it in the sky during the Clear and Bright solar term. This activity required a synthesis of different modalities, understanding how different disciplines coincide. Students learned that in the real world, activities often involved different disciplines coming together, just as the different components of these lessons synthesized learning about the solar units.

Embodied solar term related activities to contextualize the task

Lastly, these units also involved solar term related activities. Two specific solar terms were associated with each month. For instance, for February, the terms were 'Start of Spring' and 'Rainwater.' In Chinese culture, the Spring Festival usually occurs in this month, commencing the new lunar year. Specific activities for this month included putting on rain gear to play and going round a lake to observe the plum blossoms. These tasks kinesthetically reinforced the specific solar terms.

Three distinct units were focused on: March's Spring Equinox, the Waking of Insects and the significance of the pomelo fruit; June's Summer

Solstice and the Dragon Boat Festival; and December's Winter Solstice and Christmas. In March's curricular design, the four modes of language engagement – speaking, listening, reading and writing – are all integrated. The students noted the blooming of the pomelo trees in March (in Taiwan) and continued observing the trees' growth through six months, until the fruits were harvested in September before the Moon Festival. In addition to eating the fruits, the children made them into a jam, and dried their peels to make mosquito incense, a pomelo bath pack and even pomelo fragrance bags. Fresh pomelo leaves were used as a dye for cloth and made into scarves. Furthermore, pomelo leaves could even be stewed. To these students, pomelo trees became more than a plant but rather a mode connected to families and to nature. Hands-on science activities also involved many opportunities for authentic language practices.

June's Dragon Boat Festival unit specifically integrated literacy, social studies, science, math, music, health and geography. For instance, the Dumplings activity encouraged students to study science and math through making dumplings – measuring ingredients and noting the effect of heat on water and food. Furthermore, the Dragon Boat activity involved an experiment elucidating the science of sinking and floating. The Fragrance Bags (香包) activity entailed the making of scented sachets from leaves and flowers and learning how the Chinese used certain fragrances to dispel pests, thereby teaching the geometric shapes of leaves, the function of those leaves, their weight, and the process of transpiration. This activity was tied to math and science, as well as health education and Chinese culture. Additionally, the Boat Race developed teamwork concepts, push-pull forces and physical education. These tasks created opportunities for students to practice English in communicative and problem-solving situations. Through listening to and discussing Chinese classic literature like *The Legend of the White Snake* in English, children developed English listening and speaking abilities along with Chinese literacy. Moreover, the students took part in role-plays in which they participated in conversations or memorized specific dramatic scenes.

Lastly, Winter Solstice Day often coincides with Christmas Day. Warmth and Appreciation are key concepts and Hoping and Warming (希望和溫暖) are themes. For this unit, parents were invited to join in singing and praying together. There was the potential for a great deal of meaningful language use with regard to the Western and Eastern celebrations. This season involves the last vestiges of animal activity before the slumber of winter, and Cold Dew and Frost's Descent are the solar terms (in Beijing). Related activities included hiking in nature to experience the changing colors of autumn, along with observing the frost on darkening leaves. Children also made a pomegranate out of clay, integrating science and art. Students noted the changing of the world, and learned to be conscious of these changes, also gaining discipline-specific skills such as making empirical observations, as well as artistic creations in various mediums.

Discussion and Implications

The results indicated that the students engaged in vibrant multimodal learning of these solar units, in which they also integrated their background and family funds of knowledge with new semantic content. The children, with Chinese as their home language, were able to demonstrate their learning in English through multiple modalities. When distinct modalities coexist in the presentation of content, as well as displaying learning, children's multiple intelligences are activated (Gardner, 2011).

Dialogic interaction of the modalities

With greater concurrence of different information modes targeting the central concept of the solar units, learning occurs via multiple means. In this one unit, children's diverse sensorimotor skills are activated in the service of learning these 24 solar terms.

During Harvest in November, the songs in each unit correspond to each month, such as 'Row Row Row Your Boat,' and 'The More We Get Together' about the Thanksgiving story regarding the celebration of harvest for the British settlers in 1621. Thereby, the children learn about the time of the year, but they also acquire musical knowledge as well as information about the culture in the theme of the song. Also, students are taught to critically question the dominant Thanksgiving narrative, learning that the contacts between Europeans and Native people were often deleterious for Native Americans, and that the arrival of Europeans effectively signaled the end of their way of life. So, by critically examining aspects of US culture, the curriculum also teaches about important sociocultural topics around the world.

In this way, this unique cultural concept is taught in meaningful and multiple ways, in a manner more resembling how we garner experiential knowledge in our lives. The information is not merely communicated via one or two modalities, like visual and auditory, but through all of our senses and perceptions, such as the kinesthetic activities of moving like bees and butterflies in the service of March and its theme of 'Whisper of Spring.' By embodying and moving like the insects they study, the children gain firsthand awareness of the process of pollination, an important scientific concept.

Cross-cultural interdisciplinary learning

Through the multimodal learning on the solar units, the children are also engaged in the learning of multiple disciplines and acquiring diverse academic and real-life skills. Each unit involves singing, speaking, dancing and other specific physical activities, such as playing Cuju, an ancient Chinese precursor to soccer (Lan & Xing, 2008), which spawned during the Warring States period. This kinesthetic activity is rich in cultural significance, as well as coinciding with the warming of the outside temperature and the preponderance of outdoor activities during April.

Yet the social studies learning in this month is not restricted solely to Chinese culture, as other occasions, such as the Western Christian celebration of Easter, also in April, is similarly taught via music through the song, 'Five Little Easter Eggs.' Through this activity, not only are the children acquiring semantic knowledge about Easter, but also musical learning through singing and following the musical score of this song. Thus, social studies content is integrated with musical learning.

The children are also empirically discovering their local world. For example, for the month of April, the children embark on a fruit-picking tour, and note the size, shape and color of each fruit, while weighing them, dissecting them and distinguishing their unique tastes. They learn to use all their senses to characterize and categorize their world. Finally, by making and conducting experiments, like 'Do plants drink water?' and 'Can a tree grow out of a potato?', these children are engaged in hands-on, inquiry-based scientific learning, integrating science as a discipline. In fact, the calendar and seasons are also scientific concepts, and so the theme of science is deeply ingrained in this learning.

Multimodality accesses students' rich resources and various learning strengths to learn social studies content via interdisciplinary means. By engaging with so many aspects of their world, both physically, linguistically and culturally, students' learning becomes richer and more meaningful. Through multimodality, students not only understand what they are learning, but get to live and experience it as well. In a sense, they are conjoining the 'world as told' (Kress, 2003: 150) with the 'world as shown' (Kress, 2003: 152), enfolding the design of instruction with its significance.

Learning English through a multicultural, multilingual and multimodal approach

By learning the culturally specific concept of the solar units and integrating cross-cultural activities, students gain an appreciation of how cultures address and broach the natural phenomenon of the changing of the seasons and the times of the year. In a single month, for example, April, children learn about the universal holiday of Earth Day and the Christian celebration of Easter, along with the heritage celebration of the Tomb Sweeping Festival. As a kinesthetic component, students recreate the life cycle of a tree through choreographed movements. They gain a meta-perspective on how cultures around the world take note of and celebrate this season, while deeply understanding how the natural world manifests changes as well.

Children are learning cross-cultural, cross-linguistic knowledge, allowing them to gain a richer perspective on their global world. By learning these heritage notions in a second language, there is a cross-mesh of perspectives, as heritage elements are learned through a vernacular which colors its words with its distinct cultural nuances. Therefore, these children are gaining rich cultural and linguistic learning through the perspective of linguistic and cultural insiders in the readings, while reinforcing their own heritage with the solar terms. The languages and cultures synthesize awareness, which is demonstrated and reinforced in the tactile and kinesthetic activities.

Because the objective of these courses is to teach a new language, English, to Chinese-speaking students, the participatory, lived experiential learning strongly benefits learners' language acquisition (Knutson, 2003). Students engage with multiple modes, such as music, words, food and activities, to experience and internalize the phenomenon of solar units.

References

Chou, M.H. (2014) Assessing English vocabulary and enhancing young English as a foreign language (EFL) learners' motivation through games, songs, and stories. *Education 3–13* 42 (3), 284–297.

Dyson, A.H. and Genishi, C. (2005) *On the Case: Approaches to Language and Literacy Research.* New York: Teacher's College Press.

Frejd, J. (2021) Children's encounters with natural selection during an interactive read aloud. *Research in Science Education* 51 (1), 499–512.

Gardner, H. (2011) *Frames of Mind: The Theory of Multiple Intelligences.* New York: Basic Books.

Glaser, B.G. (1992) *Basics of Grounded Theory Analysis: Emergence Versus Forcing.* San Francisco, CA: Sociology Press.

Hung, Y.S. and Yeh, S.F. (2013) The aesthetics of curriculum and Taoism. *International Journal of Chinese Education* 2 (1), 54–69.

Jewitt, C. and Kress, G. (eds) (2003) *Multimodal Literacy.* New York: Peter Lang.

Knutson, S. (2003) Experiential learning in second-language classrooms. *TESL Canada Journal* 20 (2), 52–64.

Kress, G. (2003) *Literacy in the New Media Age.* London: Routledge.

Lan, L. and Xing, M.F. (2008) Study on the origin, development and extinction of Chinese Ancient Cuju [J]. *Ludong University Journal (Natural Science Edition)* 3, 23.

Lems, K. (2018) New ideas for teaching English using songs and music. *English Teaching Forum* 56 (1) 14–21.

Longhurst, R. (2003) Semi-structured interviews and focus groups. *Key Methods in Geography* 3 (2), 143–156.

Mavers, D. (2003) Communicating meanings through image composition, spatial arrangement and links in primary school student mind maps. In C. Jewitt and G. Kress (eds) *Multimodal Literacy* (pp. 19–33). New York: Peter Lang.

New London Group (1996) A pedagogy of multiliteracies: Designing social futures. *Harvard Educational Review* 66 (1), 60–93. doi:10.17763/haer.66.1.17370n67v22j160u

Pahl, K. (2003) Children's text making at home: Transforming meaning across modes. In C. Jewitt and G. Kress (eds) *Multimodal Literacy* (pp. 139–154). New York: Peter Lang.

Schatten, K. (2005) Fair space weather for solar cycle 24. *Geophysical Research Letters* 32 (2), 1.

Shin, J.K. (2017) Get up and sing! Get up and move! Using songs and movement with young learners of English. *English Teaching Forum* 55 (2), 14–25.

Stake, R.E. (2006) *Multiple Case Analysis*. New York: Guilford Press.
Strauss, A.L. (1987) *Qualitative Analysis for Social Scientists*. New York: Cambridge University Press.
Xue, J. (2012) Hao Shi Shi Hao: Food education for children in the way of exploration, which is based on 24 solar terms. Politecnico di Milano.
Yelland, N.J. (2018) A pedagogy of multiliteracies: Young children and multimodal learning with tablets. *British Journal of Educational Technology* 45 (5), 847–858.

7 For a Politically Engaged and Socioculturally Just Language Education through Critical Multimodal Literacy in Brazilian Contexts

Cláudia Hilsdorf Rocha, Fernanda Coelho Liberali and Antonieta Heyden Megale

> We are revolution's evolution. We are free like black birds. Hey Black, you are Power and with all that strength, fight. Even when mourning!
>
> Vitor Abade Silva, 2020
> Language in Activities in the School Context (LACE) Project

Where We Speak from and What We Struggle for in Language Education: A Brief Overview

As Brazilian citizens and language educators, we are sadly aware of the profound and increasingly oppressive social, cultural, linguistic, racial, gender and economic inequalities our country is built upon.[1] The inclusive growth trend Brazilians had been experiencing over past decades regarding household incomes and social inequality has faced a major reversal since 2015, when the Gini coefficient[2] declined to 0.52, as advertised worldwide (Neri, 2019).

According to the findings of recent Brazilian studies, the COVID-19 pandemic has deeply worsened the Brazilian abyssal line between the rich and the poor and, consequently, seriously aggravated inequalities on extremely important fronts such as education, the economy and the labor market.[3] Much has been discussed about the recent impacts of remote learning on Brazilian education (Liberali *et al.*, 2020; Ribeiro & Vecchio,

2020), since digital literacies, with regard to both teachers and students, need to be more consistently developed. Besides, the digital divide is still very clear in Brazil; lack of internet access remains a serious issue in the country, which needs stronger and more sustainable public policies for digital inclusion (Alves & Faria, 2020; Moreira *et al.*, 2019).

Pandemic times have accelerated the sovereignty of a contemporary authoritarian government to lead its own people toward death, allowing the devastatingemergence of *necropolitics* (Mbembe, 2016). In a world marked by extreme inequalities and led by ever-increasing waves of necropower, we all face the resurgence of social, political and economic forces that reflect fascist, racist and nationalist ideologies and that promote the structural exclusion, the silencing and the killing of minority or oppressed groups (Mbembe, 2016). Based on such premises, Liberali (2020a) claims that we have been experiencing the lethal effects of *necroeducation* in Brazil. Brazilian educational policies, in general, have deepened abyssal lines, because they have fostered the *enslavement of the oppressed* (Freire, 1987; Souza, 2017). Consequently, by reinforcing oppressive differences as far as access to teaching-learning processes are concerned, such policies have disgustingly promoted the silencing, as well as the erasure and the annihilation of socially and economically disfavored groups (Liberali, 2020a).

When discussing the Brazilian sociopolitical crisis, Pinheiro-Machado (2019) states that Freirean hope can make a better tomorrow as it can nurture resistance forces and can therefore help us to challenge conservative and authoritarian moves that potentialize fascist ideologies, atrocious alienation and cruel individualism. According to Freire (2014) and Freire *et al.* (2016), it is possible for us to experience a critically hopeful and radically transformative utopia if we are committed to *denouncing* every possible form of domination while also *announcing* alternative and, consequently, more collective, equitable and democratically just ways to live in a profoundly *pluralistic* society.

Once the idea of social, cultural and linguistic pluralism is seen through the Bakhtin Circle's lens (Bakhtin, 1981, 1986a, 1986b; Vološinov, 1986), neither culture nor language can be understood as passive, abstract or closed systems. Rather, conceptually, they are both dynamically open and in constant complex flux. Besides, the dialogic nature of social practices highlights heteroglossia as a key element in social interaction, because it reveals the multiplicity of social voices or discourses, which are tangled in very tense and complex ways as we relate to others in the world. From this perspective, language is experienced as a living dialogue and a socioculturally situated process of ideological becoming. When linked to educational realities, such principles seem to 'have the potential to free us from [...] impoverished approaches and binary thinking,' as well as to challenge simplistic and prepackaged views as far as language education practices and policies are concerned (Shields, 2007: 1). Likewise, from a dialogic and pluralistic perspective, the ideological and political nature of (language) education is highlighted (Freire, 2004). The power of dialogue, seen as the potential 'to remain open to the Other, to difference, and to the possibility of new understandings' (Shields, 2007: 9), is crucial to the process of social transformation and to the fight for a more socially, culturally, linguistically and educationally just society for all.

Therefore, challenging monolithic and monolingual ideologies, which centripetally erase plurality, within both educational landscapes and other social contexts, also seems to be of extreme importance when it comes to social justice (Fraser, 2008; Freire, 1987, 2000, 2003a, 2014). In Brazil, recent educational and language policies can be said to represent a drawback with regard to a pluralistic proposal. More specifically, as far as language education is concerned, such policies reflect authoritatarian discourses by formally excluding the teaching and learning of additional/foreign languages from primary schools and also by imposing English as a mandatory subject. Since the Brazilian National Educational Framework, which has been gradually implemented since 2017, has also been claimed to reinforce inequalities and reduce social, linguistic and cultural plurality (Gerhardt & Amorim, 2020), we strongly believe that critical and transformative literacy approaches are urgently needed to help us defy the neoliberal and oppressive educational policies that have been currently imposed on us. From this perspective, where a pluralistic language education is seen as a human right, we pose a question to guide the discussions we aim to present in this chapter: *How can multimodal literacy support a politically engaged, critically informed and socioculturally just education?*

According to Freire (2003a), in order for a libertarian education to empower people and enable them to overcome the oppressive circumstances they face, it is necessary to make it possible for learners to immerse themselves in reality and emerge from it in a historically more conscious way, so that society can be transformed. A literacy practice that aims at this kind of libertarian awareness should allow the *reading of the word and world* (Freire & Macedo, 2015) from a situated, dialogic and transformative perspective.

From this point of view, this work approaches an explicitly critical and multimodal pedagogy which aims at fostering dialogic interactions and at enhancing plurilingual and transcultural literacies (Rocha, 2012, 2014). We believe that such a pluralistic and socioculturally situated perspective can allow young emergent bilinguals to make meaning in the world through multi-layered communicational ensembles (Bezemer & Kress, 2016), which are, in their turn, produced in a specific context of power relations. In this chapter, we also explore the notion of critical and multimodal literacies (Mills, 2016), which was expanded so that the concept of an *engaged multiliteracy pedagogy* (Liberali, 2019, 2020b, forthcoming) can be introduced. Such a transformative pedagogy is aimed at raising our awareness regarding the relations of power, inequalities and social exclusion that make up part of the social practices we engage in today. This libertarian literacy pedagogy also aims at enabling marginalized voices to be made visible, while fostering students' funds of *perejivanie* (experiences) (Megale & Liberali, 2020).

In order to illustrate such principles and premises, this chapter examines pedagogical practices within a specific Brazilian educational context: a preschool class in English, which works on everyday habits, as socially situated activities, within a project in an underprivileged community in São Paulo City. In such a context, multimodality was an essential resource for understanding, analyzing, evaluating and creating new possibilities to promote a socially and culturally transformative and plurilingual educational practice, as well as to expand the students' experience repertoires, so that these young learners could act beyond their constraints, read the word and the world more critically, and transform realities in future social activities they may engage in.

Critical and Multimodal Literacies as Key Elements for a Dialogically Pluralist and Socially Engaged Language Education

In a globalized, multilingual, pluricultural and digital society, it is important to recognize the hybrid nature of social practices, which are mediated by a wide range of modes of language and media in a very complex and dynamic way. Multimodal meanings and digital epistemologies are constitutive elements of contemporary social interaction and communication that challenge rationalist, essentialist and structuralist views and profoundly impact how we express ourselves, relate to others and produce knowledge in the world. Diversity, in its most varied forms, as well as inequalities, becomes more and more visible in current social relations, which consequently reinforce the pluralized nature of literacies nowadays and highlight the urgent need for a critical (educational) response to the fast-changing textual and technology landscapes we experience (Mills, 2016).

As we see it, a critical approach to multiple and multimodal literacies calls for the recognition of the sociocultural and ideological nature of social and educational practices, as well as for an expansive view of meaning-making and knowledge production, which can offer grounds for us to challenge authoritative discourses and promote social transformation. From a discursive and critical point of view, challenging a reductive perspective with regard to multimodal literacies implies recognizing the intersections between both multimodality and subjectivity (Mills, 2016), that is, understanding how we engage in and with heteroglossia and multimodal ensembles (Bezemer & Kress, 2016) to interact and communicate within pluralistic events and practices. Also, a transformative view regarding multimodality demands critical interrogation of the intersections that exist between race, gender, whiteness (and any other oppressive elements that maintain structural inequalities and silence the voices of minority groups) and present society (Mills, 2016).

From this perspective, the idea of a critical and heteroglossic language teaching and learning process emerges. Such an approach is based upon the Bakhtinian notion of plurilingualism and, in a broad sense,

> the concept refers to the way different voices and social languages can be orchestrated in literary works. Together with heteroglossia, it is deeply related to the dialogic nature of language and, therefore, linked to the presence of otherness in one's inner self, discourses and voices. When redirected from novel to educational settings, plurilingualism implies recognizing each and every way of expressing meaning, each and every social language or each and every way of thinking and doing things in the world as equally important and valid. (Rocha, 2014: 801)

Consequently, such a proposition reveals a deep concern with a socially transformative and just form of language education, one whose main goal is to promote learning spaces that foster critical multimodal communication while also nurturing the idea of meaning-making as a rhizomatic process of interpenetration of (social) languages, discourses and cultures (Rocha, 2012, 2014). A critical, transcultural and plurilingual kind of language education seeks to promote decentered learning spaces, where monolingual and monolithic discourses can be deeply challenged, and the emergence of an exotopic, surplus view (Bakhtin, 1981) becomes a possibility.

This dialogic language education approach reveals its subversive nature as it potentializes the possibilities for us to have our understandings (of the world, of ourselves and of the other) expanded, our funds of *perejivanie* (Megale & Liberali, 2020) broadened, as well as our agency empowered. The concept of funds of *perejivanie* is a proposal to bring together the notion of funds of knowledge (Hogg, 2011; Moll & Cammarota, 2010) with the concepts of *perejivanie* (Vygotsky, 1994), of repertoire (Blommaert & Backus, 2013; Busch, 2012, 2015) and of translanguaging (García, 2009; Rocha, 2019; Rocha & Maciel, 2015). It integrates experience with knowledge, triggered by the concepts of repertoire and translanguaging, corroborating the inseparability between emotion and cognition. However, the concept of funds of *perejivanie* goes beyond the issues that underlie the discussion of funds of identity, since it integrates all the potential one has to signify and live reality.

It is the set of resources accumulated from dramatic events lived with others, which materialize (or do not) in the 'means of speaking' (Blommaert & Backus, 2013: 3). In other words, they are all the means by which the subjects interact with the world, and understand and live linguistic, cultural, emotional and social aspects. From this perspective, reading the word and the world (Freire & Macedo, 2015) can be experienced as a libertarian educative and language practice, based upon critical solidarity and rights re-vindication, as well as aimed at active citizenship, democratic awareness and critical social participation (Dei, 2013; Liberali & Megale, 2019; Rocha 2014).

Engaged Multiliteracies

The idea and the practices related to critical multimodal literacies, described in the previous section, were expanded and reframed from Vygotskian and Freirean perspectives and gave rise to what Liberali (2019, 2020b, forthcoming) named as Engaged Multiliteracies. This notion expands the processes of teaching and learning and focuses on the correlation between what the students have been able to incorporate throughout their lives and the proposals presented by the school in order to broaden their possibilities to act in the world. Supported by Gee (2000), the concept of Engaged Multiliteracies emphasizes that our presence in the world is not only silent, passive and receptive; on the contrary, it has transformative potential, which means that once we critically understand our reality, we can build possibilities to intervene in the world.

In this sense, the idea of Engaged Multiliteracies highlights some aspects so as to understand the process of teaching and learning as a possibility to transform the conditions of oppression we have been struggling with in the world. In order to do so, it is necessary that the school curriculum provides the students with opportunities to immerse themselves in reality. Moreover, the building of scientific knowledge aimed at schools has to be correlated with everyday knowledge so that students can develop critical positioning. Finally, it is important to highlight that playing should be understood as a way to appropriate and transform the social practices students may face in their lives. But how can this proposal be implemented in schools?

First, there must be an immersion in reality, which allows school knowledge to connect to students' funds of *perejivanie*, so that they can develop consciousness of potentials they still have to develop or improve (Liberali, forthcoming). Through this connection, the diversity of world and linguistic knowledge, emotions, experiences and multimodal resources are valued, at the same time as it encompasses different cultural contexts (Megale & Liberali, 2020).

Integrated with the Immersion in Reality, Liberali (forthcoming) explains that the Critical Construction of Generalizations takes place. It occurs, according to the author, through the combination and exploitation of historically accumulated school knowledge as a basis for expanding students' experiences.

In addition to this, the Critical Construction of Generalizations also includes the Critical Framework, which aims at students' critical development, based on the process they have already experienced in relation to what, why and how they learn (Liberali, forthcoming). It also implies valuing the process of choices and taking positions in the teaching-learning process. Thus, it provides students with the opportunity to interculturally perceive reality so that they can position themselves in relation to events, situations and ways of acting in the world. Taking a position in the face of reality leads to an agentive responsibility for the Production of Social Change. It involves developing ways of critically creating new practices imbued with their own goals and values so that students can apply and revise what they have learned (Liberali, forthcoming).

Thus, expanding this idea, Liberali (forthcoming) proposes that students have to engage in tasks in which they experience real or quasi-real experiences. These tasks are intended to expand their participation in society, once students through performance assume a role that enables them to think over possible ways of acting in the world. In this sense, the students' repertoires are seen as records of mobility; in other words, they allow the movement of people, linguistic resources or even social disputes (Megale & Liberali, 2020).

The integration of these three actions – Immersion in Reality, Critical Generalization Construction and Production of Social Change (Liberali, forthcoming) – and their relation with the four movements proposed by the New London Group (1996, 2000) are illustrated in Table 7.1.

These three actions must not be understood as functioning in linear hierarchy or stages to be followed. They are actions that relate with each other in a complex way; therefore, they occur simultaneously at different times or become predominant in a given situation and it should be noted that they are repeatedly revisited at different levels (Cope & Kalantzis, 2000).

To sum up, Engaged Multiliteracies aim at promoting, through educational praxis, the 'participant insertion' (Freire, 2003b: 10) of subjects often silenced and made invisible in national decision-making processes. They have as their purpose to create favorable conditions for students to move from 'inauthentic life' to 'authentic life' (Freire, 2003b: 10), which is the reason for educational processes committed to social justice.

A Preschool Project in English in an Underprivileged Community in São Paulo City

When critically approaching language education at early ages, it seems important to situate such a practice and, consequently, to discuss and challenge preconceived and stereotyped views regarding the conceptualization of a *child* and of *childhood*. In general terms, we agree with a renewed sociology approach (Matthews, 2007: 323), in which childhood is primarily seen as a time of socialization, when infants relate to others as 'social actors who are not only affected by but also affect social structures and relationships.' In this regard, children's thoughts, views, feelings and experiences cannot be universalized nor explained from an adultocentric perspective (Quinteiro, 2002). Such a time in life, consequently, should be understood within all of its plurality and heterogeneity, which would allow us to transgressively use the term in its plural

Table 7.1 Fundamental actions within the Engaged Multiliteracies framework

Engaged Multiliteracies (Liberali, forthcoming)		**Connections**	**Multiliteracies (New London Group, 1996, 2000)**	
Three actions			**Four movements**	
Immersion in Reality (Freire, 1987)	Recognize, understand and experience reality.	Experience concrete situations reframed by Vygotsky's proposal to play.	**Situated Practice**	The experience of making sense in the world, in the public domain and in the workplace.
Critical Generalization Construction (Vygotsky, 1978)	Experience discussions, tasks and games that enable students to relate the experienced knowledge to others structured as scientific.	Multicultural proposal. Different sources with different ways of understanding reality. Historical implications to reframe reality (Freire, 1987).	**Overt Instruction**	The students' development of an explicit metalanguage of design.
			Critical Framing	Interpretation and evaluation of social contexts and the purpose of projects of meaning.
Production of Social Change	From the analysis and criticism, students are summoned to concrete actions of intervention in reality.	Broader understanding of reality. Create the viable unheard of (Freire, 1987) in concrete and effective actions.	**Transformed Practice**	Students, as creators of meanings, become designers of social futures.

Source: Amorim (forthcoming)

form (*infâncias*). Within a country of extreme inequalities, as is the case of Brazil, impoverished children are deeply affected not only by the authoritarian force of reductive views, but also by the violent impacts of extreme poverty, racism and other social, cultural and economic abyssal drawbacks imposed on the underprivileged, minority groups. Given this, when discussing language education in Brazilian (public) schools it seems crucial to keep in mind such a social divide, as well as the urgent need to promote more inclusive, libertarian ways to educate young children and to expand their experience repertoire without silencing their social and cultural identities, languages and knowledges (Freire, 1987; Sousa Santos, 2007).

Taking into account this scenario, in the first semester of 2012, researchers from the 'Multicultural Project' joined sessions for playing in English with three- to four-year-old children for 30 minutes, twice a week. The idea was to offer a multilingual space for the collaborative engagement of children in everyday life situations in a different language and with multicultural possibilities to experience the world and expand their funds of *perejivanie*.

The project shared here involved working with the social activity 'going to bed,' and consisted of ten 30-minute sessions. The idea was to offer the children the opportunity to familiarize themselves with various realities of going to bed, experienced and represented in heteroglossic ways. From this perspective, *going to bed* was understood as a social activity and, as such, it was seen as 'something given and something yet to be determined' (Bakhtin, 1993: 33). In other words, this activity was approached as an event that encompassed a multiplicity of languages, discourses and voices, dialogically, historically and socioculturally orchestrated, and that, consequently, kept authoritative and centrifugal forces in a dialogic tension (Bakhtin, 1981). From this standpoint, this particular social activity could be discussed and experienced based on a wide range of themes, such as machismo, gender and/or social inequality and so on. When performed from a singular, authoring and transgressive point of view, this event should allow possibilities of participatory thinking and of affective engagement and emotional-volitive intonation (Bakhtin, 1993). In this way, one of the purposes of this educational proposal was to problematize this social practice in order to expand the possibilities of living known and unknown realities from a pluralistic perspective, of sharing and creating knowledges from an ecologic stance, and of nurturing interaction between family members when going to bed.

In its turn, the general objective of this project was to develop ways to have a good time with the family and to prepare for a peaceful sleep, besides constructing new possibilities of critical acting and awakening the imagination through stories. It also involved specific expressions of the speech genders (Bakhtin, 1986b) that circulated in the activity.

Every session was introduced with **immersion in reality** created by a song and the other activities that were developed through stories which presented different sociocultural perspectives of going to bed that the children were invited to perform. To initiate the **critical construction of generalization**, the children and teachers explored several stories and talked about the social activity, sharing ideas about the context (who, what, which, where, when, why?). The children saw examples of putting a baby to sleep, using a variety of items such as blanket, pillow, teddy bear, so on, and were invited to play 'going to sleep' with the material kits, as illustrated by the blurred picture in Figure 7.1.

In one of the meetings, for example, the children sang the 'Hello Song'[4] and heard Murray's *Snug as a Bug* 2013 story, among others. After that, they played with the idea of day and night with a game they made up together and that they named the 'Day-Night Game.' They were also introduced to the 'Twinkle, Twinkle, Little Star'[5] lullaby. While singing, they played with paper stars affixed to a stick, which they themselves had previously made. As for the performance, they were organized into two or three

Figure 7.1 Bedtime

groups and played with the social activity 'going to bed,' using the material kits. Children were encouraged to say, 'good night,' 'sleep tight' and other words related to the objects used. The teacher and the students played together, taking the time to give the baby doll a bottle, brush their teeth, read the story to the baby doll and put them to sleep. They also pretended the baby dolls were crying and it was suggested that they needed attention and affection, as we can see in the blurred picture in Figure 7.2.

As usual, the meeting ended with the 'Goodbye Song.'[6] In doing so they had the opportunity to **immerse in reality** and to **critically construct**

Figure 7.2 Taking care time

possibilities of **generalizing** ways of going to bed while using English and playing.

In other sessions, to expand this **immersion** and possibility of **generalization**, the children saw video scenes of children going to sleep in India, Ghana and Australia. Teachers paused the scenes and asked the children to mimic and say the name of the actions (drink milk, brush teeth, etc.). In their time for performance, as a means to **produce social change**, they were invited to pretend they were the children from those different parts of the world and use the words they learned while watching the scenes. In reflective moments, they were invited to share how they were affected by these different experiences. In this example, the focus was nature and societies. In other moments, different areas of knowledge were emphasized and expanded with different examples of sources and cultural possibilities.

As a way to transform realities in the final **production of social change**, at the end of the project, the teachers read to the children the books they had been asked to create in previous sessions. Such books were made with photographs taken while performing 'going to bed.' Some of the children brought their own pictures, taken from home, while preparing themselves to go to bed. The performances and creation of the books provided opportunities for the children to express their world and life experiences. They became empowered authors of their own lives with more choices of how to act and engage critically with reality. The blurred picture in Figure 7.3 shows the children interacting with the book they created.

Figure 7.3 Interacting with the book

Throughout all the projects, the children were invited to sing, dance, and play with various songs, rhythms and objects. These choices were intentionally proposed so that they could enhance the development of their funds of *perejivanie*. The variety was conceived as a conscious intent to value different forms of acting that were not only seen but played with so that the children could live through these pluralistic events and become able to make choices about their ways of acting and engaging with the world and with the word. In this way, children could **immerse** themselves in different forms of going to bed and could also **critically construct generalizations** about this social practice.

All in all, this project involved an intercultural perspective which critically supported children in exploring with a variety of possibilities to deal with very common everyday activities of children's lives, such as going to bed. By playing with this social activity, children could have access to different ways of living: ones they usually had contact with; through the stories told; and the watched videos of children going to bed in different places in the world. Also, they could engage with a wide range of practices that allowed them to experience the situation and to experiment with difference through comparing the different ways of going to bed.

Reading with the children and playing with toys, songs and images as well as engaging with them in the performance of going to bed, teachers supported the children in the process of enacting funds of *perejivanie* that expanded their possibilities of living. While they expanded their possibilities of constructing meaning in a language other than Portuguese, children could multimodally play with words, gestures, expressions, sounds, movements and artifacts. The process involved a translinguistic **immersion** in children's reality through play, its **expansion and reflection** through the stories told and the films watched, as well as the participation of the teachers in some play activities with the children. Every time the children had another opportunity to perform the same social activity again, it was possible to see how they expanded their ways of acting and creating meaning together in the group. The sessions offered children, even if from a very early situation (considering their ages), the opportunity to interculturally play different realities, so that they could position themselves in relation to events, situations and ways of acting in the world.

Concluding Remarks

The idea of thinking about a usual activity in the lives of these children and recreating it with the help of the additional language generated possibilities to reorganize the ways students lived these situations and created funds of *perejivanie*. We believe that such practices fostered opportunities for them to go beyond, not only in terms of language resources, but also in terms of their feelings, opinions and ways of interacting with others. The fact that they were invited to critically experiment with different social practices, discourses and voices made it possible for children to transcend their limits and, therefore, to expand their social-cultural mobility. Although very young, these children, often silenced, were made visible and experienced with decision-making processes that created possibilities for expanding their funds of *perejivanie* and redesigning their social futures.

Likewise, it is our belief that these types of proposals, based on an engaged multiliteracy, can potentially refract and reflect the principles upon which a more critically transformative and socially just language education relies. Such dialogic and pluralistic practices can foster children's agency in how to face unexpected challenges such as the ones we are living today, in this pandemic time. In a libertarian way, children learn to be stronger and find ways to resist and expand their possibilities of living and transforming the world while being transformed by it.

Appendix 1: 'Slam' by Vitor Abade Silva[7]

Somos Brasil, somos a beleza vasta, a evidência maquiada de desgraça, somos a tal famosa 'mulata', somos o catador de sucatas, mente de ouro, coração de prata, mas pra eles nossas vidas não valem nada

Somos buracrácia, somos democracia, somos podres se tornando burguesia, somos o POVO de valor, somos turistas no Cristo Redentor.

Somos o lugar onde a esperança prevalece, somos a liberdade e a fé
Vivenciada por nosso povo na praça da Sé.

Somos sangue escondido embaixo de tapete vermelho, somos albinos, brancos e também NÁVIOS NEGREIROS.

Fugir nunca foi uma opção
nessa deu eu que lute, nasce o luto.
É que de preto em preto vão exterminando nosso povo
Mas se os pretos se juntar?
Se os pretos se juntar você pode se preparar, porque hoje com nossas palavras iremos revidar.

Somos a evolução da revolução,
Somos livres como pássaros negros.
Hey Black você é Power e com todo esse poder lute. Mesmo de luto!

João Pedro, presente!
É tanto só corre, só corre ...
Que até esquecem de nos socorrer
E as lembranças se tornam a última que correm

Translation by Bárbara Manja

We are Brazil, we are the vast beauty, the evidence of disgrace in disguise, we are the famous 'mulatto,' we are the scavenger, the gold mind, the silver heart, but for them our lives are worthless.

We are bureaucracy, we are democracy, we are rotten becoming bourgeoisie, we are the PEOPLE of value, we are tourists in Christ the Redeemer.

We are the place where hope prevails, we are freedom and faith
Experienced by our people in 'Praça da Sé'.

We are blood hidden under a red carpet, we are albinos, whites and also slave ship.

Running away was never an option
And from 'I who fight,' mourning is born.
From black to black they are exterminating our people
But what if Black people get together?
If Black people get together you can get ready, because today with our words we will fight back.

We are revolution's evolution,
We are free like black birds.
Hey Black, you're Power and with all that strength, fight. Even when mourning!

João Pedro, presente!
It's too about running, just run ...
That they forget to help us
And memories become the last that run.

Notes

(1) The HDI (Human Development Index) figures released in 2020 indicate that Brazil sits at the 84th position in the overall ranking, with an HID value (2019) of 0.765. See http://hdr.undp.org/en/content/latest-human-development-index-ranking.
(2) The Gini coefficient is an index that is often used to measure and analyze the extent of the prevailing inequality within a country (Neri, 2019).
(3) Such studies were jointly developed in 2020 by PUCRS (Pontifical Catholic University of Rio Grande do Sul) and National Institutions of Science and Technology, such as Observatório das Metrópoles (Metropoles Observatory) and the Observatório da Dívida Social na América Latina – RedODSAL (Latin America Social Debt Observatory). See https://www.pucrs.br/en/blog/pucrs-research-inspires-series-on-social-inequality-in-brazil/.
(4) Available at https://www.letras.mus.br/cocomelon/hello-song/ (accessed 5 April 2021).
(5) Available at https://kidsongs.com/song/twinkle-twinkle-little-star/ (accessed December 2021).
(6) Available at https://www.letras.mus.br/super-simple-songs/bye-bye-goodbye-goodbye-song/ (accessed 5 April 2021).

(7) Both Vitor and Bárbara are teen researchers from the Language in Activities in the School Context (LACE) Research Group. Vitor created this slam as part of his participation in the Brincadas Project, which uses Engaged Multiliteracy as the basis for its actions.

References

Alves, E.J. and Faria, D.C. (2020) Educação em tempos de pandemia: Lições aprendidas e compartilhadas [Education in times of pandemic: Lessons learned and shared]. *Revista Observatório* 6 (2), 1–18.

Amorim, A.G.P. (forthcoming) Ações fundamentais que compõem o processo de ensino-aprendizagem no Multiletramento Engajado. In F. Liberali (ed.) *A Formação de Formadores por meio do Multiletramento Engajado como Possibilidade de Redesenhar Futuros Sociais [Teacher Education through Engaged Multiliteracy as a Possibility to Redesign Social Futures]*. Campinas: Pontes.

Bakhtin, M.M. (1981) Discourse in the novel. In *The Dialogic Imagination: Four Essays* (C. Emerson and M. Holquist, trans., pp. 259–422). Austin, TX: University of Texas Press.

Bakhtin, M.M. (1986a) Response to a question from the Novy Mir editorial staff. In C. Emerson and M. Holquist (eds) *Speech Genres & Other Late Essays* (pp. 1–9). Austin, TX: University of Texas Press.

Bakhtin, M.M. (1986b) The problem of the speech genres. In C. Emerson and M. Holquist (eds) *Speech Genres & Other Late Essays* (pp. 60–102). Austin, TX: University of Texas Press.

Bakhtin, M.M. (1993) *Toward a Philosophy of the Act* (V. Liapunov and M. Holquist, trans.). Austin, TX: University of Texas Press.

Bezemer, J. and Kress, G. (2016) *Multimodality, Learning and Communication: A Social Semiotic Frame*. London: Routledge.

Blommaert, J. and Backus, A. (2013) Superdiverse repertoires and the individual: Current challenges for educational studies. In I. Saint-Georges and J.J. Weber (eds) *Multilingualism and Multimodality* (pp. 11–32). Rotterdam: Sense.

Busch, B. (2012) The linguistic repertoire revisited. *Applied Linguistics* 33 (5), 503–523.

Busch, B. (2015) Expanding the notion of the linguistic repertoire: On the concept of Spracherleben – the lived experience of language. *Applied Linguistics* 38 (3), 340–358.

Cope, B. and Kalantzis, M. (eds) (2000) *Multiliteracies: Literacy Learning and the Design of Social Futures*. London: Routledge.

Dei, G.J.S. (2013) Democratic education, thinking out differently. In A.A. Abdi and P.R. Carr (eds) *Educating for Democratic Consciousness: Counter-Hegemonic Possibilities* (pp. 50–67). New York: Peter Lang.

Fraser, N. (2008) *Scales of Justice Reimagining Political Space in a Globalized World*. Cambridge: Polity Press.

Freire, P. (1987 [1970]) *Pedagogia do Oprimido [Pedagogy of the Oppressed]* (17th edn). Rio de Janeiro: Paz e Terra.

Freire, P. (2000) *Pedagogia da Indignação: Cartas Pedagógicas e Outros Escritos [Pedagogy of the Indignation: Letters and Other Essays]*. São Paulo: Editora UNESP.

Freire, P. (2003a) *Educação e Atualidade Brasileira [Education and Brazilian Present Times]*. São Paulo: Cortez, Instituto Paulo Freire.

Freire, P. (2003b) *Educação como Prática da Liberdade [Education as a Practice of Freedom]* (27th edn). Rio de Janeiro: Paz e Terra.

Freire, P. (2004 [1996]) *Pedagogia da Autonomia: Saberes Necessários à Prática Educativa [Pedagogy of Autonomy: Necessary Knowledges for Educational Practice]* (29th edn). São Paulo: Paz e Terra.

Freire, P. (2014 [1992]) *Pedagogia da Esperança: Um Reencontro com a Pedagogia do Oprimido* [*Pedagogy of Hope: A Reencounter with the Pedagogy of the Oppressed*] (21st edn). São Paulo: Paz e Terra.

Freire, P. and Macedo, M. (2015 [1990]) *Alfabetização: Leitura do Mundo, Leitura da Palavra* [*Alphabetization: Reading of the World, Reading of the Word*]. São Paulo: Paz e Terra.

Freire, P., Freire, N. and Oliveira, W.F. (2016 [2014]) *Pedagogia da Solidariedade* [*Pedagogy of Solidarity*] (2nd edn). São Paulo: Paz e Terra.

García, O. (2009) *Bilingual Education in the 21st Century: A Global Perspective*. Oxford: Wiley-Blackwell.

Gee, J. (2000) New people in new worlds: Networks, the new capitalism and schools. In B. Cope and M. Kalantzis (eds) *Multiliteracies: Literacy Learning and the Design of Social Futures* (pp. 43–68). London: Routledge.

Gerhardt, A.F.L. and Amorim, M.A. (eds) (2020) *A BNCC e o Ensino de Línguas e Literaturas* [*The National Educational Framework and the Teaching of Languages and Literatures*]. Campinas: Pontes.

Hogg, L. (2011) Funds of knowledge: An investigation of coherence within the literature. *Teaching and Teacher Education* 27, 666–677.

Liberali, F.C. (2019) O compromisso da Linguística Aplicada com a formação de educadores: Avanços e desafios [The commitment of applied linguistics to the education of educators: Movements and challenges]. Paper presented at the International Conference of Critical Applied Linguistics na Jornada Internacional de Linguística Aplicada Crítica, Brasília, 23–25 July.

Liberali, F.C. (2020a) Construir o inédito viável em meio a crise do coronavírus – lições que aprendemos, vivemos e propomos. In F.C. Liberali, V.P. Fuga, U.C.C. Diegues and M.P. Carvalho (eds) *Brincando em Tempos de Pandemia: Brincando com um Mundo Possível* [*Playing in Pandemic Times: Playing with a Possible World*] (pp. 13–21). Campinas: Pontes.

Liberali, F.C. (2020b) A pesquisa crítica de colaboração como forma de resistir-expandir em contextos de decolonialidade [The critical and collaborative research as a means to resist-expand in decolonial contexts]. Presented live at III Circle of Conferences – GEADEL. See https://www.youtube.com/watch?v=k973V2-Fkek&feature=youtu.be (accessed September 2020).

Liberali, F.C. (forthcoming) Multiletramento engajado na construção de práticas do bem viver. In F.C. Liberali and V. Carrijo (eds) *Necroeducação e Multiletramento Engajado* [*Necroeducation and Engaged Multiliteracies*]. Campinas: Pontes.

Liberali, F, Fuga, V., Diegues, U. and Carvalho, M. (eds) (2020) Educação em Tempos de Pandemia: Brincando Com um Mundo Possível. Campinas: Pontes.

Liberali, F.C. and Megale, A.H. (eds) (2019) *Alfabetização, letramento e multiletramentos em tempos de resistência: Por que importa?* In F.C. Liberali and A.H. Megale (eds) *Alfabetização, Letramento e Multiletramentos em Tempos de Resistência* [*Alphabetization, Literacies and Multiliteracies in Times of Resistance*] (pp. 59–74). Campinas: Pontes.

Matthews, S.H. (2007) A window on the 'new' sociology of childhood. *Sociology Compass* 1 (1), 322–334. doi:10.1111/j.1751-9020.2007.00001.x

Mbembe, A. (2016) Necropolítica [Necropolitics]. *Artes & Ensaios* 32, 123–151.

MEC (2017) *Base Nacional Comum Curricular* [*National Educational Framework*]. Brasília: Ministério da Educação Brasil. See http://basenacionalcomum.mec.gov.br/ (accessed March 2021).

Megale, A.H. and Liberali, F.C. (2020) Implications of the concept of funds of perejivanie as an alternative for multilingual education. *Revista X* 15 (1), 55–74.

Mills, K.A. (2016) *Literacy Theories for the Digital Age: Social, Critical, Multimodal, Spatial, Material and Sensory Lenses*. Bristol: Multilingual Matters.

Moll, L.C. and Cammarota, J. (2010) Cultivating new funds of knowledge through research and practice. In K. Dunsmore and D. Fisher (eds) *Bridging Literacy Home* (pp. 290–306). Newark, DE: International Reading Association.

Moreira, E.S., Lima, E.O. and Brito, R.O. (2019) Estudo comparado das políticas públicas educacionais de inclusão digital: Brasil e Uruguai [Comparative study of educational policies of digital inclusion]. *Revista de la Facultad de Educación* 1, 1–22.

Murray, T. (2013) *Snug as a Bug*. London: Simon & Schuster.

Neri, M. (2019) Inequality in Brazil: Inclusive growth trend of this millennium is over. *UNU-WIDER Policy Brief* 1, 1–19. See https://www.wider.unu.edu/publication/inequality-brazil.

New London Group (1996) A pedagogy of multiliteracies: Designing social futures. *Harvard Educational Review* 66 (1), 60–93. doi:10.17763/haer.66.1.17370n67v22j160u

New London Group (2000) A pedagogy of multiliteracies: Designing social futures. In B. Cope and M. Kalantzis (eds) *New London Group, Multiliteracies: Literacy Learning and the Design of Social Futures* (pp. 9–37). South Yarra: Macmillan Publishers Australia Pty.

Pinheiro-Machado, R. (2019) *Amanhã Vai Ser Maior: O Que Aconteceu com o Brasil e Possíveis Rotas de Fuga para a Crise Atual* [*Tomorrow Will Be Bigger: What Happened to Brazil and Possible Escape Routes for the Present Crisis*]. São Paulo: Planeta do Brasil.

Quinteiro, J. (2002) Infância e educação no Brasil: Um campo de Estudos em construção. In A.L.G. Faria, B.F. Demartine and P.D. Prado (eds) *Por uma Cultura da Infância: Metodologias de Pesquisa com Crianças* [*For a Culture of Childhood: Methodologies and Research with Children*] (pp. 19–47). São Paulo: Autores Associados.

Ribeiro, A.E. and Vecchio, P.M. (eds) (2020) *Tecnologias Digitais e Escola: Reflexões no Projeto Aula Aberta Durante a Pandemia* [*Digital Technologies and Schooling: Reflections in the Project Open Classes in Pandemic Times*]. São Paulo: Parábola Editorial.

Rocha, C.H. (2012) *Reflexões e Propostas sobre Língua Estrangeira no Ensino Fundamental I: Plurilinguismo, Multiletramentos e Transculturalidade* [*Reflections and Proposals Concerning Foreign Language Teaching in Primary School: Plurilingualism, Multiliteracies and Transculturality*]. Campinas: Pontes.

Rocha, C.H. (2014) Plurilingualism and critical literacies in the teaching of English in higher education. *Sino-US English Teaching* 11, 797–811.

Rocha, C.H. (2019) Language education in the fluidity of the burnout society: The decolonial potential of the translingual approach. *DELTA* 35 (4), 1–39. e2019350403

Rocha, C.H. and Maciel, R.F. (2015) Foreign language teaching as translingual practice: Articulations with Bakhtinian theories. *DELTA* 31 (2), 411–445.

Shields, C.M. (2007) *Bakhtin*. New York: Peter Lang.

Sousa Santos, B. (2007) Beyond abyssal thinking: From global lines to ecologies of knowledges. *Review (Fernand Braudel Center)* 30 (1), 45–89.

Souza, J. (2017) *A Elite do Atraso: Da Escravidáo à Lava Jato* [*The Drawback Elite: From Slavery to Lava Jato Operation*]. Rio de Janeiro: Leya.

Vološinov, N.V. (1986) *Marxism and the Philosophy of Language*. London: Harvard University Press.

Vygotsky, L.S. (1978) *Mind and Society: The Development of Higher Mental Processes*. Cambridge, MA: Harvard University Press.

Vygotsky, L.S. (1994 [1934]) The problem of the environment. In R. Van der Veer and J. Valsiner (eds) *The Vygotsky Reader* (pp. 338–354). Oxford: Blackwell.

Part 2

Kindergarten

8 La Tortuga Está Tiptoeing: Multimodal Storytelling in a Bilingual Kindergarten

Laura Schall-Leckrone

Introduction

Mrs Semilla clutched a sparkly microphone while narrating the archetypal race scene from *the Tortoise and Hare* in Spanish. One child pretended to nap while another crept slowly across the carpet, and Yesenia surmised, 'La tortuga está tiptoeing,' using an ingenious intra-sentential code-switch to characterize the action. Teacher- or student-initiated multimodal storytelling episodes were a common phenomenon in this bilingual kindergarten, especially in the popular classroom area where children 'played house,' with pretend kitchenware, baby dolls and costumes. Young bilingual learners (BLs) experienced storytelling using all available semiotic resources: named languages (Spanish, English), movement, classroom objects, illustrations, drawing and Chromebooks. As Lotherington (2017: 1) observes, 'early childhood education is intrinsically multimodal.' Accordingly, this chapter examines how emergent BLs used multiple communication modes to interpret and compose stories through a case study in a bilingual kindergarten where both Spanish and English were spoken. First, I briefly discuss the purpose of story genres, the use of genre pedagogy to teach them and multiple modalities to enact them. Then, I provide a detailed portrait of storytelling in one bilingual kindergarten in a multilingual community in the northeastern United States (Lawrence-Lightfoot, 2005). In the process, this chapter will illustrate how translanguaging – the flexible and resourceful use of languages demonstrated by Yesenia – embodied learning, material objects and drawing can mediate engagement in the genre of storytelling.

Storytelling and Multiliteracy Development

Modern societies tell stories through multiple modalities and digital platforms that can be harnessed to enhance students' literate identities and composing processes in schools (Vasudevan *et al.*, 2010). Often, young children are socialized into expected home, school and community literacy practices through the types of stories told to them (Heath, 1983). As Derewianka and Jones (2016: 78) explain, 'one of the major functions of language [is] to represent our experience of the world ... through stories.' The demands of 21st century literacies suggest expanding the definition of story genres to include all the media through which young children currently experience stories (New London Group, 1996).

Accordingly, this study addresses the New London Group's (1996) prescient call for research on education's role in developing multiliteracies, which are 'multilingual, multicultural, and multimodal' (Accurso *et al.*, 2019c: 2). The analysis presented here also draws from related scholarship on translanguaging (Baker & Wright, 2017; García & Kleyn, 2016), multimodal communication (Kress, 2011; Wohlwend, 2011) and genre pedagogy (Derewianka & Jones, 2016; Martin, 2009; Siffrinn & Harman, 2019).

Genre pedagogy, as described by educational linguists associated with systemic functional linguistics (SFL), is an instructional model designed to apprentice students into ways of communicating knowledge consistent with school success (Derewianka & Jones, 2016; Schall-Leckrone, 2017). From an SFL perspective, genres are regularly occurring social phenomena captured in language (Kress, 1993). They may contain anticipated organizational and linguistic features, but genres are fluid entities responsive to cultural situations (Martin, 2009).

Story genres are a central feature of all cultures; they are 'told in [...] social groupings to interpret life's chaos and rhythms [...] evaluate behavior and educate and entertain [...] children' (Martin & Rose, 2008: 49). Story genres introduce people or protagonists, a setting in time and place, and a disruptive event that is resolved (Derewianka & Jones, 2016; Martin & Rose, 2008). Even though their purpose is to entertain (Derewianka & Jones, 2016), stories also inculcate cultural values, traditions and norms, so they play a significant role in families, schools and communities. Ann Patchett (2013), an American author, even suggests that composing stories is intrinsic to the human experience:

> [W]riting should be a natural act, a function of a well-operating human body, along the lines of speaking, walking, and breathing. We should be able to tap into the narrative flow our minds provide, the roaring river of words filling up our heads, and direct it out into a neat stream of organized thought so that other people can read it. (Patchett, 2013: 21)

Patchett, a bestselling novelist, focuses on written stories.

However, literacy and storytelling are performative. Languages are always in motion: a process of doing rather than a closed system that we can possess (McWhorter, 2016). This action-oriented notion of language is encapsulated in the present progressive verb form of the term, *translanguaging*. It suggests that BLs draw upon all linguistic resources available to them in natural, holistic and evolving ways to engage with stories (Baker & Wright, 2017; García & Kleyn, 2016). Storytelling in multilingual schools and communities occurs through fluid language use: complex semiotic systems of print, oral, drawn and digital communications (Kress, 2011).

Since 21st century narratives consist of complex interplays of moving images, speech and written languages (Kress, 2011), multiliteracies pedagogy must encompass multiple communication modes (Harman & Shin, 2018). A growing body of research demonstrates how embodied learning and the arts engage EBLs in literacy instruction (Berriz *et al.*, 2019; Chappell & Faltis, 2013). On a related note, Siffrinn and Harman (2019) argue that genre pedagogy should integrate physical activity, because the body plays a key role in meaning production. They argue that embodied learning (e.g. planting a garden) can be used to build background knowledge in the first phase of the teaching learning cycle (TLC) through which genre pedagogy is enacted. The arts and embodied learning can also scaffold learning in subsequent TLC stages: supported reading; deconstructing examples of the genre; shared writing; and, finally, independent writing (Derewianka & Jones, 2016; Schall-Leckrone, forthcoming). Schall-Leckrone (forthcoming) demonstrates how a bilingual teacher used drawings, kinesthetics and singing to support reading comprehension. Multimodal pedagogy can be used to apprentice BLs into key school genres.

In summary, this investigation builds on prior work on multimodality (Kress, 2011; Wohlwend, 2011), genre pedagogy (Derewianka & Jones, 2016; Schall-Leckrone, 2017; Siffrinn & Harman, 2019) and translanguaging (García & Kleyn, 2016). Insufficient research portrays the complex communicative resources of bilingual teachers and young children in high-poverty communities as assets in literacy development (Durán & Palmer, 2014). Therefore, the purpose of the chapter is to illustrate how a bilingual kindergarten teacher used oral and written languages, drawing, material objects and movement as an intrinsic part of genre pedagogy in an early childhood classroom. In the process, I argue that young BLs should be engaged in multimodal storytelling.

Research Context

This study was part of an ethnography of the rich linguistic ecology of a multilingual school in a gateway community in the northeastern US (Geertz, 1973; Wortham, 2008). Arborway School, a K-6 elementary school ironically classified as 96% minority and 100% economically disadvantaged, serves approximately 600 learners. Most students spoke a home language other than English, including Spanish, Portuguese, Vietnamese, Nepali, Mandarin and Arabic. All children in the new bilingual program were Latinx.

Classroom observations occurred two to three times a week, beginning in mid-August of 2019 when children first arrived for kindergarten screening, and ended abruptly in March of 2020 when the school closed due to the COVID-19 pandemic. As a participant observer, I wrote copious field notes to create 'thick descriptions' of classroom discourse (Geertz, 1973). Starting in early October when all seemed accustomed to my presence, I video-taped whole-group instruction with the assistance of Nelson, a boy a head taller than the other students, already knowledgeable about digital technologies but challenged by sitting still.

As is typical with ethnography, participants were selected based on an established relationship with the principal, kindergarten teacher (both former students) and school community. Kindergarteners included newcomers and children of im/migration from the Caribbean and Central and South America. The teacher, Mrs Semilla, was originally from Puerto Rico and had significant early childhood education experience. She had worked as an ESL teacher at Arborway before assuming the role of kindergarten teacher to implement the dual immersion program. A soft-spoken individual with a firm, loving demeanor, she established an orderly environment through color-coding, oral, written and illustrated instructions, movement and music; use of multiple modalities was not unique to literacy instruction.

Data analysis

To construct a case study of multimodal storytelling in this kindergarten classroom, observation video-tapes, field notes and teacher and student work were collected and analyzed. First, I identified when storytelling figured as a prominent episode in the class, initiated either by the teacher or students. To do so, I examined field notes and observation video-tapes, creating a table with storytelling episodes: when they occurred, in which modalities (oral, written, drawn, kinesthetic and so on) and language(s), who initiated the story, and what story was being told. Teacher-created charts, posters, graphic organizers and student drawings and writing augment the case analysis. These data were analyzed through the lens of multimodal communication to illuminate the children's storytelling experiences in the classroom. As Wohlwend (2011: 243) explains, 'Multimodal analysis involves isolating, examining, and explaining an aspect of lived experience to understand how actors exploit available semiotic resources to represent meanings [and] carry out social practices.' Accordingly, storytelling episodes were interpreted using a researcher-created analytical framework (see Figure 8.1), which was adapted from Wohlwend (2011) and Schall-Leckrone (in press) to better understand how the teacher and students used 'available semiotic resources' to engage in storytelling.

Findings

The bilingual kindergarten teacher and children employed multiple simultaneous mediational tools to engage in storytelling. Oral and written languages, drawing, movement and material objects were used in storytelling episodes to retell familiar stories and compose personal and fictional narratives. Overall, drawing played a prominent role in both teacher- and student-initiated storytelling in the classroom as indicated in Figure 8.1.

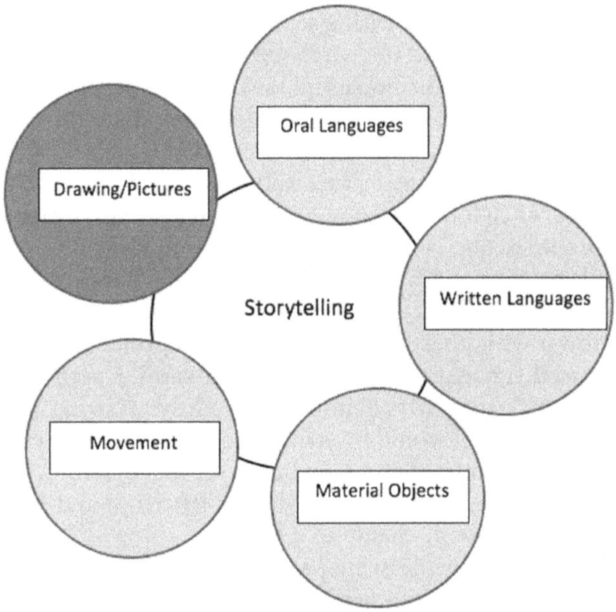

Figure 8.1 Multimodal storytelling episodes

Teacher-initiated storytelling

The teacher frequently used drawing to co-construct iconic stories with the children. Co-construction engages students in shared writing to model what skilled writers do and how they do it (Derewianka & Jones, 2016; Gibbons, 2015). Accordingly, Mrs Semilla would scribe and 'think aloud' as she prompted students to co-create stories using multimodal scaffolds. The premise of the joint construction stage is that it prepares students to write or draw a designated genre independently. In this dual immersion kindergarten, Mrs Semilla co-constructed Rapunzel to teach the organizational features of a fairytale, and the Thanksgiving legend as part of a lesson on the significance of the holiday.

Rapunzel retell through drawings

Mrs Semilla stood at the easel with a black marker, poised to retell the already familiar story of Rapunzel with the children through drawings. The paper had a large rectangle divided into three sections with horizontal lines to represent narrative stages: the orientation (setting, characters); problem or conflict; and resolution (Derewianka & Jones, 2016; Martin & Rose, 2008). First, the teacher drew a baby in a bassinet in the top section, and then the witch, but paused while drawing the witch's face to ask the class: 'How should we do her mouth, as if she is angry?': The children responded, chorally, 'Sí!' The teacher paused again, tapped the marker against her own mouth, indicating she was thinking, and said, 'But when she stole the baby, how did the witch feel?' The children shouted, 'Feliz!' [Happy]. She picked up the book and said, 'Let me see. I'm going to look for evidence in the book.' After Mrs Semilla found an illustration of the witch stealing the baby, she walked around the carpet. The children craned their necks to see the picture and murmured, 'Feliz!' Mrs Semilla asked why the witch looked happy, and a child near her responded immediately, 'Porque se robó la bebe' [because she stole the baby]. Mrs Semilla drew a smile on the witch's face, and asked, 'What happened next?' With oral prompting and pictures, the children recounted how Rapunzel was put into a tower without a door and stairs until a prince helped her escape. They discussed subsequent plot events in a similar manner until they reached the conclusion. Mrs Semilla finished the drawing with a grand castle, where Rapunzel would live with the prince and their children happily ever after. She concluded, 'Y pudieron ser felices para ...' [And, they could live happily ever ...] turning over her left hand and holding it up, and the children shouted, 'Siempre!' [After].

Mrs Semilla used the drawing process, oral language and the book to retell Rapunzel. Simultaneous use of a graphic organizer, gestures, prompting and pictures scaffolded instruction of narrative components. Afterwards, she ran her hands over the illustrated graphic organizer to reinforce the narrative stages, saying, 'This was the problem, right? What was the solution?' She emphasized that she could retell any story using pictures. Next, she explained, the children would create their own stories with what happened at the beginning, the problem, the events showing the problem, and the solution. This led to a humorous conversation about how many problems could occur in a story. Mrs Semilla said there could be two or three or just one problem, holding up corresponding fingers, and a child said, 'O cinco problemas' [Or, five problems]. The teacher laughed, held up her hand with five fingers splayed, and repeated, 'O cinco problemas!'

Drawing the Thanksgiving legend

Similar to the Rapunzel recounting, the teacher reminded the class that they had already read the story and said, 'Ustedes saben que a Mrs Semilla, le encanta dibujar?' [You know Mrs Semilla loves to draw]. The children responded, 'Sí!' and a child added in Spanish, 'Me too.' Complete with a map of the continents, a book, chart paper, markers, and the children's active contributions, Mrs Semilla drew the Thanksgiving story. This time, indicating that this was a historical legend instead of a fairy tale, she wrote a number beside each image to underscore the event sequence. The story began with (1) Pilgrims with sad faces and the label, 'Inglaterra' [England], then (2) a ship labelled 'Mayflower' and (3) the Commonwealth of Massachusetts, also labelled with its name. She drew wavy lines under the Mayflower, emphasizing that the Pilgrims sailed for a long time. Then she asked what the weather was like when the Pilgrims arrived, folding her arms across her chest and shaking to indicate cold.

The children shouted, 'Frio!' Mrs Semilla asked, 'What happened?' 'Se enfermaron' [They got sick], the children responded, so Mrs Semilla wrote the number 4 and drew an adult and child Pilgrim looking ill. She continued, 'It was snowy and very windy,' drawing snow over the Pilgrims' heads with wavy lines. She opened the book again and asked, 'Who helped them?' A child replied, 'Esquante.' Mrs Semilla repeated, 'Who helped them?' 'Esquante,' the child repeated, and Mrs Semilla said, 'Esquanto,' subtly changing the final phoneme to a long o sound, but reproducing the Spanish-influenced start to the name with the addition of an 'E' sound. However, she wrote the number 5 and 'Squanto,' next to it, and the children said, 'Esquanto!' Then she showed a book illustration, which displayed Squanto and a Pilgrim in the classic hat and brown suit shaking hands. Then she asked, 'How did Squanto help them? What did he teach them?' She wrote the number 6. One child volunteered that he taught them to grow plants, and when the teacher said, 'And what else?', another child offered, 'He helped them to catch fish.' Mrs Semilla drew plants and a fish on the surface of the water next to the number 6. Then she wrote the number 7, and said, 'The Pilgrims felt very happy,' drawing a picture of smiling Pilgrims. And, 'What did the Pilgrims decide to do with the Americans?', she asked and then held up another illustration in the book. One child said, 'They ate,' and another child shouted, 'And shared.' Mrs Semilla elaborated, 'They shared a big feast.' She wrote the number 8 and drew a long table, saying 'To give thanks …' A child finished the sentence, 'A dios!' (to god). And Mrs Semilla continued, 'To give thanks to god and for the food.' They had corn and pumpkins, she said, adding images of the vegetables to the table. Then, she held up the book again, saying, 'Miren' [Look], showing an illustration of the first Thanksgiving feast. The class concluded that portion of the lesson by discussing what foods their families consume to celebrate Thanksgiving. When a child said 'pavo,' Mrs Semilla circulated around the carpet, displaying a photo of a turkey family on her phone. Then, she unfolded a drawing of a large turkey that she had created earlier with the sentence starter in Spanish, 'I give thanks for …' on its body. She proceeded to record student responses: essentially family members including pets. Finally, the class was given cardstock to create Thanksgiving cards. These teacher-led storytelling episodes also prompted original compositions by children.

Student-initiated storytelling

Students combined drawing and translanguaging to retell known stories and construct creative solutions to personal and societal issues. They were familiar with common fables (e.g. *The Tortoise and the Hare)* and their features: animal characters, a problem, a solution and a moral. Their drawings typically depicted animals and plot elements, and might be labeled, 'habia una vez' [once upon a time] with animal names. The fable unit prepared students to create original stories with orientations, problems and solutions. Their stories often comprised everyday problems: dropping an ice cream, wanting a pet or toy, with some fictional elements. For instance, unicorns were quite popular. Nonetheless, one child considered the climate crisis and another imaginatively conveyed a solution to a troubling situation. These stories are more fully illustrated here because of the originality of their efforts and because Yesenia and Angelito represented opposite ends of the kindergarten developmental spectrum.

Yesenia was one of the strongest pre-readers/writers in the class in both Spanish and English. A bright-eyed child, she engaged fully in learning activities without the nearly constant motion of her peers. Toward the end of the narrative unit, she used a graphic organizer with the organizational framework of the story genre to draw a picture of a penguin on a melting iceberg (see Figure 8.2).

The first story panel, prelabeled 'Characters,' illustrates a penguin with snow falling around it. The letters, 'FRSiWZOW' and 'iN,' on the next line suggest that Yesenia was writing, 'First, it was snowing,' in English. In the next panel, the penguin appears to be immersed in water. The author has switched to Spanish, but uses an English syntactical pattern, 'Yo soy nado,' with 'soy,' the 'I' form of the verb 'to be,' functioning as an auxiliary verb linked to 'nado,' suggesting she was writing, 'I am swimming,' giving voice to the penguin. Long rays of the sun are also depicted. In the next panel, prelabeled, 'Problem,' the circle of the sun has grown larger and water has risen around the penguin. Tears appear to be cascading from the penguin's left eye. In the 'Solution' panel, the sun is gone. Snow is falling again, and the penguin is no longer crying. The illustration even features a snowball with a happy face beside the penguin. Yesenia uses an evocative combination of pictures, letters and translanguaging to illustrate how a penguin is affected by global warming. Her use of Spanish, English and drawings to tell this story are interconnected and coexisting, which supports a holistic and heteroglossic perspective of bilingualism (Baker & Wright, 2017).

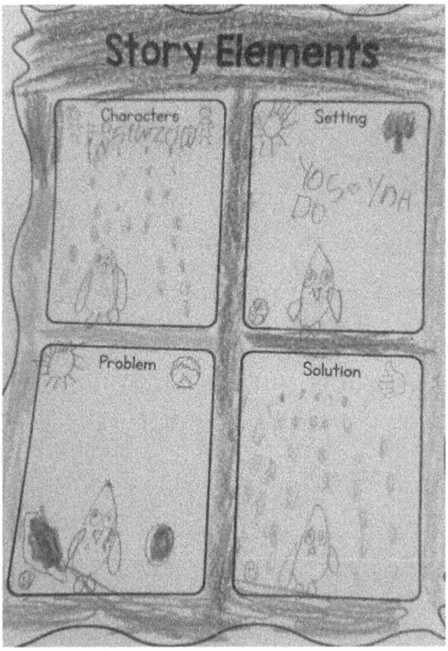

Figure 8.2 Yesenia's depiction of global warming

Angelito's creative resolution to a personal dilemma

Angelito, the smallest class member, was unable to sit still for most learning activities. During kindergarten screening, he did not count or identify letters or sounds. He spoke in single words and simple sentences interspersing Spanish with English. However, he also created an impromptu magic trick that revealed a creativity that later manifested in storytelling episodes. He took the wordless picture book by Mercer Mayer used to elicit conversation, and said, 'Close your eyes!' Then, he turned the page, commanded 'Open your eyes,' and said, 'Poof, magic!', laughing loudly, repeating this trick several times, seemingly delighted by how the pictures changed when he turned the pages.

During the Thanksgiving story co-construction, Angelito had his head down at first, crying quietly then working playdoh through his fingers. He had returned from outdoor recess visibly upset but did not want to talk. When cardstock was distributed with instructions to depict what they were grateful for, first he drew friends in the schoolyard. Then, he turned the paper over and drew a bed with himself in it and said, 'I'm tired,' and used a pencil on its side to put gray slashes all around the bed, indicating night time. Mrs Semilla later explained that his mother had just begun working nights. She was unsure who was watching him. His simple drawing indicated gratitude for school and a resolution to a troubling situation: he put himself to bed. There was a certain magic to being able to draw his own conclusion through pictures.

Implications for students

A multimodal approach to storytelling for young BLs positions them as knowers, doers and agentive learners (Harman & Shin, 2018), who can creatively construct solutions to personal and global challenges. Angelito's drawing illustrates that even young children can be authors of their own experience. Yesenia depicted a global crisis in her climate change drawing. As Wohlwend (2011) observes:

> A multimodal perspective recognizes young children as designers who talk, act, and create texts, images, and artifacts and who make strategic use of available materials, social spaces, school cultures, and global discourses. (Wohlwend, 2011: 245)

Recognition of the strategic ways in which BLs use multiple semiotic resources can guide literacy pedagogy.

Teaching implications

Multimodal ensembles can be used as an intrinsic part of genre pedagogy to apprentice BLs, including newcomers, into key genres such as storytelling, as illustrated by Mrs Semilla's example. Certainly, drawing can play a prominent role in the co-construction phase of the TLC, not just for young learners, but for multilingual individuals of any age at earlier stages of English proficiency to gain familiarity with academic genres. Given the proliferation of multimodal communication in a digital world, students would benefit from an early foundation and growing skills in how to interpret and create images as part of critical literacy development (Accurso *et al.*, 2019; Derewianka & Jones, 2016; Kress, 2011; Lotherington, 2017; New London Group, 1996).

Conclusion

With multimodal analysis, the challenge is to record and make sense of simultaneous communication forms that coexist in a single episode (Wohlwend, 2011). Because this research focuses on the development of literacy and school-based ways of knowing for multilingual individuals, I highlighted the role of drawing in genre pedagogy. Analysis of imaginative use of material objects in dramatic play would have yielded different conclusions. While the results of this case study cannot be generalized, its in-depth view of how to promote storytelling through multiple modalities can be instructive. Various pedagogical practices Mrs Semilla employed in her first year as a bilingual kindergarten teacher could be taken up by teachers working with school newcomers and in teacher education programs to promote multiliteracies development for multilingual learners.

This case study of multimodal storytelling in a bilingual kindergarten supports prior work in genre pedagogy that integrates images and embodied learning (Derewianka & Jones, 2016; Harman & Shin, 2018). The construct of translanguaging recognizes that multilingual individuals use all their linguistic resources to make meaning (Baker & Wright, 2017). Young learners in early childhood settings can engage in multimodal and bilingual communication strategies as they develop literacy. It is my hope that this small-scale study may encourage teachers, teacher educators and researchers to also explore the learning opportunities when multimodal genre pedagogy is coupled with translanguaging. Early childhood teachers can integrate holistic views of bilingualism (García & Kleyn, 2016) with multimodal communication (Kress, 2011) to engage students in learning critical school and community genres, such as storytelling. All available semiotic resources – named languages, material objects, embodied learning and drawing – should be employed to support the multiliteracies development of young BLs and other school newcomers in the multilingual schools of the 21st century.

References

Accurso, K., Muzeta, B. and Pérez-Battles, S. (2019) Reflection multiliteracies: Teaching meaning-making across the visual and language arts. *SPELT Quarterly* 34 (2), 2–16.

Baker, C. and Wright, W.E. (2017) *Foundations of Bilingual Education and Bilingualism* (6th edn). Bristol: Multilingual Matters.

Berriz, B.R., Wager, A.C. and Poey, V.M. (2019) *Art as a Way of Talking for Emergent Bilingual Youth: A Foundation for Literacy in PreK-12 schools.* New York: Routledge.

Chappell, S.V. and Faltis, C.J. (2013) *The Arts and Emergent Bilingual Youth: Building Culturally Responsive, Critical, and Creative Education in School and Community Contexts.* New York: Routledge.

Derewianka, B. and Jones, P. (2016) *Teaching Language in Context* (2nd edn). Melbourne: Oxford University Press.

Durán, L. and Palmer, D. (2014) Pluralist discourses of bilingualism and translanguaging talk in classrooms. *Journal of Early Childhood Literacy* 14 (3), 367–388.

García, O. and Kleyn, T. (eds) (2016) *Translanguaging with Multilingual Students: Learning from Classroom Moments.* New York: Routledge.

Geertz, C. (1973) Thick description: Toward an interpretive theory of culture. In *The Interpretation of Cultures* (pp. 3–30). New York: Basic Books.

Gibbons, P. (2015) *Scaffolding Language, Scaffolding Learning: Teaching Second Language Learners in the Mainstream Classroom* (2nd edn). Portsmouth, NH: Heinemann.

Harman, R. and Shin, D. (2018) Multimodal and community-based literacies: Agentive bilingual learners in elementary school. In G. Onchwari and J. Keengwe (eds) *Handbook of Research on Pedagogies and Cultural Considerations for Young English Language Learners* (pp. 217–238). Hershey, PA: IGI Global.

Heath, S.B. (1983) *Ways with Words: Language, Life, and Work in Communities and Classrooms.* New York: Cambridge University Press.

Kress, G. (1993) Genre as social process. In. B. Cope and M. Kalantzis (eds) *The Powers of Literacy: A Genre Approach to Teaching Writing* (pp. 22–37). Pittsburgh, PA: University of Pittsburgh Press.

Kress, G. (2011) Discourse analysis and education: A multimodal social semiotic approach. In R. Rogers (ed.) *An Introduction to Critical Discourse Analysis in Education* (2nd edn, pp. 205–226). New York: Routledge.

Lawrence-Lightfoot, S. (2005) Reflections on portraiture: A dialogue between art and science. *Qualitative Inquiry* 11 (1), 3–15.

Lotherington, H. (2017) Elementary language education in digital, multimodal, and multiliteracy contexts. In S. Thorne and S. May (eds) *Language, Education, and Technology: Encyclopedia of Language and Education*. Cham: Springer International.

Martin, J.R. (2009) Genre and language learning: A social semiotic perspective. *Linguistics and Education* 20, 10–21.

Martin, J.R. and Rose, D. (2008) *Genre Relations*. London: Equinox.

McWhorter, J. (2016) *Words on the Move: Why English Won't – and Can't – Sit Still (Like, Literally)*. New York: Holt.

New London Group (1996) A pedagogy of multiliteracies: Designing social futures. *Harvard Educational Review* 66 (1), 60–93. doi:10.17763/haer.66.1.17370n67v22j160u

Patchett, A. (2013) The getaway car: A practical memoir about writing and life. In A. Patchett (ed.) *This is the Story of a Happy Marriage* (pp. 19–60). New York: Harper Collins.

Schall-Leckrone, L. (2017) Genre pedagogy: A framework to prepare history teachers to teach language. *TESOL Quarterly* 51 (2), 358–382.

Schall-Leckrone, L. (forthcoming) Multimodality and translanguaging as scaffolding: Sensemaking in a bilingual kindergarten. In L.C. de Olivereira and R. Westerlund (eds) *Scaffolding for Multilingual Learners in Elementary and Secondary Schools*. New York: Routledge.

Siffrinn, N. and Harman, R. (2019) Toward an embodied systemic functional linguistics pedagogy. *TESOL Quarterly* 53 (4), 1162–1173.

Vasudevan, L., Schultz, K. and Bateman, J. (2010) Rethinking composing in a digital age: Authoring literate identities through multimodal storytelling. *Written Communication* 27 (4), 442–468.

Wohlwend, K.E. (2011) Mapping modes in children's play and design: An action-oriented approach to critical multimodal analysis. In R. Rogers (ed.) *An Introduction to Critical Discourse Analysis in Education* (2nd edn, pp. 242–266). New York: Routledge.

Wortham, S. (2008) Linguistic anthropology of education. *Annual Review of Anthropology* 37, 37–51.

9 Move, Play, Language: A Translanguaged, Multimodal Approach to Literacies with Young Emergent Bilinguals

Laura Ascenzi-Moreno, Cecilia M. Espinosa and Alison Lehner-Quam

> Languages grow, travel, shift, carry, teach, change minds, comfort, heal, hurt, scare, tickle, move, produce. We craft, tinker, record, copy, paste, move, and then move them again with/through blocks, pencil, or digital device. Languages demand, encourage, woo, wound, play, and dance with/through the prosody of our voices. We sing, scream, laugh, or whisper them aloud with/through emotion as they are shaped by and reshape the history of our own and our mothers' tongues.
>
> (Zapata *et al.*, 2018: 492)

While many teachers are aware that multimodality within literacy, such as drawing or playing, is critical to rich experiences in literacy across all ages, multimodality has most often been explored within monolingual learning environments (Blackledge & Creese, 2017; Kusters *et al.*, 2017). Until recently, scholarship on emergent bilinguals has focused on students' language practices and has not probed how a broader range of emergent bilinguals' communicative repertoire including gestures, art, dance, drawings, play and out-of-school texts are instrumental both in students' learning and in teachers' understanding of students. As Zapata *et al.* (2018) describe above, understanding, valuing and leveraging the dynamism of emergent bilinguals' practices offers educators the opportunity to reimagine literacy when multilingualism and multimodal engagements are the norm.

Educational scholars who study multimodalities and translanguaging converge in thinking that these lenses offer teachers an opportunity to think about and develop curriculum which is not solely teacher directed, but can also be shifted and shaped by students' interactions with texts and objects with the fullness of their entire beings (Espinosa & Lehner-Quam, 2019; Leander & Bolt, 2012; Lenters, 2018; Serafini, 2015). An integrated view of translanguaging and multimodality also allows educators to understand how emergent bilinguals' resources are recognized and valued in schools. This chapter addresses, through two classroom vignettes, how translanguaging and multimodalities are lenses to understand students' strengths and to both challenge and offer up alternatives of what literacy instruction can be like for young emergent bilinguals.

An Integrated View of Translanguaging and Multimodality

For many years, researchers who study multimodality in classrooms focused on monolingual environments, while translanguaging research has focused on the linguistic repertoire, resulting in scant 'cross-generation' between these fields. Recently, there has been a call to find the commonalities that the two fields share and thus more broadly understand how students engage in literacy by calling forth all of their resoures – linguistic, semiotic and embodied.

The call for integrating multimodalities and translanguaging is undergirded by an evolving understanding of what language is. Lin (2019: 8) offers the following description of a 'dynamic, distributed view of language, seeing language as embodied, emplaced, and ensembled in its physical and social environments.' Translanguaging scholars have advocated that the definition of translanguaging must expand beyond the linguistic (García & Li, 2014; Otheguy *et al.*, 2015; Vogel *et al.*, 2018). Rather than viewing translanguaging as beginning with the speaker, it begins with the *person*. In making the person the center of translanguaging, it is acknowledged that translanguaging encompasses social practices, embodied experiences and context (Blackledge & Creese, 2017; Kusters *et al.*, 2017). In this light, Blackledge and Creese (2017: 253) write that 'whenever people enter into social action, they bring along their own biographies.' In essence, we are not superimposing translanguaging upon multimodalities or vice versa, but rather we advocate for an integrated understanding of the two, where they are inseparable from each other, just as the person is an integrated whole.

Because an expanded notion of languaging is centered on the person, *who* the person is matters. Flores and Rosa's (2015) notion of raciolinguistics draws attention to the politicized nature of how racialized emergent bilinguals are perceived by white listening subjects. They assert that it is the white listening subject that imposes perceived deficiencies upon racialized emergent bilinguals. Therefore, the perceived deficiencies are not real, but rather reside in overarching ideologies that shape how people think about and value others' resources. Flores (2020) adds that emergent bilinguals perceived through this gaze are viewed as lacking academic language and as in need of remediation and policing, and therefore what needs 'fixing' are the systems that sustain this gaze. It is critical to understand raciolinguistics in relation to translanguaging and multimodality as it describes how students' embodied and emplaced resources are valued and given power in school. In this chapter, we take up multimodalities and translanguaging as they exist in early childhood classrooms through read-alouds and play-based center time.

Context and Methods for the Studies

We draw upon data from two separate research studies. Both studies were carried out in large urban communities with Latinx students in early childhood grades. One study investigated how researchers integrated multilingualism and multimodality with read-alouds with kindergarten and first- and second-grade students in transitional bilingual classrooms. The other study consisted of teachers and researchers in a professional learning community as they reflected about how to incorporate play into literacy instruction through text-based extensions through centers in dual language bilingual classrooms. While these two studies were entirely separate, researchers in both studies used grounded theory to analyze their respective data. In the two cases, the researchers analyzed their data first by reading through observational field notes and then by identifying themes that emerged from the data. In each study, researchers subsequently revisited the data and found excerpts that represented themes identified in the analysis, which are featured here.

Context for Study 1: Exploring bilingual texts through multimodal experiences

The first study we describe was carried out by two researchers, Cecilia, an early childhood/childhood college professor, and Alison, library faculty member and liaison to the school of education. The site for this project was La Colina Elementary School (proper nouns referring to study sites and participants are pseudonyms). The school has students from Grades PreK through fifth and is located in a large urban setting. It offers a transitional bilingual program to second grade. This site was selected because it has a mixed population of English and Spanish speakers with most of the families in the community coming from the Dominican Republic, Puerto Rico, Mexico, Central America and South America (NYC Population FactFinder, 2020). The student population is 85% Latinx, with 29% of the students designated as English Language Learners/Multilingual Learners (NYC Department of Education, 2020).

The researchers, Cecilia and Alison, met at least three consecutive times for 45 minutes each with four small groups of five children between the grades of kindergarten and second grade during their literacy class time. During these sessions, the researchers and children explored children's books, written by Latinx bilingual authors, through multimodal experiences. The aim in interviewing the children was to identify students' reading preferences and experiences with bilingual books.

In this chapter we share our experience with children in a second-grade class with the book, *Salsa: Un poema para cocinar/A Cooking Poem.*

Vignette 9.1: Opportunities for constructing deeper meanings with a culturally, linguistically relevant and sustaining text

We selected *Salsa* by Jorge Argueta (2015), a native Salvadoran and Pipil Nahua Indian, illustrated by Duncan Tonatiuh, a Mexican-American writer/illustrator, to share with the second-grade class. It is a bilingual book written in English and Spanish and in poetry form. If one does not look attentively, it is simply a book about making salsa. Yet, *Salsa* holds much more complexity. Argueta's use of language invites the reader to savor the words and pictures with one's senses. This bilingual poem sits alongside Tonatiuh's artwork and is influenced by Pre-Columbian Mixtec codices (http://duncantonatiuh.com/about-me/) and their connections to a present-day family coming together to cook. If one looks carefully, as second-grader Daniel did, one realizes that this text offers readers ample opportunities not only to explore metaphors and rich imagery, but also to learn about the origins of an ancient cooking tool, the molcajete (Figure 9.1).

Rather than reading the entire book, we decided to focus on a few stanzas. As soon as the book *Salsa* was introduced to the small group of children, Alison noticed Daniel's keen interest in the molcajete and that

Figure 9.1 A molcajete

he had so much to share. Until then, Daniel had been mostly quiet in our previous visits to the class. Below is an excerpt of the conversation:

Daniel: So, this [book] is about salsa. And ... is about a mom that makes salsa. And ... the kids like salsa, but it wasn't enough spicy, so they go to get tomatoes and jalapeños and onions and pepinos. And then, they cut the tomatoes in pieces. They cut the onions. They cut the pepinos and they put the jalapeños and then they smash it.
Alison: They smash it.
Daniel: My grandmother knows how to make salsa, too. ... she has a lot of jalapenos, a lot of tomatoes, and a lot of onions. And she even makes delicious food.
Alison: What else does she make?
Daniel: She can make tacos.
Alison: Delicious! And you say she has a bowl like this? (points to the molcajete in the illustration) Made out of the lava? The lava from the mountain? ... Do you want to read it to me?
Daniel: 'En mi casa hay una piedra de moler.' [In my house there is a stone bowl.] (Argueta *et al.*, 2015)
(**Transcription of child interview, second grade, 22 November 2016**)

Daniel shared how his grandmother also makes salsa using a molcajete. In this instance, his worlds of home and school are joined. We learn not only that his grandmother uses a molcajete to make salsa, we also learn that he loves how she cooks. As the conversation continued, Daniel volunteered to read from the book. He opted to share a passage in Spanish, although he could be considered a student who had already transitioned to English. In this small group, Daniel felt the freedom to use his entire linguistic repertoire.

As we made plans for the next reading, we noticed that not all of the children had experiences with a molcajete. We decided to bring one to share with the small group in the next session. On this day, the children explored a real molcajete. As they engaged in this exploration, we helped them make connections to the illustrations of the volcano in the book *Salsa*: 'a molcajete comes from the volcano,' we explained, as we pointed to the pictures in the book. The children had opportunities to touch it and feel its texture and shape, and to lift it as they felt its weight. They talked about its color. We reminded them that it has the color of the lava that comes from the volcano. Then, they were invited to grind pepper and explore how the peppercorns' texture and smell was transformed as they crushed them in the molcajete with the tejolote, the small stone. We helped the children extend this experience by asking them to look closely and draw the details they noticed, moving from a tactile experience to observation and reflection. Our intention was to offer the children various opportunities to enrich their connections to the text we were reading.

Reading *Salsa* by Argueta was not just about lifting the beautiful language the author utilized, but it was also about grounding the children's experiences in the deeper layers of meaning the text offers. This was in many ways also the intent of the author, Argueta *et al.* (2015), who talks about the molcajete and heritage in his poem *Salsa*, 'My mother tells me molcajetes were our ancestors' blenders.' For Daniel the molcajete also reminded him of his grandmother, her love for cooking and her expertise in cooking with it. The poem, the visuals, the molcajete, the grinding of the peppercorns, the conversation with his peers and with us strengthened and affirmed his home experiences, while deepening the understanding of his own cultural background. Daniel learned about his people's ancestral relationship to the molcajete, while he shared his expertise with his classmates. If we had read this culturally relevant book to the class, but not included the opportunity and time for a student like Daniel to interact with the molcajete, the experience of reading the book aloud might not have led to the engagement and conversations that we relate in this anecdote.

For us as educators and researchers, witnessing this instance was a powerful moment. We understood what it means to be intentional about the texts we select, why it matters that we pay attention and respond to children's noticings and interests and, most importantly, that we should be mindful that when we engage children as readers, we need to move beyond simply reading the text, talking about vocabulary, looking at the illustrations, to experiencing texts in new ways so that we can all deepen the possibilities for constructing meanings as readers, while we invite children to capitalize on their entire linguistic repertoire.

Context for Study 2: Reclaiming play in a dual language bilingual kindergarten classroom

Play sits at the intersection of translanguaging and multimodalities – as it integrates students' languaging, movement and objects. In this second study, early childhood teachers in a Spanish-English dual language bilingual program start the year with an inquiry: 'How can we infuse more play into the day?' This question stemmed from teachers' concerns that, over the years, the time for play had been reduced due to the demands of mandated curriculum.

This collaborative research took place at the Oak Elementary School, an entirely dual language Spanish-English school located in the heart of a residential portion of a large city. The majority of residents in the neighborhood where the school is located are Latinx (around 60.8%), but there are also sizable numbers of African American (25.2%) and Asian (8%) residents (NYC Population FactFinder, 2020). In many schools in low-income neighborhoods, where students are deemed to be in need of intense academic support, there has been an adoption of mandated literacy curricula in early childhood. For schools with dual language bilingual programs, this move has particularly negative effects, as the literacy curriculum used for intervention often favors instruction in English over languages other than English.

Members of the CUNY-NYSIEB (City University of New York-New York State Initiative on Emergent Bilinguals) team – Gladys Aponte, Kate Seltzer and Laura Ascenzi-Moreno – led a Professional Learning Community to assist kindergarten teachers at the Oak School with their inquiry (Seltzer *et al.*, 2020). Our process started with teacher interviews focused on strengths and challenges when working with young emergent bilinguals. After a joint study of articles about play and how to extend books into play, teachers and CUNY-NYSIEB members collaboratively chose books that would be read to students in Spanish and English and planned out how these books would extend to the centers. The teachers chose fairy tales such as the *Three Little Pigs*. Once the teacher had read the books multiple times with the children, we introduced options for students to play with props and puppets from the books within the centers. We video- and audio-taped students at play and then analyzed these together in after-school meetings. The collaborative analysis consisted of watching excerpts of videos of students playing. Group members started by making several rounds of low inference observations and noticed patterns in these observations. These discussions led to recommendations in practice. We met a total of ten times spanning over five months. All teachers in the Professional Learning Community were Latinx and the students in their classrooms were also all Latinx or Afro-Latinx.

Vignette 9.2: Studying young emergent bilinguals at play

At the beginning of the study, we learned from the teacher interviews that they were concerned about the children's ability to produce language and to sustain their play. In her initial interview Franny stated, 'the biggest challenge has been language. To have them [students] produce the language in a way that makes sense. It's hard for them to develop an idea. When they have an idea, it doesn't make sense.' Her partner teacher, Ana, also chimed in that they needed assistance to 'help kids talk more during play and teach us how to help students sustain their play.' These statements, viewed through a raciolinguistics perspective, show that teachers deemed their emergent bilingual students as 'not having language' and 'not being able to sustain play.' Flores and Rosa (2015) argue that the social status of the 'speaker,' and we would add 'do-er,' impacts the listener, in this case the teacher. Thus, students and their play are framed through a deficit lens: the children do not talk or play as the teachers imagine they should be able to. We stress that this framing is not related to these particular teachers but permeates many teachers' thinking because of the pervasiveness of the idea that racialized emergent bilinguals' language practices and ways of being are a problem in need of remediation.

Our design consisted first of enhancing centers to include props and items that were reflective of the books that were read in addition to adding a new center – the theater – to the menu of choices. For example, one way in which the centers changed is that after reading the *Three Little Pigs/Los Tres Cochinitos* to students, the teachers placed the English and Spanish versions of the story in the theater along with puppets. They also included puppets in the block center. After each of these shifts was made, we observed the children at play.

The following transcript of children playing in the block area demonstrates how they took up the narrative of the *Three Little Pigs* and integrated it with their language practices, experiences and embodied play.

Jorge: Let's go to outer space. I'm going to make the rocket ship.
Alex: Listen to me please. Excuse me guys. Go to my house. I live in Ludum Street.
Jorge: What's the number of your house?
Alex: I live in the basement. Want to know what number I live in? I live in the number 3.
Gloria: But this is the rocket ship. This is the pool. Come on let's go into the pool. [Pink container doubles as a rocket ship and as a pool.]
Wilfredo: ¿Pero dónde … ?
Gloria: Knock, knock. Pretend they didn't know. Knock, knock. Pretend it's your sister. Pretend they didn't know. He's in disguise.
Wilfredo: Es el lobo. They are married [the lobo and the pig].
Gloria: [Moving the spaceship with the pig.]
Jorge: Help us brother, we are stuck.
Alex: I have a hammer. I am going to break the hammer.
Wilfredo: Let me go.
Jorge: No, no. Wait for us. The little pig's feet is out. You are never going to get us. Help us.
Alex: Now it's time for dinner!
Gloria: I'll save my sister.
Alex: You can never save them now! You know these blocks are made of strong metal.
(**Transcript of kindergarten children, 23 January 2018**)

In the excerpt above, children transform the story of the *Three Little Pigs*, through interaction and by remixing the story. The scene is in outer space with both a rocket ship and a pool. The pig is married to a lobo [wolf], and rather than the wolf being a threat, she is part of the family. The children also make personal connections to the story with Alex telling the others where he lives and Gloria asks the others to put 'a sister' into the story. All the while the children keep some elements of the story – the pigs, the houses and the materials that the house is made of. Children communicate with each other through words, movement and using their named languages fluidly. This story remix allows the children to make personal connections to the story and to be authors by inserting new characters and settings. In this small snippet of classroom interaction, we can see that the children are enthusiastic about playing with elements of the *Three Little Pigs* and build on one another's ideas to create a fantastical version of the story.

When teachers viewed this work, they began to rethink their initial thoughts that students did not have language and could not sustain their play. Marlena, a PreK teacher at the school, noted after viewing the videos of kindergarten students: 'The videos helped me see how to support kids during play ... taking them where they're at and expanding from there. And having something in your mind already and expanding from there. Now in the dramatic play it's beautiful. A lot is happening that wasn't before.' There was a distinct shift between what teachers thought about and valued in their students' play before planning for play and observing it and afterwards. Prior to closely observing their students play, they considered the students as not being able to speak any language 'well' nor being able to play in sustained ways, and thus determined that their students were not ready 'academically.' After several observations, the teachers realized that the children were engaged in skills such as retelling and remixing stories that are considered 'academic.' Shifting the opportunities for children to play with characters, plots and themes of texts from the space for reading and writing to a broader and more dynamic platform such as play allowed children to bring their resources to this task. Teachers realized when they were involved in setting up lively and engaging centers where students could dynamically interact with texts, their classmates and objects, children could exercise their linguistic and semiotic resources alongside their knowledge of story.

Watching the students play supported a shift in how the teachers both thought about students' competencies and how they planned experiences for them. Franny noted that watching the children play made her rethink her role in supporting students' play. She said, 'They have gotten us to think deeper about how to plan and move forward with the kids, in a different way that's not academic. Getting us to analyze language through play and expand the work beyond the 40 minutes, like building blocks throughout the week.' Through this experience, teachers began to see that they could create connections between stories that students read and their opportunities for play, thus leveraging students' multimodal and multilingual resources.

While teachers demonstrated an increased attention to and surprise at the way that students' play around texts demonstrated their language practices and their engagement in texts, teachers continued to mark students' play-based engagement with texts as not being 'academic.' Rather than seeing what students can do as being academic, academic is defined as being able to perform given a certain context that is less familiar to these students. Therefore, maintaining the idea that 'academic' literacy can only be achieved through traditional learning – listening to a story, sitting at a desk and writing, or orally answering questions – means that educators may make the decision to skew literacy performance in favor of students who are used to these practices rather than to enlarge them for students who have diverse practices, such as emergent bilinguals.

Discussion

The vignettes presented in this chapter – Daniel connecting to Jorge Argueta's book *Salsa* and kindergarteners remixing the *Three Little Pigs* in the block area – point to the importance of the role of the whole person in literacy development. By this we mean that students bring all of their language, cultural, family and contextual resources into an embodied literacy experience. The showcased vignettes demonstrate what literacy development and engagement *can be* when emergent bilinguals are given the opportunity to go beyond the text through multilingual and multimodal interaction with objects and play. In what follows, we flesh out three themes emerging from our analysis of the vignettes and how they impact educators' understanding of what students 'are doing and can do' with literacy (Lenters, 2018).

Expanding possibilities for literacy and the question of academic language

Often academic learning for young racialized emergent bilinguals is conceived of as learning literacy skills in isolation. Students are asked to engage in drills where they memorize letters and letter sounds in isolation but disregard the words and languaging practices that are important to the child (Espinosa & Ascenzi-Moreno, 2021). Play, authentic exploration and imaginative use of materials are absent from these curricula. Therefore, in this climate, making room in literacy instruction for the integration of multilingualism and multimodality is a necessary step toward equity. When literacy instruction is constrained to monolingual and monomodal means of engagements, many students, particularly emergent bilinguals, cannot participate fully, and therefore are deemed deficient, unprepared and underperforming. Falchi *et al.*'s (2014) work demonstrates that emergent bilinguals' resources can remain latent or uncaptured by a monomodal and monolingual literacy curriculum.

The work described in this chapter demonstrates that when children are given the time and space to engage with texts through play and exploration, they seamlessly engage in the higher thinking skills that are valued in literacy instruction. For example, when a kindergartener asserts that the pig is married to the lobo [wolf], this child creates a remixed fairy tale that offers possibilities of understanding the narrative in a new way. We concur with Compton-Lilly *et al.*'s (2020: 2) argument that 'reductive and singular models of reading fail to honor the cultures, experiences and humanity of readers' and, therefore, position emergent bilinguals at a disadvantage when engaging in literacy. In contrast, when literacy is expanded to include room for multilingualism and multimodalities, children have more time to creatively explore and to forge deep and dynamic connections to texts.

Part of expanding what literacy means must incorporate a raciolinguistic lens and question what is considered academic in early childhood education. Flores (2020) and Flores and Rosa (2015) challenge us to shift the focus 'that frames the home language practices of racialized communities as inherently deficient' (Flores, 2020: 24) and in need of change. At the Oak School we saw a change in how teachers saw students' language practices from a strengths-based lens; they were better able to value children's play. However, what is considered academic runs deep; while teachers recognized students as engaged in more talk and play, they still did not consider that students were involved in academic tasks. A next step would be to dialogue with teachers about interrogating the concept of 'academic' and to focus on what students can do and how they engage in literacies.

The role of the adult: Noticing, sustaining, expanding possibilities

Teachers play an essential role in crafting the literacy environment and valuing young emergent bilinguals' engagements. This role is grounded in the ideologies that teachers hold; to shift teachers' ideas of what type of literacy experiences students need, Furman (2018) advocates that schools and teacher communities 'cultivate a particular ethos' (Foucault, 1997, as cited in Furman, 2018) to enhance our capacities to attend and respond to children. Furman (2018: 431) calls these moments 'Stopping Time,' with the capacity to 'act with practical wisdom.' Carini and Himley (2010) also advocate slowing down and learning to attend to children with care while being mindful of one's assumptions and ideologies. In this chapter, we demonstrate that these reflective practices are essential to develop intentional engagements in our literacy work with racialized emergent bilinguals.

For example, when teachers at the Oak Elementary School reviewed recordings of kindergarteners playing, they were able to 'Stop Time' and recognize the children's capacities to draw on their entire linguistic repertoire and their funds of knowledge to remix and recreate the *Three Little Pigs*. Because of this reflection, long-held assumptions about what children need and who they are could then begin to be challenged. Also, when Alison witnessed Daniel's interest in the molcajete, it allowed her and Cecilia to create a literacy experience that affirmed and deepened his knowledge and connection to his family's background. Both of these experiences demonstrate the importance of an intentional space for teacher reflection – one that is steeped in understanding and valuing the resources that all emergent bilinguals bring to literacy events.

What could literacy be?

In most classes, children would have experienced the texts featured in this chapter as read-alouds. The children would certainly have enjoyed them, particularly if the teacher read with voice and gestures, and offered opportunities to talk after the read-aloud. The experiences with multimodality and translanguaging added ample possibilities for exploration and deeper meaning-making. The children enacted their agency with regard to how to capitalize on their language practices. Exploration of open-ended materials served as tools to share their knowledge, to play with others while making something new.

Yet, was it enough? In looking back, we think about what other experiences would have positioned the children as critical readers, as bilingual/multilingual composers of new multimodal narratives for whom their bilingualism is the norm. We reflect, for example, about what experiences would have helped them challenge the notion that someone who builds a house of wood is not building a strong house or is not hard-working enough. A teacher could invite them to think about why and where someone would need to build such a house. They would then learn about weather, choices of materials, or geography. By taking a different perspective, the children can begin to experience the notion that these narratives can be deconstructed and reimagined.

In our own work, the exploration of the molcajete could have been extended to the ways in which people from other geographical places use similar tools, the name used to refer to this tool, an interview in Spanish with a maker of molcajetes in Mexico or a parent who uses them. The class could prepare a salsa recipe using a molcajete, use clay to shape their own molcajetes, and they could study what tools their families use to cook. They could develop a study about how another culture uses the materials available to make tools and utensils to sustain their lives, just as the people from Mexico do with the lava and the molcajete.

These examples are possibilities that invite us as educators both to stop time and listen attentively to children and to pay attention to the texts, the multimodal experiences and the authentic opportunities we offer our young emergent bilingual students to engage with all their resources. When we do this, we begin to reimagine what we mean by a translanguaging, raciolinguistic and multimodal stance toward literacy. In this way, we remain wide awake and continually reflective about the types of texts we read to students, how we provide students with opportunities to engage with their whole selves, and how we invite them to critically examine and reflect. Having the story read aloud then becomes the bare minimum in engaging young emergent bilinguals in literacy.

Implications for Practice

As educators committed to working with emergent bilingual students, we stress that it is critical that young emergent bilinguals are offered opportunities to engage in literacy multilingually and multimodally. As young emergent bilinguals learn literacy in schools, it is critical that:

- Teachers plan intentionally for multimodal experiences with young bilingual children that capitalize on their entire linguistic repertoire and that are culturally and linguistically sustaining.
- Teachers need opportunities to continuously develop their capacities to take a resource-based stance to question practices, curriculum and materials. As they become keen observers of children who engage multimodally and with their entire linguistic repertoire, teachers can support and guide students to express new meanings about topics of interest and help them imagine 'what it could be.' By attending with care, teachers can deconstruct old narratives and reimagine new ones with students.
- Teachers need opportunities to develop new listening subject-positions (Flores, 2020) with regard to how young emergent bilingual children grow as literate beings by taking a stance that challenges deficit perspectives and positions *all* children as fully capable.
- Multimodal experiences enrich children's development, sense of agency and voice, as they develop as readers and writers, and as creators of new narratives. These experiences offer a broader space for children's self-expression as critical readers, writers and creators.
- The whole child, the person, fully participates in the learning event: physically, emotionally, socially, intellectually and linguistically. Multimodal experiences broaden the possibilities of developing the whole person.

Conclusion

We advocate, along with others (Compton-Lilly *et al.*, 2020; Falchi *et al.*, 2014), for a reshaping of literacy instruction which normalizes and incorporates students' multilingual and multimodal repertoires. Literacies are dynamic and must shift to take into account the diverse linguistic and sociocultural realities of emergent bilinguals by valuing students' full participation and varied resources in meaning-making. By embracing this dynamism in literacy, we ensure that emergent bilingual students are positioned as agents who can imagine 'what is not yet' (Blair *et al.*, 2018), and through this engagement develop literacy as whole selves. We concur with Lenters (2018) that when children engage in exploring ideas in texts through multilingual means, the teachers' role is to reflect and create rich literacy environments where children control the experience and, therefore, the outcome of that engagement is open to where students take the lead.

References

Argueta, J., Amado, E. and Tonatiuh, D. (2015) *Salsa: Un poema para cocinar.* Toronto: Groundwood Books/House of Anansi Press.

Blackledge, A. and Creese, A. (2017) Translanguaging and the body. *International Journal of Multilingualism* 14 (3), 250–268.

Blair, A., Haneda, M. and Bose, F. (2018) Re-imagining English-medium instructional settings as sites of multilingual and multimodal meaning-making. *TESOL Quarterly* 52 (3), 516–539.
Carini, P. and Himley, M. (2010) *Jenny's Story: Taking the Long View of the Child: Prospect's Philosophy in Action*. New York: Teachers College Press.
Compton-Lilly, C., Mitra, A., Guay, M. and Spence, L. (2020) A confluence of complexity: Intersections among reading theory, neuroscience, and observations of young readers. *Reading Research Quarterly* 55 (S1), 185–195.
Espinosa, C. and Ascenzi-Moreno, L. (2021) *Rooted in Strength: Using Translanguaging to Grow Multilingual Readers and Writers*. New York: Scholastic.
Espinosa, C. and Lehner-Quam, A. (2019) Sustaining bilingualism: Multimodal arts experiences for young readers and writers. *Language Arts* 96 (4), 265–268.
Falchi, L., Axelrod, Y. and Genishi, C. (2014) Miguel es un artista – and Luisa is an excellent student: Seeking time and space for students' multimodal practices. *Journal of Early Childhood Literacy* 14 (3), 345–366.
Flores, N. (2020) From academic language to language architecture: Challenging raciolinguistic ideologies in research and practice. *Theory into Practice* 59 (1), 22–31.
Flores, N. and Rosa, J. (2015) Undoing appropriateness: Raciolinguistic ideologies and language diversity in education. *Harvard Educational Review* 85 (2), 49–171.
Furman, C. (2018) Stopping time to attend as a care of the teaching self. *Philosophy of Education* (1), 429–441.
García, O. and Li, W. (2014) *Translanguaging: Language, Bilingualism and Education*. New York: Palgrave Macmillan.
Kusters, A., Spotti, M., Swanwick, R. and Tapio, E. (2017) Beyond languages, beyond modalities: Transforming the study of semiotic repertoires. *International Journal of Multilingualism* 3, 219–232.
Leander, K. and Bolt, G. (2012) Rereading 'A pedagogy of multiliteracies': Bodies, text, and emergence. *Journal of Literacy Research* 45 (1), 22–46.
Lenters, K. (2018) Multimodal becoming: Literacy in and beyond the classroom. *The Reading Teacher* 71 (6), 643–649.
Lin, A. (2019) Theories of trans/languaging and trans-semiotizing: Implications for content-based education classrooms. *International Journal of Bilingual Education and Bilingualism* 22 (1), 5–16.
NYC Department of Education (2020) *2019–20 School Quality Snapshot*. Retrieved December 30, 2021, from https://tools.nycenet.edu/snapshot/2020
NYC Population FactFinder (2020) *Demographic Profile*. See https://popfactfinder.planning.nyc.gov.
Otheguy, R., García, O. and Reid, W. (2015) Clarifying translanguaging and deconstructing named languages: A perspective from linguistics. *Applied Linguistics Review* 6 (3), 281–307.
Siebert, P. and Elena, H. (2007) *Three Little Pigs*. New York: Brighter Child.
Seltzer, K., Ascenzi-Moreno, L. and Aponte, G. (2020) Translanguaging and early childhood education in the USA: Insights from the CUNY-NYSIEB Project. In J. Panagiotopoulou, L. Rosen and J. Strzykala (eds) *Inclusion, Education and Translanguaging* (pp. 23–39). Wiesbaden: Springer.
Serafini, F. (2015) Multimodal literacy: From theory to practice. *Language Arts* 92 (6), 412–423.
Tonatiuh, D. (2020) *Duncan Tonatiuh: Sobre mi*. See http://duncantonatiuh.com/about-me/.
Vogel, S., Ascenzi-Moreno, L. and García, O. (2018) An expanded view of translanguaging: Leveraging the dynamic interactions between a young multilingual writer and machine translation software. In J. Choi and S. Ollerhead (eds) *Plurilingualism in Teaching and Learning: Complexities Across Contexts* (pp. 89–106). Abingdon: Taylor & Francis.
Zapata, A., Kuby, C.R. and Thiel, J.J. (2018) Encounters with writing: Becoming-with posthumanist ethics. *Journal of Literacy Research* 50 (6), 478–501.

10 'Being Bilingual is Cool': Co-Constructing Bilingual Identities with Dual Language Kindergarteners

Ruth Flores Bañuelos and Leslie C. Banes

Introduction

At the beginning of the year, Maestra Flores, a kindergarten teacher in a dual language (DL) bilingual program, reflected on her students' comments about the use of two languages in her classroom:

> They would ask, 'Maestra, why are we doing extra work? The other class doesn't have Spanish time.' or '¿Por qué tengo que aprender inglés si mi mamá no lo ha aprendido?' I realized the majority of my students were not *excited* about the opportunity to develop their Spanish, which is an opportunity that I could only have dreamed of as an English Learner in English-only schools. In first grade, I was asked to read a passage aloud, which contained the name 'Luis.' I used the Spanish pronunciation to read the name and was immediately stopped. I will never forget how the teacher said, '*You are doing it again. Remember that here, at school we have to talk in English because we are American. At home you can say it like that, but here and in most places that is not okay.*' I will never forget the sense of shame that I felt.

By contrasting her own experiences of linguistic oppression in early elementary school with those of her students, Maestra Flores reflects her understanding of DL programs as a gift with incredible promise, where her students are invited to bring their full selves into the classroom, to grow and flourish using both of their languages for academic learning. Her students, however, often articulated their view of learning two languages as simply 'extra work.'

Background

One of the primary goals of DL programs is to develop high levels of bilingualism and biliteracy (Lindholm-Leary, 2001). While research demonstrates many benefits of bilingualism (Callahan & Gándara, 2015), DL teachers face challenges in their endeavor to support high levels of bilingualism. One challenge is reinforcing use of the partner language beyond the early grades. In Spanish-English programs, studies found that by sixth grade, students generally use much less Spanish than English (Tarone & Swain, 1995), and a survey of native Spanish-speaking fifth graders indicated that although the school delivered 50% of instruction in Spanish, students preferred English both academically and socially (Babino & Stewart, 2017). Scholars point to the dominant power of English (de Jong & Howard, 2009) and language ideologies that position monolingualism as the norm (Lippi-Green, 2012) as key factors in students' diminishing use of Spanish throughout the grades. This is alarming given the negative emotional, social and academic consequences of losing one's first language (Baker, 2011).

An ongoing goal of DL teachers and programs should be to elevate the status of the partner language in the school and classroom context and ensure that students understand the importance of bilingualism (LaVan, 2001). This points to the need for research on pedagogical innovations that create openings for students to explore their understandings and beliefs about bilingualism and develop strong bilingual identities. In this chapter, we describe Maestra Flores' attempts to engage her students in a multimodal exploration of their own bilingual identities. As part of her graduate degree which included teacher inquiry, Maestra Flores asked: (a) How can I support young learners' bilingual identities? and (b) How can tools from multimodal literacy create openings for students to explore and communicate ideas about bilingualism?

Literature review

Views of bilingualism

A search of the literature returned 40 different definitions of bilingualism and a collective understanding of 'who counts as bilingual' that continues to shift (Li, 2000). Many define bilingualism as having or using two languages with a 'native-like fluency' (Hamers & Blanc, 2000). While this definition emphasizes the need for bilinguals to work toward fluency, it reflects an idealized notion of a 'perfect bilingual,' and does little to help our youngest students make sense of their own developing proficiency in two languages.

Grosjean (1989) posited that bilinguals are not simply two monolinguals in one. This holistic view of bilingualism, taken up by many bilingual education scholars, views bilinguals as having complex and interrelated language practices, with languages that develop in different ways and to different degrees, contradicting the myth of the perfectly balanced bilingual.

Other definitions emphasize what one can *do* with language, such as a view of bilingualism as the ability to use two languages to meet the demands of self and society to communicate and interact (Hamers & Blanc, 2000). However, this view positions bilingualism primarily in relation to one's resources for communication, ignoring what bilingual individuals feel or believe, or their connections to the languages, and the cultures and communities associated with them.

Rather than dichotomizing what does and does not count as 'bilingual,' in this project we emphasize 'bilingual identity,' which we define, drawing on Fielding and Harbon (2013), as seeing oneself as part of a community that uses two languages in meaningful ways, shaping the way individuals see themselves, think, communicate and understand the world.

Developing bilingual identities

The way students see and position themselves (as smart or not, good at school or not) is essential to success in school and to acquiring another language (Norton, 2000; Peirce, 1995). To meet the goal of developing content and academic language proficiency in both languages, students must be personally invested in learning and using both languages. In a study of first-graders, García-Mateus and Palmer (2017) found students' bilingual identity was co-constructed as teachers and students discussed bilingual poetry. Providing students with opportunities to reflect on, share and better understand their emerging ideas about bilingualism allows students to validate their own linguistic experiences and those of others. Further, because school is the primary place in which societies negotiate what counts as knowledge, who may define and display knowledge, and in which language (Heller & Martin-Jones, 2001), teachers have a responsibility to consider how experiences in their classrooms may directly or indirectly impact students' bilingual identities, and to act with intentionality.

Identity development through multimodal literacy

In contrast to traditional views of literacy as reading and writing, multimodal approaches align with calls for a broadened, pluralistic conception of literacy (Cope & Kalantzis, 2000) and engage students in learning through multiple representations (e.g. visual, audio, movement) as resources for meaning-making (Jewitt & Kress, 2003). Because the properties of different modes facilitate various kinds of learning, multimodal texts create opportunities for leveraging culturally and linguistically diverse students' academic and linguistic strengths (Hull & Nelson, 2005; Smith *et al.*, 2020).

Several scholars have explored using multimodal literacy practices for understanding and shaping identities in young students. In one such study, Binder and Kostopoulos (2011) described the identity journeys of kindergartners as they engaged in writing 'I am from' poems and creating quilt squares. Students' understanding of literacy expanded beyond 'print only' and their understanding of themselves shifted from 'I can't draw' to seeing themselves as creative communicators across modalities. Similarly, Cummins and Early (2010) explored the creation of 'identity texts,' or multimodal texts that represent important aspects of students' background, shared with varied audiences. Identity texts provide opportunities for students to explore different modes of expression as a way to develop understanding of self, other and community. Kim (2018) found translanguaging across modes in digital spaces offered more comprehensive representations of transnational students' identities than any single mode could offer.

Three-phase multimodal framework for exploring bilingual identity

We designed a multimodal approach that begins with exploring bilingualism in self/family and expands outward to literature/music, and then to bilingual community/world (Figure 10.1). We adapted a framework from Athanases *et al.* (2019) for exploring language ideologies of preservice teachers 'from the inside out,' starting with self-reflection. Beginning

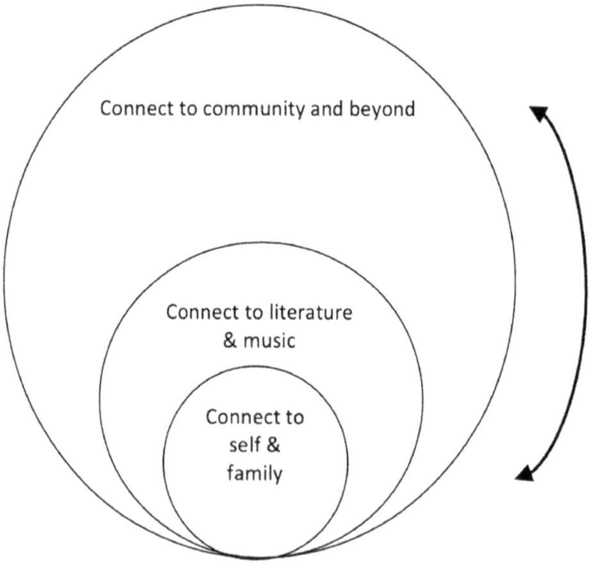

Figure 10.1 A three-phase, multimodal approach for exploring bilingual identity

with a focus on self/family seemed particularly appropriate for kindergarteners who, at five to six years old, are just beginning to understand themselves as individuals and their role in familial and social relationships (Harter, 1999).

Methods

Context

This classroom inquiry takes place in an elementary school in California with a 50-50 Spanish-English DL track and a traditional track. The focal class is kindergarten in the DL track, with 50% of instruction taking place in each language. Students included 25 emerging bilinguals, with 16 classified as English Learners (ELs) and 9 as Spanish Learners (SLs), although many students were likely simultaneously bilinguals from homes where both languages are used.

At the time of the study, the first author, Maestra Flores, was a first-year teacher conducting classroom inquiry as part of a graduate degree. She identifies as a first-generation Latina, who learned English alongside her family when she started elementary school. The second author, Leslie Banes, is a White, former DL teacher, who learned Spanish as an adult to better support her students. She was the instructor of Maestra Flores' research methods course. As course instructor, Dr Banes guided Maestra Flores through her inquiry project and continued to collaborate with her afterward, encouraging her to share what she learned by co-authoring this chapter.

Classroom activities

Key features of the framework and activities Maestra Flores tried out are described below. The intention behind these activities was to create opportunities for students to explore their *own* identities, not to tell them what to believe. Handouts and lesson plans can be found at https://tinyurl.com/FloresBanesAppendices.

Phase 1: Connect to self and family

The primary goals for Phase 1 were to create opportunities for students to begin to reflect on their own bilingualism and for Maestra Flores to gain a deeper understanding of students' beliefs about bilingualism. Using a self-reflexive language portrait (Dressler, 2014), she asked students to color representations of their languages on a body outline, using the body as a metaphor to prompt students' self-reflection on uses of and feelings about their languages in their everyday lives. Maestra Flores asked guiding questions to help students reflect. For example, she asked, 'When you use your ears to listen, do you hear things in Spanish, English or both?' and 'In your heart, to be a good friend, do you use Spanish, English or both?' She also individually interviewed students, asking what they think it means to be bilingual, who they know that is bilingual, and how they feel when they speak each language. This interview was repeated in Phases 2 and 3.

Phase 2: Connect to literature and music

This stage included a three-day lesson with a read-aloud and discussion of bilingual children's literature and music. The focus was on using literature and music as 'windows, mirrors, and sliding glass doors' (Bishop, 1990), creating opportunities for students to reflect on their own experiences and those of others. The bilingual text was *Mango, Abuela, and Me* by Meg Medina (2015), which depicts an English-speaking child interacting with her Spanish-speaking grandmother. Maestra Flores facilitated whole-class discussion about the characters becoming bilingual. Each day opened and closed with a multilingual song with greetings from around the world. On Day three, students were given a template titled *I Am Bilingual/Yo Soy Bilingüe* to write and/or draw something they can do because they are bilingual.

Phase 3: Connect to school, community and beyond

The goal for Phase 3 was to provide opportunities for reflection on bilingualism beyond the self, family and classroom. Maestra Flores invited three guests to discuss their bilingual experiences with the class. Speakers included a parent who had immigrated from Mexico during childhood and went to English-only schools, a fifth grader at the school, and a college-age, volunteer tutor. Speakers were selected to reflect a range of ages and experiences. Speakers visited on separate days for roughly 15 minutes and were asked to use both languages. Maestra Flores moderated the discussion, asking: (a) How did you become bilingual? (b) How do you use Spanish and English? (c) Why is it important to be bilingual? and (d) What advice would you give us about learning Spanish and English? Students asked follow-up questions and interacted with the speakers.

Next, Maestra Flores introduced a service-learning project. At the time, there were no bilingual posters or signs around the school indicating the presence of the DL program or recognizing the diversity of students' home languages. Maestra Flores and her students created posters to raise awareness of what it means to be bilingual. Student quotes about bilingualism collected from previous phases were written on poster paper for students to decorate in groups. Posters were hung around the school and Maestra Flores led her class on a scavenger hunt to see how they were being seen and discussed across the school.

Table 10.1 Coding scheme: Students' understandings of bilingualism

Code	Description	Examples
Definition-based	Student answers by explaining that they know two languages.	'Yo sé hablar español e inglés.' 'I know two languages.'
Bilingual identity validated	Student explains how they have talked to a separate individual to confirm bilingual status.	'My mom told me I am bilingual.'
Language history	Student explains how they have learned two languages.	'When I was little I only knew English, now I am learning Spanish.'
Language contexts	Refers to using language in specific language situations or contexts.	'I use Spanish at home and English at school.'
Proficiency/expertise	Aspect of linguistic identity built upon how much of a language a child knows.	'I know more English than Spanish.'
Affiliation	Expressed as identification or attachment to a language.	'I like Spanish more.' 'I don't like English that much.'
Inheritance	Refers to having a familial connection to a language.	'My mom speaks Spanish.' 'My brother knows English and Spanish.'

Data collection and analysis

Maestra Flores engaged in three cycles of inquiry in which she: (a) developed a wondering; (b) implemented a pedagogical innovation; (c) collected and analyzed evidence; and (d) documented, shared and celebrated her new understandings, using them to guide her actions in the classroom and her next round of inquiry (Dana, 2013). The inquiry process was guided by the instructor and supported by a resource-rich environment including collaboration with peers and research literature.

To capture students' thinking as fully as possible, Maestra Flores allowed students to select which language(s) they would use to participate. An individual student interview was conducted in each phase to capture students' developing understandings. To analyze data from the language portrait questionnaire and interviews, Maestra Flores transcribed audio-recordings and used a coding scheme, adapted from Dressler (2014), to capture variation in the ways students understand bilingualism (Table 10.1). Students' written, spoken and visual representations of bilingualism from the *I Am Bilingual/Yo Soy Bilingüe* activity were analyzed to surface patterns in what students shared that being bilingual enabled them to do. Responses were coded as talking to others, listening to music or playing.

Findings

Students' understanding of bilingualism and expression of their bilingual identities evolved across phases.

Shifts in understanding of bilingualism and bilingual identity

How I use my languages

In Phase 1, most students understood that they used two languages and that they did not interact in exactly the same ways in each language, but they did not realize that this ability has a name or that it represents a special skill. When discussing their language portraits, more than 50% of students indicated that they use both languages for each body part and shared specific activities they do in each language, often including where or with whom. For example, one student shared, 'Yo veo películas en español con mi hermanito' [I watch movies in Spanish with my little brother], while another student reflected, 'We talk a lot of English at home. Mommy and me are the only ones who can talk in secret, because we both know a little bit of Spanish.' Several students shared their feelings about activities in each language, such as, 'A mi me gusta música en español más que en inglés' [I like music in Spanish more than in English].

Learning what it means to be bilingual

At the end of Phase 1, when asked, 'What does it mean to be bilingual?', only one student correctly described it as speaking two languages. Twenty students responded they did not know what the word meant, and five students provided unrelated responses. The student who indicated an understanding of the term was also the only student to self-identify as bilingual. This is significant because, although the majority of students recognized that they used both Spanish and English in different and sometimes overlapping domains of their lives, only one student was able to name it as bilingualism. Psychologists point to the importance of naming ideas for understanding them, discussing them and shaping the way we think (e.g. McConnell-Ginet, 2020). Thus, in order to explicitly self-identify as bilingual and to understand bilingualism as something important and worthy of attention, students needed first to understand what it means to be bilingual.

More than Spanish and English

By the end of Phase 2, after discussing bilingualism portrayed in the book, *Mango, Abuela, and Me*, and singing a song about languages around the world, 21 students were able to correctly define the term bilingual, describing it as 'talking two languages' or 'hablar en español y inglés' (speak in Spanish and English). Interestingly, nearly half (12 students) referenced languages other than Spanish and English. One student explained, 'it's speaking both languages, Spanish and English, maybe even German and French if you are lucky.' Students likely took up this expanded understanding of bilingualism from the multilingual song they sang each day in Phase 2. Three of the four students who incorrectly defined the term bilingual described it as 'to speak Spanish,' which may reflect an understanding of bilingualism as learning a language other than English, as if English were a given.

'Not bilingual enough'

At the end of Phase 2, all but seven students self-identified as bilingual. Of these, four were those who were unable to define the term bilingual. The other three students who did not self-identify as bilingual communicated a belief that they were not proficient enough in one or both languages. For example, one student reflected, 'No soy bilingüe porque yo todavía estoy aprendiendo mis sonidos' [I'm not bilingual because I'm still learning my sounds]. Further exploration of what it means to be bilingual, with an emphasis on how language proficiency or literacy alone does not determine one's bilingual identity, may support these students to see themselves as bilingual.

Expanding understandings of bilingualism

In Phase 3, after meeting the guest speakers and participating in the poster-making service-learning project, all 25 students correctly defined the term bilingual *and* self-identified as bilingual. When asked, 'How do you know you are bilingual?', 11 students provided definitions that went beyond restating the definition to include other elements, such as connecting to other people or expressing what they do with their bilingualism. One student explained, 'Hablé con mi papá, y el me dijó que yo sí soy bilingüe' [I talked with my dad and he said that I am bilingual], indicating that ideas about bilingualism discussed at school were also being discussed at home, helping shape his bilingual identity. Another student included a reflection on her language history, 'En casa solamente hablan español, y en escuela empecé a aprender más inglés' [At home they only speak Spanish, and at school I started to learn more English].

These responses represent an important shift from previous phases in which all students used a definition-based response, such as, 'I am bilingual because I know two languages.' Students' responses were beginning to reflect more nuanced understandings of their bilingual identity, such as having a language history or a community, an important part of validating one's own linguistic identity.

What can you do because you are bilingual?

Communicating with others

In discussion of the book, *Mango, Abuela, and Me*, students were asked to reflect by writing, drawing and explaining what they can do because they are bilingual and why it is important. Sixty-eight percent of students related the usefulness of bilingualism to family members, as shown in Figure 10.2. One student reflected anger at a family member for

Figure 10.2 Student's writing: I Am Bilingual/Yo Soy Bilingüe

Note: This student phonetically wrote, *'I can talk to my papá. Yo puedo hablar con mi mamá'* [I can talk to my dad. I can talk with my mom].

not 'wanting to learn Spanish.' When prompted further, the student stated, 'he always needs me or my mom's help to talk to people in Spanish.' For this student, Spanish was a necessary tool for language brokering.

YouTube and movies are in Spanish, too?

Listening to music and playing in two languages were other common applications of bilingualism that students communicated in Phase 2. Two of the students who shared that being bilingual allowed them to listen to music in both languages had previously reflected a belief that YouTube, television shows and movies are only available in English. It is possible that exposure to bilingual songs and books in Phase 2 may have prompted some students to realize that entertainment media can be multilingual. This speaks to the importance of exposing students to authentic and relevant multilingual media and begs the question for teachers and parents: If students are not exposed to bilingual media at home, school or in their communities, how will they know they exist? How will they learn to search for them?

Making public how I think and situate myself as a bilingual

Not everyone gets to learn two languages

In Phase 3, two students began to demonstrate awareness of issues related to bilingualism. When asked, 'Are there a lot of people who are bilingual?', 22 out of 25 students responded 'yes.' Two students who responded 'no' provided insightful explanations. One reasoned that there are not many bilingual people, because 'mi mami dice que no hay muchos niños que pueden aprender español y ingles en escuela' [my mom says that there are not many kids who can learn Spanish and English at school]. This student went on to express sympathy for a friend who wanted to be in this class because her class only spoke English. This represents a shift from student discourse at the beginning of the year that reflected learning two languages as 'extra work,' to the creation of a classroom culture where students see learning two languages as a privilege.

Being bilingual is cool!

Several parents shared that students had begun asking questions and starting conversations about bilingualism at home, about what it means to be bilingual, or how family members became bilingual. At school, students were excited to share what they were learning about themselves and several students used their posters as conversation starters to discuss bilingualism with peers. Other students, unprompted, decided to give parents, siblings and others a tour around the school to explain the posters. One day, Maestra Flores saw one of her students approach a peer from an English-only class looking at the posters. Her student stated, 'I'm bilingual. I know two languages, Español and English. Are you bilingual?' and then said, 'Being bilingual is cool! Come, I can show you!' Students demonstrated agency in taking up bilingual identities in their own way, and used their portraits, drawings and posters as tools for sharing understandings of bilingualism and of themselves. These experiences provided varied multimodal resources to communicate complex ideas as fully as possible, empowering students to make public how they think and situate themselves in the world.

Conclusion

Through inquiry, Maestra Flores reflected deeply on the messages she and others were sending students about bilingualism. She found that she could create opportunities for exploration that helped shape the way students understood bilingualism and themselves as bilinguals using multimodal resources including portraits, literature, music, writing, drawing and discussion to negotiate and communicate meaning. Students expressed agency in co-constructing bilingual identities both inside and outside the classroom. Like Kim (2018), we found communicating across modes offered more comprehensive representations of students' identities than any single mode could offer. This is crucial. Students spoke from their portraits, posters and drawings, and incorporated ideas gleaned from literature, music and guest speakers into their own thinking. If we had narrowed participation to print and oral language only, students likely would not have engaged as deeply or explored as broadly, and their developing ideas may have gone unseen and unsupported.

There is much still to be done if we are to take full advantage of the benefits of DL programs. When we situate DL programs in the larger sociopolitical climate, we see that our programs and students may still be very much limited by the dominance of English. Students often feel social pressure to acquire English quickly, or even to replace their first language with English (Valdés, 2004), while teachers and parents, feeling pressure for students to perform well on high-stakes tests, often prioritize English in subtle or overt ways that students pick up on (Shannon, 1995). Helping students view their own bilingualism through a positive lens could prompt them to invest more in their DL learning (Pierce, 1995) and develop a sense of who they are and where they belong in the world (García-Mateus & Palmer, 2017). Starting with a strong foundation may help develop the resistance necessary to counteract the pull toward the dominance of English and monolingual ideologies they are likely to experience as they grow up. Although this study features a DL classroom, it is equally important to engage bilingual students in English-as-language-of-instruction classrooms in understanding and exploring bilingual identities. We encourage other teachers to use and adapt our framework to create rich, varied, sustained, multimodal and multilingual opportunities for students to explore and communicate their developing ideas about bilingualism.

References

Athanases, S.Z., Banes, L.C., Wong, J.W. and Martinez, D.C. (2019) Exploring linguistic diversity from the inside out: Implications of self-reflexive inquiry for teacher education. *Journal of Teacher Education* 70 (5), 581–596.

Babino, A. and Stewart, M.A. (2017) 'I like English better': Latino dual language students' investment in Spanish, English, and bilingualism. *Journal of Latinos and Education* 16 (1), 18–29.

Baker, C. (2011) *Foundations of Bilingual Education and Bilingualism* (5th edn). Bristol: Multilingual Matters.

Binder, M. and Kotsopoulos, S. (2011) Multimodal literacy narratives: Weaving the threads of young children's identity through the arts. *Journal of Research in Childhood Education* 25 (4), 339–363.

Bishop, R.S. (1990) Mirrors, windows, and sliding glass doors. *Perspectives* 6 (3), ix–xi.

Callahan, R.M. and Gándara, P.C. (2015) *The Bilingual Advantage: Language, Literacy and the US Labor Market*. Bristol: Multilingual Matters.

Cope, B., Kalantzis, M. (2000) *Multiliteracies: Literacy Learning and the Design of Social Futures*. London: Routledge.

Cummins, J. and Early, M. (2010) *Identity Texts: The Collaborative Creation of Power in Multilingual Schools*. Stoke-on-Trent: Trentham Books.

Dana, N.F. (2013) *Digging Deeper into Action Research: A Teacher Inquirer's Field Guide*. Thousand Oaks, CA: Corwin Press.

de Jong, E. and Howard, E. (2009) Integration in two-way immersion education: Equalising linguistic benefits for all students. *International Journal of Bilingual Education and Bilingualism* 12 (1), 81–99.

Dressler, R. (2014) Exploring linguistic identity in young multilingual learners. *TESL Canada Journal* 32 (1), 42–42.

Fielding, R. and Harbon, L. (2013) Examining bilingual and bicultural identity in young students. *Foreign Language Annals* 46 (4), 527–544.

García-Mateus, S. and Palmer, D. (2017) Translanguaging pedagogies for positive identities in two-way dual language bilingual education. *Journal of Language, Identity and Education* 16 (4), 245–255.

Grosjean, F. (1989) Neurolinguistics, beware! The bilingual is not two monolinguals in one person. *Brain and Language* 36 (1), 3–15.

Hamers, J.F. and Blanc, M.H.A. (2000) *Bilinguality and Bilingualism*. Cambridge: Cambridge University Press.

Harter, S. (1999) *The Construction of the Self: A Developmental Perspective*. New York: Guilford Press.

Heller, M. and Martin-Jones, M. (2001) *Voices of Authority: Education and Linguistic Difference*. Westport, CT: Greenwood.
Hull, G.A. and Nelson, M.E. (2005) Locating the semiotic power of multimodality. *Written Communication* 22 (2), 224–261.
Jewitt, C. and Kress, G.R. (eds) (2003) *Multimodal Literacy*. New York: Peter Lang.
Kim, S. (2018) 'It was kind of a given that we were all multilingual': Transnational youth identity work in digital translanguaging. *Linguistics and Education* 43, 39–52.
LaVan, C. (2001) Help! They're using too much English! The problem of L1 vs. L2 in the immersion classroom. *ACIE Newsletter* (4) 2.
Li, W. (2000) *The Bilingualism Reader*. New York: Routledge.
Lindholm-Leary, K.J. (2001). *Dual Language Education*. Clevedon: Multilingual Matters. https://doi.org/10.21832/9781853595332
Lindholm-Leary, K. (2016) Students' perceptions of bilingualism in Spanish and Mandarin dual language programs. *International Multilingual Research Journal* 10 (1), 59–70.
Lippi-Green, R. (2012) *English with an Accent: Language, Ideology, and Discrimination in the United States*. New York: Routledge.
McConnell-Ginet, S. (2020) *Words Matter: Meaning and Power*. Cambridge: Cambridge University Press.
Medina, M. (2015) *Mango, Abuela, and Me*. Somerville, MA: Candlewick Press.
Norton, B. (2000) *Identity and Language Learning: Gender, Ethnicity, and Education Change*. Buenos Aires: Editorial Dunken.
Peirce, B.N. (1995) Social identity, investment, and language learning. *TESOL Quarterly* 29 (1), 9–31.
Shannon, S.M. (1995) The hegemony of English: A case study of one bilingual classroom as a site of resistance. *Linguistics and Education* 7 (3), 175–200.
Smith, B.E., Pacheco, M.B. and Khorosheva, M. (2020) Emergent bilingual students and digital multimodal composition: A systematic review of research in secondary classrooms. *Reading Research Quarterly* 56 (1), 33–52.
Tarone, E. and Swain, M. (1995) A sociolinguistic perspective on second language use in immersion classrooms. *The Modern Language Journal* 79 (2), 166–178.
Valdés, G. (2004) Between support and marginalisation: The development of academic language in linguistic minority children. *International Journal of Bilingual Education and Bilingualism* 7 (2–3), 102–132.

Part 3

Primary Grades

11 Multimodality as a Pathway to Bilingual Learners' Funds of Knowledge

Adriana Alvarez

This chapter discusses an analytical approach to examining bilingual students' expressions and meaning-making processes through drawings and artifacts using a multimodal social semiotics lens (Hodge & Kress, 1988; Kress, 2010) as a vehicle to discover, understand and integrate children's funds of knowledge, experiences and lives outside of school in classroom learning (Moll *et al.*, 1992). This chapter explores the following inquiries: (1) How does a multimodal approach support the meaning-making processes of young bilingual students? (2) How can a multimodal approach facilitate insights into children's funds of knowledge? and (3) How can educators integrate multimodal opportunities with effective meaningful instruction? I present data examples from two separate research studies in which students created personal multimodal artifacts to demonstrate how this analytical approach can be operationalized.

A Multimodal Social Semiotics Approach toward Bilingual Students' Funds of Knowledge

Engaging culturally sustaining pedagogies in classrooms largely builds on affirming and connecting classroom learning to students' lives and identities (Ladson-Billings, 1995; Paris, 2012). Understanding effective approaches to accomplishing this integration has been a pressing need considering the growing diverse student population who are often seen through a deficit lens and denied opportunities in schools (Valencia, 1997). For bilingual students in particular, students make use of and demonstrate their full linguistic repertoire, including multimodal resources that contribute to a sense-making process across languages (Gort, 2006; Kenner, 2004; Kenner & Kress, 2003), as well as how their sociocultural experiences and identities contribute to their biliteracy development (Dworin, 2006; Moll *et al.*, 2001).

Funds of knowledge has been one useful construct for thinking about the links between students' experiences outside of school and classroom learning and biliteracy development (Dworin, 2006; Moje *et al.*, 2004). The original approach involved teachers conducting home visits to document sources of learning in students' homes with the intention of making concrete connections to their classroom pedagogy (Moll *et al.*, 1992). While this approach is ideal and enriching in many ways, with the current time and curricular limitations teachers face, we must expand pedagogical approaches to seek and integrate students' funds of knowledge as learning resources in alternative ways. Children's multimodal expressions provide important insights into their lives and experiences, yet these are often unnoticed and missed opportunities. A multimodal social semiotics approach offers a pathway to examine bilingual students' creative expressions in order to unveil and integrate students' funds of knowledge in classrooms, and to better understand how visual modes can be tools as they make sense of their worlds, their transnational experiences and their bilingualism. There is much to learn about students' lives by engaging modalities beyond language. This chapter argues that bringing together a multimodal social semiotics perspective to seek children's funds of knowledge in daily classroom opportunities presents an alternative approach for educators to learn from their students' lives (Figure 11.1). This analytical approach stands on the following premises:

(1) Children's sociocultural experiences cultivate their resources and funds of knowledge (Moll *et al.*, 1992; Vygotsky, 1978).
(2) Children engage in meaning-making processes shaped by their sociocultural experiences, including social interpretations, cultural contexts, literacy and language (Freire & Macedo, 2005; Kress, 2010).

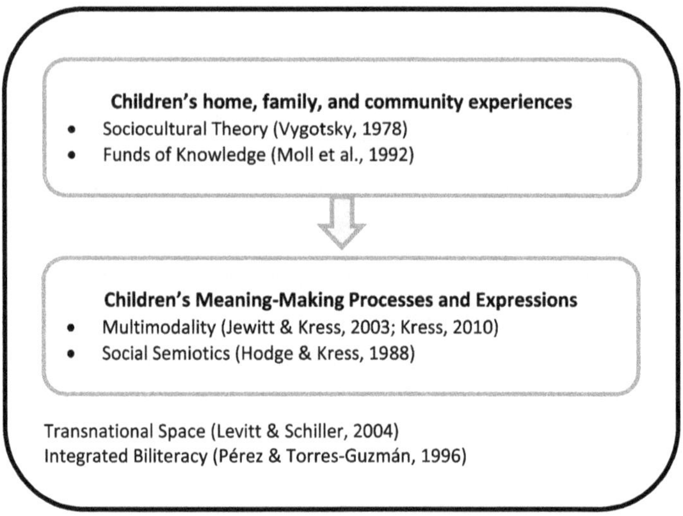

Figure 11.1 A multimodal social semiotic approach toward funds of knowledge
Source: Adapted from Alvarez (2018).

(3) Children's multimodal expressions reveal these meaning-making processes and funds of knowledge (Hodge & Kress, 1988; Kress, 2010).
(4) These processes connect to and occur within broader sociopolitical contexts that include transnational spaces and integrated forms of biliteracy (Levitt & Schiller, 2004; Pérez & Torres-Guzmán, 1996).

Multimodality and social semiotics

A multimodal social semiotic theoretical lens and analytical approach centers meaning-making in all modes of communication and representation (Kress, 2010). Multimodality goes beyond language as a form of communication, just as literacy goes beyond reading, encompassing a wider selection of resources as contributions to the process. Although multimodality refers to the modes a child engages in their communication, including sounds, gestures or illustrations, it is the notion of social semiotics that refers to the child's process of meaning-making that considers sociopolitical and sociocultural contexts. Kress (2010: 8) explains, 'Semiotic resources are socially made and therefore carry the discernible regularities of social occasions, events and hence a certain stability; they are never fixed, let alone rigidly fixed.' In social semiotics theory there is a 'signifier' and a 'signified,' where one uses a 'sign' (through a variety of modes) and the 'signifier' receives the message through mutual understandings (Hodge & Kress, 1988). This mutual understanding depends on social and cultural constructions of meaning and relationships. For example, when a child chooses to draw a flower to depict love, multimodality would refer to the choice of pictorial illustration as expression, as opposed to a hug (gesture) or a song (sound). In this manner, it is through a social semiotics perspective that the flower represents a 'sign' that carries meaning depending on the context, such as a symbol for love on Mother's Day where the 'signified,' or the child's mother, shares the understanding of the 'sign.' Kress (2010) describes a multimodal social semiotic theory as:

> a fork with two prongs, so to speak – the semiotic and the multimodal prong. The former attends to signs, meaning, to sign and meaning-making [...] The latter attends to the material resources which are involved in making meaning, the modes. (Kress, 2010: 105)

Visual features in drawings and artifacts, as modes, can be signifiers of children's meaning-making, or semiotic signs, that encompass ideologies, social interactions and contexts.

Funds of knowledge and biliteracy

Funds of knowledge in children's lives refer to the 'historically accumulated and culturally developed bodies of knowledge and skills essential for household or individual functioning and well-being' (Moll *et al.*, 1992:

133). A funds of knowledge approach aims to 'develop both theory and methods through which educators can approach and document the funds of knowledge of families and re-present them on the bases of the knowledge, resources, and strengths they possess, thus challenging deficit orientations that are so dominant, in particular, in the education of working-class children' (Moll, 2019: 131).

Students' literacies also develop and are shaped by interactions in meaningful contexts as they make sense of the world and their experiences (Freire & Macedo, 2005). An integrated biliteracy approach shares this perspective and considers the additional layers of social and cultural processes associated with learning bilingually, including language ideologies and power asymmetries (Pérez & Torres-Guzmán, 1996). Correspondingly, children's literacies and multimodal resources also become 'signifiers' that carry meaning and depict their socially and culturally constructed understandings of their worlds. Sociopolitical and sociocultural contexts also contribute to these processes, such as their transnational and biliteracy experiences, and must be considered. Transnational experiences are those in which students' daily lives and routines occur or connect across countries (Levitt & Schiller, 2004). Although many students do not share physical border-crossing experiences, they do keep emotional and communicative ties to their parents' country of origin.

Understanding these relationships provides insights to identify and integrate children's funds of knowledge via multimodal literacy practices which are also a valuable resource as they develop biliteracy and consider children's sociocultural and sociopolitical experiences. The analytical approach presented in this chapter contributes to the growing body of work that examines the intersections of multimodality and social semiotics with bilingual students' learning processes and funds of knowledge (Becker, 2014; Brown, 2017; Marshall & Toohey, 2010; Soto & Garza, 2011; Wessels & Herrera, 2014).

When visuals speak: Funds of knowledge in students' creations

In this chapter, I rely on data from two separate research studies to show how multimodal creations offer an effective pathway to identify, understand and engage students' funds of knowledge and, thus, have a valuable place in classrooms and integration in students' learning processes. The first body of data includes 220 written narratives and drawings collected once a month in Spanish during one school year from 22 bilingual students in my own first-grade classroom. I analyzed how students' illustrations contributed to and complemented their narratives in supplementary ways to depict their social understandings of their family and community and their own role as contributors (Alvarez, 2018a). The second data set includes 61 biliteracy family projects created in Spanish and English from 22 bilingual students in a first-grade bilingual classroom in Colorado. The biliteracy family projects included story books based on family experiences and a visual timeline of significant events in the children's lives and their envisioned future timeline (Alvarez, 2018b). In both studies, visual data were coded inductively and deductively through two coding cycles. The first coding cycle identified patterns, and the second coding cycle condensed these patterns to themes (Miles *et al.*, 2014). Both research studies examined the experiences that bilingual students' visual creations (drawings and artifacts) portrayed.

Camila

Camila was a six-year-old first-grader whose home language was Spanish; her parents had immigrated to the US from Mexico. One afternoon her mother shared that their family was experiencing the devastating terminal illness of Camila's aunt, her mother's younger sister. Camila's mother was concerned about Camila and described the hardship and pain the family was suffering during this time. The opportunity to illustrate and write about her experience provided a space for Camila to process and share her understandings and the ways she was contributing to her family (Figure 11.2).

Camila expressed pictorially and in her written narrative the many caretaking activities that she participated in, and expressed her ownership by using 'I' and not 'we' to describe who was completing these activities. In the written narrative, she said 'I am my aunt Lupita's doctor' and described her contributions, such as bathing her and providing love and care. The text also revealed her aunt's deteriorating condition when Camila said she was sleeping a lot and not taking her medicine. Camila's drawing displays visual features that also revealed her meaning-making process in this difficult experience. In the illustration, Camila was positioned as a colorful, healthy figure, larger in size and smiling. Her aunt

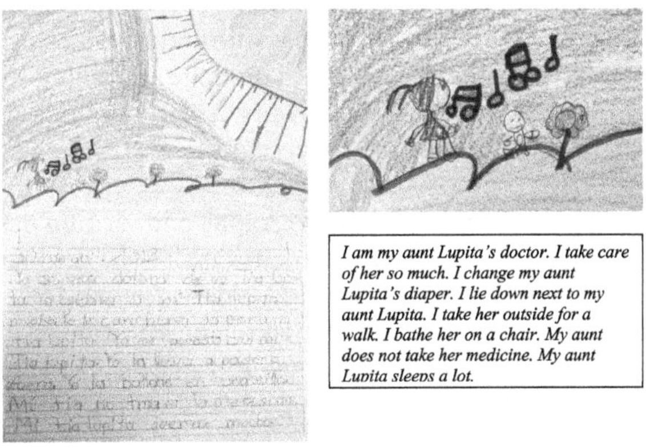

Figure 11.2 Camila's narrative and illustration
Note: With permission from the *Journal of Early Childhood Literacy.*

was represented by a smaller and pale fragile figure that portrayed an anguished facial expression. She was protected between Camila, a large flower, and the musical notes above her. Pictorially, Camila encompassed her aunt with beauty and vibrant life. From a multimodal social semiotics perspective, Camila surrounded the weakness and dullness of 'illness' by a colorful and picturesque setting and positioned herself as larger and stronger, providing alleviating musical notes to ease her aunt's pain and anguish. From these multimodal expressions, Camila perceived herself as a caretaker with the role of ameliorating pain by providing a happy environment with visual and musical joy to her terminally ill aunt.

The roles children hold in their families and the many ways they contribute to the family's well-being represent important funds of knowledge and insights about their sociocultural perceptions. Children in immigrant households contribute in many ways to their family, including providing care, translating, completing household chores and being responsible with schoolwork (Orellana, 2003). It is important to recognize the learning that takes place within these experiences as forms of familial funds of knowledge and, in this case, the difficult situation that Camila was facing with an active and affirmative demeanor. As González and Moll (2002: 638) explain, 'students' learning is bound up in networks of relationships that extend beyond the nuclear family. By tapping into the extended networks and social capital of students, teachers can not only validate knowledge, but can also activate these networks for pedagogical purposes.' For Camila, the illustration provided an additional multimodal resource in her meaning-making process that conversely supported the written narrative of her experience, and revealed her familial funds of knowledge and how she viewed her role as an active contributing member in her family.

Ana

Ana was a first-grader who had recently arrived in the US with her family from Torreón, México, and was continuously making sense of her new contexts – a new country, school, language and living situation with extended family. Ana's projects included two picture books depicting personal experiences and a timeline depicting the most important events in her life.

Ana's life timeline combined photographs and written descriptions to tell her story (Figure 11.3). The close relationships she held with extended family were evident, as were her schooling experiences in Mexico and the US – both of which represent important funds of knowledge. Ana and her family used photographs to depict recent and significant events in her life: immigrating to the US and first days of school in both countries.

One event showed a photograph of Ana standing by her mother in what looks like a town square with an illuminated Christmas tree. While this photograph may seem like a common event in a family, for Ana this

Figure 11.3 Ana's timeline project

was her last Christmas in her hometown, as the caption reads with a nostalgic tone, 'Última Navidad que pasamos en Torreón' [Last Christmas we spent in Torreón]. The following event showed Ana posing with her mother in front of a jeep-like limousine by a stone building. The photograph represented a life-changing moment – their first day in Colorado, where they would seek a new life. The caption reads: 'Nuestro primer día en Colorado' [Our first day in Colorado]. These two events were in close proximity physically on the project and also in composition, with mother and child posing in front of a point of interest, marking the point in time and in Ana's life when they moved. Ana's mother explained the sadness Ana felt:

> El otro día empezamos a hablar de los proyectos y ella dijo que acaba de llegar a Estados Unidos. Que sus abuelitos se habían quedado en México y luego dice que ella estaba muy triste.
>
> [The other day we started talking about the projects and she said that she had just arrived to the US. That her grandparents had remained in Mexico, then said that she was very sad.]

From a multimodal social semiotics perspective, these two events positioned together embody social contexts and rely on a process in which meaning is co-constructed and exchanged in different planes (Hodge & Kress, 1988). The first semiotic meaning plane likely took place among family members as they created the project, and the second was when this message was shared between Ana and her classmates in school. Ana and her family portrayed an important event in their lives with visuals, and subsequently engaged in a literacy practice to write a description. This is evident in that the written descriptions would be incomplete without the photographs, which in this case are important visuals to convey meaning.

Although all children in this classroom, except Ana, were born in the US, most shared transnational connections to Mexico through their parents, who had all immigrated to the US. These shared experiences facilitated an understanding between the multimodal symbols on the project as 'signifiers' and the audience as 'signified.' Ana's visuals of her immigration experience as 'signs' were very well understood by her classmates. These transnational connections and experiences fostered significant funds of knowledge as part of their lives that were present in everyday classroom interactions, from heated debates about the latest results of the Mexican soccer league, to side conversations in which a child confided with another that she knows her parents cannot go to Mexico because 'they don't have papers.' Ana's project represents one example of the ways in which children engaged visuals to depict their transnational connections to Mexico and their border-crossing experiences. Children's projects revealed both relevant experiences and interests, as Moll (2019: 137) explains: 'a funds of knowledge approach helps teachers understand the cultural–historical basis of household life and other formative experiences, such as students' interests, from which additional pedagogical innovations may emerge.' The peer relationships that Ana was building during her first few months in the US were of great importance to her. This was evident when in a classroom interaction she responded to a classmate's question, 'No, no tengo hermanos, pero mis amigos son como mis hermanos' [I don't have siblings, but my friends are like my siblings]. She shared with her mother that the two things she liked best about being in the US were making new friends and becoming bilingual.

For Ana, moving to Colorado involved the opportunity to become bilingual, which she excitedly expressed during a focus group, 'yo siempre quise ser bilingüe' [I always wanted to be bilingual]. Interestingly, when presenting her project to a kindergarten student in Spanish, she shifted her pronunciation of 'Colorado' from Spanish to English. Hodge and Kress (1988: 82) explain that accent refers to a metasign that marks 'solidarity, group identity and ideology.' Metasigns carry meaning connected to broader systems of power and solidarity, and relationships between groups (Blom & Gumperz, 2000; Hodge & Kress, 1988). In this example, Ana may be resorting to English pronunciation in discourse to mark her membership among peers who have been exposed to English since birth or longer than Ana. Her desire to become bilingual and make new friends occurs within an environment where English is dominant and peers' extended access to English may be perceived as an advantage and valuable from her perspective. Ana may be affirming her emerging membership of a bilingual community as a way to facilitate her social relationships. Ana further made sense of her experience of acquiring bilingualism and the role of welcoming friends as sources of support in her picture book (Figure 11.4).

In Ana's book, the main character experiences moving, attending a new school, not speaking the dominant language, meeting friendly and supportive friends, and a recognition of her effort by the teacher. All were experiences that Ana has recently lived. Ana's mother described the sense-making process that took place orally between them as they created her book:

> Se estaba reflejando ella, dice, 'sí mamá, que le da miedo ir a la escuela porque no sabe hablar como los demás animales.' Le digo 'sí hija, pero sus amigos le dijeron que le van a ayudar,' y responde 'como a mí me dijeron

The Jungle, Written by: Ana, Illustrated by: Ricardo

Once upon a time there was a little monkey that moved to live in another jungle

The animals at the jungle welcomed him happily

The next day the little monkey was afraid to go to school since he didn't know how to speak the language of the other animals, but his friends helped him study

The hippopotamus teacher congratulated the little monkey for his effort and good grades.

Figure 11.4 Ana's picture book

> mis amigos.' […] 'Así mamá, como yo, el changuito también tenía miedo, pero sus amigos le ayudaron.' […] Estaba bien emocionada y sí la vi como que ella estaba viéndose en la historia, que estaba reflejándose. Le digo, 'sí hija, pues es tu historia.'
>
> [She was reflecting herself, she said, 'yes mom, that he is afraid of going to school because he doesn't speak like the other animals.' I told her, 'yes sweetheart, but then his friends tell him they are going to help him,' and responded 'just like my friends told me.' […] 'Like this mom, like me, the little monkey was also afraid, but his friends helped him.' […] She was so excited and I did see how she would see herself in the story, it was reflecting her. I tell her, 'yes sweetheart, well it is your story.']

Ana's meaning-making process of her experiences and contexts was supported by the opportunities a multimodal approach offered by engaging creative storytelling, the use of artifacts and visuals, and oral interactions with peers.

A Multimodal Approach to Support the Meaning-Making of Bilingual Children

Centering children's experiences in their learning experiences is a significant aspect of culturally sustaining pedagogy, and multimodality as a pedagogical resource in classroom instruction supports children's meaning-making processes about their social contexts and lives. The examples presented in this chapter illustrate the ways in which multimodal opportunities supported young bilingual students who are not only making sense of their social and familial contexts, but also of their emerging biliteracy and bilingualism. Camila's illustrations served as a canvas that captured her feelings and understandings of the challenging situation her family was facing, and how she perceived her role in ameliorating the pain and illness. In Ana's case, engaging visuals, artifacts and creative storytelling became resources for her expressions that reflected her recent experiences of immigration and bilingualism, while also fostering a sense of belonging, mutual understanding and 'compañerismo' [comradeship] with her peers. In both cases, multimodal pedagogical resources served as pathways for students to share aspects of their lives orally and visually, accessing various forms of literacies.

Multimodality as Pedagogical Tools to Seek Children's Funds of Knowledge

This chapter delineates alternative and viable multimodal pathways, such as project-based approaches, creative storytelling, artifacts and illustrations, to learn from and about children's life experiences and funds of knowledge. A multimodal social semiotics perspective to seek funds of knowledge is relevant as it merges two central literacy and sociocultural constructs –multimodality and funds of knowledge – to offer educators an approach that values and creates inviting spaces for students to engage with multimodal resources in their learning while revealing aspects of their home lives.

Children's multimodal expressions and creations are speaking to us, offering insights into their funds of knowledge and social understandings, which are part of their meaning-making processes but are seldom prioritized in classroom instruction. Of even more concern, we may be limiting students' multimodal resources for the sake of 'instructional time' to focus solely on assessed skills. An inevitable consequence is that teachers focus on developing those skills that are formally assessed, which also affect their own teaching evaluations, having a detrimental impact on instructional practices (Menken, 2006). Yet, children's worlds are not experienced only in print modes, and thus instruction should not be limited to print modes either. Rather, multimodality becomes a vehicle and support to develop much more than the assessed skills. Children's multimodal expressions also represent an opportunity to foster teacher-student relationships which are central in effective culturally sustaining pedagogical approaches.

Fostering Opportunities to Integrate Multimodality with Instruction

An important implication revolves around the common time and curricular restrictions educators face. Integrating multimodal opportunities for bilingual students and effective instruction are not mutually exclusive, but rather these build on one another. Educators can begin by examining their classroom practices to first identify the opportunities students currently have to explore and express through multimodal ways beyond print. Teachers can engage in a self-reflective process that asks: What can I learn about students' lives by paying attention to these multimodal expressions and creations? Secondly, educators can evaluate their instruction and curriculum to seek opportunities to embed multimodality in learning experiences. During the design of lessons, educators can keep in mind ways to integrate children's full communicative modes, for example, considering instances where students can engage visuals, photographs, drawings and artifacts as resources to access and promote other forms of literacies. Educators can also consider the kinds of opportunities students have to interact with one another or with family members, using visuals or artifacts as prompts. Finally, educators can evaluate their own learning about students' lives to make further concrete curricular connections in a continuous generative process. This emphasis on connecting theory to practice and using the knowledge learned about and from students to guide instruction and learning experiences can have remarkable results and, in this process, multimodality becomes an additional tool to access funds of knowledge.

Conclusion

In conclusion, this chapter explored inquiries that centered on examining a multimodal social semiotics approach toward seeking students' funds of knowledge, and on understanding it as a resource in their meaning-making. The data examples presented showed how two bilingual first-graders depicted their lives and social understandings through creative multimodal opportunities in classroom instruction, offering insights into their meaning-making processes and funds of knowledge as they experienced contextual circumstances. Multimodal expressions incorporated photographs, artifacts, creative storytelling and illustrations that delineated important funds of knowledge in their lives, such as familial and peer relationships of support, transnational experiences, and their emergent bilingualism. These findings demonstrate the importance of integrating multimodal opportunities in classroom instruction for bilingual learners who are making sense of their lives and bilingualism in environments that may not be supportive of their experiences. If our lives and learning experiences are not limited to print, classroom learning experiences should not be either.

References

Alvarez, A. (2018a) Drawn and written funds of knowledge: A window into emerging bilingual children's experiences and social interpretations through their written narratives and drawings. *Journal of Early Childhood Literacy* 18 (1), 97–128.

Alvarez, A. (2018b) Experiential knowledge and project-based learning in bilingual classrooms. Occasional Paper No. 39, 8.

Becker, A. (2014) Funds of (difficult) knowledge and the affordances of multimodality: The case of Victor. *Journal of Language and Literacy Education* 10 (2), 17–33.

Blom, J.P. and Gumperz, J.J. (2000) Social meaning in linguistic structure: Code-switching in Norway. *The Bilingualism Reader* 2000, 111–136.

Brown, S. (2017) Building on emergent bilinguals' funds of knowledge using digital tools for literacy. In E. Ortlieb and E.H. Cheek (eds) *Addressing Diversity in Literacy Instruction* (pp. 171–192). Bingley: Emerald.

Dworin, J. (2006) The Family Stories Project: Using funds of knowledge for writing. *The Reading Teacher* 59 (6), 510–520.

Freire, P. and Macedo, D. (2005) *Literacy: Reading the Word and the World*. Westport, CT: Bergin & Garvey.

González, N. and Moll, L.C. (2002) Cruzando el puente: Building bridges to funds of knowledge. *Educational Policy* 16 (4), 623–641.

Gort, M. (2006) Strategic codeswitching, interliteracy, and other phenomena of emergent bilingual writing: Lessons from first-grade dual language classrooms. *Journal of Early Childhood Literacy* 6 (3), 323–354.

Hodge, R. and Kress, G. (1988) *Social Semiotics*. Oxford: Polity Press.

Kenner, C. (2004) Living in simultaneous worlds: Difference and integration in bilingual script-learning. *International Journal of Bilingual Education and Bilingualism* 7 (1), 43–61.

Kenner, C. and Kress, G. (2003) The multisemiotic resources of biliterate children. *Journal of Early Childhood Literacy* 3 (2), 179–202.

Kress, G.R. (2010) *Multimodality: A Social Semiotic Approach to Contemporary Communication*. New York: Routledge.

Ladson-Billings, G. (1995) Toward a theory of culturally relevant pedagogy. *American Educational Research Journal* 32 (3), 465–491.

Levitt, P. and Schiller, N.G. (2004) Conceptualizing simultaneity: A transnational social field perspective on society. *International Migration Review* 38 (3), 1002–1039.

Marshall, E. and Toohey, K. (2010) Representing family: Community funds of knowledge, bilingualism, and multimodality. *Harvard Educational Review* 80 (2), 221–242.

Menken, K. (2006) Teaching to the test: How No Child Left Behind impacts language policy, curriculum, and instruction for English language learners. *Bilingual Research Journal* 30 (2), 521–546.

Miles, M.B., Huberman, A.M. and Saldana, J. (2014) *Qualitative Data Analysis: A Methods Sourcebook*. Thousand Oaks, CA: Sage.

Moje, E.B., Ciechanowski, K.M., Kramer, K., Ellis, L., Carrillo, R. and Collazo, T. (2004) Working toward third space in content area literacy: An examination of everyday funds of knowledge and discourse. *Reading Research Quarterly* 39 (1), 38–70.

Moll, L.C. (2019) Elaborating funds of knowledge: Community-oriented practices in international contexts. *Literacy Research: Theory, Method, and Practice* 68 (1), 130–138.

Moll, L.C., Amanti, C., Neff, D. and Gonzalez, N. (1992) Funds of knowledge for teaching: Using a qualitative approach to connect homes and classrooms. *Theory into Practice* 31 (2), 132–141.

Moll, L.C., Saez, R. and Dworin, J. (2001) Exploring biliteracy: Two student case examples of writing as a social practice. *Elementary School Journal* 101 (4), 435–449.

Orellana, M.F. (2003) Responsibilities of children in Latino immigrant homes. *New Directions for Youth Development* 100, 25–39.

Paris, D. (2012) Culturally sustaining pedagogy: A needed change in stance, terminology, and practice. *Educational Researcher* 41 (3), 93–97.

Pérez, B. and Torres-Guzmán, M. (1996) *Learning in Two Worlds*. White Plains, NY: Longman.

Soto, L.D. and Garza, I. (2011) Latino/a immigrant children's drawings and writings. *Contemporary Issues in Early Childhood* 12 (2), 118–133.

Valencia, R.R. (1997) *The Evolution of Deficit Thinking: Educational Thought and Practice*. New York: Routledge.

Vygotsky, L.S. (1978) *Mind in Society: The Development of Higher Psychological Processes* (M. Cole, V. John-Steiner, S. Scribner and E. Souberman, eds). Cambridge, MA: Harvard University Press.

Wessels, S. and Herrera, S.G. (2014) Drawing their way into writing: Culturally and linguistically diverse students finding voice through mini-novelas. *TESOL Journal* 5 (1), 105–119.

12 Creative Creations: Self-Authoring Multimodal Stories

Heidi R. Bacon and Moneerah Al Jabr

> Children's immersion in digital communication occurs at a critical period in their lives when their emerging literacy skills (speaking, listening, reading and writing) and identities as effective and competent learners are being moulded by the conventions of the social and cultural worlds in which they live.
>
> (Flewitt *et al.*, 2015)

This chapter describes a qualitative case study of two Arabic-dominant seven-year-old bilingual children using StoryKit®, a mobile storytelling app. We illustrate the children's use of retelling stories in multiple modalities to author and make meaning using the app. Their retellings were created in a playful, imaginative context with Moneerah, one of the children's mothers. Our research exemplifies the potential of iPads and open-source apps to support emergent bilinguals' multimodal literacies.

The Shifting Landscape of Early Childhood Literacies

Flewitt *et al.* (2015) call attention to the landscape of children's shifting sociocultural worlds. Touchscreen devices and open-content apps are changing the nature of early literacy learning (Rowsell, 2014; Wohlwend, 2018). To conceptualize this shift, Rideout (2017) estimated that 98% of children aged eight years and under have access to digital devices in the home. Despite the proliferation and affordances of digital devices, however, early childhood instruction continues to focus on print-centric literacies defined as 'skills and practices associated with traditional, paper-based texts' (Burnett, 2010: 253). Although schools are tasked with fostering children's 21st century literacies, the emphasis on print-centric practices does not effectively address the complexities of early childhood literacies in today's world (Henning, 2020).

Moreover, print-centric literacies position emergent bilinguals at a particular disadvantage because they constrain or limit opportunities for expression (Rodriguez-Mojica, 2019; Taylor & Leung, 2020). Emergent bilinguals benefit from expressing their ideas in multiple modalities in collaborative spaces. Digital technologies and multimodal literacies strengthen their repertoires of meaning-making (Smith *et al.*, 2021). As such, Maureen *et al.* (2020: 57) argue that literacies can 'no longer be limited to traditional text-based reading and writing'; they must include multimodal texts.

Relatedly, the use of touchscreen devices offers increased opportunities for multimodal composing. Brown and Allmond (2021) found that teachers understood more about emergent bilinguals' story comprehension when children produced pictures using tablets to demonstrate linguistic competence and story comprehension. Story-creating apps and touchscreen devices can help children connect languages, reading, writing, listening, audio and video in a single storytelling event (Quinn & Bliss, 2021; Rowe & Miller, 2016). As children compose, new layers of meaning are added, creating an 'ensemble' (Brown & Allmond, 2021: 219).

Nonetheless, in classrooms, children's story comprehension is typically assessed through comprehension questions and oral retellings in English. Kucer (2014) points out that predetermined comprehension questions focus on specific information a reader might not understand or remember and retellings depend on what the child constructed from reading or listening to a story. As Lotherington (2020: 23) explains, children must be able to access the symbols on a page, but there are other means of telling and retelling through 'pictures, words, actions, songs, puppetry, and in mixed media limited only by the imagination.' Likewise, Goodman *et al.* (2005) agree that conventional retellings may not represent what readers comprehend and suggest that incorporating different modalities may reveal more about children's interpretations of text. Therefore, in this chapter, we demonstrate how multimodality supports emergent bilinguals' language and literacies.

Perspectives on Multimodality and Play

Sociocultural perspectives on multimodality and play framed this study. Literacies are socially constructed and mediated by resources to construct meaning (Flewitt, 2013). Multimodality extends sociocultural perspectives and challenges the assumption that language is the most important mode for meaning-making. In this study, multimodality is conceptualized as 'print based and digital texts that utilize more than one mode or semiotic resource to represent meaning potentials' (Serafini, 2015: 412). Multimodality emphasizes socially and culturally shaped worlds and semiotic resources including linguistic, visual, audio and gestural modes for communication and learning (Kress, 2010; Oakley *et al.*, 2018). Rather than focusing on one mode, such as linguistic or visual, multimodality represents the interrelationship between multiple modes and how they work together in sense-making (Kress, 2010).

Young children's multimodal expressions are linked through gestures and play (Taylor & Leung, 2020), forming a 'play-literacy nexus,' a space where play, literacy and language coalesce (Roskos & Christie, 2011: 204). In these spaces, children engage their imaginations through reading, writing and making. As such, play is a way for children to make sense of their world (Short & Acevedo, 2016; Wohlwend, 2015). When children tell stories, they create a 'narrative playground' (Dyson, 2020: 121), sharing connections and responding to the ideas of others through storying and creating new stories (Flint, 2020). Through play, children imagine, explore and learn, using bodies and materials to rework or make new meaning (Wohlwend, 2018). Thus, play enhances emergent literacies by breathing life into children's imaginaries.

Storytelling can also build children's story schema and aid comprehension (Stevens *et al.*, 2010). Children use their knowledge of story schema to comprehend story events (Rowe, 2013). Citing Whitmore and Goodman (1995), Wohlwend (2018) notes that children pretend to read through dramatic play by tracking print, turning pages, acting out the voices of storybook characters and creatively narrating their own meanings. When composing, children make choices about story elements, media and resources to support their authoring. They turn 'work into play' through their authoring of stories (Dyson, 2016: 9).

Opportunities for multimodal authoring are critical for emergent bilinguals (Gillanders, 2018). Constructing stories through multiple modes can enhance children's linguistic confidence and writing. For example, Rowe and Miller (2016) studied the digital composing of bilingual/biliterate four-year-olds. They found the children shared their cultural backgrounds with other children and used the vocabulary they were learning at school to talk about familiar artifacts and activities. These kinds of creative literacy experiences position emergent bilinguals as active producers of knowledge. Creating spaces for bilingual children to playfully and creatively combine multiple modes to author their own stories is key to their language and literacy development.

Contextualizing the Study

This study took place in a small university town in the midwestern United States. Layla, a first grader, moved to the US five years ago with her family, and Rosa, also a first grader, is Layla's friend (Layla and Rosa are pseudonyms). The children attended the same school where English was the language of instruction. Layla and Rosa's first-grade teachers described their reading as 'above-average' based on benchmark assessment scores. Moneerah, Layla's mother, worked with the children in her home. Reading, retelling and composing took place in Layla's bedroom. Layla had a standing whiteboard, a bookcase with a variety of books, and a table with two chairs where the children sat while they listened to the stories, played or worked.

Researchers' positionality

Moneerah, an Arabic-English bilingual, biliterate woman, grew up in Saudi Arabia and came to the US to attend graduate school. She is a doctoral candidate specializing in early childhood literacies and a close friend of Rosa's mother. Throughout her graduate program, she has worked closely with Heidi, and they have collaborated on several research projects. Heidi is the daughter of German immigrants who came to the US after World War II. She is a white, monolingual associate professor who teaches courses in language, literacies and culture, and qualitative research methods.

Data sources and collection

Data sources included field notes of observations that Moneerah collected during audio-recorded oral retellings, digital story retellings, retelling guides to score each retelling, and informal audio-recorded interviews after each retelling session. Moneerah read four paper-based stories which the children then retold. The stories were read and retold in English because Layla and Rosa attended an English-only school. The children participated in two oral and two iPad retellings. For the oral retellings, Moneerah read the story to each child separately, after which the child retold the story. Moneerah then read two other stories to both children and asked them to retell the stories using StoryKit®. Layla and Rosa had their own iPads but were unfamiliar with the app. Moneerah introduced the app and showed the children how it worked. She encouraged the children to practice with the app to ensure they knew how to use it.

A conventional retelling guide was developed for each story. The guides, adapted from Goodman *et al.* (2005), were used to evaluate the children's story comprehension (see Figure 12.1). Once each child had finished her unaided oral retelling, Moneerah asked open-ended questions and encouraged them to continue retelling the story. Forty points were given for mentioning the characters, and 60 points were given for recalling events in the story. Total points were compared between the oral and iPad retellings.

Observational field notes were captured by Moneerah to document the children's interactions during their digital retellings. In addition to observations, Moneerah conducted informal interviews after each retelling session. She asked the children questions to evaluate their comprehension of the stories, such as: What is the story about? What do you think the author wanted you to learn from this story? The children were asked to talk about their experiences retelling the stories. Open-ended questions such as 'What did you notice about the oral retelling and the iPad retelling?' prompted the children to respond.

Audio-recorded data were transcribed verbatim by Moneerah. We read through the field notes and interview transcripts and wrote margin notes to get a sense of the data. The data were coded using first and second

Retelling Guide #1: *The Snowy Day*
By: Ezra Jack Keats

Reader: Date:

Character Analysis:
(40 points)
20- Peter (Boy) -----
10- Mother (Woman) -----
5- Big boys -----
5- Peter's friend -----

Events:
(60 points)

- One winter morning, Peter woke up and saw the snow covering everything. After breakfast, he put on his snowsuit and ran outside. (10 points) ------
- He made tracks in the snow with his feet and a stick. He used the stick for smacking a snow-covered tree and the snow fell on top of Peter's head (5 points) ------
- He tried to join a snowball fight with the big boys, but he thought that he wasn't old enough. (5 points) ------
- He made a snowman and snow angles. He climbed up a snow mountain and slid all the way down. (10 points)
- He picked a snowball and put it in his pocket for tomorrow. Then he went inside his warm house and took a bath and told his mother about his adventures while she took off his wet socks. (10 points) ------
- Before Peter got into bed, he looked in his pocket and the snowball wasn't there. He felt sad. He went to sleep and dreamed that the sun had melted all the snow away. (10 points) ------
- When he woke up, the snow was still everywhere and it was falling. After breakfast, he went out with his friend into the deep, deep snow. (10 points) ------

Points - character analysis ------
Points- events ------
Total points ------
Comments

Figure 12.1 *The Snowy Day* retelling guide
Source: Adapted from Goodman *et al.* (2005).

cycle coding (see Saldaña, 2016). Open coding was used to identify patterns that seemed important or meaningful, such as playful learning, children's perceptions of using the tablet, differences between oral and digital retelling, writing using iPads and the app, collaborative learning and the use of multimodal features. We next initiated second cycle coding to eliminate marginal or unnecessary codes. Focused coding was used to group and categorize the codes. Four themes were interpreted from the data, which we present in the findings.

Findings

Using an iPad for story retelling was a new and exciting experience for Layla and Rosa. Findings showed that digital tools provided unique experiences not available through traditional print-centric literacies. In this section, we elaborate on four prominent experiences we identified: self-authoring, oral and digital retellings, playful learning and engagement in multimodal literacies.

Self-authoring

Rosa and Layla viewed themselves as authors who produced their own versions of the stories. During the informal interviews, Rosa referred to her multimodal retelling as 'My story; *my* words,' and when asked if retelling the story using the app helped her understand the story, Rosa responded, '*Yes*, because it's with my *own* writing and I can understand it more because I wrote it down.'

Moneerah encouraged Rosa and Layla to develop titles for their multimodal retelling of *The Empty Pot* (Demi, 1990). In the story, Ping, a young boy, participated in a competition planned by the Emperor of China to find his successor. The emperor gave every child a special flower seed and whoever grew the best flower would become the next Emperor, but the seeds were cooked and could not grow. Ping won and became Emperor because he had the courage and honesty to tell the truth that his seed would not grow. Layla named her digital retelling 'The Strange Seed,' in response to wondering why the seeds would not grow even when carefully planted and faithfully watered. On the other hand, Rosa titled her story 'King,' to reflect her understanding of the story. Rosa understood the story as a contest to see who would become king, and the main character won the contest. Naming the stories suggested that the children creatively innovated. They changed words and drew pictures that differed from the original stories to represent their own narrations. Layla explained that she could write 'whatever words I do' and 'use my imagination' whenever she did not remember the exact story events. She added, 'it can be different beginnings and different endings, but it needs to match the same information to show we get it.'

Oral and digital retellings

When we compared the children's oral and digital retellings, Layla and Rosa's comprehension scores were above 80% (see Table 12.1). While the oral retellings summarized and explained story events, Layla and Rosa's digital retellings were playful and included illustrations that

Table 12.1 Layla and Rosa's retelling scores

	Oral retelling (*The Snowy Day*)	**Oral retelling (*Odd Velvet*)**	**Digital retelling (*Fish is Fish*)**	**Digital retelling (*The Empty Pot*)**
Layla	82%	91%	95%	86%
Rosa	95%	87%	93%	88%

suggested new stories. When asked to compare the digital and oral retellings, Layla said, '[oral retelling] is just like reading it [the story], but this one [digital retelling] is how to make it all happen.' The children used the iPad's affordances to transform their stories. As they composed, Moneerah noticed Layla and Rosa reading and rereading their stories to each other, taking on the role of authors as they searched for 'good' words that made sense within the context of their stories to make them understandable.

Layla and Rosa saved their stories in Storykit®. They asked if they could share them with family, and Moneerah showed them how to enter family members' emails and send links to the stories. The children liked being able 'to go back and look at it' whenever they wanted. Layla reasoned, 'if we want to read the story and we don't have it, we can just see the iPad. It's there.' The children demonstrated their knowledge of digital affordances as they knew the stories could be saved and shared electronically with others. Touchscreen affordances and multiplicity of resources shaped and enhanced Layla and Rosa's authorship.

Playful learning

Although Layla and Rosa created their own stories, Moneerah observed them socially interacting and playfully learning together. The tablets' mobility allowed the children to move around the room as they composed. Layla and Rosa engaged in conversations, complimented one another's pictures, and asked questions about each other's stories. In the first digital retelling, Rosa complimented Layla's drawing and offered suggestions as she said, 'Your picture is lovely but try to ....' In addition, the children helped one another solve problems. When Layla accidently erased her drawing of the fish, frog and pond from *Fish is Fish* (Lionni, 1970), Rosa suggested making a blue background and then drawing the fish and frog. Throughout their composing, the children's conversations were anchored in their drawings and the visual modes available on the app. When recording their retellings, they used different character voices to express feelings and ask questions. Layla and Rosa created text boxes and played with picture sizes, fonts and colors to imagine what the stories would look like on each page.

The children also helped one another with spelling, as this seemed to be a concern for both girls. When Layla had trouble spelling 'grew,' 'each' and 'legs,' Rosa offered to help her. The children took weekly spelling tests and participated in spelling bees, which led us to wonder if Layla and Rosa's concern about correct spelling stemmed from their school experiences. Unlike learning and spelling decontextualized words, digital retelling provided a context that fostered writing and collaboration.

The use of tablets for storytelling seemed to encourage the girls to discuss, share and jointly solve problems that often arise during play. The collaborative nature of their composing allowed Layla and Rosa to remember different parts of the stories. For example, when the girls were typing their retelling of *Fish is Fish* (Lionni, 1970), Layla attempted to spell the word 'argue.' When Rosa heard her, she remembered an event in the story about an argument between the fish and the frog, which she included in her digital story. Layla declared, 'you are probably copying from me,' and Rosa replied, 'maybe we have the same idea.' Layla and Rosa's social interactions and playful learning supported collaborative meaning-making.

Engagement in multimodal literacies

The Storykit® app combined verbal, visual and audio modes for authoring and interpreting stories. Both girls typed text on each page, drew their own illustrations and recorded their own narration. They used the 'Edit' function to edit every page and chose the 'Read' option to read their completed stories by swiping to turn the pages. These young bilinguals understood the notion that meaning-making is more than just written words and that pictures also carry meaning. In her informal interview, Layla commented, 'we look at the pictures if we can't understand the words,' and Rosa explained that words could tell them what was illustrated on the page.

Brown and Allmond (2021) maintain that emergent bilinguals move their information and understanding to a visual mode to communicate their understanding using oral or written language. Drawing seemed to provide a supportive scaffold for Layla and Rosa's authoring. To this end, Rosa stated, 'You can just draw because drawing it makes it like [pointing at a page of her story] ...see pretend I have no words, but you can already tell those are the kids. That's the king talking to him. You see automatically and don't need words' (see Figure 12.2 for Rosa's digital story retelling of *The Empty Pot*).

The girls also understood that stories have themes. In their retelling of *The Empty Pot* (Demi, 1990), Rosa stated that the author wants readers to learn from the story to 'Always tell the truth. Never tell a lie.' Layla chimed in, saying, 'We don't need to cheat.'

The children's writing reflected knowledge of English conventions. Layla and Rosa capitalized titles and used periods, quotation marks and quite a few exclamation points. Furthermore, when a red line appeared beneath a word, they looked up the spelling in StoryKit® and chose from the word list displayed on the screen, a helpful affordance for emergent bilinguals (Brown & Allmond, 2021). Digitally retelling their stories enabled the girls to 'do a better thing.' According to Rosa, 'You can see more difference because I'm drawing and I'm typing stuff with my words and I'm recording.' Drawing, writing and recording enriched Layla and Rosa's retellings.

Figure 12.2 Rosa's digital retelling of *The Empty Pot*

Discussion and Implications

Retelling a story requires children first to interpret the story and then to reconstruct it using appropriate vocabulary and accurate ordering of events (Lucero, 2018). The findings of our study aligned with Rowe's (2013) review of research to demonstrate Rosa and Layla's knowledge of genre, story structure and their ability to self-author. In her retellings, Rosa used words such as 'the main characters,' 'illustrations' and 'the lesson' to indicate her familiarity with stories that have moral lessons for readers. The children evidenced their knowledge of reading and writing as composing meaning.

Rowe (2018: 235) argues that people concerned with school 'readiness' tend to 'equate writing with conventional spelling and handwriting' and focus on 'the conventional readability of children's products rather than their meaning-making processes.' When value is placed on written language in schools to the detriment of playful literacies, emergent bilinguals will continue to struggle (Brown & Allmond, 2021). Schools that focus on tested skills marginalize emergent bilinguals and children whose writing may not match mainstream expectations (Rowe, 2013; Wohlwend, 2015). Conversely, multimodality counters the notion that written language is the most valuable mode to represent knowledge (Brown & Allmond, 2021). Therefore, we believe that teachers should be mindful of the knowledge, experiences and language repertoires of emergent bilinguals in becoming bilingual meaning-makers (D'warte, 2020).

Composing multimodal texts in early childhood classrooms using drawing, playing and writing is not new, as teachers often provide children with paper, markers and objects to support their literacy development (Rowe & Miller, 2016). As writing is influenced by social and cultural contexts, today's children not only write on paper; they also read and write on screens (Flewitt *et al.*, 2015). As Layla and Rosa have shown, multimodal authoring can empower children who are learning English to express themselves (Rowe & Miller, 2016). Open-content apps are playful and allow for rich storytelling, whereas closed-content apps with drill-and-skill activities position children as consumers by imposing boundaries and limiting possibilities for authentic, imaginative language learning.

The importance of play cannot be minimized. Play involves children using their minds, materials and bodies to make their own meanings (Wohlwend, 2018). Children demonstrate agency through playful literacies, taking on new roles, using languages, collaborating with peers and reimagining themselves and their world (Dyson, 2020). When engaged in multimodal storytelling, Layla and Rosa playfully became authors and teachers. They appropriated the modes available through the app to construct their understanding of texts and to author their words and world.

Multimodal composing helps emergent bilinguals build on their sophisticated and abundant linguistic resources, but more research is needed. How might opportunities be provided to engage children's multimodal, digital authoring? How can we give children creative space to ideate beyond and imagine new stories and worlds? We think these questions are essential to address the complexities of 21st century early childhood literacies.

Concluding Thoughts

This study demonstrates that creating stories in multiple modalities enhanced Layla and Rosa's oral language, literacies and social interaction. They made choices, acted on their thoughts, took ownership of their learning and collaborated with each other (Oakley *et al.*, 2018). In doing so, they entered a zone of possibilities extending what each could do by herself (Moll, 2014). Digital apps are generative authoring tools for engaging with texts and communicating with others. They expand and enrich print-centric practices, allowing children to document their story comprehension through creative, imaginative retellings. Multimodal and digital literacies support emergent bilinguals' semiotic meaning-making and are valuable tools for language and literacy learning in homes and classrooms.

References

Brown, S. and Allmond, A. (2021) Constructing my world: A case study examining emergent bilingual multimodal composing practices. *Early Childhood Education Journal* 49 (2), 209–221. doi:10.1007/s10643-020-01062-4

Burnett, C. (2010) Technology and literacy in early childhood educational settings: A review of research. *Journal of Early Childhood Literacy* 10 (3), 247–270.

Demi, H. (1990) *The Empty Pot*. New York: Henry Holt.

D'warte, J. (2020) Recognizing and leveraging the bilingual meaning-making potential of young people aged six to eight years old in one Australian classroom. *Journal of Early Childhood Literacy* 20 (2), 296–326.

Dyson, A.H. (2016) Introduction: Gathering textual children. In A.H. Dyson (ed.) *Child Cultures, Schooling, and Literacy: Global Perspectives on Composing Unique Lives* (pp. 3–13). New York: Routledge.

Dyson, A.H. (2020) 'We're playing sisters on paper!': Children composing on graphic playgrounds. *Literacy* 54 (2), 3–12.

Flewitt, R. (2013) Multimodal perspective on early childhood literacies. In L. Larson and J. Marsh (eds) *The Sage Handbook of Early Childhood Literacy* (pp. 295–309). Thousand Oaks, CA: Sage.

Flewitt, R., Messer, D. and Kucirkova, N. (2015) New directions for early literacy in a digital age: The iPad. *Journal of Early Childhood Literacy* 15 (3), 289–310.

Flint, T.K. (2020) Responsive play: Creating transformative classroom spaces through play as a reader response. *Journal of Early Childhood Literacy* 20 (2), 385–410.

Gillanders, C. (2018) ¿Cómo Lo Escribo en Inglés o en Español? Writing in dual-language learners. *The Reading Teacher* 71 (4), 421–430.

Goodman, Y.M., Watson, D.J. and Burke, C.L. (2005) *Reading Miscue Inventory: From Evaluation to Instruction*. Katonah, NY: Owen.

Henning, L. (2020) I'm gonna get it for my birthday: Young children's interpretive reproduction of literacy practices in school. *Journal of Early Childhood Literacy* 20 (4), 706–731.

Keats, E.J. (2011) *The Snowy Day*. New York: Viking.

Kress, G.R. (2010) *Multimodality: A Social Semiotic Approach to Contemporary Communication*. New York: Routledge.

Kucer, S.B. (2014) What retellings can tell us about the nature of reading comprehension in school children. *Australian Journal of Language and Literacy* 37 (1), 31–44.

Lionni, L. (1970) *Fish is Fish*. New York: Dragonfly Books.

Lotherington, H. (2020) Remixing emergent literacy education: Cross-age, plurilingual, multimedia adventures in narrative teaching and writing. In O. Erstad, R. Flewitt, B. Kümmerling-Meibauer and I.S.P. Pereira (eds) *The Routledge Handbook of Digital Literacies in Early Childhood* (pp. 227–241). New York: Routledge.

Lucero, A. (2018) Oral narrative retelling among emergent bilinguals in a dual language immersion program. *International Journal of Bilingual Education and Bilingualism* 21 (2), 248–264.

Maureen, I.Y., van der Meij, H. and de Jong, T. (2020) Enhancing storytelling activities to support early (digital) literacy development in early childhood education. *International Journal of Early Childhood* 52 (1), 55–76.

Moll, L.C. (2014) *L.S. Vygotsky and Education*. New York: Routledge.

Oakley, G., Wildy, H. and Berman, Y.E. (2018) Multimodal digital text creation using tablets and open-ended creative apps to improve the literacy learning of children in early childhood classrooms. *Journal of Early Childhood Literacy* 20 (4), 655–679.

Quinn, M. and Bliss, M. (2021) Moving beyond tracing: The nature, availability and quality of digital apps to support children's writing. *Journal of Early Childhood Literacy* 21 (2), 230–258.

Rideout, V. (2017) *The Common Sense Census: Media Use by Kids Age Zero to Eight* (pp. 1–56). San Francisco, CA: Common Sense Media.

Rodriguez-Mojica, C. (2019) Instructional supports: Facilitating or constraining emergent bilinguals' production of oral explanations? *International Multilingual Research Journal* 13 (1), 51–66.

Roskos, K. and Christie, J. (2011) The play–literacy nexus and the importance of evidence-based techniques in the classroom. *American Journal of Play* 4 (2), 204–224.

Rowe, D.W. (2013) Recent trends in research on young children's authoring. In L. Larson and J. Marsh (eds) *The Sage Handbook of Early Childhood Literacy* (pp. 423–447). Thousand Oaks, CA: Sage.

Rowe, D.W. (2018) The unrealized promise of emergent writing: Reimagining the way forward for early writing instruction. *Language Arts* 95 (4), 229–241.

Rowe, D.W. and Miller, M.E. (2016) Designing for diverse classrooms: Using iPads and digital cameras to compose eBooks with emergent bilingual/biliterate four-year-olds. *Journal of Early Childhood Literacy* 16 (4), 425–472.

Rowsell, J. (2014) Toward a phenomenology of contemporary reading. *Australian Journal of Language and Literacy* 37 (2), 117–127.

Saldaña, J. (2016) *The Coding Manual for Qualitative Researchers*. Thousand Oaks, CA: Sage.

Serafini, F. (2015) Multimodal literacy: From theories to practices. *Language Arts* 92 (6), 412–423.

Short, K.G. and Acevedo, M.V. (2016) Creating global understandings through play. In R. Myers and K. Whitmore (eds) *Reclaiming Early Childhood Literacies* (pp. 165–168). New York: Routledge.

Smith, B.E., Pacheco, M.B. and Khorosheva, M. (2021) Emergent bilingual students and digital multimodal composition: A systematic review of research in secondary classrooms. *Reading Research Quarterly* 56 (1), 33–52.

Stevens, R.J., Van Meter, P. and Warcholak, N.D. (2010) The effects of explicitly teaching story structure to primary grade children. *Journal of Literacy Research* 42, 159–198.

Taylor, S.V. and Leung, C.B. (2020) Multimodal literacy and social interaction: Young children's literacy learning. *Early Childhood Education Journal* 48 (1), 1–10.

Whitcomb, M.E. (1998) *Odd Velvet*. San Francisco, CA: Chronicle Books.

Whitmore, K.F. and Goodman, Y.M. (1995) Transforming curriculum in language and literacy. In S. Bredekamp and R. Teresa (eds) *Reaching Potentials: Transforming Early Childhood Curriculum and Assessment* (pp. 145–146). Washington, DC: National Association for the Education of Young Children.

Wohlwend, K.E. (2015) One screen, many fingers: Young children's collaborative literacy play with digital puppetry apps and touchscreen technologies. *Theory into Practice* 54 (2), 154–162.

Wohlwend, K. (2018) Play as the literacy of children: Imagining otherwise in contemporary childhoods. In D.E. Alvermann, N.J. Unrau, M. Sailors and R.B. Ruddell (eds) *Theoretical Models and Process of Literacy* (7th edn, pp. 301–317). New York: Routledge.

13 Teaching a Picturebook Author Study to Support Narrative Composing Processes of Emergent Bilinguals

Ted Kesler

Today's minilesson focuses on the writing skill, show, not tell. *Yvonne opens to a full-page spread from* Lilly's Big Day (Henkes, 2014) *that shows Ginger, as flower girl, is frozen in fear as the wedding ceremony is starting, and Lilly stands beside her and knows just what to do. This is a book her second graders have read several times so far. 'Listen and look for how Kevin Henkes SHOWS us in WORDS and PICTURES how Ginger is feeling.' She displays the full-page spread on the screen, using the document camera, so all children can see as she walks to the back of the meeting area and reads aloud this scene.*

Afterwards, Yvonne waits 10 seconds, tapping her chin, whispering 'you're thinking.' Yvonne returns to her stool. 'Kevin Henkes is SHOWING us how Ginger is feeling. Kevin Henkes is doing it in a COUPLE of ways. [Yvonne flashes two fingers.] What's Kevin Henkes doing to SHOW how Ginger is feeling?' [She points to the words and pictures.] She calls on students with raised thumbs. Rabia (all children's names are pseudonyms) comes up and embodies Ginger's expression in the illustration, with Ginger's big, round eyes, turned toward us, stiff body, and outstretched arms grasping the bouquet. Yvonne also wants attention to the words. She calls Raveena to come up and show 'ONE place in the words that SHOWS us how Ginger feels.' Raveena comes up and searches. Raveena points to the line, 'Ginger was as still as a stone.' Yvonne reads it aloud. 'Let's all do that,' and she and the students embody 'still as a stone.'[1]

This was an excerpt from a minilesson that lasted 15 minutes. In her minilesson, Yvonne demonstrated several practices of explicit instruction. She connected writing to reading. She guided the children to analyze *show, not tell* in one explicit example in a Kevin Henkes (KH) book. She restated the strategy multiple times and in multiple ways. Her teaching emphasized the why behind the what (Hindley, 1996), for the purpose of making the story interesting to the reader, emphasizing the audience. She established clear expectations for their work. She modeled prosocial behaviors, such as 'stand and teach your colleagues' and her response to students' suggestions.

Equally important were all of Yvonne's pragmatic and multimodal cues to express instruction. She modulated her voice and consistently emphasized terms that were central to the lesson. She scanned the class and moved around the meeting area, adjusting her proximity to various students to catch their attention. She used consistent gestures to indicate expectations, such as tapping her chin for thinking, and to emphasize concepts, such as when she held up two fingers to emphasize words and pictures. She encouraged children to embody characters' feelings to support their inferential thinking. She practiced wait time for children's responses, and skillfully moved them between whole-class and partnership work to generate more thinking. She displayed the full-page spread so all children could easily reference the words and pictures. She was establishing and reinforcing specific, contextual language and tools that were central for the application of *show, not tell*, for children's own picturebooks.

Yvonne's instruction was part of a second-grade KH author study that she and her three second-grade colleagues conducted for six weeks. I am the ELA staff developer at their school. After watching videos of KH's composing process, the teachers and I committed to making art and design integral parts of each day's work, transforming the writing workshop into a composing workshop in our second-grade KH author study. (We provide the complete unit plans at https://tinyurl.com/KHUnitofStudy, including our LbD objectives.) We used the Learning by Design (LbD) framework, based in multiliteracies theory (Cope & Kalantzis, 2015), applying a reflexive pedagogy that melded both didactic and authentic methods responsively to students' learning needs. Briefly, in didactic methods, the teacher, in position of authority, transmits knowledge to students. Rather than knowledge that is imposed, authentic methods take the lead from students, pursue their interests and motivations and promote the social participation of learners. This framework was supportive for teaching students to use KH books as mentor texts: texts that would teach them the many craft moves he uses.

In this chapter, I address the following questions based in the work we did:

(1) What does a multimodal approach to writing instruction look like?
(2) How does a multimodal approach support the composing processes of young emergent bilinguals?
(3) What are the challenges of multimodal literacy teaching?
(4) What are the implications of multimodal composing for young children?

I begin with the theoretical framework that guided our work. I then provide context for the study which describes what a multimodal approach to writing instruction looks like. Next, I report some of the findings of implementing this unit of study that demonstrate how our composing workshop supported young emergent bilinguals. In this discussion I address both challenges and implications of our multimodal approach to composing workshop.

Theoretical Framework

The 'multi-' prefix in a multiliteracies framework embraces specific sociocultural contexts for every literacy event and multimodality. When creating multiliteracies theory, the New London Group (1996: 74) emphasized design work to demonstrate that any semiotic activity 'is an active and dynamic process, and not something governed by static rules.' They described three elements to design: available designs ('resources for meaning; available designs of meaning'), designing ('the work performed on/with available designs in the semiotic process') and the redesigned (the products of design work) (New London Group, 1996: 77). They explained, 'designing always involves the transformation of Available Designs; it always involves making new use of old materials' (New London Group, 1996: 76). Moreover, the redesigned produces 'new meaning, something through which meaning-makers remake themselves' (New London Group, 1996: 76). Concurrently, the redesigned relies on 'historically and culturally received patterns of meaning' and 'is the unique product of human agency: a transformed meaning' (New London Group, 1996: 76).

Design work is inherently multimodal. Modes refer to historical, social and cultural sign systems that are available for making and representing meaning, including speech, writing, still and moving images, gestures, music. Each mode has affordances, or 'what it is possible to express and represent readily, easily, with a mode' (Jewitt & Kress, 2003: 14), based on its material features (such as writing and drawing tools in two-dimensional space across pages for picturebooks) and on the social and cultural history of that mode. Each mode enables a system of signs – 'the fusions of meaning and form' (Jewitt & Kress, 2003: 10) – that are used purposefully within a specific sociocultural context and, in their use, signs are transformed or newly made.

Kress (2003) defines texts as the products of social action. Composing is a more apt term than writing to describe the process of creating a text using one or more modes of expression, as it avoids valuing writing over other modes. Composing then is the deliberate use of signs, using specific modes and media, to generate meaning for what the sign-maker intends to represent of the world. A more apt term for this deliberate composing process is design work, or 'how people make use of the resources that are available at a given moment in a specific communicational environment to realize their interests as makers of a message/text' (Jewitt & Kress, 2003: 17). Through this deliberate act, the sign-maker's potential for meaning is changed. 'That change to a person's inner resource, both through representation to the outer-world and through representation to their inner world, can be thought of as learning' (Jewitt & Kress, 2003: 13). Our author study with our second-grade students raises the following question: 'how does learning happen differently or in the same way when we engage with "knowledge" – or the world much more generally – through different modes?' (Jewitt & Kress, 2003: 4). We realized that analysis of the second graders' use of signs would reveal 'the learning engaged in by the maker-of-the-sign-as-learner' (Jewitt & Kress, 2003: 12).

Picturebooks are a particularly powerful form of semiotic representation. Sipe (1998) explained a synergy of words and pictures. By synergy, Sipe means that 'the total effect depends not only on the union of the text and illustrations but also on the perceived interactions and transactions between these two parts' (Sipe, 1998: 98–99) and is greater than either the text or illustrations alone. To emphasize this synergy, Sipe (2001) blends the words as picturebooks. Picturebooks are multimodal because they include three primary modes for constructing meaning: visual images, design elements (e.g. layout, typography, color) and written language. Sipe (1998: 106) explains that, because of the multimodal construction of picturebooks, readers oscillate between the visual, textual and design elements 'in a potentially endless process' of meaning-making. As students designed their own picturebooks, influenced by KH's work, we anticipated oscillation of narrative expression in their multimodal constructions.

These outcomes were what we were aiming for in our KH unit of study. We wanted our second graders to study available designs in KH's picturebooks, and actively engage in design work for their own narratives, resulting in redesigned picturebooks. For transformed meaning of redesigned work, the New London Group (1996: 77) called on teachers and students to develop and apply a metalanguage: 'a language for talking about language, images, texts, and meaning-making interactions.' A metalanguage is 'a tool kit for working on semiotic activities' (New London Group, 1996: 77) such as picturebooks, applied flexibly and creatively to serve authors' intentions. The opening vignette depicts Yvonne's reflexive pedagogy to develop her students' metalanguage.

Study Context

This study took place in a public early childhood school (Grades pre-K through 3) in a large northeast city. The school serves the local community. The school population is 87% Asian, 1% Black, 8% Hispanic or Latinx and 2% White. Fifty-nine percent of students are English language learners, and 11% are students with special needs. The school serves a

Table 13.1 Second-grade class demographics

Class 2A	Class 2B	Class 2C	Class 2D
Yvonne (22 years teaching)	Jessica (12 years teaching)	Angela (12 years teaching)	Karen (4 years teaching + 10 years as assistant teacher)
22 Students 9 ENLs 1 special needs student	22 Students 7 ENLs	23 Students 8 ENLs	23 Students 9 ENLs

predominantly immigrant and economically disadvantaged population (67% free or reduced-price lunch). Seventy-eight percent of families are Chinese immigrants. Mandarin is the predominant language in the home. Fifty-five percent of students are emergent English learners and 20% speak two or more languages other than English.

The four teachers are experienced, general education second-grade teachers and White, cis-gendered women, with an average of 12.5 years as lead teachers. Table 13.1 shows their years of experience, class sizes and demographics at the time of this study ($n = 90$). Yvonne had a paraprofessional to serve one student with learning dis/abilities at the time of this study. I am a White, cis-gendered man, who also is an associate professor at the local college. None of us speaks other languages. During field work for this study, my role shifted to observer-participant, in which I 'observe[d] and interact[ed] closely enough with members to establish an insider's identity without participating in those activities constituting the core of group membership' (Adler & Adler, 1998: 85). During workshop time, I sometimes offered instructional ideas, or asked clarifying questions, or also conferred with students as they worked. These were interactions the teachers were used to in our ongoing work. I had 12 visits during six weeks of implementation of the author study, from February through mid-March.

Our Kevin Henkes Study

Prior to this redesigned unit, the teachers had conducted a KH author study for several years. Consistent with social cognition (Vygotsky, 1978; Wertsch, 1991), the teachers valued writing workshops, which provide extended time for students' authentic writing projects within a writing community that enables writers' perspectives and readers' demands (Harwayne, 1992). The writing workshop generally has three phases: it begins with a mini-lesson of approximately 10–15 minutes; followed by workshop time of approximately 25 minutes; and ends with a sharing session of approximately 10 minutes.

I now highlight a few ways in which we valued design and turned the writing workshop into a composing workshop, building on Kress (2003).

Consistent with author and picturebook studies with children (Hindley, 1996; Maderazo *et al.*, 2010; Martens *et al.*, 2012; Pantaleo, 2016a, 2016b; Zapata *et al.*, 2015), we emphasized an inquiry stance. First, we immersed our students in KH's picturebooks, making sure our students paid attention to his craft of art and design as much as his writing. We gave a balance of minilessons focusing on elements of art and design principles, making sure they learned '*what* the writing conveyed, *how* [Kevin Henkes] employed text and image to create meaning, and *why* the text and images moved us as readers' (Dawes *et al.*, 2019: 164). Consequently, the children learned 'a disposition towards inquiry' in addition to the craft of picturebook making. For example, we would ask, 'How does Kevin Henkes show character emotions?' Students would notice facial expressions, such as the shape of characters' eyes or eyebrows, the shape of mouths, and body positions. We taught them peritextual elements such as the dedication, the title page and about the author.

In our LbD pedagogy, we explored the following elements of art and design in KH's picturebooks: layout, details in drawings, speech bubbles and labels, color, use of lines, framing, patterns, balance, movement, proportion, typography and perspective. We also explored craft moves that often oscillated between words and pictures, such as his use of ellipses, repetition, show not tell, vivid verbs and 'sparkly language,' ways of showing elapsed time, sound words (onomatopoeia), and ending with a twist. We made sure our anchor charts, checklists and rubrics equally valued both writing and design. For example, we gave children a checklist of art elements to search for in KH's books, with space to add new ones. Consistent with writing workshop educators' advice, we provided copies of his books for students' investigation and application during workshop time. We encouraged them to explore the books alone, in dyads and in small groups, and to be influenced by his composing decisions.

We put blank 11½" × 17" paper in the writing center which children folded in half to draft their picturebooks. We provided various sized strips of blank white paper for writing. We also cut out many blank frames, consistent with the range of framing KH uses, such as ovals, small and large squares, rectangles and circles, and put out sticky putty at tables. We taught children to use sticky putty on the back of their writing strips and illustrations, so they could move them around on their pages as they designed their picturebooks, exploring layout and typography choices that they noticed in KH picturebooks. For their final products, we invited children to 'glue them down,' which gave permanence to their design decisions. Children also had access to drawing supplies, such as markers, colored pencils and crayons. During composing workshop, children were free to compose: to 'use your time wisely' to draw, write, design and discuss their stories, as we conferred one-on-one, with dyads or in small groups to support their work.

A multimodal approach to writing instruction

Table 13.2 shows an inventory of all writing instruction practices I observed and teachers also documented, based in the three phases of the writing workshop. I documented 41 minilessons, 39 shares, 80 teacher-student conferences, 16 peer-to-peer conferences and 27 small-group conferences. The opening vignette is an example of one of these minilessons. It provides some insights into mediators teachers used to make their teaching explicit. In addition to Yvonne's display of the full-page spread from *Lilly's Big Day*, she used embodiments, gestures, gaze, proximity, modulation of her voice, and several charts and signs to convey her teaching.

Table 13.2 Explicit instruction during composing workshop

Phases and location	Explicit instruction	Environmental mediators
Minilesson (approx. 15 min.) *Location*: meeting area, including benches, pillows, rug area	• Teacher demonstrating application of writing, art and design • Delving into mentor texts • Students' examples of skills and strategies at work • Inquiry question (e.g. 'What craft moves does Kevin Henkes use in one of his books to tell the story?') • Experiencing, conceptualizing, analyzing and applying anchor charts and checklists	• Interactive displays, such as videos, specific pages of KH books, teacher's writing sample, etc. • Teacher's writing sample • Kevin Henkes books • Students' work in writing folders • Whiteboard easel and dry erase markers • Anchor charts and checklists
Workshop time (approx. 25 min.) *Location*: classroom, including: desk areas, two rug areas, floor chairs and cushions to spread out in various areas	• Independent composing time • Teacher-student small group work • Teacher-student conferences • Peer-to-peer conferences • Mid-workshop teacher instruction	• Art supplies, including: colored pencils, pencils, pens (green revision pens, red editing pens, black and blue writing pens), markers, sticky putty, different shaped frames, blank paper for words • Writing folders, including checklists, high-frequency words, blend and digraphs chart, story flow map plan, dummy book • Flexible seating • Anchor charts on display • Kevin Henkes books
Share (approx. 10 min.) *Location*: meeting area, including benches, pillows, rug area	• Author's chair, featuring up to three children who share their work and ask for feedback • Partner shares • Teacher shares student examples to highlight specific skills and strategies • Try-its • Advice • Reflections	• Interactive display board • Kevin Henkes books • Students' work in writing folders • Whiteboard easel and dry erase markers • Anchor charts and checklists

I provide more details about teachers' explicit instruction in another paper (Kesler, forthcoming).

Mediational tools were central to supporting the work of teachers and students in every phase of the composing workshop. Teachers co-constructed these tools with students, providing mediational means for developing social cognition (Vygotsky, 1978; Wertsch, 1991). A prime example was the story flow map they used to plan their stories. We designed this flow map to replicate the narrative structure of many KH stories. Figure 13.1 shows three displays that Jessica actively uses in her minilesson. On the interactive display screen is the flow map of her story, and each child is using the same flow map for their story plans. On the easel chart is 'Writers can plan for and rehearse their stories before drafting.' The chart specifies the procedural steps: first, on their own; then with a partner; then make revisions. Teachers demonstrated speaking into a pretend microphone as they rehearsed their stories, using their flow maps. My data sources show students doing this practice for their own stories: internalizing the use of these mediational tools for their own authentic purposes. For revision work, teachers specified use of a green pen. In Figure 13.1, Jessica is holding and pointing out details on a second chart that elaborates constructive feedback partners should provide. The chart values art and design: 'What pictures might go along with this part of the story?' 'What kind of layout might you use?' 'Think about setting details, clothing details, facial expressions, layout, use of fonts.' Jessica was explaining, and building conceptual and procedural understandings, using reflexive pedagogy. These charts remained on display as children worked.

Figure 13.1 Jessica's mediational displays

Figure 13.2 Students at work

Figure 13.2 shows children during composing work. Both proximal and distal are two partnerships with one flow map between them, in peer-to-peer conferences, applying mediational tools that Jessica explained for their own authentic purposes. At their tables are stacks of KH books for reference. In the upper right corner, the charts are on display on the easel. One boy looks up at an anchor chart (not pictured), hanging from a clothesline, for direction as his partner waits in the distance. The anchor chart displays a Tree Map of 'What are Kevin Henkes' Craft Moves We Know?' which was work they did previously. Figure 13.3 shows one child's

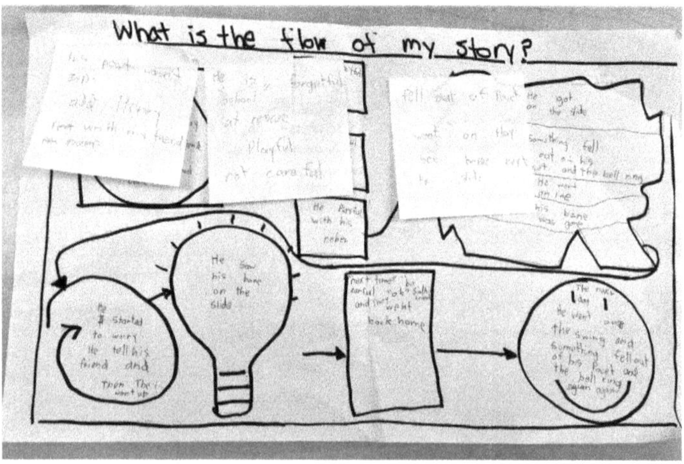

Figure 13.3 Student's flow map with revisions

revised flow map, with sticky notes and green pen revisions overlaying his plans from the previous session. Reflexive pedagogy supported students' social cognition as they applied these mediational tools for their story development (Vygotsky, 1978; Wertsch, 1991).

How Our Multimodal Approach Supported the Composing Processes of Young Emergent Bilinguals

To show how our multimodal approach supported the composing processes of young emergent bilinguals, I analyze one opening from one student's picturebook. (We go into more detail of this analysis in another paper; Kesler *et al.*, 2021.) Nadine was an emergent bilingual, with Mandarin as her primary language. She was shy and reluctant to speak English in class and with me. Nevertheless, she was a diligent student and was performing on grade level in both reading (Level N, DRA 28/30) and writing (Level 3). She has a little sister. Both her parents are Chinese speaking, and her teacher had a translator for conferences with Nadine's mom. In Nadine's story, 'Mimi The Kindist Person of the World!' [sic], the two central characters, Mimi and her older sister, Amy, are pandas. Mimi and Amy go to the cupcake store, when Mimi is attracted to the beautiful blossoms outside and wanders off. She then is lost, until Amy finds her. In the fourth opening (Figure 13.4), Amy finds Mimi, which is the resolution of her story.

Figure 13.4 Full-page spread from Nadine's story

The written description on this page is, 'Suddenly Amy dindin't saw Mimi! So she herd a voise calling out, "Amy! Amy!"' Nadine shows tension with the jagged frame she drew around the words.

45 T: So, tell me, {you made this. That's really cool!} {I trace the jagged lines again}. Why did you do that? # Just to show that they couldn't find each other and they were SCARED? [Nods.] So, {this helps show they were scared?} {I trace the jagged lines again.} [Nods.][1]

The illustration enhances this plot development. In the top left circular frame, both Amy and Mimi are looking directly at the viewer at eye level, making a demand for our involvement. The trees and the swirly clouds and the horizon line establish that they are both now outdoors, where Mimi wandered on the previous page, attracted to the blossoms. Nadine shows distance by drawing Amy at a public distance and Mimi small and distant in the upper left quadrant. In addition to Amy's speech tag, 'What is that noise?' Nadine makes two question marks to show Amy's concern and wonder as she searches for her lost sister. She draws Amy's arms outstretched downwards in supplication. Nadine shows Mimi's anxiety in a few ways. She draws parallel curved lines under Mimi's speech tag, 'Amy! Amy!' She draws a downturned mouth on Mimi to indicate her concern, and her arms outstretched and waving as she calls. I asked Nadine about the parallel curved lines:

43 T: So you're showing that it's LOUD, that she's calling her from a DISTANCE, and that it's traveling, her voice is TRAVELING? [Nadine nods.]

Nadine therefore used the lines to show sound waves traveling to indicate that Mimi was shouting for Amy. It is only in the illustration that Nadine conveys the worry and anxiety of the sisters as they search for each other. Nadine therefore shows the tension of the climactic moment of her story in the synergy of words, picture and design elements.

The bottom picture in the rectangular frame on the verso shows their reunion. Nadine zooms out, showing the cupcake store partially off-frame on the right. She keeps both Amy and Mimi at a distance, with their full frontal eye-level gaze at the viewer, on a horizontal, with a mountain in the background. The tree where Mimi stood, the swirly cloud with the yellow sun peeking through also establish the outdoor setting. Amy has an open smile and Mimi has a smile with the speech tag, 'Yay!' Their downward turned outstretched arms are inviting a hug.

This illustration is coupled with the diagonal words on the recto: 'She herd the voise and rellize that it was Mimi's voise, so she followed that voise, then .... She is found! "Horray!"' What is interesting is Nicole's design decisions for the layout of these words. The words fall diagonally, then are paused by the ellipses after *then*, to the grand resolution: 'She is found!' The quotation marks around *Horray!* indicate that both sisters shout it. Nadine indicated that she got the idea for this layout from studying KH books, and in particular *Wemberley Worried* (Henkes, 2010). For example, we had the following exchange about her use of small smiley faces on the recto:

54 T: {THIS!} {I find the page and point to details on the page.} Oh! With {all the QUESTION MARKS} {I point to the question marks on the page.} Is that what you meant? So, you did all the SMILEY faces like that. {Is that what you're talking about?} {I remove *Wemberley Worried*, so we can again focus on her p. 7} ['Yeah.'] Oh. Wow! That's smart. And is that why {you made the, the PRINT BIGGER?} {I point to 'Hooray!'} / Like, {the print} {I trace the diagonal writing}, did you try to make the print BIGGER? [Nods.] Is that also why {you underlined HERE?} {I point to the underline under 'Hooray!'} ['Yeah.'] Like they do {HERE?} {I focus again on the writing in *Wemberley Worried*}, like Kevin Henkes did? [Nods.] Okay. So, they found each other.

Nadine and I establish her intentions to transform KH's available designs for her re-designed narrative purposes. Her design decisions of font, typography, layout and bright yellow smiley face icons scattered around the page enhance the joyful resolution of her story.

Discussion

This study shows the equal attention teachers gave to words, art and design, for narrative understandings (Martens *et al.*, 2012), developing children's semiotic landscapes (Jewitt & Kress, 2003). It was equally valid to show sadness by drawing a downturned mouth, or to express worry with question mark icons, or to use a cluster of yellow smiley faces in the background to show the joy of reconciliation. In our LbD framework, teachers were explicit in all their practices and mediational tools, blending didactic and authentic pedagogy (Cope & Kalantzis, 2015), for the *synergy* of words, pictures and design (Sipe, 1998).

They supported this synergy in the design of their learning environments. Each workshop time, teachers played soothing music in the background. Children had choices of where to do their work: lying on the floor, sitting on scoop rockers or stools or cubes or bean bags or cushions or benches, using portable desks or at their desks. They had choices of whether to work alone or with a partner (see Figure 13.2). They had choices of using composing materials purposefully. They had choices of how to use their workshop time for drawing, layout, writing. While teachers monitored and directed these choices, they always gave it back to the children, by having them evaluate if they used their time wisely, if they were productive in their work, if they gave their best effort, or how they might improve tomorrow.

This explicit instruction enabled children's knowledge transformation (Bereiter & Scardamalia, 1987) and metalinguistic awareness (Kesler, 2020; Kesler *et al.*, 2021; Maderazo *et al.*, 2010; Martens *et al.*, 2012; New London Group, 1996; Pantaleo, 2016a, 2016b). Children learned to draft, revise, and edit recursively, supported by the tools of their learning environment. For example, in Angela's class reflection, the children discussed how mistakes were 'no big deal' because they had correction tape to fix up. Sticky tack also made it easy 'to move things around.' They learned to play around with their design decisions prior to publishing. This process of revising their texts and rethinking rhetorical choices provided 'a strong indication of increasing compositional maturity' (Bereiter & Scardamalia, 1987: 266).

The challenges of multimodal literacy teaching

It is important to return to the term *reflexive*. Cope and Kalantzis (2015) explain that reflexive pedagogy is:

> the constant vigilance teachers must have, in order to gauge which pedagogical move is appropriate at different moments of the learning process, for different students, and for different subject matters. The mix and the sequence can always vary, and teachers need to be constantly reading student reactions to each move in order to determine the next best move. (Cope & Kalantzis, 2015: 16)

Implementing reflexive pedagogy was challenging, as the teachers expressed in their reflective entries and in our grade group reflective discussion. Each lesson took lots of preparation: preparing materials and mediational tools; finding and marking relevant examples in KH books; reading through students' work for strengths and needs. They made decisions 'on the fly,' such as announcing mid-workshop for children to use blank paper for their words instead of writing words directly in their draft picturebooks, so that words could more easily be designed. The teachers expressed 'next time,' 'moving forward,' 'I need to work on …'. But they also expressed what surprised them, what inspired children, what they would definitely do again next year. They expressed their efforts to be intentional. For example, Jessica wrote: 'I wanted to be intentional that all students were able to identify and understand the purpose of each craft move' and 'I made sure to be more intentional of how writing partners help each other.'

Implications of multimodal composing for young children

This study contributes to studies that report positive outcomes of infusing multimodal work within reading and writing processes and workshops (e.g. Dawes *et al.*, 2019; Maderazo *et al.*, 2010; Martens *et al.*,

2012; Pantaleo, 2016a, 2016b; Zapata *et al.*, 2015), for author studies using mentor texts (e.g. Graves, 1983; Harwayne, 1992; Hindley, 1996). I showed the value of enabling students to express their narrative understandings across multiple sign systems (Kenner & Kress, 2003). Emergent English language users especially need consistent opportunities to develop multimodal repertoires to generate meaning (Bengochea *et al.*, 2017; Kenner & Kress, 2003). Many more classroom-based studies are needed, particularly with emergent bi- and multilingual populations such as ours. For example, how do they coordinate their language repertoires with their use of other modal resources to facilitate design work? We also wonder how children might respond to authors with cultural backgrounds similar to their own, who use narrative structures that 'conform to the structure of the kind of stories they have heard at home' (McCabe, 1997: 463). We hope the positive outcomes in our study will encourage more teacher teams to take these transformational risks.

Note

(1) Transcription conventions: ALL CAPITALS = spoken louder, with emphasis; { } { } = coupled brackets to show overlapping speech and actions; [ ] = actions; descriptions; ['']= interjections; # = approx. 5-second pause

References

Adler, P.A. and Adler, P. (1998) Observational techniques. In N.K. Denzin and Y.S. Lincoln (eds) *Collecting and Interpreting Qualitative Materials* (pp. 79–109). Thousand Oaks, CA: Sage.

Bengochea, A., Sembiante, S.F. and Gort, M. (2017) An emergent bilingual child's multimodal choices in sociodramatic play. *Journal of Early Childhood Literacy* 18 (1), 38–70.

Bereiter, C. and Scardamalia, M. (1987) *The Psychology of Written Composition*. Hillsdale, NJ: Lawrence Erlbaum.

Cope, B. and Kalantzis, M. (2015) The things you do to know: An introduction to the pedagogy of multiliteracies. In B. Cope and M. Kalantzis (eds) *A Pedagogy of Multiliteracies: Learning by Design* (pp. 1–36). New York: Macmillan.

Dawes, E.T., Cappiello, M.A. and Magee, L. (2019) Portraits of perseverance: Creating picturebook biographies with third graders. *Language Arts* 96 (3), 153–166.

Graves, D.H. (1993) *Writing: Teachers & Children at Work*. Portsmouth, NH: Heinemann.

Harwayne, S. (1992) *Lasting Impressions: Weaving Literature into the Writing Workshop*. Portsmouth, NH: Heinemann.

Henkes, K. (2010) *Wemberley Worried*. New York: Greenwillow.

Henkes, K. (2014) *Lilly's Big Day*. New York: Greenwillow.

Hindley, J. (1996) *In the Company of Children*. York, ME: Stenhouse.

Jewitt, C. and Kress, G. (2003) *Multimodal Literacy*. New York: Peter Lang.

Kenner, C. and Kress, G. (2003) The multisemiotic resources of biliterate children. *Journal of Early Childhood Literacy* 3 (2), 179–202.

Kesler, T. (2020) Does it have to be a real story? Assessing an emergent writer. *Language and Education* 34 (5), 440–468.

Kesler, T. (forthcoming) Explicit instruction in the teaching of writing in a 2nd grade author study.

Kesler, T., Darrell, K., Moss, Y., Pasternak, J. and Valco, A. (2021) Designing on the page: Composing picturebooks in a Kevin Henkes author study. *Journal of Early Childhood Literacy*. doi:10.1177/1468798421995527

Kress, G. (2003) *Literacy in the New Media Age*. London: Routledge.

Maderazo, C., Martens, P., Croce, K., Martens, R., Doyle, M., Aghalarov, S. and Noble, R. (2010) Beyond picture walks: Revaluing picturebooks as written and pictorial texts. *Language Arts* 87 (6), 437–446.

Martens, P., Martens, R., Doyle, M.H., Loomis, J. and Aghalarov, S. (2012) Learning from picturebooks: Reading and writing multimodally in first grade. *The Reading Teacher* 66 (4), 285–294.

McCabe, A. (1997) Cultural background and storytelling: A review and implications for schooling. *Elementary School Journal* 97 (5), 453–473.

New London Group (1996) A pedagogy of multiliteracies: Designing social futures. *Harvard Educational Review* 66 (1), 60–93. doi:10.17763/haer.66.1.17370n67v22j160u

Pantaleo, S. (2016a) Primary students' understanding and appreciation of the artwork in picturebooks. *Journal of Early Childhood Literacy* 16 (2), 228–255.

Pantaleo, S. (2016b) Primary students transgress story world boundaries in their multimodal compositions. *Journal of Research in Childhood Education* 30 (2), 237–251.

Sipe, L.R. (1998) How picture books work: A semiotically framed theory of text-picture relationships. *Children's Literature in Education* 29 (2), 97–108.

Sipe, L. (2001) Picturebooks as aesthetic objects. *Literacy Teaching and Learning* 6 (1), 23–42.

Vygotsky, L. (1978) *Mind in Society*. Cambridge, MA: Harvard University Press.

Wertsch, J.V. (1991) *Voices of the Mind: A Sociocultural Approach to Mediated Action*. Cambridge, MA: Harvard University Press.

Zapata, A., Valdez-Gainer, N., Haworth, C. and Zapata, I.F.B. (2015) Bilingual picturebook making in the elementary classroom. *Language Arts* 92 (5), 343–358.

14 A STEERS Model of Literacy to Tackle the Challenges of the Digital for Young Bilingual Learners

Sara Hawley

Introduction

This chapter is about the experience of young bilingual learners when an online writing intervention, a wiki, was introduced into classroom practice. It proposes a model of literacy which highlights the importance of sponsors, tools, emotions, experiences, reflexivity and syncretism (STEERS) when navigating the boundaries between home and schooled literacy practices. This model arises from a detailed case study which I carried out as a teacher-researcher to examine the impact of using the wiki, with its affordances for collaborative online publishing, in a diverse inner London elementary classroom with over 70% bilingual learners. The wiki was set up in response to the ongoing concern of many commentators (Buckingham, 2007; Ito *et al.*, 2013) about the apparent disconnect between the classroom and the vibrant and connected multimodal world outside. Because of the large number of bilingual learners, my intention was to follow the advice of Cummins (2015: 243) for educators to create 'interactional spaces that affirm students' identities in association with literacy.' Thus, it was a space where boundaries between work and play and between home and school were deliberately blurred, where pupils could continue at home what they had started both in the classroom and in the playground. Children were shown how to build up texts that incorporated different modes such as image and video in keeping with their practices and interests outside the school gates.

As I carried out the research, I started to look for new ways to theorize literacy that go beyond the notion of a 'literacy event,' problematizing sociocultural accounts of literacy and analyzing the complex interplay between people and objects – a sociomaterial perspective (Burnett & Merchant, 2020). The main aim of my study was to explore the ways in which the integration of the wiki influenced students' writing practices, with particular reference to the way in which their literacy learning was affected by social and material factors. The principal questions guiding the research were: (1) How do the social and material become woven or imbricated over time to shape literacy practices when a wiki is integrated into a classroom of eight- to nine-year-olds? and (2) Does this weave result in the same outcomes for all children and if not, why not?

Inspired by my own children's interactions with digital technology and the work of Ito *et al.* (2013: 6) on the potential for digital media to expand 'reach and accessibility ... so it is not just privileged youth who have these opportunities,' I was optimistic about the potential of the wiki to improve outcomes for all children because of the focus on their interests. I hoped to find, as Kalantzis and Cope (2012: 11) did, that Generation P (participatory) would, 'when given more engaging and more varied learning spaces, more relevant to the kind of world that [they] already inhabit ... take greater responsibility for their learning.' However, during the pilot study for the research, it became clear that not all children were benefiting from the intervention in the same way. It became clear that not all children were able to thrive in this space because the *function* of technology, that is, the perception of what it can be used for, differs across homes. The data in this study (like Lemphane & Prinsloo's 2014 work with families from different households) point to the 'complex and socially variable nature of form-function relationships' and the fact that 'the same interactive multimedia screen might ... not be functionally the same across these settings' (Lemphane & Prinsloo, 2014: 15).

Wikis in education

Broad claims have been made about the potential benefits of wikis to change our approach to writing because of their functionality, the ease of editing and revision, as well as the possibility for asynchronous collaborative communication that can blur the boundaries between home and school and between formal and informal learning. According to Lundin (2008: 445), a wiki 'could broaden the definition of writing to include new media elements and deep collaboration.' Research on wikis in education has mainly focused on their affordances for collaborative writing. Several studies in higher education and secondary school (Li & Zhu, 2017; Mak & Coniam, 2008) investigate the dynamics of collaboration as second language (L2) learners plan, draft and revise texts in small groups. One of the main themes emerging from the small number of wiki studies carried out in primary schools is the importance of a pedagogy that scaffolds the collaborative process (Pifarré & Fisher, 2011; Pifarré & Li, 2018). Other wiki studies in primary settings (Pifarré & Fisher [2011] with first language learners; Woo *et al.* [2011] with L2 learners) have focused on the affordances of wikis to encourage revision and editing.

Although introducing students to collaborative writing was one advantage of adding a wiki to my pedagogy, the main draws for me were first the possibility the wiki afforded for students to merge home and school literacy practices through asynchronous communication, and second the potential for them to incorporate multimodal elements into their texts. As Lundin (2008: 441) argued, 'the technology can open writing to easy and rhetorically sensitive incorporation of new media elements.' Thus, a pedagogy for the use of the wiki was devised in line with the ethos of New Literacy Studies, which sees literacy as a culturally embedded social practice that values informal literacies with the idea of allowing 'identities of competence' (Manyak, 2004) to develop.

Learning activities

The pedagogy that underpinned the intervention in the current study followed many of the principles in Burnett and Merchant's (2015: 272–273) Charter for Literacy Education. The aim of the wiki was to: 'recognise and build on students' repertoires of textual practices, acknowledge the role of multimodality in meaning making ... encourage improvisation and experimentation as well as the need to produce intelligible texts ... recognize the affective, embodied and material dimensions of meaning making ... promote collaboration around and through texts in negotiating meaning [and] ... ensure opportunities.' A *Wikispaces Classroom* was set up which offered me and the pupils the chance both to generate a set of linked pages and to add comments beneath each page. As a teacher, I could also invite selected users to a smaller 'wiki within the wiki' in order to customize work for different groups and promote collaborative work. The wiki pages were editable, with each version being saved.

The wiki was introduced during a two-hour lesson at the outset of the intervention: students were shown how to create their own pages and insert multimodal elements such as images, hyperlinks and videos, and groundrules were set for accurate and respectful contributions. Pupils were told that they could make their own pages on topics of their own interests, provided the content was appropriate and linked to learning. The aim was to encourage independent writing by creating a space that children could add to during out-of-school hours. In subsequent weeks, during regular weekly sessions, pupils were supported with text drafting, working with peers and individually to familiarize themselves with the software. Some class-based writing tasks that would normally be carried out in exercise books were done on the wiki with teacher modelling and scaffolding of the genre during lesson-time. Students were encouraged to continue working on these from home while also being allowed to draft unsolicited pages. Scaffolded homework tasks were also set on the wiki, such as drafting pages about their own countries, choosing and sharing favorite poems and writing about favorite authors or famous Greek historical characters. In all of these cases, pupils had prompts and models to follow. Lessons were also set aside in class for students to write collaboratively in pairs about non-fiction classwork topics. Fiction writing (versions of the Narnia story) from their exercise books was also published on the wiki. Students spent a lesson reading each other's stories on the wiki. In a subsequent lesson, they were asked to edit and improve their original work using ideas they had gleaned from one another. Thus, throughout the intervention, the wiki was woven into classroom practice in order to make use of the affordances for collaboration, revision, peer feedback and asynchronous communication to improve attitudes to and outcomes in writing.

Methodology

Research design

The current study was preceded by a pilot study with a different class of children. In response to what was observed online and in class during the pilot study, a theoretically informed research design was constructed that would afford insights into the complex relationships between the social and the material and the way in which they are layered across online and offline spaces. The aim was to explore how, when a wiki is integrated into classroom practice, the social and material become woven or imbricated (Leonardi, 2013) over time to shape literacy practices.

Participants

The present study was conducted over two academic years in a class of eight- and nine-year-olds (third and fourth grades) with the author working as a teacher-researcher and using ethnographic methods. A large variety of different languages were spoken by the children at home including languages from South and East Asia and the Middle East as well as European languages. Around 75% of students received pupil premium funding (a measure of social deprivation). Data were collected from the 27 pupil participants and five of their parents during the 12-month wiki intervention and over the following year when I continued to teach the same children.

Data collection

Data collection methods involved participant observation including online observation. Because of my role as teacher, I was 'participant as observer' rather than 'observer as participant' (Gold, 1958). Other data included interviews with pupils, parents and teachers, semi-structured individual interviews and focus groups (Flewitt, 2014). The choice of children to interview in the first term focus group interviews was made using purposive sampling techniques: the children who were participating most enthusiastically in the wiki were the ones chosen. At the end of the second term of the wiki, theoretical sampling was used to select the children for an interview. Data from interviews and observation were also triangulated with documents and texts, both those that were 'produced independently of any research project,' known commonly as 'found materials' (Hearn & Thomson, 2014: 157), and those generated by the research process such as the writing on the wiki.

Data analysis

The data were analyzed using a combination of NVivo software and manual color coding. The initial codes involved participant codes such as *fun or enjoyment*, process codes such as *peer scaffolding*, activity codes such as *handwriting versus typing*, strategy codes such as *revision/editing*, and relationship codes such as *community of practice*. Archer's (2000) identification of emergent properties of the 'people' and the 'parts' were used in conjunction with Leonardi's (2013) concept of sociomaterial imbrication to identify categories once the initial coding had taken place. The categories *social* and *material* were seen as analytically distinct as advised by Archer (2000) and Leonardi (2013), with further subcategories *online* and *offline* for each of these. The category *emergent properties* branched off each of these four categories in a mind map which helped me

Table 14.1 Case matrix (all names are pseudonyms)

Child	Demographic data	Mechanism/vector	Outcome
Morphogenesis – high extensibility			
Vladimir	EAL (English as an additional language) Pupil premium*	Own response to affordances/emergent properties of technology Parental reflexivity or response to affordances/emergent properties of technology	Enhanced engagement with schooled literacy Positive attainment outcomes
Katerina	EAL Pupil premium	Own response to emergent properties of technology Parental response to emergent properties of technology	Enhanced engagement with schooled literacy Positive attainment outcomes
Morphogenesis –moderate extensibility			
Zachary	EAL	Own response to technology Very limited home support	Improved outcomes in schooled literacy
Celine	EAL Pupil premium	Own response to emergent properties of technology Parental support around literacy	Improved outcomes in schooled literacy

Note: *Pupil premium denotes a child who receives or has received free school meals during their school career – an indicator of socioeconomic deprivation.

to unpick the distinct factors for each child and try to fathom the answer to why different children's outcomes and practices differed.

The theoretical sampling of children led to the development of three themes categorizing their practices according to high, moderate or low levels of extensibility. The case matrix in Table 14.1 shows the cases of high and moderate extensibility which led to morphogenesis (Archer, 2000), and will be discussed in detail in the Findings section below.

Findings

Cases of highly extensible practices

Vladimir was a child who was often disruptive in writing lessons, saying 'I feel sick in literacy' and requesting a writing frame to scaffold his work (see Figure 14.1). Yet he immediately applied himself to writing on the wiki, excited by the chance of adding images and videos to pages. His mother noted in an interview that, when given the choice at home during his 'device time' of whether to play games or work on the wiki, he chose

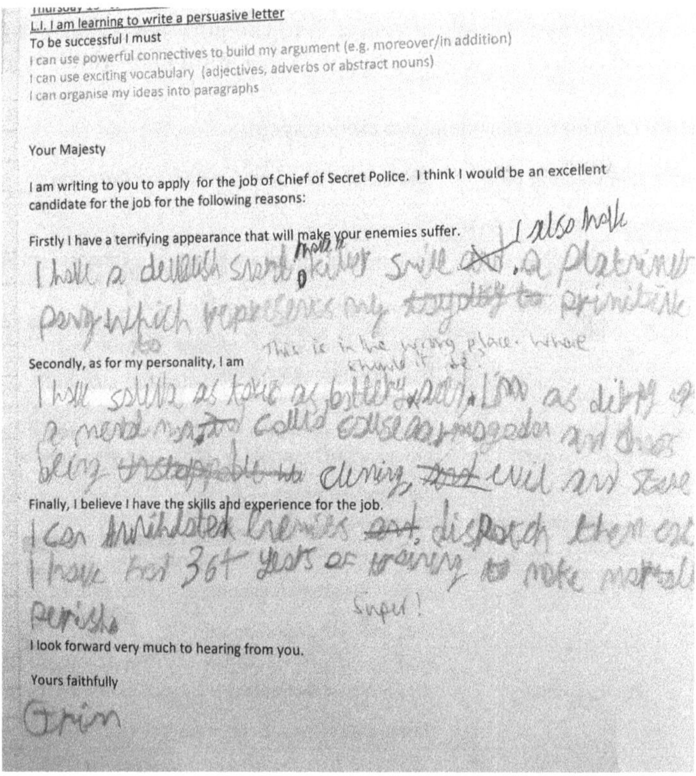
L.I. I am learning to write a persuasive letter
To be successful I must
I can use powerful connectives to build my argument (e.g. moreover/in addition)
I can use exciting vocabulary (adjectives, adverbs or abstract nouns)
I can organise my ideas into paragraphs

Your Majesty

I am writing to you to apply for the job of Chief of Secret Police. I think I would be an excellent candidate for the job for the following reasons:

Firstly I have a terrifying appearance that will make your enemies suffer.

Secondly, as for my personality, I am

Finally, I believe I have the skills and experience for the job.

I look forward very much to hearing from you.

Yours faithfully

Figure 14.1 Vladimir's writing at the start of the intervention

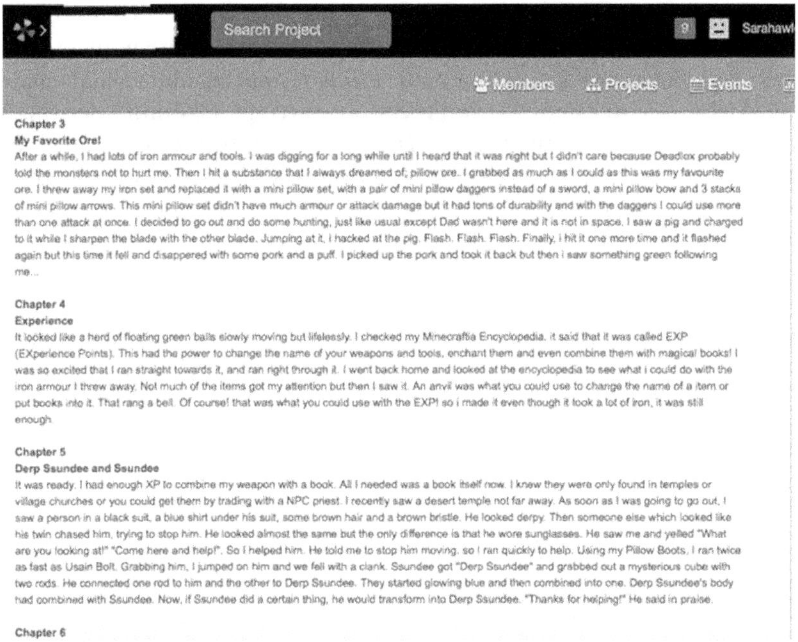

Figure 14.2 Vladimir's Minecraft narrative

the wiki. Within weeks, Vladimir and two friends were involved in building their own collaborative spaces on the wiki where they focused on a narrative based on their Minecraft play, each of them writing a different page in character on a mini-wiki (see Figure 14.2).

During focus group interviews, he spoke about how the wiki's affordance of asynchronous communication facilitated the social aspect of learning with peers:

> V: For example, it's the weekend, then you can just communicate with them on wikispaces, meet up with them and communicate with them. … What you are learning is you are learning how to learn from other people.

He spoke enthusiastically about the material elements of writing on the wiki, in particular liberation from his struggles with pen and paper:

> V: I prefer to type more than anyone else in the whole world … When you write on paper … you have to cross it out and it will be quite messy and with technology you can delete things without losing it with just a few clicks.

In cases of highly extensible literacy practices like Vladimir's, the unboundedness of the wiki allowed offline relationships to be taken up online in a way that was linked to learning. He and his friends moved between their online play on Minecraft to offline discussions about this in the playground in school, back online to the wiki where texts were composed collaboratively, and back to an offline discussion with parents where they were mentored and with me, the teacher, praising and taking notice.

Within six weeks of the intervention starting, Vladimir's writing in class had improved dramatically (see Figure 14.3). By the end of the intervention, he was transformed from one of the class's most reluctant writers to its highest achiever, generating large numbers of extended multimodal texts on subjects linked to his own interests as well as to topics being studied in class such as space.

Another case of high extensibility was Katerina, who arrived in class a few weeks after the wiki intervention started from southern Europe. New to the school and new to the UK, she spoke and wrote very little English. She quickly started contributing regularly to the wiki in response

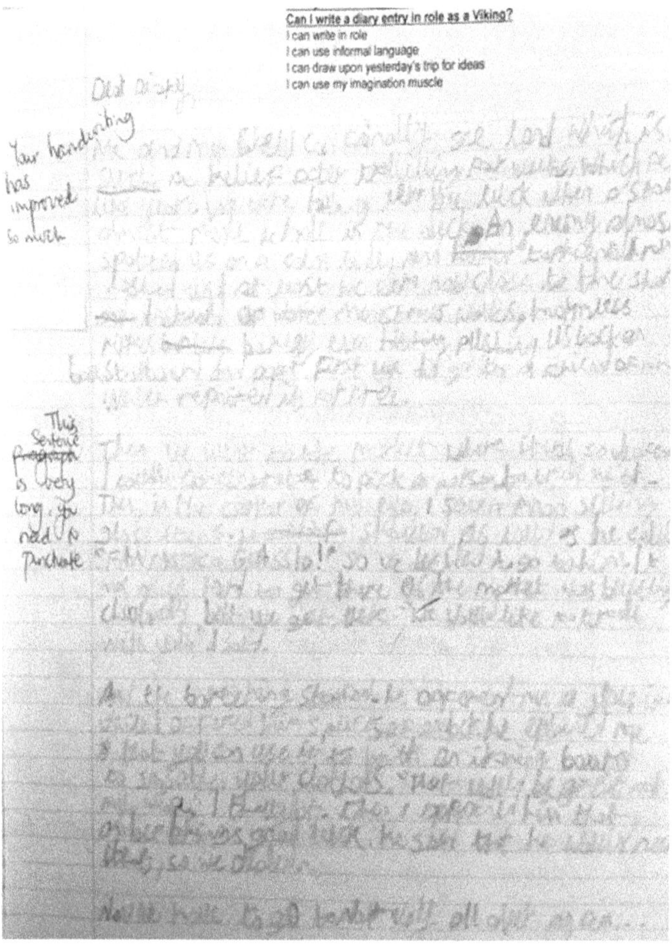

Figure 14.3 Vladimir's writing in class after six weeks

to the scaffolded tasks. However, in interviews, the role of her mum as literacy *sponsor* (Brandt, 1997) became clear.

K: The first time I made some mistakes, my mum said we need to do it together and then she helped me. I saw everybody's work and then I learned.

For parents like Katerina's, the material elements of the wiki, namely its affordance of making texts visible across time and space, provided an insight into what was going on at school, what was required in this project and what other children were capable of producing. A TV presenter in her home country, Katerina's mother spoke in an interview about how she saw wikispaces as beneficial not just in supporting her child's writing but in preparing her for the future:

S: What I noticed was that because she was new, she was able to access a lot of material outside school. Do you think that was helpful?
M: I also worked with her a lot ... I wanted her to catch up with other children because now secondary school is coming and people don't know when she came but they want results. So I was trying hard.
S: Why is it good from a parent's perspective?
M: Because at the same time they learn the new technology – it's good for the future of our kids.

Katerina continued to use the wiki for homework and writing about her own interests over the next 18 months. She went on to meet the expected standard in writing at the end of the following year and was in the top third of the class for writing by the time she left the school. One important factor in these cases of high extensibility was parental use of the computer for work at home and parental support as their child used the computer. This became evident when the children were asked to draw a picture or diagram of their family technology use at home (see Katerina's notes in Figure 14.4).

In cases like Katerina's and Vladimir's, morphogenesis took place: the imbrication of the social and the material and the reflexivity of the parents about the function of technology in their children's lives allowed something new to take shape and emerge – a positive feedback loop which was transferable across space and time back into the classroom. The function of the digital tools in these households was very different from the function in some other homes. The children with highly extensible practices were supported by knowledgeable, empathetic sponsors. They, like the Boltons in Lemphane and Prinsloo's (2014) study, were operating with the 'sociocultural backgrounds' and 'linguistic resources' (Lemphane & Prinsloo, 2014: 29) which led to their successes. But there was also a particular flexibility on the part of their parents who allowed the children's sense of fun and enjoyment to flourish while also managing to introduce mentoring moments. This allowed the emergence of something dynamic and transformative. What we may be seeing is a re-run of Lareau's (2003)

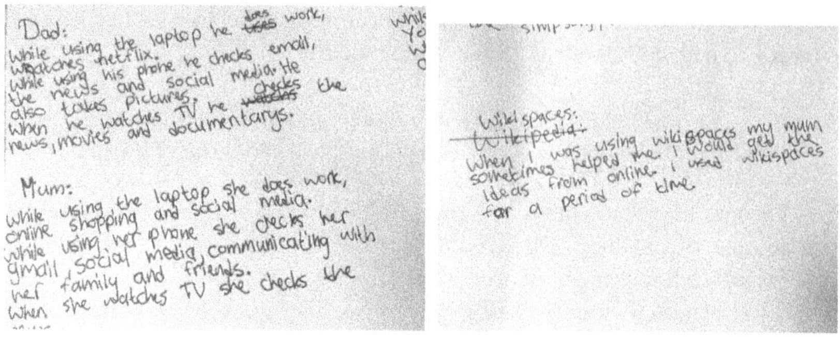

Figure 14.4 Katerina's notes about home computer use

natural growth and *concerted cultivation* models of parenting, re-characterized by Gee (2015) to keep up with the times. The concerted cultivators described by Lareau invest heavily out of school in supporting their child's education. In the digital age, such parents, often working themselves in technology-rich environments, 'encourage their children to develop mastery with digital tools, using things like games as a gateway, and help their children relate this mastery to literacy and knowledge development' (Gee, 2015: 73).

Cases of moderate extensibility

In cases of moderate extensibility, children produced a variety of developed multimodal texts on the wiki and were also observed making progress in class-based offline literacy as judged by conventional assessment data. From interviews with the children and their depictions of technology use at home, it was clear either that they had direct support or that the function of technology in the home was oriented toward work. However, what marks them out from the cases in the previous section is the absence of parental reflexivity about and support for online play as a gateway to learning.

One child who showed moderately extensible practices was Celine. She produced wiki pages about interior design and fashion (Figure 14.5). She grew up in a household where it was clear that computers were to be used purposefully. In her diagram of technology use at home (Figure 14.6), her mother is seen 'doing her teacher work.' Her mother may have lacked the professional networks and imbrication in technology-rich workplaces of the parents of Vladimir and Katerina. Nevertheless, a part-time language teacher, she had a strong work ethic and enthusiasm for education which she transmitted to her daughter and, in the initial stages of the project, she allowed her daughter some leeway in the use of the computer. However, because of her own sponsors – her education in another system – she did not see the value of playful use of technology as

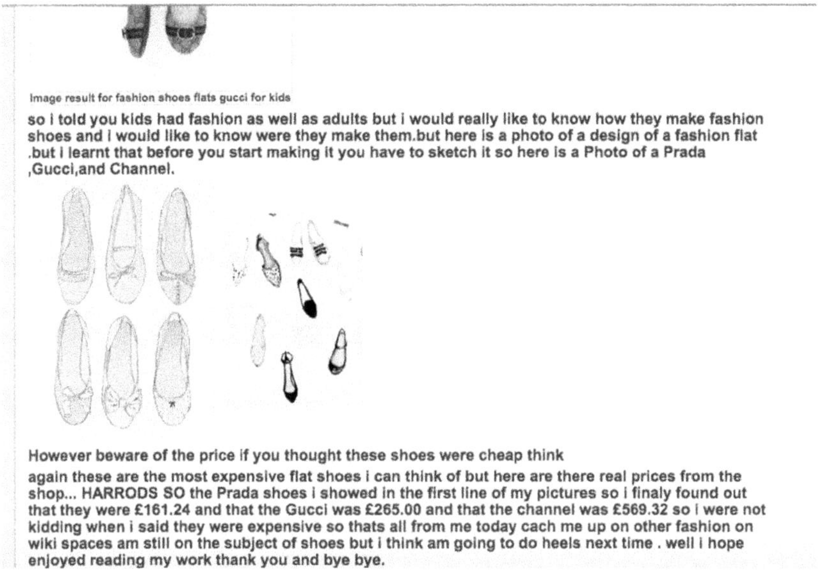

Image result for fashion shoes flats gucci for kids

so i told you kids had fashion as well as adults but i would really like to know how they make fashion shoes and i would like to know were they make them.but here is a photo of a design of a fashion flat .but i learnt that before you start making it you have to sketch it so here is a Photo of a Prada ,Gucci,and Channel.

However beware of the price if you thought these shoes were cheap think again these are the most expensive flat shoes i can think of but here are there real prices from the shop... HARRODS SO the Prada shoes i showed in the first line of my pictures so i finaly found out that they were £161.24 and that the Gucci was £265.00 and that the channel was £569.32 so i were not kidding when i said they were expensive so thats all from me today cach me up on other fashion on wiki spaces am still on the subject of shoes but i think am going to do heels next time . well i hope enjoyed reading my work thank you and bye bye.

Figure 14.5 Celine's fashion wiki page

a springboard for learning. She was willing to support learning at home in spelling, handwriting and arithmetic but did not manifest the reflexivity about popular culture and digital know-how of the parents in the previous section. For her, Celine's elaborate pages about interior design and fashion were a waste of time and were distracting her from 'real' work. Thus, Celine was not being mentored or supported at home around literacy practices involving technology that were of interest to her.

At the other end of the scale in terms of parental response is the case of Zachary. Zachary was the youngest child of two professional parents – his mother worked in the software industry. His parents encouraged him to

Figure 14.6 Celine's diagram of her home technology set-up with mum 'doing her teacher work'

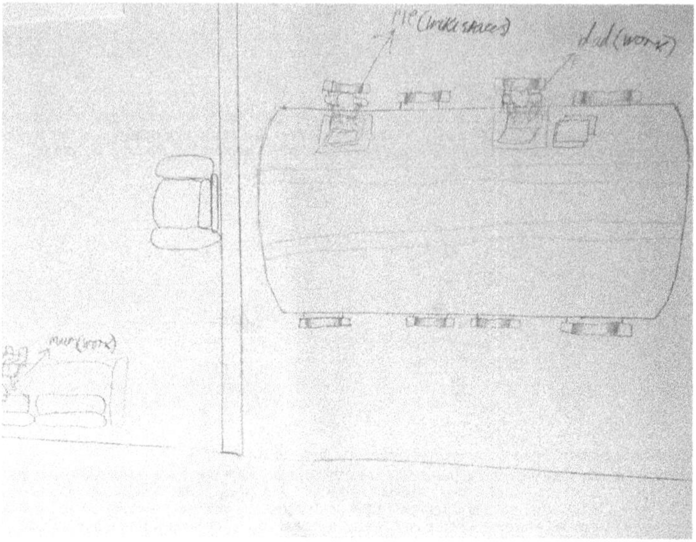

Figure 14.7 Zachary's drawing of home technology use

use the wiki but, as is clear from his pictorial representation of technology use in the home (Figure 14.7), other family members sat working alongside him on separate devices rather than supporting him as he worked.

In conversations with his parents in which the teachers asked why he was not completing his homework, they replied that they had assumed he was getting on with it independently when he told them he was working on the wiki. However, it is likely that, perhaps because of deterministic assumptions about technology, they overestimated his capacity for independent work, displaying a Papertian confidence that the 'children's machine' could on its own lead to self-directed learning. Far from hovering over him like concerted cultivators, they adopted a natural growth model of parenting, allowing him to get on with his thing while they did theirs.

The response to technology of Celine's and Zachary's parents was not the same and it was different from that of the parents in the previous section. In one household, there was skepticism and disapproval and in the other there was over-optimism about the power of technology, yet the effect was the same. These parents did not hover, intervene or attempt discussions with their children around what they were doing online. Nevertheless, these children were imbricated in households where the parents made clear that the function of technology was to produce work. Celine and Zachary could see how their parents were using computers and this influenced their own perception of its function. Thus, there was also a positive feedback loop and morphogenesis – something dynamic and transformative did emerge although these children's practices could be characterized as less extensible than those of the children in the previous section.

Conclusion

The benefit of being in a classroom and being responsible for the progress of all the children is that it brings into focus not only the dids but also the did-nots. The home-school boundary was key in this research and extensible practices only emerged for some children. Those children who were mentored by experienced sponsors were able to build on their digital literacy practices at home and extend them back into the school environment where they made progress in offline tasks too.

To teach literacy is to teach the ability to move between different spaces and to empower people so that everyone steers their own courses and potentially navigates away from their pre-allocated roles in society. Reflecting on what I had seen during the intervention, I devised a heuristic, a STEERS model of literacy, to help me frame my thoughts about how to take forward my findings.

Literacy practices, including multimodal composing practices, are about:

- **Sponsors**. Schools will need to identify the level of support (or sponsorship) that children receive at home and supplement it if necessary.
- **Tools** that we can build up mastery of. Educators need to recognize the way different tools for literacy can suit different children and allow them to achieve a feeling of competence and mastery.
- **Emotional** response to the sponsors and tools we encounter. Teaching and learning in literacy is an affective experience. Previous imbrications between children's embodied selves and their digital devices as they played games produced affect which they brought to their multimodal literacy practices on the wiki.
- **Experiences**. The richer our experiences the more we have to talk and write about. As Gee (2015: 81) notes, 'experience and language bootstrap each other.' Literacy pedagogy must take account of this and build in rich experiences as a stimulus.
- **Reflexivity** about our own position in the world. Through reflexivity we can become empowered and have greater capacity for action. Pupils' reflexivity about their role in the classroom and the possibility the wiki gave them to transform into more active engaged learners was important for some learners. Parental reflexivity about the function of technology use also plays an important role in extensible practices.
- **Syncretism** (ways of reconciling different systems so that we can build on home and informal literacies). Educators need to value and understand the behavior and beliefs around computer use in their pupils' homes in order to support their digital literacy practices effectively in school.

A STEERS model of literacy may be one way to problematize some of the celebratory discourse around children's multimodal and digital literacy practices, making us more aware of issues of equity.

References

Archer, M. (2000) *Being Human: The Problem of Agency*. Cambridge: Cambridge University Press.

Brandt, D. (1997) *The Sponsors of Literacy*. See https://doi.org/10.2307/358929

Buckingham, D. (2007) *Beyond Technology: Children's Learning in the Age of Digital Culture*. Cambridge: Polity Press.

Burnett, C. and Merchant, G. (2015) The challenge of 21st-century literacies. *Journal of Adolescent and Adult Literacy* 59 (3), 271–274.

Burnett, C. and Merchant, G. (2020) *Undoing the Digital: Sociomaterialism and Literacy Education*. London: Routledge.

Cummins, J. (2015) Literacy policy and curriculum. In J. Rowsell and K. Pahl (eds) *The Routledge Handbook of Literacy Studies*. London: Routledge.

Flewitt, R. (2014) Interviews. In A. Clark, R. Flewitt, M. Hammersley and M. Robb (eds) *Understanding Research with Children and Young People*. London: Sage.

Gee, J. (2015) *Literacy and Education*. New York: Routledge.

Gold, R. (1958) Roles in sociological field observations. *Social Forces* 36 (3), 217–223.

Hearn, H. and Thomson, P. (2014) Working with texts, images and artefacts. In A. Clark, R. Flewitt, M. Hammersley and M. Robb (eds) *Understanding Research with Children and Young People* (pp. 154–168). London: Sage.

Ito, M., Gutiérrez, K., Livingstone, S., Penuel, B., Rhodes, J., Salen, K., Schor, J., Sefton-Green, J. and Watkins, S.C. (2013) *Connected Learning: An Agenda for Research and Design*. DML Research Hub. See https://dmlhub.net/publications/connected-learning-agenda-for-research-and-design/index.html.

Kalantzis, M. and Cope, B. (2012) *Literacies*. Cambridge: Cambridge University Press.

Lareau, A. (2003) *Unequal Childhoods: Class, Race and Family Life*. Berkeley, CA: University of California Press.

Lemphane, P. and Prinsloo, M. (2014) Global forms and assemblages: Children's digital literacy practices in unequal South African settings. In C. Burnett, J. Davies, G. Merchant and J. Rowsell (eds) *New Literacies Around the Globe: Policy and Pedagogy*. New York: Routledge.

Leonardi, P. (2013) Theoretical foundations for the study of sociomateriality. *Information and Organization* 23 (2), 59–76.

Li, M. and Zhu, W. (2017) Good or bad collaborative wiki writing: Exploring links between group interactions and writing products. *Journal of Second Language Writing* 35, 38–53.

Lundin, R. (2008) Teaching with wikis: Toward a networked pedagogy. *Computers and Composition* 25 (4), 432–448.

Mak, B. and Coniam, D. (2008) Using wikis to enhance and develop writing skills among secondary school students in Hong Kong. *System* 36 (3), 437–455.

Manyak, P. (2004) 'What did she say?': Translation in a primary-grade English immersion class. *Multicultural Perspectives* 6, 12–18.

Pifarré, M. and Fisher, R. (2011) Breaking up the writing process: How wikis can support understanding the composition and revision strategies of young writers. *Language and Education* 25 (5), 451–466.

Pifarré, M. and Li, L. (2018) Characterizing and unpacking learning to learn together skills in a wiki project in primary education. *Thinking Skills and Creativity* 29, 45–58.

Woo, M., Chu, S., Ho, A. and Li, X. (2011) Using a wiki to scaffold primary school students' collaborative writing. *Educational Technology and Society* 14 (1), 43–54.

15 Listening to the Stories of Refugee Children from Burma: A Positioning and Multimodal Study

Aijuan Cun and Mary B. McVee

Introduction

The United States has a long history of resettling refugees, both individuals and whole families (Dettlaff & Fong, 2016). Between 2007 and 2018, people from Burma comprised the largest population of resettled refugees in the US, with over 170,000 such people arriving in the country over the course of that period of time (Masaad, 2019). Individual refugees and refugee families from Burma who reside in the US include different ethnic groups, such as Burmese, Karen and Mon (Lee *et al.*, 2015). Similar to refugee children from other countries, many children from Burma are required to acquire English by attending English as a second language (ESL) classes. Although intended to help students transition or acculturate to US schools, these classes are often grounded in restrictive educational language policies that 'undermine bilingual education and multilingualism' (Hornberger & Link, 2012: 262).

When they enter US contexts, newcomer children and their families bring various kinds of family literacy practices and funds of knowledge (Moll *et al.*, 1992), but these literacy practices are often ignored or marginalized in American schools. In particular, academic school literacies usually depend on print texts (e.g. writing or reading) (Shanahan, 2013). Often school literacy practices are not closely related to the multimodal and linguistic practices in the children's families. However, family literacy practices can become significant educational resources to help students engage in literacy learning and to help teachers know their students better (Li, 2000, 2007). The first step in this process is to explore how newcomer children from Burma and their families engage with texts in their home literacy practices. Previous literature has explored the literacy practices of refugee students (Gilhooly *et al.*, 2019; Johnson & Kendrick, 2017;

Kennedy *et al.*, 2019; Perry, 2007, 2009), but little research has focused on the family literacy of children from Burma. To help contribute to the literature, this study examines how three refugee children from Burma draw upon multiple semiotic resources to make sense of themselves and their family stories in a family literacy project.

Theoretical Framework

Two theoretical frameworks are used in this study: positioning theory and the social semiotics multimodal perspective. Positioning theory was originally developed by Davies and Harré (1990) in the field of social psychology, and has been used in different areas of social science to 'study all kinds of social situations' (van Langenhove, 2017: 9). Positioning is about 'the appropriate expression with which to talk about the discursive production of a diversity of selves' (Davies & Harré, 1990: 47). There are various kinds of positioning. This study focuses on *self and other positioning*. Harré and van Langenhove (1991: 398) point out that 'within a conversation, each of the participants always positions the other while simultaneously positioning him- or herself.'

The positioning triangle – 'position, speech-act, storyline' is also crucial to positioning (Harré & van Langenhove, 1991: 405) in order to understand how people position themselves in conversation. As Harré and Moghaddam explained, position is defined as a cluster of rights and duties to perform certain social acts. Speech and other acts are viewed as 'every socially significant action, intended movement, or speech that must be interpreted as an act, a socially meaningful and significant performance' (Harré & Moghaddam, 2003: 6). A person's discursive social actions are not randomly developed, but rather 'follow established patterns of development,' which are called 'storylines.' Most research related to positioning theory has focused on speech acts or linguistic modes only; few positioning studies have examined multimodal positioning (McVee *et al.*, 2021). To help address this gap, the present study explores three children's positions through their speech acts and multimodal artifacts.

The other supporting theoretical framework is the social semiotics multimodal approach, which is used to examine how meaning is made through various semiotic resources, also defined as 'modes' (Kress & van Leeuwen, 2002). Modes can be sounds, images, words or layouts (Jewitt, 2009). Each mode has its own affordances and 'potentials for making meaning' (Kress, 2010: 20). One mode (e.g. word) may serve a unique function distinct from that provided by another mode (e.g. image). The multimodal approach highlights how multiple modes interact to produce representation or communication through 'orchestration' (Shanahan & Flury-Kashmanian, 2014). For example, when designers create multimodal artifacts that include both words and images, viewers may comprehend part of their meaning based on reading the words only. However, they may understand the full story if they consider both words and images.

The multimodal perspective can also help readers or viewers understand a designer's interests. Kress (2010: 59) states that 'social semiotics and the multimodal dimension of the theory, tell us about interest and agency; about meaning (-making); about processes of sign-making in social environments.' This statement prompts scholars to consider how individuals who are sign-makers have options to combine different modes to make meanings based on their interests or everyday lives. As meaning-makers, children choose which modes to use to create a representational meaning with their multimodal artifacts. These theoretical perspectives enable scholars or educators to understand the ways in which the participants draw upon various modes to make meanings associated with their family stories.

Historical context of refugee families from Burma

All the participants' families self-identified as ethnic Burmese and were originally from Burma – a country in Southeast Asia with numerous ethnic groups. Its military government changed the name of the country from Burma to Myanmar after the former British colony gained its independence in 1989 (Banki & Lang, 2008). However, based on the participants' preferences, 'Burma' was used in this chapter. Due to political and anti-Muslim violence, many people have fled Burma for neighboring countries (Mahmood *et al.*, 2017; Oh & Van Der Stouwe, 2008). Even as this chapter was being published, a new round of violence erupted (Paddock, 2021). As refugees, Burmese reside in neighboring countries (i.e. countries of transit) before moving to more permanent host countries such as the United States. These neighboring countries include Thailand (Bowles, 1998) and Malaysia (O'Neal *et al.*, 2018). Due to religious and political persecution, the families in the present study moved through transit countries before reaching the United States.

Methodology

Research context and participants

This study was part of a dissertation research project investigating the language and literacy learning of immigrant and refugee families (Cun, 2020). This study used a case study design to explore 'a real-life contemporary bounded system (a case) or multiple bounded systems (cases) over time, through detailed in-depth data collection involving multiple sources of information' (Creswell, 2013: 97). The focal participants for this book chapter were three refugee children in Grades K-3. All three children and their families were recruited through contact with a community center in a middle-sized city in the northeastern United States. At the time of data collection, one of the children's parents was an adult learner attending ESL classes for adults at the community center. The first author, Aijuan, knew the parent, Ni Ni (a pseudonym), and built a trusting relationship with her through data collection in the adult ESL class. Ni Ni indicated that her family was willing to open their house to Aijuan to visit and conduct the family literacy project. Additionally, Ni Ni invited her neighbors and friends to participate in the study, and Aijuan met the second and third families through Ni Ni. Aijuan received approval from the university's Institutional Review Board (IRB) before conducting the study. Consent and assent to participate were provided by the parents and children, respectively, in the three families prior to home visits and data collection.

The focal participants for this chapter are three children from Burma: Gawa, Swe Lin and Su Su. At the time when the data were collected in 2018, Gawa, from the first family, was a third-grader. She was born in Burma and stayed in a refugee camp in Thailand with her parents and younger brother. Gawa spoke Burmese as her first language and English as a second language. She also spoke a limited amount of Thai. Swe Lin, from the second family, was a second-grader born in Malaysia. His parents were originally from Burma. Swe Lin spoke Burmese as his first language and English as a second. He also spoke a limited amount of Malay. Similarly, Su Su, from the third family, had also been born in Malaysia. Her parents were from Burma but stayed in Malaysia for several years before resettling in the United States. She also spoke Burmese as her first language and English as a second. At the time of the study, she had just completed kindergarten. All three children also spoke Arabic for religious purposes.

Data collection

Data included field notes based on home visits, ethnographic interviews with the participants during the home visits, and artifacts created by the participants. These data sources contributed to the case of the investigation of the stories of three children from Burma. Twelve home visits were conducted with each participant's family. Each visit took about two hours. During each visit, Aijuan invited the families to share their family and community literacy practices. The children initiated the topics of conversations and then created multimodal artifacts to share their life experiences. Topics that were initiated by the children included culture, religion and educational experiences. Field notes were taken during each home visit. Conversations were video- and audio-recorded. Artifacts included multimodal drawings made by the participants.

Data analysis

Before data analysis, the video- and audio-recordings of conversations were transcribed. The transcripts were then encoded using *initial coding*, which is 'a first cycle, open-ended approach to coding' (Saldaña, 2016: 115). *Self and other* positioning (Harré & van Langenhove, 1991) was employed in order to understand how the participants positioned themselves and their family members when they created their multimodal drawings. Additionally, the social semiotics multimodal perspective (Kress, 2010) was used to understand what modes were chosen by the participants and how these modes comprised meaning-making tied to the participants' stories. Moreover, triangulation of data (Glesne, 2011) was carried out by comparing the conversation transcripts, field notes and artifacts.

Findings

The children positioned themselves in different ways when they created their multimodal drawings. Additionally, the children's multimodal artifacts represented their family stories related to culture, religion and education.

Gawa's favorite drawing and cultural artifacts

Participants liked to share stories related to their culture. In the first family, Gawa's mother often sewed Burmese-style clothes for her family, so Gawa liked to present dresses made by her mother. During one home visit, Gawa was excited to share one of her favorite Burmese-style dresses as an artifact (i.e. the actual dress). When presenting the dress, she said:

Gawa:	I wanna draw, my favorite drawing is [name of the dress in Burmese], my mom made it, and I'm gonna show you! It's pretty.
Gawa's brother:	It's so little.
Gawa:	Right here! Right here!
Gawa's mother:	[Talks to Gawa in Burmese]
Gawa:	Excuse me. I got it here.
Aijuan:	Wow, this one is pretty.
Gawa:	My mom made for me long time ago. [Gawa shows the dress made by her mother to Aijuan]

This conversation positioned Gawa as a bilingual child who was able to present her favorite dress and share her happiness with her family members and the researcher. She used English to provide information, such as who had made the Burmese-style dress. On the other hand, she used Burmese to name the dress, keeping the unique meaning tied to her culture. *Self and other positioning* (Harré & van Langenhove, 1991) allowed us to find that Gawa also positioned her mother in this excerpt. While positioning herself in relation to the dress, she positioned her mother as a cultural expert who was skillful at making Burmese-style dresses. In an informal conversation, Gawa's mother stated that she gained the knowledge and skills to make Burmese-style clothes in her home country and

Figure 15.1 Gawa's drawing: A unique dress

brought them over to the United States, where she makes dresses for their family members and friends in the local community.

On another day, Gawa created a drawing of another favorite dress made by her mother (see Figure 15.1). She especially drew upon visual modes (i.e. images, shapes and colors) to create the artifact. Pride in her mother's dressmaking ability and the beautiful dress, a physical representation of her culture and identity, influenced her choice to work on a drawing of the dress in the study. This example of sharing a cultural artifact and drawing highlights a story of the cultural identity and family strengths of Gawa's family. Her family carried their cultural knowledge and skills over to the United States and maintained and shared them in the local community of their new US city.

Swe Lin's artifact and religious literacy practices

Religious literacy practices played an essential role in all the families, who self-identified as Muslims. The families carried their religious literacy practices from their home country to the United States and continued to develop them. During the home visits, the children created multimodal artifacts to represent their religious holidays and literacy practices. Swe Lin, for example, made several drawings related to religion. The drawing

Figure 15.2 Swe Lin's artifact: Ramadan

shown in Figure 15.2 illustrated how his family observed a significant religious month in Islam – Ramadan.

The artifact includes both linguistic and visual modes and illustrates three ways in which Swe Lin and his family engaged with religious actions and literacy practices during Ramadan: fasting, reading the Quran and praying. In addition to the drawing, he also provided verbal descriptions. While pointing to the first two sections on the left side, he stated, 'If you're fasting, you can't eat in the morning.' Swe Lin's mother explained that their family did not eat after sunrise; they needed to fast during the day, and broke their fast after sunset, usually around 8:45 in the evening. To emphasize the practice, his mother added the word 'fasting' to Swe Lin's drawing.

The third section represents a book, the Muslim religious text, the Quran, and the fourth section refers to praying. Reading the Quran and praying are important religious literacy practices in Swe Lin's family every day. Swe Lin said that his family used Arabic to read the holy book and to pray. The drawing and his description positioned himself as a religious expert who was skillful at sharing his religious knowledge.

Su Su's artifact and daily educational experience

Daily educational experience was another topic the participants liked to share during data collection. During a home visit with Su Su's family, she shared her daily schooling experiences and created a multimodal artifact: 'My School' (see Figure 15.3).

This artifact includes both linguistic and visual modes. Two sentences included in the upper area of the artifact explain where Su Su's school is located. Following IRB guidelines, the names of Su Su's school and her

Figure 15.3 Su Su's multimodal artifact: My school

city of residence were removed from this artifact. If readers only read the two sentences, it would be difficult to obtain additional meaning and understanding. Visual modes, such as the images, colors and shapes, provide a specific view of her version of the school based on her current daily schooling experiences. The layout of this artifact follows the 'reading path from top to down [which] means ideal to real' (Jewitt & Oyama, 2001: 148).

In addition to the artifact, Su Su provided a verbal description to elaborate on its meaning during the home visit:

Aijuan: Su Su, this shape means? [Aijuan points to the 'heart' on the drawing]
Su Su: I like school.
Aijuan: This heart means you like school?
Su Su: Yeah, and green; let me think for a minute, these, the green are classrooms.
Aijuan: Classrooms?
Su Su: I'm gonna put these as my classrooms, this is the lounge, this is the library, this is, this is playground, and this is um, gym. [The whole green area includes all these rooms]

Aijuan: OK. These are the classrooms?
Su Su: Yeah. All the classrooms and the lounge.
Aijuan: This is? [Researcher points to the flower]
Su Su: To my teacher.
Aijuan: This is to your teacher? The flower?
Su Su: Yeah.

This excerpt illustrates Su Su's understanding of what school looked like based on daily experiences associated with her school. The shape 'pink heart' was to express her feelings about school, which meant *she liked school*. In this case, Su Su positioned herself as a student who enjoyed schooling following her resettlement in the United States.

In addition to her own multimodal artifact, she also asked Aijuan to help her use Google Maps on a laptop to find the route from her home to her school. While looking at the route on Google Maps, Su Su stated, 'school to home very close, like three minutes. If you walk, like 12 minutes. The school bus pick me up in the morning, 7:45, then school starts 8:00.' In this case, Su Su used her speech acts and multimodal drawing to position herself as a student who was skillful at displaying her knowledge in relation to time, space and schooling.

Discussion and Conclusion

The findings described above demonstrate the ways in which three refugee children from Burma positioned themselves when making and sharing their multimodal drawings and artifacts. This is important because 'every object tells a story' (Pahl & Rowsell, 2019). Positioning theory, in particular *self and other positioning* (Harré & van Langenhove, 1991), was used to help us examine how children's identities and cultural practices were embedded within these objects or artifacts (Rowsell & Pahl, 2007). The idea of storytelling through artifacts is not new, but what is important to note is how the children position themselves in relation to the artifact and others around them. Even though positioning theory has been utilized to study people's positions through speech acts in different social sciences fields, few studies have explored multimodal positioning (McVee *et al.*, 2021). The present study built on the previous literature on positioning theory and added perspectives on examining three children's positions through their speech acts and multimodal artifacts.

All three children's stories shared a similar storyline. In that storyline, these multilingual children positioned themselves as experts who represented their cultural knowledge, religious literacy practices and daily educational experiences to others. That is, through artifacts and multiple modes, children conveyed their funds of knowledge (Moll *et al.*, 1992).

Einarsdottir *et al.* (2009: 217) note that children's drawings are windows to help 'access young children's views and experiences.' Drawing upon funds of knowledge, artifacts and multiple modes, teachers can support children in tapping into their family literacy practices. This repositions children to draw upon home literacy practices and funds of knowledge as resources with which to build and share knowledge. Describing multimodal storytelling with immigrant children, Ghiso and Low (2013: 33) note that 'students are often sorted by their abilities to decode print and produce personal narratives along with essay conventions for the genre.' In contrast, using drawing and other modalities can disrupt school processes positioning students as learners and contributors, contrasting with the deficit-oriented positions often ascribed to students who are emerging bilinguals.

US schools are dominated by standardized testing which heavily relies upon print-based texts (Bhattacharyya *et al.*, 2013). Often, there is no time for the stories of refugee children to be shared in school settings. While Taylor (2012: 165) prompts teachers to consider 'the process of learning and text-making as multimodal, rather than linguistic activities,' the change to shift student learning opportunities is not contingent upon teachers alone. All the children in this study spoke more than one language, but their multilingual identities were not empowered in English-only classrooms due to restrictive language policies (Hornberger & Link, 2012). It is up to language policy makers to re-examine current policies and open up spaces and approaches for language learning that benefit both the children and their teachers. Under these policies, schools can provide more effective programs to encourage the children to exercise their agency and share their own stories in relation to cultural knowledge, family literacy practices and their bilingual (or multilingual) identities.

Educational researchers also need to continue the dialogue on exploring refugee children's family stories and their multiple identities, and to advocate for the children's families. A limited amount of literature has examined the family literacy practices of refugee students (Gilhooly *et al.*, 2019; Karam, 2018; Perry, 2007). Few studies have focused on refugee children from Burma (Roof & McVee, 2020). This book chapter serves as an example of further research through an exploration of three children's family stories, positions and multimodal artifacts. At the same time, it calls for researchers' attention, urging them to continue the discussion on refugee children's multimodal literacy learning and the construction of their identities.

References

Banki, S. and Lang, H. (2008) Protracted displacement on the Thai-Burmese border: The inter-related search for durable solutions. In H. Adelman (ed.) *Protracted Displacement in Asia: No Place to Call Home* (pp. 59–82). New York: Routledge.

Bhattacharyya, S., Junot, M. and Clark, H. (2013) Can you hear us? Voices raised against standardized testing by novice teachers. *Creative Education* 4 (10), 633–639.

Bowles, E. (1998) From village to camp: Refugee camp life in transition on the Thailand-Burma border. *Forced Migration Review* 2, 11–14.

Creswell, J.W. (2013) *Qualitative Inquiry and Research Design: Choosing Among Five Traditions.* Thousand Oaks, CA: Sage.
Cun, A. (2020) Capturing the lived experiences of refugee families: A positioning, literacies, and multimodal perspectives study. Published doctoral dissertation, State University of New York at Buffalo.
Davies, B. and Harré, R. (1990) Positioning: The discursive production of selves. *Journal for the Theory of Social Behaviour* 20 (1), 43–63.
Dettlaff, A. and Fong, R. (2016) *Immigrant and Refugee Children and Families: Culturally Responsive Practice.* New York: Columbia University Press.
Einarsdottir, J., Dockett, S. and Perry, B. (2009) Making meaning: Children's perspectives expressed through drawings. *Early Child Development and Care* 179 (2), 217–232.
Ghiso, M.P. and Low, D.E. (2013) Students using multimodal literacies to surface micronarratives of United States immigration. *Literacy* 47 (1), 26–34.
Gilhooly, D., Amos, M. and Kitson, C. (2019) Reading the ink around us: How Karen refugee youth use tattoos as an alternative literacy practice. *Journal of Research in Childhood Education* 33 (1), 145–163.
Glesne, C. (2011) *Becoming Qualitative Researchers* (4th edn). London: Longman.
Harré, R. and van Langenhove, L. (1991) Varieties of positioning. *Journal for the Theory of Social Behavior* 21 (4), 393–407.
Harré, R. and Moghaddam, F. (2003) Introduction: The self and others in traditional psychology and in positioning theory. In R. Harré and F. Moghaddam (eds) *The Self and Others: Positioning Individuals and Groups in Personal, Political, and Cultural Contexts* (pp. 1–12). Westport, CT: Praeger.
Hornberger, N.H. and Link, H. (2012) Translanguaging and transnational literacies in multilingual classrooms: A biliteracy lens. *International Journal of Bilingual Education and Bilingualism* 15 (3), 261–278.
Jewitt, C. (2009) *The Routledge Handbook of Multimodal Analysis.* New York: Routledge.
Jewitt, C. and Oyama, R. (2001) Visual meaning: A social semiotic approach. In T. van Leeuwen and C. Jewitt (eds) *Handbook of Visual Analysis* (pp. 134–156). Thousand Oaks, CA: Sage.
Johnson, L. and Kendrick, M. (2017) 'Impossible is nothing': Expressing difficult knowledge through digital storytelling. *Journal of Adolescent & Adult Literacy* 60 (6), 667–675.
Karam, F.J. (2018) Language and identity construction: The case of a refugee digital bricoleur. *Journal of Adolescent & Adult Literacy* 61 (5), 511–521.
Kennedy, L.M., Oviatt, R.L. and De Costa, P.I. (2019) Refugee youth's identity expressions and multimodal literacy practices in a third space. *Journal of Research in Childhood Education* 33 (1), 56–70.
Kress, G. (2010) *Multimodality: A Social Semiotic Approach to Contemporary Communication.* New York: Routledge.
Kress, G. and van Leeuwen, T. (2002) Colour as a semiotic mode: Notes for a grammar of colour. *Visual Communication* 1 (3), 343–368.
Lee, S., Choi, S., Proulx, L. and Cornwell, J. (2015) Community integration of Burmese refugees in the United States. *Asian American Journal of Psychology* 6 (4), 333–341.
Li, G. (2000) Family literacy and cultural identity: An ethnographic study of a Filipino family in Canada. *McGill Journal of Education/Revue des sciences de l'éducation de McGill* 35 (1), 9–30.
Li, G. (2007) Second language and literacy learning in school and at home: An ethnographic study of Chinese Canadian first graders' experiences. *Literacy, Teaching, and Learning* 11 (2), 1–31.
Mahmood, S.S., Wroe, E., Fuller, A. and Leaning, J. (2017) The Rohingya people of Myanmar: Health, human rights, and identity. *The Lancet* 389 (10081), 1841–1850.

Masaad, N. (2019) *Refugees and Asylees: 2018*. Washington, DC: Office of Immigration Statistics. See https://www.dhs.gov/sites/default/files/publications/immigration-statistics/yearbook/2018/refugees_asylees_2018.pdf (accessed October 2019).

McVee, M., Silvestri, K., Schucker, K. and Cun, A. (2021) Positioning theory, embodiment, and the moral orders of objects in social dynamics: How positioning theory has neglected the body and artifactual knowing. *Journal for the Theory of Social Behaviour* 51 (2), 192–214

Moll, L.C., Amanti, C., Neff, D. and Gonzalez, N. (1992) Funds of knowledge for teaching: Using a qualitative approach to connect homes and classrooms. *Theory into Practice* 31 (2), 132–141.

Oh, S.A. and Van der Stouwe, M. (2008) Education, diversity, and inclusion in Burmese refugee camps in Thailand. *Comparative Education Review* 52 (4), 589–617.

O'Neal, C., Atapattu, R., Jegathesan, A., Clement, J., Ong, E. and Ganesan, A. (2018) Classroom management and socioemotional functioning of Burmese refugee students in Malaysia. *Journal of Educational and Psychological Consultation* 28 (1), 6–42.

Paddock, R.C. (2021) 'It's better to walk through a minefield': Victims of Myanmar's army speak. *The New York Times*, 9 March. See https://www.nytimes.com/2021/03/09/world/asia/myanmar-military-tatmadaw-violence.html (accessed March 2021).

Pahl, K. and Rowsell, J. (2019) *Artifactual Literacies: Every Object Tells a Story*. New York: Teachers College Press.

Perry, K.H. (2007) Sharing stories, linking lives: Literacy practices among Sudanese refugees. In V. Purcell-Gates (ed.) *Cultural Practices of Literacy: Case Studies of Language, Literacy, Social Practice, and Power* (pp. 57–84). Mahwah, NJ: Lawrence Erlbaum.

Perry, K.H. (2009) Genres, contexts, and literacy practices: Literacy brokering among Sudanese refugee families. *Reading Research Quarterly* 44 (3), 256–276.

Roof, L. and McVee, M.B. (2020) *The Experiences of Refugee Youth from Burma in an American High School: Countering Deficit-Based Narratives through Student Voice*. New York: Routledge.

Rowsell, J. and Pahl, K. (2007) Sedimented identities in texts: Instances of practice. *Reading Research Quarterly* 42 (3), 388–404.

Saldaña, J. (2016) *The Coding Manual for Qualitative Researchers*. Thousand Oaks, CA: Sage.

Shanahan, L.E. (2013) Composing 'kid-friendly' multimodal text: When conversations, instruction, and signs come together. *Written Communication* 30 (2), 194–227.

Shanahan, L. and Flury-Kashmanian, C. (2014) Orchestrating semiotic resources in explicit strategy instruction. *Pedagogies: An International Journal* 9 (2), 99–115.

Taylor, R. (2012) Messing about with metaphor: Multimodal aspects to children's creative meaning making. *Literacy* 46 (3), 156–166.

van Langenhove, L. (2017) Varieties of moral orders and the dual structure of society: A perspective from positioning theory. *Frontiers in Sociology* 2 (9), 1–13.

16 Black Girls' Multimodal Manifestations: Exploring the Multimodal Flexibility of Black Language in Dual Language Bilingual Education

Vivian E. Presiado and Brittany L. Frieson

Since the 1960s, dual language bilingual education (DLBE) programs have increased in popularity with goals to cultivate bilingual, bicultural and biliterate citizens (García, 2009; Lindholm-Leary, 2012). However, with the rapid growth of DLBE programs in the US, critical scholarship has pointed to the urgency of attending to issues of power and privilege within these programs (Cervantes-Soon *et al.*, 2017; Chaparro, 2019; Valdés, 2018). Particularly, critical scholars have stressed the need for examining how the curricularization of language in bilingual programs continues to linguistically marginalize Black children, specifically Black language (BL) speakers. Typically, DLBE spaces function with a Latinx/Anglo dualism (Valdés, 2018), with language policies that promote standardized languages such as Spanish and White Mainstream English (WME), often overlooking the rich artistry of BL speakers (Frieson, 2021).

Classrooms function with a single-axis approach to language practices that privilege a 'rightness to whiteness' perspective (Lyiscott, 2019), rejecting the rich nuances of BL speakers including Black girl literacies. Black girls' discourses are 'ways of knowing and acting and the development of skills, vernacular expressive arts and crafts that help females to advance and protect themselves and their loved ones in society' (Richardson, 2003: 77). Furthermore, Black girls' language practices encompass multiple modes that represent the 'nuanced spectrum of Black girl/womanhood in a racially and politically charged world' (Muhammad & Haddix, 2016: 310) which often rejects their personhood while insisting on learning institutionalized languages such as WME and Spanish in bilingual education without considering the harmful impact on Black girls and their identities (Baker-Bell, 2020). We seek to call attention to the ways in which Black girls in DLBE programs continue to assert the brilliance of their language practices across multiple modes despite society's invalidation of it in educational contexts. From this perspective, we draw upon qualitative data to highlight how Black girls utilize multimodal manifestations and semiotic tools of BL to traverse across supposed linguistic margins in their social worlds to amplify their multilingual skills.

Literature Review and Theoretical Framing

Critical scholarship in bilingualism and bilingual education has documented the ways in which the rich language and literacy practices of speakers of BL are often erased or reduced compared to those of their Anglo, WME-speaking peers in Spanish/English DBLE programs (Flores & Rosa, 2015; Palmer, 2010). We extend that notion to specifically name the cultural and linguistic erasure of Black girls in bilingual programs in order to interrogate the ways in which DLBE programs go without recognizing the multimodal brilliance of Black girls. Through theorizing the language and literacy practices of Black girls rooted in Black girl literacies and translanguaging frameworks, we seek to disrupt traditional notions of literate brilliance via multimodal resources with BL and urgently call attention to the various semiotic tools that Black girls regularly utilize to explore their identities and social worlds (Muhammad & Haddix, 2016).

Reconsidering translanguaging

Originally, translanguaging referred to social practices where students intentionally utilized various languages for specific, productive purposes (García & Li, 2014; Williams, 1994). More recently, scholars adopted the term to describe the dynamic practices of multilingual speakers that are mobilized for various aspirations (Canagarajah, 2011; García, 2009; García & Li, 2014; Otheguy *et al.*, 2015). Translanguaging can be further defined as 'the deployment of a speaker's full linguistic repertoire without regard for watchful adherence to the socially and politically defined boundaries of named (and usually national and state) languages' (Otheguy *et al.*, 2015: 283).

We take up and operationalize translanguaging (García & Li, 2014) to delineate the complex linguistic practices of BL speakers that often transcend presumed language and cultural margins that are generated by institutional norms, such as DLBE programs (Frieson, 2021). Few published studies have taken up translanguaging to describe the fluid and dynamic deployment of BL speakers' language practices in DLBE spaces, as many studies typically associate translanguaging practices with features from standardized named languages. However, we assert that BL speakers also engage in translanguaging practices. For example, multilingual Black girls often deploy multiple linguistic registers and modes in order to negotiate their gendered, racialized and linguistic identities (García, 2009) which are generally prohibited from academic spaces. This often forces BL speakers to choose between systematic boundaries of their repertoires rooted in colonial and racist practices that do not embody the richness of their identities, histories and experiences (Flores & Rosa, 2015; Lyiscott, 2019). From this perspective, pedagogies that value whiteness invalidate the richness of multilingual Black girl literacy practices which are often perceived as deficit in academic settings. Moreover, multilingual Black girl language practices then challenge static notions of languaging by engaging in dynamic ways of communication.

Black girls' multimodal manifestations

Traditional notions of scholarship on multimodality define it as a 'field of work, a domain for inquiry, a description of the space and the resources which enter into *meaning*, in some way or another' (Kress, 2011: 242). In conjunction with research grounded in semiotics and Black girl literacies, multimodal resources that are available to Black girls include their distinct cultures, identities and histories, which constitute affordances that are necessary in facilitating meaning-making (Kress, 2011; Muhammad & Haddix, 2016; Richardson, 2003). Although there are shared experiences among Black children participating in DLBE programs as BL speakers, the ways that knowledge and signs are 'produced, and shaped, and constituted distinctly in different modes' (Kress, 2011: 242) emanate uniquely from multilingual Black girls' literacy practices. From this perspective, the multimodality and social semiotics of Black girls are specific to the interests of the sign-maker, multilingual Black girls and their needs, in relation to power and agency within the embodied space that they exclusively create for their literacies.

The intersection of Black girl literacies and multimodality frameworks provides an entry to disrupt traditional research with multimodality in defining multiple modes as associated with written and oral modes, visual images, sound, streamed video, and various other modes through electronic or digital literacy (Hornberger, 2007). We challenge these approaches and theorize multimodality through the lens of multilingual Black girls traversed across various spaces such as the DLBE classroom and the Black church. BL is a complex language system composed of patterns of various linguistic, grammatical, rhetorical and functional features. 'Though linguists have produced detailed accounts of the pronunciation and grammatical system of Black Language since at least the 1960s, Black children are often not formally taught the linguistic features of their own language' at school (Baker-Bell, 2020: 71). We argue that young Black multilingual children embody multimodal practices when engaging with BL, as speakers of BL often simultaneously engage in multiple modes traversed among various spaces (Sembiante *et al.*, 2020; Smith *et al.*, 2017).

From this perspective, these unique multiple modalities that Black girls engage in are reflective of their intentional selection of organizing modes and are inherently tied to symbols representative of their intersectional identities (Price-Dennis *et al.*, 2017). Employing Black girl literacies and multimodality frameworks, the research questions that guided this study were: (1) What are the language and literacy practices of multilingual Black girls participating in a two-way immersion (TWI) program? and (2) How do multilingual Black girls use multimodal resources to navigate their social worlds?

Research Methods

This study converges findings from two larger ethnographic case studies focused on the language and literacy practices of Brieanna and Blessing (pseudonyms), two young Black girls, who were in the same elementary midwestern Spanish/English DLBE program (Frieson, 2019; Presiado, 2020). Ethnographic methods, including in-depth, audio-recorded individual interviews, pláticas/hangouts, audio and video-recorded observations with ethnographic field notes, and artifacts, were utilized to explore how both children employed translanguaging practices in various spaces to move across languages and modalities. This includes a first-grade DLBE classroom (Brieanna), church (Blessing) and home (Blessing). These data collection methods reflect the importance of foregrounding participants' linguistic and experiential knowledge as valid (Cook & Dixson, 2013), as these sources provide insight into the historical nature of how Black girls' voices have traditionally been dismissed. In highlighting various contexts, we seek to address how messages from school also permeate home and community spaces (Chaparro, 2019).

Data analysis occurred throughout the study (Bhattacharya, 2017), with audio-recording transcripts by both authors in their respective research studies to construct data intimacy (Saldaña, 2011) with the data sources. To triangulate our data, we used an inductive analysis to analyze the data, reviewed the raw data for coding, and clustered categories of coding to look for salient patterns or themes (Bhattacharya, 2017). Once themes were identified, we collaboratively re-engaged with both data sets to highlight where participants engaged in multimodal literacies, using BL to develop a deeper understanding of the function of their translanguaging practices in contextual situations. We agreed upon codes that represented multimodal resources and developed broader themes that were representative of the data set.

Challenging Norms and Exploring the Brilliance of Multilingual Black Girls' Literacies

In this section, we present findings from our ethnographic research studies across various dynamic spaces, highlighting the brilliance of Blessing and Brieanna's use of multimodal resources with BL by challenging linguistic norms and employing translanguaging practices.

'Like a boss': Black girlhood language and literacy practices

Blessing started her journey in the Spanish/English DLBE program in kindergarten where she quickly began to use the Spanish she learned, often reminding classmates to 'get them luces [lights]' upon exiting the classroom. Years later, as a nine-year-old fourth-grader, Blessing maintained strong connections to her linguistic identity with BL and intertwined those features with Spanish and WME, as WME was a language of instruction in her classroom. Whether she was playing at home with her brother wearing her 'Like a Boss' T-shirt, or microphone in hand at her church, Blessing often engaged in multimodal practices as she braided visual images, gestures, music and artifacts fluidly across languages and modes (Sembiante *et al.*, 2020; Smith *et al.*, 2017).

In Blessing reflecting on her own language use, she considered herself a speaker of WME, Spanish and some French. At her church, Blessing participated in body movements, gestures, and visual and linguistic expression. The preacher at her church often incorporated artifacts and gestures in addition to call-response and testifying to make a point during sermons (Smitherman, 1977). During a sermon, the preacher picked up a basketball and bounced it to emphasize his message. He called attention to the ball and said, 'There is something inside this ball that is not allowin' it to change its shape ... when we fill ourselves with God, you will not lose your form.' Incorporating artifacts was a practice used within Blessing's Black church and one she utilized in conversation with her sibling and peers as seen in the following excerpt from the children's Bible study:

Blessing:	Oooh! We gettin' Skittles! [taking a skittle between her pointer finger and thumb and looking at it closely] They will not lose their form!
Child at Bible Study:	Yup!
Blessing:	Jesus be inside us. [still looking closely at the skittle between her fingers] I want all these Skittles! [sitting up and nodding toward a pile of skittles in front of her] You want them maestra [teacher]?

Blessing referenced the sermon she had heard earlier that day by paralleling two artifacts as she engaged in conversation with other children. Multimodal literacy exists within a sociocultural context where social interactions and practices influence and inform the use of particular signs (Taylor & Leung, 2020). Artifacts became meaning-making tools that held stories, messages and connections for Blessing to participate and create her own narrative (Sembiante *et al.*, 2020). Blessing also continued to vibe to the music by bouncing her head, as the music from the main area continued to play and trickled into the children's bible study room. Music was a major component of the service, as Blessing and the church members would sing, sway, dance, clap and call out during songs, a practice that Blessing continued at home and in the community. In the excerpt below from hanging out with her in the community, Blessing continued to use BL as she preached to her church congregation.

Blessing:	[microphone in hand] Genesis 43:25 … Forgiveness, no matter what you **be** in. You can always forgive.
Congregation:	Yes baby! Preach! /Mhm/Yes girl! [waving hand in air and shaking head]

Blessing often took on the role of teacher at her church as church elders provided a space for children to serve as teachers to their peers and church congregation. The church space created an atmosphere that embraced Blessing's multiple identities, including her role as big sister. Using her repertoires of practice, she made sure that her younger brother Rasheed participated in Bible study by volunteering him to read a passage to the children's Bible group, often with a gaze. Rasheed would comply with what Blessing would nonverbally ask after catching sight of the shift in her stance, tilt of her head, and wide eyes staring at him. Multimodal literacies often generate leverage for students to draw upon their cultural worlds that allow for students to express themselves in empowering ways (Pacheco & Smith, 2015). Blessing used her 'spiritual literacy practices' to help her read the world (Compton-Lilly & Greene, 2010; Freire & Macedo, 1987). Specifically, this Black community space provided a refuge where Blessing could freely use BL and amplify its resourcefulness in various literacy practices.

In a hangout with Blessing, she had just taught about King Solomon and wanted to read during a break. In the following excerpt, she flowed between linguistic resources embodied through three language systems.

> Blessing got a book from the bookshelf and sat next to me. The title of the book she chose was *The Magic Tree House: Blizzard of the Blue Moon*. She opened the book to a page that had a corner folded to where she had previously left off. She then said to me, 'Vamos a leer' [Let's read]. She then pointed to the right side of the book that was closest to me and said, 'You **finna** read this side, and I **finna** read this side.' She pointed to the left side, which was closest to her. She then began to read the text with 'expression.' 'Jack charged back downstairs …' She then turned to me and said, 'What will it say? Let's see.' Her tone reminded me of a teacher leading a guided reading group.

Translanguaging practices represent an 'additional unique semiotic resource that students wield in tandem with their other modal resources to experiment with hybrid languaging and identities' (Sembiante *et al.*, 2020: 2). Blessing had a clear understanding of the multiple language patterns she used. She also negotiated when to use certain linguistic features, as she chose to initiate conversation in Spanish and then flowed into BL by using 'finna' and then ended with WME as she shifted into the role of reading buddy. Although there was no direct acknowledgment of these shifts, she demonstrated clear options and navigation of her language tools. A translanguaging space has its own transformative power, with endless bounds that combine and generate new identities, values and practices (García & Li, 2014). In the examples presented, Blessing engaged in multiple modes of communicating and representing language beyond speaking and writing in ways that displayed her brilliance (Love, 2019).

Black girl literate brilliance and translanguaging practices

Brieanna, a six-year-old first-grader with a vibrant personality, loved to socialize with her friends and always sought to connect her identities and social world. She often recontextualized her classroom assignments to provide insights into her identities as a young Black girl who spoke BL. Whether she was writing about playing on the playground, telling stories with friends, or revoicing narratives that she read in books and listened to on the tablet with her own storytelling that featured BL, we were reminded that her dialogic negotiation was deeply personal, intertwined with her multiple identities.

Leer solitos was a center intended for independent reading; however, Brieanna often engaged in buddy reading with her friends and myself by inviting the words on the page to come alive by engaging in translanguaging using BL, Spanish and various semiotic tools. In this example, Brieanna chose a pattern book titled *Yo Quiero* [I want]. She often liked to read with me during visits as we both used BL and gestures to 'make the book not so boring,' as she would say. As we were sitting on the carpet reading the book, she started reading the words on the first few pages, 'Yo quiero, yo quiero un girafe' [I want, I want a giraffe]. As she turned the page with laughter, Brieanna pointed at the illustration of the big crocodile looking at the tub. She said to me:

Brieanna: [*to me*] Look for yourself [pushing the book so I can see the pages] ... and this gone be a problem.

Brieanna: [reading the book] Yo quiero, yo quiero los ... un cocodrilo [I want, I want ... a crocodile]. Look that's gone be a problem cause she too big. She biiiiiiig and the tub is the same size as him! How she gon' get in? [looking at the picture of the crocodile trying to get into the tub]

In this example, you can see how Brieanna flexibly drew on her linguistic repertoire, including features of BL and Spanish. It was evident that she was reading the author's text, but she also demonstrated how her verbal dexterity afforded tools to construct meaning-making during reading. The author's intent was for readers to gain fluency with word patterns, which she accomplished, but it was not absent of BL to engage in meaning-making. Instead of suppressing BL at the expense of learning Spanish, like most language allocation policies in DL encourage Black children to do (Sánchez *et al.*, 2018), she demonstrated how BL was a valuable resource.

Following Brieanna's inquiry about the uncertainty of the crocodile fitting into the tub, I responded, 'I don't know.' Brieanna said, 'So she might have to take a bath in the tub ... not in the tub, but in the basket. Not a basket, but like a bucket.' Brieanna shared how this illustration reminded her of growing up in a low-income community. I was not surprised by this as we often exchanged stories about our Black girlhoods. She vocalized these experiences to me by recalling how she took turns using the bathroom in the studio apartment shared with family. She told me, 'The big black bucket is for you to stand in and the little white bucket is for water and soap. And we got a cup and a towel.' With that interaction, Brieanna demonstrated how literacy is more than a social practice for Black girls; it helped her make sense of living in a racialized and classed world too (Muhammad & Haddix, 2016).

She continued to read, 'Pero los cocodrilos tienen demasiados dientes [But the crocodiles have so many teeth]. Im'a count how many they are.' She started to count the teeth in the crocodile's mouth, swinging her fingers vigorously back and forth. Using multimodal resources, she also fluidly selected various features to compose an alternative narrative between reading in Spanish and narrating in BL while using her fingers to engage in number sense. This is more complex than the standardized language practices that DLBE programs encourage with language policies that promote selection of features from one named-language system at a time.

As she turned the page, there were two penguins in water that had two symbolic squiggly lines, representing hot water. Brieanna shared that it was going to be an issue with the penguins and the hot water. Shimming her shoulders, she said, 'Oooh ... this gone be a problem with the two *pingüinos* [penguins] in the hot water.' Based on her knowledge that penguins live in cold climates, she shared her concerns with the storyline. Although the author's intent was for her to practice the phrase '*yo quiero*,' she opted for a more complex reading of the word by using translanguaging while she was reading the book in Spanish, using gestures and movement. In the examples, Brieanna also engaged in multimodal manifestations by interacting with visual cues from images, recontextualizing the story and using gestures, to understand her identity as a Black girl within broader local and socioeconomic contexts. She also utilized features of BL and Spanish as valuable resources to forge a space for cultural and linguistic identities, asserting their importance (Baker-Bell, 2020).

Discussion and Conclusion

This chapter explored the multimodal practices of two elementary-aged Black girls participating in a Spanish/English DLBE program, adding to the literature about the brilliance of BL speakers in DLBE programs. Blessing and Brieanna drew from their multimodal resources in varying ways where different identities and practices coexisted, using BL as a powerful linguistic tool for the production of new knowledge and practices. As the examples illustrate, translanguaging, gestures, artifacts and visuals served as devices that facilitated learning and interaction for multilingual Black girls to navigate and explore their identities as literate and capable enactors of knowledge in spaces that typically 'valorize a proper English' (Muhammad & Haddix, 2016: 311). Although Brieanna's experience in the DLBE program did not provide explicit instruction or acknowledgment of BL, Brieanna powerfully incorporated BL with the languages of instruction, leveraging it with multimodal resources in complex ways to add meaning to her literate world (Sembiante *et al.*, 2020). Blessing continued to embrace BL in various spaces to engage in broader forms of literacy and she used agency to create and communicate knowledge creatively rather than selecting from pre-existing signs (Kress, 2011). Blessing's literacy practices were dynamic, multiple and adaptive to her knowledge, experiences and audiences, as seen when she engaged with the congregation versus her brother (Sembiante *et al.*, 2020).

Multimodal studies have provided important insights into how children engage with a repertoire of resources for meaning-making, with less being known about the ways in which multilingual children engage with multimodal resources (Sembiante *et al.*, 2020). Although Black multimodal devices are already a part of Black communities and have been flowing through their minds and spirits for generations (Muhammad, 2020), we argue that DLBE programs are not leveraging the multimodal ways of knowing of BL speakers. Brieanna and Blessing engaged in practices that have been reverberating for ages, such as storytelling and testifying (Smitherman, 1977).

We can learn a lot from how Brieanna and Blessing engaged in multimodal practices in ways that echoed the richness, complexity and dynamism of BL that has been cultivated throughout generations (Love, 2019; Muhammad, 2020). Antiracist Black language education and pedagogies are humanizing and are needed to abolish the systematic structures of schooling that continue to oppress Black children (Baker-Bell, 2020; Love, 2019). DLBE language policies continue to center whiteness and monolingualism, yet Black children continue to demonstrate their brilliance and artistry regardless (Frieson, 2021). An antiracist Black language education and pedagogical approach to literacy teaching and learning provides a sphere for understanding the specificity of needing to center Black identities and language practices to critically interrogate the anti-Black linguistic racism and white language hegemony that is often perpetuated in schools and in DLBE spaces (Baker-Bell, 2020). We conclude that taking up an antiracist Black language education and pedagogy honors the brilliance of multilingual Black girls' language practices, identities and social worlds.

References

Baker-Bell, A. (2020) *Linguistic Justice: Black Language, Literacy, Identity, and Pedagogy*. New York: Routledge.

Bhattacharya, K. (2017) *Fundamentals of Qualitative Research: A Practical Guide*. New York: Routledge.

Canagarajah, S. (2011) Translanguaging in the classroom: Emerging issues for research and pedagogy. *Applied Linguistics Review* 2, 1–28.

Cervantes-Soon, C.G., Dorner, L., Palmer, D., Heiman, D., Schwerdtfeger, R. and Choi, J. (2017) Combating inequalities in two-way language immersion programs: Toward critical consciousness in bilingual education spaces. *Review of Research in Education* 41 (1), 403–427.

Chaparro, S.E. (2019) But mom! I'm not a Spanish boy: Raciolinguistic socialization in a two-way immersion bilingual program. *Linguistics and Education* 50, 1–12.

Compton-Lilly, C. and Greene, S. (2010) *Bedtime Stories and Book Reports: Connecting Parent Involvement and Family Literacy*. New York: Teachers College Press.

Cook, D.A. and Dixson, A.D. (2013) Writing critical race theory and method: A composite counterstory on the experiences of Black teachers in New Orleans post-Katrina. *International Journal of Qualitative Studies in Education* 26 (10), 1238–1258.

Flores, N. and Rosa, J. (2015) Undoing appropriateness: Raciolinguistic ideologies and language diversity in education. *Harvard Educational Review* 85 (2), 149–171.

Freire, P. and Macedo, D.P. (1987) *Literacy: Reading the Word and the World*. London: Routledge & Kegan Paul.

Frieson, B.L. (2019) (Re)mixin' and flowin': Examining the literacy practices of African American language speakers in an elementary two-way immersion bilingual program. Unpublished doctoral dissertation, University of Illinois at Urbana-Champaign.

Frieson, B.L. (2021) Remixin' and flowin' in centros: Exploring the biliteracy practices of Black language speakers in an elementary two-way immersion program. *Race Ethnicity and Education*. doi:10.1080/13613324.2021.1890568

García, O. (2009) *Bilingual Education in the 21st Century: A Global Perspective*. Malden, MA: Basil Blackwell.

García, O. and Li, W. (2014) *Translanguaging: Language, Bilingualism, and Education*. London: Palgrave Macmillan.

Hornberger, N.H. (2007) Biliteracy, transnationalism, multimodality, and identity: Trajectories across time and space. *Linguistics and Education* 18 (3–4), 325–334. doi:10.1016/j.linged.2007.10.001

Kress, G. (2011) 'Partnerships in research': Multimodality and ethnography. *Qualitative Research* 11 (3), 239–260.

Lindholm-Leary, K. (2012) Success and challenges in dual language education. *Theory into Practice* 51 (4), 256–262.

Love, B.L. (2019) *We Want to Do More than Survive: Abolitionist Teaching and the Pursuit of Educational Freedom*. Boston, MA: Beacon Press.

Lyiscott, J. (2019) *Black Appetite. White Food: Issues of Race, Voice, and Justice within and Beyond the Classroom*. New York: Routledge.

Muhammad, G. (2020) *Cultivating Genius: An Equity Framework for Culturally and Historically Responsive Literacy*. New York: Scholastic.

Muhammad, G.E. and Haddix, M. (2016) Centering black girls' literacies on the multiple ways of knowing of black girls. *English Education* 48 (4), 299–336.

Otheguy, R., García, O. and Reid, W. (2015) Clarifying translanguaging and deconstructing named languages: A perspective from linguistics. *Applied Linguistics Review* 6 (3), 281–307.

Pacheco, M.B. and Smith, B.E. (2015) Across languages, modes, and identities: Bilingual adolescents' multimodal codemeshing in the literacy classroom. *Bilingual Research Journal* 38 (3), 292–312.

Palmer, D. (2010) Race, power, and equity in a multiethnic urban elementary school with a dual-language 'strand' program. *Anthropology & Education Quarterly* 41 (1), 94–114.

Presiado, V.E. (2020) 'We about to be real' ... 'Literacy is everywhere' ... 'Ya somos expertos': Documenting and learning from families' language and literacy practices. Unpublished doctoral dissertation, University of Illinois at Urbana-Champaign.

Price-Dennis, D., Muhammad, G.E., Womack, E., McArthur, S.A. and Haddix, M. (2017) The multiple identities and literacies of black girlhood: A conversation about creating spaces for black girl voices. *Journal of Language and Literacy Education* 13 (3), 1–18.

Richardson, E. (2003) *African American Literacies.* New York: Routledge.

Saldaña, J. (2011) *Fundamentals of Qualitative Research.* New York: Oxford University Press.

Sánchez, M.T., García, O. and Solorza, C. (2018) Reframing language allocation policy in dual language bilingual education. *Bilingual Research Journal* 41 (1), 37–51.

Sembiante, S., Bengochea, A. and Gort, M. (2020) 'Want me to show you?': Emergent bilingual preschoolers' multimodal resourcing in show-and-tell activity. *Linguistics and Education* 55, 1–11.

Smith, B.E., Pacheco, M.B. and de Almeida, C.R. (2017) Multimodal codemeshing: Bilingual adolescents' processes composing across modes and languages. *Journal of Second Language Writing* 36, 6–22.

Smitherman, G. (1977) *Talkin and Testifyin: The Language of Black America.* Detroit, MI: Wayne State University Press.

Taylor, S.V. and Leung, C.B. (2020) Multimodal literacy and social interaction: Young children's literacy learning. *Early Childhood Education Journal* 48 (1), 1–10.

Valdés, G. (2018) Analyzing the curricularization of language in two-way immersion education: Restating two cautionary notes. *Bilingual Research Journal* 41 (4), 388–412.

Williams, C. (1994) Arfarniad o ddulliau dysgu as addysgu yng nghyd-destun addysg uwchradd ddwyieithog [An evaluation of teaching and learning methods in the context of bilingual secondary education]. Unpublished doctoral thesis, University of Wales, Bangor.

17 Theory of Mind: A Missing Piece in Understanding Emergent Bilinguals' Comprehension of Multimodal Narrative Texts

Ana Taboada Barber, Susan Lutz-Klauda, Mayra Cruz and Jerae Kelly

Teachers and parents usually focus on either children's academic achievement *or* their emotional development at a given point in time. Hardly ever are these two dimensions of child development seen as intertwined or instruction designed to cater to both simultaneously. The domain of socioemotional learning (SEL) merges these two areas of development as it involves the processes through which individuals acquire and apply the attitudes, knowledge and skills necessary to understand and manage their emotions, feel and show empathy, develop positive relationships and make responsible decisions (Schonert-Reichl *et al.*, 2017). Knowledge and skills are needed to manage one's own emotions and others' – making it evident that cognition is part of SEL. However, SEL is often called the 'missing piece' in schools because, crucial as it is to school success, it has not received much attention from practitioners in schools until the last decade. Within SEL, social awareness, or the ability to take the perspective of and empathize with others from diverse backgrounds and cultures (Schonert-Reichl *et al.*, 2017), is one key dimension for success in both academic settings and life in general.

In this chapter, we focus on social awareness by spotlighting a specific sociocognitive skill that is amenable to teaching through the use of narrative texts throughout the primary grades, and beyond: Theory of Mind (ToM). Although ToM is sometimes used interchangeably with perspective taking, ToM is a more specific construct, one that has been studied empirically in relation to reading comprehension in elementary school children and adolescents in general populations as well as among students with autism (McIntyre *et al.*, 2018; Ricketts *et al.*, 2013; Tong *et al.*, 2020) and with emergent bilinguals (EBs) of various language backgrounds in kindergarten and Grade 4 (Pelletier, 2006) and in Grades 3–5 in our own work, as we describe in this chapter.

Theory of Mind

ToM is a sociocognitive skill that refers to a child's development of understanding that others have beliefs, thoughts and intentions – different from one's own. ToM is generally indicated by the capacity to infer the particular mental states that others are experiencing. This knowledge of others' mental states is key to enabling perspective taking (Wellman, 2002). Past research has emphasized that narrative texts, stories or literature, in particular – as opposed to expository or informational texts – can play a significant role in fostering ToM in various student populations through their inclusion of content featuring social situations (Mar & Oatley, 2008; Martucci, 2016; Pelletier, 2006; Tompkins *et al.*, 2018). Only one study to our knowledge, however, has focused specifically on the relation between ToM and reading comprehension in EBs (Pelletier, 2006). The relation between ToM and text comprehension stems from the premise that there are shared skills between ToM and the ability to comprehend narratives. People form models of the minds of those with whom they interact, allowing them to infer people's mental states, to which they have no direct access, which in turn affords insight into the motives for others' behavior (Frith & Frith, 2001) and how that behavior may impact our own lives. In narrative texts or literature – similar to what happens in ordinary life – people ascribe mental states to characters, such that they can know or infer what characters might be wanting, thinking and feeling (Mar & Oatley, 2008).

As educational psychologists and a current principal in a multicultural language immersion school (Spanish-English) with a trajectory of beating the odds, especially for children who are EBs, we propose that ToM may be a potential missing piece in reading comprehension instruction. As such, in this chapter we first build the case for the relations between ToM and reading comprehension of narrative texts. Second, we analyze how multimodal texts in particular may support the development of ToM and thereby strengthen reading comprehension, highlighting key issues for research in this understudied area. Third, we provide empirical evidence from others' research on the development of ToM in bilinguals, EBs in particular, and describe our own empirical work on the relation between ToM and reading comprehension in elementary Spanish-English EBs. We then move on to implications for classroom instruction, focusing on the interplay of ToM and inference making while reading narrative texts, including multimodal texts. Lastly, we conclude our chapter with thoughts on the positive academic and broader socioemotional consequences of emphasizing ToM in instruction for EBs as well as students of all language backgrounds.

Theory of mind and reading comprehension of narrative texts

The relation between ToM and the understanding of narratives – of characters' perspectives specifically – is one that merits our attention in this volume on multimodal literacies. As noted above, with the sociocognitive skill of ToM, individuals are able to recognize and infer that others may have mental states different from their own in order to determine the motives for other people's behavior (Wellman, 2002). Performance on ToM tasks involves coordinated executive control processes, reasoning and conceptual skills (Carlson & Moses, 2001; Carlson *et al.*, 1998; Wellman *et al.*, 2001). The claim behind research on ToM is that our everyday understanding of people is fundamentally 'mentalistic'; that is, we think of people in terms of mental states, namely their beliefs, thoughts, hopes, goals and emotions (Wellman & Lagatutta, 2004). When we read stories, our understanding of characters' perspectives and their motives is central to our understanding of the story as whole. ToM supports readers' narrative reading comprehension by helping them integrate plot actions with characters' thoughts and beliefs. Children learn mental concepts such as 'belief,' 'desire' and 'knowledge' during their preschool years, largely by listening to, observing and interacting with others during their everyday activities (Wellman & Liu, 2004) as well as through narrative texts (Dore *et al.*, 2018; Pelletier & Beatty, 2015). When a teacher reads a story aloud, or when a child explores a story on their own, by examining the words, pictures, or both, the reader (or listener) builds a mental representation of the text that goes beyond its basic text base, by building a text representation that integrates text information and the reader's (or listener's) background knowledge and experiences (Kintsch, 1988). A child's development of ToM assists beginning readers with understanding narratives by supporting their inference-making skills about the mental states of characters in the stories (Cartwright, 2015; Kim, 2020).

For example, when listening to the fragment from the book *Owl Moon* by J. Yolen (1987), a rich story about a girl and her dad's 'owling experience' in the woods of New England at night, Lucas (all names are pseudonyms), a six-year-old EB, asked: *Does the girl think her dad thinks she is excited about the owl?* Lucas's question reveals that he was not only trying to determine the main character's (the girl's) mental state, but also trying to infer what she thinks her dad thinks about her own thinking and feelings (mental state). This sort of double inference reflects Lucas's use of ToM when interpreting the characters' emotions. His younger friend, Marion, a four-year-old, was also applying ToM when she asked*: Does the dad think the girl is scared?* Marion was trying to figure out how the dad feels about his daughter's experience. In this way, because ToM captures one's reasoning about other people's mental states, such as their thoughts, desires and emotions (Astington & Edward, 2010; de Villiers &

Pyers, 2002), and this thinking is inferential by nature, ToM assists with oral (listening) and reading comprehension by helping readers make inferences about characters' mental states and their motives for behaviors in narratives. Further, because ToM reflects one's ability to identify a contingency between characters' mental states, such as their thoughts, desires and emotions (Astington & Edward, 2010; de Villiers & Pyers, 2002), *and* subsequent behaviors, ToM serves the comprehension of narratives by supporting a more cohesive understanding of the story structure (Dore *et al.*, 2018).

Researchers have also suggested that as children manifest indicators of early development of ToM (around three to four years of age) they can adopt the mental perspectives or mental states of the main character when listening to narratives. In time, these perspectives become more elaborate and more complex as ToM, listening comprehension and reading comprehension develop (Fecica & O'Neill, 2010; see also Dore *et al.*, 2018). Others have concluded that less skilled readers who are taught perspective taking are better able to adopt character perspectives and exhibit better comprehension (Emery, 1996; Hodges *et al.*, 2018; McTigue *et al.*, 2015) than non-trained readers. This latter finding has implications for the use of culturally relevant materials, ideally representative of all students' backgrounds within a class (e.g. characters and plots that reflect the diverse ethnicities and races of a community of learners), so that students can deepen their empathy for others who come from different backgrounds from themselves.

The Use of Multimodal Texts to Foster Theory of Mind and Reading Comprehension

Characteristics of multimodal texts that may leverage theory of mind skills

Most of the empirical research on ToM and reading comprehension has been done with traditional, print-centered texts. To our knowledge no empirical research has considered the influence of multimodal texts on ToM or, vice versa, the impact of ToM on comprehension of multimodal texts, either with monolingual or EB students. Thus, we consider some possible avenues for future research on these relations, particularly with respect to instructional practices.

Multimodal texts have been broadly defined as 'ensembles that incorporate combinations of visual images, written language, and design features, blurring simple distinctions among them' (Serafini *et al.*, 2018: 311). Such ensembles may appear in either print or digital environments, and may convey stories, concepts, information or a combination thereof (Serafini *et al.*, 2018). Multimodal texts include but are not limited to: printed picture books; digitized picture books with or without such features as animations, voiceovers and integrated activities; graphic novels; and textbooks (Sembianti *et al.*, 2019; Serafini, 2012b). We adhere to Serafini's (2012b) view that when individuals interact with multimodal texts they are 'reader-viewers' who attend to the visual images and other design elements of the multimodal texts in addition to the written language.

While multimodal texts are highly individualized, there are some features they often share, including, in particular, multimodal narratives, which may facilitate ToM as a reader-viewer. For example, for beginning reader-viewers especially, digital multimodal narrative picture books often offer oral story narration. Narration may cue young reader-viewers to focus on particular characters, and draw attention particularly to their mental states through the use of unique voices for different characters, and variations in tone, pitch, volume and pacing that convey shifts in characters' feelings and perceptions. Digital multimodal picture books additionally sometimes include animated body movements and facial expressions that can help foster inferential thinking about mental states and ToM. For example, on one page of the digital version of *Enemy Pie* by Derek Munson (2000), the expression of the protagonist/narrator – a young boy whose dad offers to help him get rid of his perceived enemy, Jeremy Ross, by baking an 'enemy pie' for Jeremy – grows into a frown and his eyes blink, conveying his sadness about Jeremy stealing his best friend away. Further, throughout the text, the dad bears a continual warm smile, which serves as a motif – a consistent, repeated image – which can play an important role in supporting text comprehension (Youngs & Serafini, 2011). In this case, the dad's smile may hint that what the boy thinks about his dad's intentions (i.e. that the dad plans to poison Jeremy with the pie) is inaccurate. Instructional attention to such features may not only help students to understand the mental states of the characters in *Enemy Pie*, but also to gain broader insight into the importance of nonlinguistic features in multimodal narrative texts. Research is needed, though, on the characteristics of multimodal narratives that foster inferential thinking about mental states, and thereby deeper comprehension, as well as on instructional techniques for fostering the use of those characteristics.

Roles of the multimodal reader-viewer: Story participant and designer

We would also like to highlight two roles that multimodal texts afford the reader-viewer, which may enhance ToM and perspective taking. The first role is that of *story participant*, specifically in multimodal narratives that fall into the burgeoning genre of 'metafictive' picture books (Serafini *et al.*, 2018), that is, picture books in which the characters are aware of being in a book, such as *Chester* by Mélanie Watt (2007) and *We Are in a Book!* by Mo Willems (2010). In the latter, Willems initiates an interactive experience with his two classic characters, the elephant Gerald and his best pal Piggie, in the opening pages, as Gerald notes to Piggie, ‘I think someone is looking at us.’ The dialogue, illustrations (e.g. close-up views of the characters gazing directly at the reader-viewer) and varying font (e.g. tiny type for whispers) each offer young readers support for inferring a multitude of mental states – none of which is explicitly identified in the text – such as surprise, joy and even distress. An area ripe for future research, however, is whether metafictive narratives are a multimodal genre that may be especially effective at facilitating ToM and understanding of how mental states shape both characters’ and readers’ behaviors, as they engage reader-viewers by giving them a personal stake in the story.

The second role that many multimodal texts invite the reader-viewer to play that could lead to stronger ToM skills is that of *designer* (Serafini, 2012a, 2012b). In this role, reader-viewers create their own text, as they ‘design the way the text is read, its reading path, what is attended to and, in the process, construct a unique experience during their transaction with a text’ (Serafini, 2012a: 157). For example, consider Lucia, a first-grader encouraged by her teachers and parents to explore digital and print multimodal texts while learning remotely during the COVID-19 pandemic. Lucia became enchanted with the American Girl print book *Kit’s World: A Girl’s-Eye View of the Great Depression* by Harriet Brown and Teri Witkowski (2008), a text with a mix of narrative and expository passages portraying life for a young girl during the Great Depression, which also included such multimodal features as historic photos, standard and pop-up illustrations, and flaps that when lifted revealed further pictures or text. Lucia designed her own text, as she determined what sections to explore, in what order to view them, how long to spend on them, and when to ask a parent to read portions for her. Thus, the designer role seems to afford great potential for active engagement in multimodal narrative, which may help power the processes of making inferences about characters’ mental states and developing empathy for them. In this realm, research is needed on the efficacy of instructional practices, such as discussing the role of designer with students and its potential for helping them develop insight into characters’ mental states, for strengthening ToM and reading comprehension, within both print and digital multimodal texts, and in both monolinguals and EBs.

Theory of mind development in bilinguals

As co-authors of this chapter, our writing reflects the fusion of our experiences as researchers and practitioners. That is, we apply our collective understanding as researchers with expertise in bilingual learners and as a school principal of a bilingual school with a strong history of leveraging the benefits of Spanish immersion language instruction for children who are EBs from various home language backgrounds. Given our collective interests, we cannot overlook the research on ToM in bilinguals which has become a notable, growing area of study within the field of socioemotional development in the past two decades. In this section, we offer a brief overview of past research and then describe our own recent empirical work with EBs in the elementary grades in the United States.

Bilinguals' sociocognitive skills: Theory of mind as a strength

Overall, the literature on ToM and bilinguals indicates that bilinguals perform better on perspective-taking tasks compared to monolinguals. For instance, a recent review of 16 empirical studies conducted since 2003, involving 1283 children, compared bilingual and monolingual children, primarily in the range of three to five years, on ToM and other perspective-taking tasks. This review found a small advantage for the bilinguals when variables that may explain performance differences were *not* taken into account (Schroeder, 2018). However, when the children's language proficiencies were statistically accounted for, the findings favoring the bilingual children were even stronger.

This pattern of results indicates that language skills (perhaps especially bilinguals' ability to use vocabulary that relates to mental states) contribute substantially to the ability to perform well on ToM and perspective-taking tasks, but that there is an important factor beyond children's language proficiency, likely related to children's bilingual versus monolingual experience, that contributes to their ability to take others' perspectives. Other work suggests that this factor may be that bilingual children are stronger in their control of attention than monolingual children. This strength is attributed to evidence showing that both languages are always active in bilinguals, necessitating that attentional control skills are continually recruited by their language processing system to help them communicate in the appropriate language with others (Bialystok, 2015; Kroll *et al.*, 2014). With regard specifically to ToM, other scholars have indicated that the supposed enhanced attentional control abilities of bilinguals could be used to suppress their own mental states (i.e. their own beliefs and knowledge; Schroeder, 2018), while up-regulating others' mental states. In fact, bilinguals' strong metalinguistic awareness – as evinced in their knowledge that there can be two labels for the same concept – might facilitate their understanding that two people can have different mental states in relation to the same event, or a mental state that differs from their own (Goetz, 2003; Schroeder, 2018).

Theory of mind and reading comprehension in emergent bilinguals

The burgeoning literature on ToM in bilinguals usually includes samples of children and adults who are either full or simultaneous bilinguals (i.e. those who are exposed to two languages from birth; Luk & Bialystok, 2013), but not EBs or sequential bilinguals (i.e. those who speak one language from birth and then learn another language in school; García *et al.*, 2008). Our recent empirical work included a sample of Spanish-English EBs in the elementary grades (specifically, Grades 3–5), a population that is often identified as struggling with reading comprehension in US schools (Mancilla-Martinez & Lesaux, 2010), and for whom the study of socio-cognitive skills, such as ToM, is often missed given the stronger emphasis on their cognitive achievement needs. All EBs in our sample spoke English and Spanish to various degrees and were from Hispanic/Latino families. More than 90% of the students were receiving Free and Reduced Meals (FARMs), indicating that they were vastly from low-SES backgrounds.

Specifically, we addressed the question of whether ToM contributed to oral comprehension and reading comprehension, beyond grade level, word recognition and vocabulary. That is, we wanted to know if ToM would be a significant, unique predictor of the variance in each of the two comprehension variables (oral and reading) when other common correlates of comprehension were statistically controlled. All assessments were administered in English. For ToM, we used a subtest from a standardized battery, the NEPSY-II, which includes a combination of answering questions orally about other people's perspectives and selecting photos that depict others' most likely feelings in social situations (Korkman *et al.*, 2007). Oral and reading comprehension, word recognition and vocabulary were assessed with the Woodcock-Johnson IV Tests of Achievement (Schrank *et al.*, 2014): the reading comprehension measure involves completing brief passages by supplying a missing word based on syntactic and semantic clues; the word recognition subtest entails reading a list of words aloud; and the vocabulary subtest requires naming pictured objects.

Using hierarchical linear regression, we found that ToM was indeed a unique predictor of both oral and reading comprehension in this group of EBs. When ToM was included as a predictor alongside grade level, word recognition and vocabulary, ToM statistically significantly predicted oral and reading comprehension. For oral comprehension, ToM was the only significant predictor besides the typically strong predictor of vocabulary. Even more notably, for reading comprehension, ToM and vocabulary – which is well established as a key contributor to reading comprehension – were equally strong predictors (i.e. they had identical β-values).

Altogether, these analyses support our contention that the ability to take others' perspectives – as evinced here through performance on ToM tasks – plays an important role in the ability to make meaning of oral and text material. Our study demonstrated this for young EBs in the elementary grades, for whom ToM specifically, and perspective-taking in general, may be strengths as they are for other types of bilinguals as noted in prior literature. Our findings applied to the understanding of texts presented in written form, as well as material presented orally. While it is a key avenue for future research, we believe these findings would extend to the comprehension of multimodal narrative texts. ToM performance may be even more strongly related to comprehension of such texts, as they call for synthesizing material from different modalities, similar in a sense to how many perspective-taking tasks benefit from recognizing and integrating the multiple perspectives that individuals may have in a given context.

Implications for Instruction: Making Theory of Mind Explicit during Reading Instruction

Our contention, throughout this chapter, which follows that of others (Nathanson *et al.*, 2013; Pelletier & Astington, 2004; Ziv *et al.*, 2015), is that children's engagement with narrative reading supports ToM development. Less, however, is known about whether multimodal narrative texts in particular may lend a favorable format for the development of ToM. Of particular interest is whether EBs may be uniquely able to benefit from literacy instruction that considers ToM, given evidence showing that ToM is a strength in bilingual populations. As with other cognitive and sociocognitive skills, we know that for ToM to develop, children must be explicitly shown the process of using knowledge of mental states to reason, and to make inferences about human behavior (Cutting & Dunn, 1999; Slaughter *et al.*, 2007). With other scholars, we contend that mere exposure to mental states in narratives is too passive a process for a child to garner meaningful learning from the exposure; rather, we posit that conversational interaction around narrative text is critical to fostering ToM (Devine & Hughes, 2019). Therefore, modeling the inferential process of mental state attribution to characters in stories and how such attributions help explain character behavior is an important aspect of leveraging the affordances of shared reading for ToM development (Devine & Hughes, 2019). This conversational interaction about narratives supports the development of ToM regardless of modality – oral stories and narrative reading, as well as multimodal texts as we proposed. In fact, the cross-modal features of this genre suggest that multimodal texts may be particularly effective in supporting children's ToM development, as we addressed earlier.

Teachers are in a prime position to support ToM development through the typical reading comprehension instruction that occurs within classrooms. Whether in monolingual or multilingual classrooms, teachers can ask text-based questions about mental states and offer feedback on the accuracy of students' attributions, such that they explicitly show their reasoning about the relation between mental states and possible behaviors. As a second step, teachers can ask inferential questions that allow students to connect mental states with character behavior. For example, returning to the story of *Owl Moon* and Lucas's reference to the mental state of *excitement*, once the teacher discusses this feeling as experienced by the girl, she can ask leading questions about how we as readers (or the girl's dad) can infer this feeling (mental state). She can follow this with questions that guide children to infer about the girl's behaviors that evince excitement. Teachers may also call attention to character illustrations within the text to help accurately attribute characters' mental states from the story's context to further support ToM development (Dyer *et al.*, 2000). Specifically, teachers can guide students by making this inferencing process visible to them. Too often, the identification of characters' mental states is an overlooked step in teachers' instruction on character traits because it is generally assumed that students will be naturally intuitive about such mental states. However, research shows that children vary in ToM skills (Devine & Hughes, 2019) and tend to be more successful in the inferencing process engendered by ToM when teachers are explicit about their own thinking about characters' mental states. As such, by making the thought process of identifying character traits and their mental states transparent, teachers can enhance students' text comprehension as well as foster ToM development.

Concluding Thoughts

The possible advantage that EBs or simultaneous bilingual children have in ToM and perspective taking does not lead us to propose that this population should benefit *more* than monolingual students from narrative comprehension instruction or other tasks that foster this sociocognitive skill. On the contrary, we advocate that explicit language about mental states in narratives, whether single or multimodal, print or digital, is beneficial for all children, irrespective of language background or language dominance. However, we believe, given that in the United States there is a significant emphasis on EBs' struggles to acquire English, and reading comprehension in particular, that EBs' ToM and other perspective-taking abilities should be seen as an important resource, and perhaps an untapped knowledge fund to wield for this population. As such, we think it would be beneficial for all children, and especially EBs, if educators were to target ToM as a malleable sociocognitive skill in the context of narrative text comprehension. This type of emphasis on ToM could be accomplished by establishing multimodal narrative texts as a focal point of instruction, as they especially afford students opportunities to use their nonlinguistic skills (i.e. visual analysis and general reasoning skills) for oral and reading comprehension. Further, emphasis on perspective taking, and ToM in particular, as part of comprehension instruction may help all students not only become more astute and savvy readers (or reader-viewers), but help enhance the sociocognitive skills needed for positive, productive functioning in the highly interconnected, multicultural, multimodal milieu of the 21st century.

References

Astington, J.W. and Edward, M.J. (2010) The development of theory of mind in early childhood. In R.E. Tremblay, M. Boivin and R.DeV. Peters (eds) *Encyclopedia on Early Childhood Development*. See http://www.child-encyclopedia.com/social-cognition/according-experts/development-theory-mind-early-childhood.

Bialystok, E. (2015) Bilingualism and the development of executive function: The role of attention. *Child Development Perspectives* 9, 117–121.

Carlson, S.M. and Moses, L.J. (2001) Individual differences in inhibitory control and children's theory of mind. *Child Development* 72 (4), 1032–1053.

Carlson, S.M., Moses, L.J. and Hix, H.R. (1998) The role of inhibitory processes in young children's difficulties with deception and false belief. *Child Development* 69 (3), 672–691.

Cartwright, K.B. (2015) *Executive Skills and Reading Comprehension: A Guide for Educators*. New York: Guilford Press.

Cutting, A.L. and Dunn, J. (1999) Theory of mind, emotion understanding, language, and family background: Individual differences and interrelations. *Child Development* 70 (4), 853–865.

de Villiers, J.G. and Pyers, J.E. (2002) Complements to cognition: A longitudinal study of the relationship between complex syntax and false-belief-understanding. *Cognitive Development* 17 (1), 1037–1060.

Devine, R.T. and Hughes, C. (2019) Let's talk: Parents' mental talk (not mind-mindedness or mindreading capacity) predicts children's false belief understanding. *Child Development* 90 (4), 1236–1253.

Dore, R.A., Amendum, S.J., Michnick Golinkoff, R. and Hirsh-Pasek, K. (2018) Theory of mind: A hidden factor in reading comprehension? *Educational Psychology Review* 30, 1067–1089.

Dyer, J.R., Shatz, M. and Wellman, H.M. (2000) Young children's storybooks as a source of mental state information. *Cognitive Development* 15 (1), 17–37.

Emery, D.W. (1996) Helping readers comprehend stories from the characters' perspectives. *The Reading Teacher* 49 (7), 534–541.

Fecica, A.M. and O'Neill, D.K. (2010) A step at a time: Preliterate children's simulation of narrative movement during story comprehension. *Cognition* 116 (3), 368–381.

Frith, U. and Frith, C. (2001) The biological basis of social interaction. *Current Directions in Psychological Science* 10 (5), 151–155.

Garcia, O., Kleifgen, J.A. and Falchi, L. (2008) *From English Language Learners to Emergent Bilinguals. Equity Matters: Research Review No. 1*. New York: Campaign for Educational Equity, Teachers College, Columbia University.

Goetz, P.J. (2003) The effects of bilingualism on theory of mind development. *Bilingualism: Language and Cognition* 6 (1), 1–15.

Hodges, T.S., McTigue, E., Wright, K.L., Franks, A.D. and Matthews, S.D. (2018) Transacting with characters: Teaching children perspective taking with authentic literature. *Journal of Research in Childhood Education* 32 (3), 343–362.

Kim, Y.S.G. (2020) Hierarchical and dynamic relations of language and cognitive skills to reading comprehension: Testing the direct and indirect effects model of reading (DIER). *Journal of Educational Psychology* 112 (4), 667–684.

Kintsch, W. (1988) The role of knowledge in discourse comprehension: A construction-integration model. *Psychological Review* 95 (2), 163–182.

Korkman, M., Kirk, U. and Kemp, S.L. (2007) *NEPSY II. Clinical and Interpretative Manual*. San Antonio, TX: Psychological Corporation.

Kroll, J.F., Bobb, S.C. and Hoshino, N. (2014) Two languages in mind: Bilingualism as a tool to investigate language, cognition, and the brain. *Current Directions in Psychological Science* 23 (3), 159–163.

Luk, G. and Bialystok, E. (2013) Bilingualism is not a categorical variable: Interaction between language proficiency and usage. *Journal of Cognitive Psychology* 25 (5), 605–621.

Mancilla-Martinez, J. and Lesaux, N.K. (2010) Predictors of reading comprehension for struggling readers: The case of Spanish-speaking language minority learners. *Journal of Educational Psychology* 102, 701–711.

Mar, R.A. and Oatley, K. (2008) The function of fiction is the abstraction and simulation of social experience. *Perspectives on Psychological Science* 3 (3), 173–192.

Martucci, K. (2016) Shared storybook reading in the preschool setting and considerations for young children's theory of mind development. *Journal of Early Childhood Research* 14 (1), 55–68.

McIntyre, N.S., Oswald, T.M., Solari, E.J., Zajic, M.C., Lerro, L.E., Hughes, C., Devine, R.T. and Mundy, P.C. (2018) Social cognition and reading comprehension in children and adolescents with autism spectrum disorders or typical development. *Research in Autism Spectrum Disorders* 54, 9–20.

McTigue, E., Douglass, A., Wright, K.L., Hodges, T.S. and Franks, A.D. (2015) Beyond the story map: Inferential comprehension via character perspective. *The Reading Teacher* 69 (1), 91–101.

Nathanson, A.I., Sharp, M.L., Aladé, F., Rasmussen, E.E. and Christy, K. (2013) The relation between television exposure and theory of mind among preschoolers. *Journal of Communication* 63 (6), 1088–1108.

Pelletier, J. (2006) Relations among theory of mind, metacognitive language, reading skills and story comprehension in L1 and L2 learners. In A. Antonietti (ed.) *Theory of Mind and Language in Developmental Contexts* (pp. 77–92). New York: Springer.

Pelletier, J. and Astington, J.W. (2004) Action, consciousness and theory of mind: Children's ability to coordinate story characters' actions and thoughts. *Early Education and Development* 15 (1), 5–22.

Pelletier, J. and Beatty, R. (2015) Children's understanding of Aesop's fables: Relations to reading comprehension and theory of mind. *Frontiers in Psychology* 6, 1448.

Ricketts, J., Jones, C.R., Happé, F. and Charman, T. (2013) Reading comprehension in autism spectrum disorders: The role of oral language and social functioning. *Journal of Autism and Developmental Disorders* 43 (4), 807–816.

Schonert-Reichl, K.A., Kitil, M.J. and Hanson-Peterson, J. (2017) *To Reach the Students, Teach the Teachers: A National Scan of Teacher Preparation and Social and Emotional Learning. A Report Prepared for the Collaborative for Academic, Social, and Emotional Learning (CASEL)*. Vancouver: University of British Columbia.

Schrank, F.A., Mather, N. and McGrew, K.S. (2014) *Woodcock-Johnson IV Tests of Achievement*. Rolling Meadows, IL: Riverside.

Schroeder, S.R. (2018) Do bilinguals have an advantage in theory of mind? A meta-analysis. *Frontiers in Communication* 3, 36.

Sembianti, S.F., Ramírez, J.A. and de Oliveira, L.C. (2019) Using multimodal practices to support students' access to academic language and content in Spanish and English. In L.C. de Oliveira (ed.) *Expanding Literacy Practices Across Multiple Modes and Languages for Multilingual Students* (pp. 38–51). Charlotte, NC: Information Age Publishing.

Serafini, F. (2012a) Expanding the four resources model: Reading visual and multi-modal texts. *Pedagogies: An International Journal* 7 (2), 150–164.

Serafini, F. (2012b) Reading multimodal texts in the 21st century. *Research in the Schools* 19 (1), 26–32.

Serafini, F., Kachorsky, D. and Reid, S. (2018) Revisiting the multimodal nature of children's literature. *Language Arts* 95 (5), 311–321.

Slaughter, V., Peterson, C.C. and Mackintosh, E. (2007) Mind what mother says: Narrative input and theory of mind in typical children and those on the autism spectrum. *Child Development* 78 (3), 839–858.

Tompkins, V., Benigno, J.P., Kiger Lee, B. and Wright, B.M. (2018) The relation between parents' mental state talk and children's social understanding: A meta-analysis. *Social Development* 27 (2), 223–246.

Tong, S.X., Wong, R.W.Y., Kwan, J.L.Y. and Arciuli, J. (2020) Theory of mind as a mediator of reading comprehension differences between Chinese school-age children with autism and typically developing peers. *Scientific Studies of Reading* 24 (4), 292–306.

Wellman, H.M. (2002) Understanding the psychological world: Developing a theory of mind. In U. Goswami (ed.) *Blackwell Handbooks of Developmental Psychology* (pp. 167–187). Hoboken, NJ: Blackwell.

Wellman, H.M. and Lagattuta, K.H. (2004) Theory of mind for learning and teaching: The nature and role of explanation. *Cognitive Development* 19 (4), 479–497.

Wellman, H.M. and Liu, D. (2004) Scaling of theory-of-mind tasks. *Child Development* 75 (2), 523–541.

Wellman, H.M., Cross, D. and Watson, J. (2001) Meta-analysis of theory-of-mind development: The truth about false belief. *Child Development* 72 (3), 655–684.

Youngs, S. and Serafini, F. (2011) Comprehension strategies for reading historical fiction picturebooks. *The Reading Teacher* 65 (2), 115–124.

Ziv, M., Smadja, M.L. and Aram, D. (2015) Preschool teachers' reference to theory of mind topics in three storybook contexts: Reading, reconstruction and telling. *Teaching and Teacher Education* 45, 14–24.

Children's books cited

Brown, H. and Witkowski, T. (2008) *Kit's World: A Girl's-Eye View of the Great Depression*. Middleton, WI: American Girl Publishing.

Munson, D. (2000) *Enemy Pie*. San Francisco, CA: Chronicle Books. See https://www.tumblebooklibrary.com/ for digital version.

Watt, M. (2007) *Chester*. Toronto: Kids Can Press.

Willems, M. (2010) *We Are in a Book*. New York: Disney Books.

Yolen, J. (1987) *Owl Moon*. London: Penguin.

18 Cultivating Language and Identity through Multimodal Literacies: Back to the StoryBoard

Marisa Ferraro and Kristin Bengtson Mendoza

Introduction

Our chapter shares an ethnographic case study which explores how emergent bilingual learners engage in multimodal literacy practices that promote language acquisition, cultivate academic identities and validate lived experiences in a fourth-grade classroom. Pedagogies that draw upon multiliteracies (Cope & Kalantzis, 2009; New London Group, 1996) provide learners with opportunities to access and engage with languages, cultures and identities. This ethnographic case study problematizes how multiliteracy practices are enacted throughout a graphic memoir writing project in a sheltered language arts classroom (Calkins & Chiarella, 2006). We analyze multimodal literacy practices through the lens of Cummins' *et al.* (2012) literacy engagement framework. This chapter examines ways in which emergent bilingual learners engage with multimodal literacy practices through graphic text production.

Pedagogies that engage language learners in multimodal literacy practices create sacred spaces in which lived experiences can be narrated, shared and validated within elementary classrooms. Students' creation of multimodal texts, from storyboard to publication, that reflect personal struggles and successes is powerful; the subsequent sharing of these stories is transformative. In this chapter, we share an ethnographic case study which afforded students the opportunity for literacy and identity development through multiliteracy practices that privileged text production. We call for a shift in how educators approach literacy, away from a linear, text-based approach that makes visible inequities of agency to a multimodal, multicultural construction that will benefit emergent bilingual youth (Cummins *et al.*, 2005; Street, 1995).

Pedagogies that reflect the concept of multiliteracies provide emergent bilingual students with rich and varied opportunities to access and engage in literacy practices (Cope & Kalantzis, 2009; New London Group, 1996). Literacy practices are encoded within language, culture and identity. The stories children share, the positionality they take up through images and illustrations, and the meaning conveyed through languages are *as* important as the writing process itself. Elementary teachers engage in multiliteracies by inviting students to share their values, families and experiences through writing workshops. Students create illustrations frequently accompanying print-based narratives, adding depth and dimension. It has become common practice to recount and sequence lived experiences, with thick description by magnifying small moments (Stagg Peterson *et al.*, 2007). While considerable curricular attention has been dedicated to crafting memoirs that rely on print practices in elementary classrooms, we believe that less attention has been dedicated to exploring how multimodal narratives can be powerful tools of educational justice, giving students voice and visibility.

Theoretical Framing

Multiliteracies theory expands our notion of literacy as a print-only practice rooted in reading and writing to a multimodal experience, integrating visuals and orality (Cope & Kalantzis, 2015; Kress, 2010; New London Group, 1996). In this new experience, emphasis is placed on social contexts and the meaning-making processes learners negotiate within such spaces. Literacy is reconceptualized to encompass multiple forms, or modes, of communication that may be realized through writing, illustrating, gesturing and speaking, without necessarily using written language as a primary mode of expression (Cope & Kalantzis, 2015; Kress & van Leeuwen, 2001). Viewing literacy in the broader scope of multiliteracies allows educators to make visible the myriad of ways learners engage with and produce texts, both inside and outside of the classroom environment.

It is within the broader theory of multiliteracies that we draw upon Cummins *et al.*'s (2012) literacy engagement framework. In his framework, Cummins (2006) views access to print as synonymous with engagement, both resulting in literacy achievement. In order for engagement to be realized, Cummins *et al.* (2012) enumerate four essential criteria: scaffolded instruction to make lessons accessible for language learners; connection to students' lives; affirmation of identity; and metalinguistic growth in competence and use. Although all four instructional dimensions were at play throughout our ethnographic study, we chose to center students' lived experiences and identity affirmation in our investigation of how language and identity are cultivated through multimodal practices.

This framework offered a lens to make visible the moves that contributed to the student investment in the multimodal memoir project and, specifically, how these moves were enacted. Cummins *et al.*'s (2012) framework is unique in that it positions investment and negotiation of learners' identities as primary indicators of cognitive engagement.

Cummins *et al.* (2005) reported on a study of language learners deeply engaged in the construction of 'identity texts.' Cummins *et al.* (2005: 2) concluded that the engagement in literacy through identity texts 'is fueled as much by affect as by cognition.' Cummins (2006) argues that the texts become sites for meaning-making and identity construction. 'Identity texts highlight the importance of identity negotiation and societal power relations in understanding the nature of classroom interactions' (Cummins, 2006: 52). Identity texts reflect positive images of the writers, serving as tools of empowerment. Identity texts have the potential to be incredibly powerful. Such a resource brings together a collective group including peers, parents and educators. The learning is collaborative within groups of native language speakers. English learners showcase their native language and identities while learning English and resituating their identities within the context of their new lives.

In our study, we follow six language learners throughout a memoir writing workshop unit in a fourth-grade classroom. Research questions guiding our inquiry were: (1) How does student engagement with multimodal literacies provide resources for literacy and language learning, for meaning-making, specifically around text production? and (2) How do graphic memoirs afford language learners opportunities to engage in transformative practices, to reimagine, reshape and resituate identities?

While connecting students' lives to storying and affirming identity were critical to the success of this writing project, we believe text *production* and *identity transformation* were paramount to literacy achievement. In the last section of this chapter, we revisit Cummins *et al.*'s (2012) literacy engagement construct to synthesize the ways in which the practices created opportunities for engagement with language and identity throughout the graphic memoir project.

Through a grounded theory analysis of classroom interactions, student-created texts and interviews over the course of 12 visits spanning three months, our study illustrates how aspects of language, culture and identity have been interwoven to create opportunities to engage in rich, literacy experiences, in both text consumption and production. The findings of the project suggest that cultivating a community of respect and care, one that makes visible the culture, background knowledge and language repertoires, is a *prerequisite* to cognitive engagement, to literacy and to language learning.

Methodology

Data for this study were collected ethnographically through participant observation and action research in the classroom (Emerson *et al.*,

2011). We engaged in ethnographic action research, with Marisa as researcher and Kristin as classroom teacher. On several visits, Marisa interviewed Kristin and the seven students listed as participants in this study and collected student writing samples to include the published graphic memoirs. Throughout the study, field notes, artifacts, transcripts of classroom interaction and student writing were analyzed using a reflexive thematic analysis approach (Braun & Clarke, 2021).

As we uncovered patterns in the field notes, classroom activities and interactions, we were guided by Cummins *et al.*'s (2012) literacy engagement framework. In analyzing the data, we initially coded thematically and subsequently categorized using inductive approaches to identify sites of language learning and identity construction throughout the graphic memoir writing project (Braun & Clark, 2021; Gibbs, 2007). This recursively yielded seven focused codes, which constitute our findings, each of which includes assertions as supporting evidence.

Kaleidoscoping communities, cubed

(1) Community in the neighborhood

Our ethnographic case study took place in an urban, bilingual K-8 school serving 750 students. The school ranks among the largest school districts in the northeast. Over 50% of the students speak English as a nonnative language. The diverse neighborhood surrounding the school consists of multi-family homes inhabited by recently arrived immigrants. *Bodegas*, churches, community health centers, *panaderías*, libraries, and several community-based, nonprofit organizations that promote advocacy through immigrant rights and cultural appreciation make up the city center.

(2) Community in the school

At first approach to the school, guests are greeted by bilingual signage. A banner hangs in the foyer promoting the Celebración Annual de la Herencia Hispana de la Escuela, a student performance to celebrate Hispanic Heritage Month. Attached to this banner are student-produced representations of peace and liberty, 'paz y libertad', alongside a more in-depth description of national Hispanic heritage month. A large painting of a hand gesture peace sign hangs, with boldly hand-painted words: **We are Latinos. We are proud of where we come from.** Two large posters hang outside the main office. The first reads: What is a community? The second poster is the mirror image, in Spanish, bordered by additional teacher photos. The lobby signage points to the office, 'la oficina'. In la oficina, the wall directly across from the main desk is covered with greetings in at least 20 languages, reflecting the diversity of its students.

The school's revised mission statement appears throughout the building: *Through an authentic education, this school empowers passionate multicultural learners to cultivate their individual strengths and inspires them to be resilient and purposeful community members.* In classrooms throughout the school, the mission is chunked into more comprehensible sound bites:

> Authentic education: real-life experiences, meaningful subject matter, engaged learners. Empowerment: be confident, be yourself, fight for what you believe in. Multicultural learning: be open-minded, value other languages, treasure our cultures. Purpose: be an advocate, be involved in your community, make the world a better place. **Be Your Best.**

(3) Community in the classroom

Despite the institutional hum of fluorescent lights, Room 227 (Kristin's classroom) was inviting, calm and peaceful. Two themes emerged that would prove impactful to the learning environment. At the classroom level, there was an energy, a palpable buzz around the blue book bin that housed graphic novels. At the school level, the theme that permeated the hallways, stairwells and classrooms centered around the mission, **Be Your Best.** Although seemingly disparate at the onset of our inquiry project, these two themes would intersect to shape the curriculum weeks later.

Room 227 was comprised of 17 emergent bilingual students spanning the fourth and fifth grades. For the purpose of our inquiry project, we followed seven students during the writing workshop memoir project (see Table 18.1).

The language proficiencies range from intermediate to low advanced, according to standardized language assessment data. Kristin designed much of her literacy block around the standards and skills of the fourth- and fifth-grade curriculum, but relied upon lower Lexile and scaffolded instruction.

Table 18.1 Kristin's students, English language arts sheltered class

Student (F = female, M = male)	Country of origin	Native language	Years in US
F1	Mexico	Spanish	6
M1	Iraq	Arabic	2.5
F2	Sudan (moved to Egypt)	Rutana, Arabic	2
F3	Syria	Arabic	2
F4	Iraq	Arabic	1.5
M2	Iraq	Arabic	1.5
F5	Syria (moved to Iraq)	Arabic	<1.5

Space to reflect, to refine

Throughout our project, Kristin simultaneously facilitated a professional learning community (PLC) with grade level peers. It was in these meetings that Kristin began to second-guess the depth of engagement her students demonstrated during the writing project's initial phase. We offered three hypotheses:

(1) The practice of using graphic organizers as a prewriting tool to brainstorm ideas as the first step of the writing process is common in American schools. This practice is embedded in the culture of how we prepare teachers to approach pedagogy and practice. We question their use outside of our culturally specific contexts.
(2) Memories shared in the semantic mapping activity included in the writing workshop curriculum recount pleasant experiences with people, places and things, e.g. house, family, nature/hiking, music lessons, pets and vacations (Calkins & Chiarella, 2006). Newly arrived immigrant students may not share similar, positive experiences.
(3) The brainstorming exercise relied on students' ability to write. When students lack the proficiency to fluently generate ideas in writing, the medium itself may be the barrier, more so than the mode.

In one of these PLC meetings, a colleague shared her success with storyboarding as a segue to writing. Kristin reflected on the medium (drawing) and mode (graphics) of storyboarding and the increased accessibility it could offer her emergent bilingual students. Kristin abandoned the heart-shaped graphic organizer and the written drafts of students' memoirs and pivoted to storyboarding. Referring to the significance of her membership in the PLC, Kristin shared:

> We talked about storyboarding one day and that was something I brought back and used in a different way the second time around with the narrative. It was what made me feel like ok about abandoning what I was doing and starting something new, just because normally I'd spend two weeks in the computer lab publishing. If this wasn't really great writing, is this the best use of their time?

Back to the storyboard: Evolution from print-centric to multimodal literacies

It was here that Kristin's narrative writing project took two critical turns. Recall the two themes that had played out, within both the school and the classroom, concurrent with the redesign of the narrative writing project:

(1) The school discourse, oral and written, had taken up the idea of being your best, echoing the words of the school's mission. Teachers dedicated class time to deconstructing this notion by identifying ways students demonstrated their best.
(2) Students devoured graphic novels, perhaps because of the content, perhaps because of the accessibility of text, with visuals.

Table 18.2 Revised memoir project timeline to include multimodal meaning-making processes

Writing process	Original (print-centric) memoir project	Revised (multimodal) memoir project
Phase 1: Prewriting	Heart-shaped graphic organizer	Theme: Be Your Best. Storyboard, with visuals and native language
Phase 2: (Re)drafting	Sensory charts to add details	Storyboard, with added abbreviated text
Phase 3: Revising	Draft memoir, in writing	Expand each storyboard tile into a paragraph, creating five-paragraph essay
Phase 4: Editing	Peer editing/teacher conference	Peer editing (attention to linguistic proficiency)/teacher conference
Phase 5: Publishing	Time to type in computer center, usually one week	Produced graphic text, synthesized from five-paragraph essay
Celebration	Full class share	Sharing with K newcomers

Kristin capitalized on the discourse of being your best and interwove that theme into student narratives. As the students began to storyboard, they reflected on a time in their life that epitomized their best, an experience in which they persevered. Over two weeks, the storyboard activity was scaffolded through the writing process to culminate in a five-paragraph essay. Table 18.2 details the revisions Kristin made to include multimodal elements. At the students' request, they created graphic memoirs, using the graphic novels they had read – *Amulet, Babymouse, The Magic Pickle, Lunch Lady* – as mentor texts.

The most significant changes made to the revised memoir project included:

(1) the focus on memoirs that illustrated students at their best, as having persevered, as being competent;
(2) the graphic representation of that memoir with text *and* imagery; and
(3) the idea that the memoirs would be shared with the kindergarten newcomer class on the ground floor.

Summary of Findings

Our approach in sharing the findings combine the use of integrative and excerpt strategies. Some of the findings, as Emerson *et al.* (2011: 211) describes, 'weave together the interpretation and the excerpt' and, in doing so, we illustrate evidence to illustrate the claim. However, some claims are instantiated through student discourse and in such cases we delineate between quotes from the field notes and/or students and our commentary and interpretation (Emerson *et al.*, 2011). Themes that emerged from our analysis suggest that while the required four components of Cummins *et al.*'s (2012) literacy framework were upheld throughout the project, there were several other ideas that contributed to language, literacy and identity development.

(1) Scaffold instruction

Scaffolding was applied in the modification of input, leveraging graphic novels as mentor texts, ensuring access to print and contextualizing the small moment memoir within the broader context of the school's mission, to include modifying the mission itself. Scaffolding was embedded in the opportunities created for output, for production, by storyboarding to generate writing with visuals, by offering modeled language during editing and revising and by giving students a voice through oral presentations at the publishing party.

(2) Connect to students' lives

Although this is inherent in any memoir writing project, we would argue that focusing on a lived experience that portrayed students at their best offered them the opportunity to reposition perceived identities. It offered students the opportunity to share times of challenges and vulnerability and make visible instances of strength and perseverance.

(3) Affirm identity and (4) extend language

Through their own multicultural illustrations of lived experiences, students had authorship, ownership and investment throughout the process. Incorporating native language was encouraged during drafts and revisions as a way to extend ideas and language, negotiate meaning, and bridge oral language and English print-based literacy. Students incorporated culturally specific visuals, e.g. national flags and colors and general appearance of family members, including cultural and religious dress. 'My favorite part was when we draw because I can draw people like they look from my country' (F5).

In addition to the four components outlined in the literacy engagement framework (Cummins *et al.*, 2012), we enumerate several factors that contributed to language and literacy development and identity negotiation throughout text production.

(5) Leverage academic communities

The PLC in which Kristin participated provided a space for reflection, critique and revision. Through conversation and collegial support, Kristin abandoned the original memoir project. She decided to incorporate the discourse of deconstructing the school mission. Kristin listened as her colleague shared a project in which students experienced success with storyboarding. Kristin communicated at the beginning of the project that the stories would be shared with newcomers in kindergarten and Grade 1. Excerpts from student interviews are enumerated below which suggest an investment in the production *and* celebration of sharing their graphic memoirs:

F4: I wonder if in some ways that I get to be a big brother, big sister, and I can teach this value to younger kids.
M2: I teach them [newcomers] not to be scared because they don't speak English. It teaches kids that even if you can't do it, you have to … if you don't do it, you won't be proud of yourself.
F2: Sometimes when I read at home, not everyone listens to me but the little kids were really paying attention. They real know what I am talking about.
F5: We are gonna read it to a lot of kids … And they're gonna know more about what happened to them, what happened to us when we get the first day of school and we were like scared, too.
F3: We taught the kids to never give up and they were happy, about what we read them.
M1: It was important to me to show them to never give up, like make an example. The class was paying attention a lot to the story and then … they started talking about it.

(6) Provide multiple ways to share multimodal productions

The students expressed a sense of community, a special bond between themselves and the newcomers. Students elaborated on their preference of modalities. 'My favorite part of the project was drawing and making it colorful, because I don't like to write that much' (F1). During the publishing party, a student (M2) used his hands to gesture the actions in his story because he knew the young kids didn't speak English, just like him a year before. As he presented, his posture was erect, more confident as he told the newcomers not to be scared if they don't speak English that much. Just try your best to learn, he said.

Although another student was initially asked to translate, she reported, 'I didn't have to translate for the newcomers because when they she saw the pictures, they understood' (F4). One student who had planned to use Arabic felt that she didn't need to because she 'showed them with my hands' (F2). A girl proudly recounted, 'They understood [the newcomers] because they speak Arabic so I translate some of the things they didn't understand' (F3). One boy, in particular, interwove both Arabic and English in his reading, 'I used Arabic to make them understand' (M1). Knowing they could use their native language, their most powerful tool in making sense of their story, assuaged students' concerns.

(7) Empower through storying

The seven students included in our study were born outside of the United States. Each had learned English as a second or third language. Each had faced great hardship on their journeys to Room 227. Many had experienced failure in school. In a school of more than 700 students, those most invisible are often students who lack capital: economic, social, cultural or linguistic. The graphic memoir and, specifically, the theme of perseverance, presented an opportunity to share success.

Given the lived experiences of emergent bilinguals, especially newcomers, reliance on writing within culturally normed, semantic maps may be an ineffective starting point. We must problematize print-centric writing and welcome multimodal forms of representation in storying and in countering perceived narratives. By focusing on perseverance in multimodal literacies, the students' strengths of character became more visible than their linguistic deficits. Weeks after the project had ended, Kristin reflected on the experience:

> Sometimes you have to sacrifice other things in a way that you might think you're sacrificing quality of work to give more choice or promote engagement. Like someone might say a graphic novel isn't the same as something that is all formatted in paragraphs and it's true but I think long term it's worth it ... you get more rigor out of them in the end.

Closing Thoughts

Multiliteracies pedagogy offers ways to understand and affirm the communities emergent bilingual students participate in and contribute to inside and outside of the classroom. By creating communities within classroom and school, students are afforded opportunities to engage in literacy and identity development and begin to take on new, academic identities, empowering them in other contexts. Within communities, Kristin cultivated a community of care, of respect, through listening, validating students' stories. Cummins *et al.* (2005) concluded that acknowledging and promoting linguistic and cultural capital in a pedagogy of respect leads to deeper meaning and engagement.

Our findings suggest that cultivating a community of respect and care, one that makes visible the culture, background knowledge and language repertoires, is a *prerequisite* to cognitive engagement, to literacy and language learning. This chapter reported on the significance of storyboarding within graphic narrative storytelling, of giving bilingual learners voice through illustration and by celebrating perseverance through sharing stories within school communities. Throughout the memoir project, participants negotiated identities as learners, as readers, as writers, as consumers of texts, as cultural ambassadors, as community members and as producers of texts. Membership in these communities is critical to language and literacy learning.

As learners negotiated, reconstructed and co-constructed new identities, they expanded and (re)connected to their communities. In doing so, they (re)shaped their positionality. Our collaboration highlights how educators can create opportunities to meaningfully practice pedagogies of multiliteracies within the communities where they live and learn (Cope & Kalantzis, 2015). In creating access, students cultivate investment in the process of language and literacy development and identity work that is critical to their academic success (Cummins *et al.*, 2012).

Our engagement with transformative pedagogies throughout this project afforded bilingual youth the opportunity to *rewrite* how they are perceived in the classroom and school community, perhaps to match more closely to the identities they reveal in their neighborhood community. Through their stories of perseverance, they *countered* the dominant deficit narrative. Students positioned themselves as winners even when they did not win the race. They tried their best. They persevered. And a space was created to reimagine themselves.

References

Braun, V. and Clarke, V. (2021) One size fits all? What counts as quality practice in (reflexive) thematic analysis? *Qualitative Research in Psychology* 18 (3), 328–352.

Calkins, L. and Chiarella, M. (2006) *Memoir: The Art of Writing Well.* Portsmouth, NH: FirstHand/Heinemann.

Cope, B. and Kalantzis, M. (2009) 'Multiliteracies': New Literacies, new learning. *Pedagogies: An International Journal* 4 (3), 164-195.

Cope, B. and Kalantzis, M. (2015) The things you do to know: An introduction to the pedagogy of multiliteracies. In B. Cope and M. Kalantzis (eds) *A Pedagogy of Multiliteracies: Learning by Design* (pp. 1–36). London: Palgrave.

Cummins, J., Bismilla, V., Chow, P., Giampapa, F., Cohen, S., Leoni, L., Sandhu, P. and Sastri, P. (2005) Affirming identity in multilingual classrooms. *Educational Leadership* 63 (1), 38–43.

Cummins, J. (2006) Identity texts: The imaginative construction of self through multiliteracies pedagogy. In O. García, T. Skutnabb-Kangas and M. Torres-Guzmán (eds) *Imagining Multilingual Schools: Languages in Education and Glocalization* (pp. 51–68). Clevedon: Multilingual Matters.

Cummins, J., Mirza, R. and Stille, S. (2012) English language learners in Canadian schools: Emerging directions for school-based policies. *TESL Canada Journal* 29, 25.

Emerson, R., Fretz, R. and Shaw, L. (2011) *Writing Ethnographic Fieldnotes* (2nd edn). Chicago, IL: University of Chicago Press.

Gibbs, G.R. (2007) *Analyzing Qualitative Data.* London: Sage.

Kress, G. (2010) *Multimodality: A Social Semiotic Approach to Contemporary Communication.* London: Routledge.

Kress, G. and van Leeuwen, T. (2001) *Multimodal Discourse: The Modes and Media of Contemporary Communication.* New York: Oxford University Press.

New London Group (1996) A pedagogy of multiliteracies: Designing social futures. *Harvard Educational Review* 66 (1), 60–93. doi:10.17763/haer.66.1.17370n67v22j160u

Stagg Peterson, S., Botelho, M., Eunice, J. and Kerekes, J. (2007) Writing assessment: What would multiliteracies teachers do? *Literacy Learning in the Middle Years* 15, 29–35.

Street, B. (1995) *Social Literacies: Critical Approaches to Literacy Development, Ethnography, and Education.* New York: Longman.

19 Legos: A Multimodal Approach to Storytelling for a Young African Emergent Bilingual

Sally Brown and Ling Hao

> Legos helped me think about my story. I kept on thinking what I wanted to make next. What was Rapunzel and the witch going to do? ... I made it, and wrote it into a book.
>
> (Bem)

Introduction

This chapter features the multimodal literacy practices of Bem (pseudonym), a young African emergent bilingual, as she engaged with reading, Lego construction, oral storytelling, digital photography and book making. The fields of sociomateriality, multimodality and New Literacy Studies provide a framework for understanding her practices. Bem's work is presented in the form of learning stories as a means of showcasing the vast complexities associated with her meaning-making processes.

Theoretical Underpinnings: A Blended Perspective

Sociomateriality creates a space for open-ended thinking about the ways in which children enter into relations with objects and technology as part of their literacy practices (Fenwick, 2012). In other words, there is a need to examine all of the 'stuff' that facilitates literacy development. Kress (2005) uses the term materiality to collectively describe the resources a child uses for meaning-making, which may include paper, words, actions, etc. The non-human objects or resources are transformed based on the ways in which the child morphs their use. Burnett and Merchant (2020) refer to the shape-shifting quality of objects as *liveliness*. Children often use environmental objects in unexpected ways which offer new learning opportunities that are unique for each child. This generates different ways of knowing and being that highlight the instability of reality and the moment-to-moment nature of human and non-human interactions, the resulting conclusion being that meaning is 'distributed between people and things' (Burnett & Merchant, 2020: 33).

As human and non-human entanglements occur, many semiotic systems are involved. For example, images, movement and language use are intertwined to construct meaning. As the child intentionally manipulates objects through sociomaterial relations, the resulting efforts may be referred to as texts. These texts are influenced by the agency of the learner and their cultural and social making skills. A multimodal perspective sheds light on the materials serving as signs or forms of meaning expression (Kress, 2005). Signs are purposely manipulated by the child in their inter-active engagement, taking into account the affordance of the materials or resources. Kuby and Rucker (2016: 13) refer to this as a state of becoming where the 'dialogue between the child and the material produces newness.' In their work with young children, they found a curriculum offering flexibility in terms of inter-activity between humans and non-humans to be essential for the unfolding nature of learning where children changed paths as they generated their own multimodal texts.

Wohlwend's (2013) literacy playshop is an example of this pedagogy in practice. She connects play and storying in a way that allows students to select humans (friends/classmates) and non-human objects (paper, props, popsicle sticks, etc.) in order to make meaning. In this model, collaboration and collective meaning-making are valued as students engage in the multimodal composing process where the children make choices about how they want to tell their stories. This positions children as knowledgeable and having expertise in a multitude of areas including the use of technology for filming purposes. Students utilize their imaginations in ways that transform materials in personally relevant ways. In Kervin and Comber's (2021) study of five-year-old Ruben, they noted his use of movement, material and sound, the use of technology, and peers as resources in order to compose a multimodal text using Book Creator. The fluidity of the learning context afforded Ruben a multitude of possibilities for navigating his construction of a text.

Context of the Research

This case study presents the multimodal literacy practices of Bem, arising out of several learning events designed and implemented by Sally in a third-grade classroom. The data were part of a larger study involving the whole class (Brown, 2020). A 'literacy-as-event' (Burnett & Merchant, 2020) approach was used to guide the analysis of data in a way that recognized literacy as being emergent rather than prefigured. This perspective allowed a focus on the ways humans and non-humans intermingled to affect one another. In addition, a learning stories method was applied to the data as a way to emphasize Bem's experiences. Learning stories were developed by New Zealand researchers Carr and Lee (2019) and are an integral part of the Te Whäriki curriculum as a way to value the complex learning of young children with a focus on assets and strengths. Carr and Lee (2019: 4) acknowledge that 'learning is entangled with, and made possible through, the material, social, cultural, and historical features of the context for learning.' Writing stories about children as learners affirms children and families. Three elements of this framework guided the creation of Bem's learning stories: (1) enhancing a child's sense of themselves as capable people and competent learners; (2) reflecting the holistic way that children learn; and (3) reflecting the reciprocal relationships between the child, people and the learning environment (Lee & Carr, 2002). Bem's learning stories address the following research questions:

- How did Bem use human and non-human resources to tell her story?
- In what ways was Bem agentive and intentional in her use of resources?

Bem

Bem was a nine-year-old third-grade student in an urban elementary school in the southeastern United States. Two years ago, she moved to the US from Liberia, Africa. Bassa was her first language, and she was learning English at school. According to school testing, her English language proficiency was rated at an *expanding level*, meaning that she knew and could use social English and specific academic language without support. Her English reading level was regarded as one half-year below level, which resulted in a label indicating that she needed improvement. Her first language literacy skills were not evaluated.

The school setting had English-only policies with limited resources in other languages. She received English for speakers of other languages (ESOL) services in the form of pull-out instruction for 30–40 minutes per day. By the end of the school year, Bem's reading performance had improved, allowing her to be promoted to the next grade level. The learning stories featured below represent a three-month period of time when Bem engaged with paper-based Lego books, built stories with Legos, took photographs using a digital camera and crafted a story including her recorded voice.

Sally served as an additional teacher in Bem's classroom during small-group center time. While some students met with the classroom teacher for guided reading instruction, the rest of the class rotated among learning centers. Sally's work with Legos was one of the centers that the children could choose to attend. The goal was to promote language development for emergent bilinguals and to motivate students to write. In order to entice students, Sally gathered Lego sets as the materials to inspire writing. The sets had various building blocks, minifigure heads and accessories (i.e. food, animals, tools, weapons), with enough pieces for small groups of students. Each child had their own base block where they could construct story scenes, and this remained intact from day to day. In other words, the students could pick up where they left off from the previous day. The overall structure of the *literacy-as-events* involved collaborative readings of Lego books in order to gain insight into story elements as well as the way professional authors photographed Legos for their books. Second, there was time for the students to build their stories. As each story scene was completed, the students took digital photographs of their scenes and, upon completion, the students inserted their images into the computer to compose a digital story.

Transcripts of video-taped small-group interactions, researcher field notes, digital photographs and work samples (student books) were used to develop the learning stories. Each story contains multimodal elements from the collected data.

Bem's Learning Stories

The three learning stories featured below document Bem's literacy learning and should be interpreted as a work in progress. Taken together, the stories draw from her multiple learning repertoires that showcase her as a thoughtful, reflective learner. In addition, the stories include the voice of Bem herself as she makes decisions about human and non-human resources in her meaning-making processes.

Learning story 1: Reading Lego books

An eager Bem arrived at the series of desks pushed together as a table along with her peers, Ruthie, Jalen and Brad. The paper-based early reader Lego books were laying with the covers facing upwards. Bem quickly sat down, grabbed Lego Friends: Perfect Pets *(Stock, 2014), and motioned for Ruthie to sit next to her. Without any direction from the researcher, the girls began talking about the book cover which was situated between them. Bem initiated the conversation, 'Hey, look here. This book has two girls. One has yellow hair like Rapunzel,' and smiled. Ruthie followed, 'Yes, like us. They have pets too. What do you have?' 'A dog at my house,' replied Bem. This was followed by a close examination of the Lego images on the pages where the girls continued talking about the storyline in the book as well as other ideas for using the Legos. Then, Bem took the book in her hand once they arrived at page five. She read the first sentence with help from Ruthie, 'Mia's friends Olivia, Emma, Stephanie, and Andrea ...,' and pulled the book close to her face and began talking mainly to herself. 'This story's giving me, well, some ideas. It's kind of like an adventure or something. That's what I can do.' Ruthie replied, 'That would be great. What will you call it?' Later, Bem commented while laughing, 'It will be Rapunzel and the Ugly Witch! I want to have a bad character.' Bem was immersed in her story based on the ideas she was receiving from the book. She was already thinking ahead to her own story, and this was basically an oral rehearsal for her writing which included identifying characters and a plot.*

In this learning story, Bem immediately took independent action as she sat down. She was familiar with the non-structured routines of the researcher and knew there was flexibility in how the learning would unfold at this center. Students were guided by 'thin pedagogies,' which encouraged more diverse learning options (Baroutsis, 2020). She used the book as a non-human resource for extended thinking about stories, and took the initiative to invite a human resource, Ruthie, for collaborative meaning-making. The actual images in the book were the focus of much of the dialogue, and the girls never read the book from cover to cover as one might traditionally expect. But, they viewed this time as an opportunity to gather ideas for their independent stories which they understood to be the goal of the center. Bem was clearly an effective communicator even though her school positioned her as less able during traditional school work. Her ways of acting and being showed a very capable composer who carefully considered options for her storyline. Connections were built upon her home experiences where she went to the movie theater to see *Rapunzel*. She effectively used visual images in the book along with the written words at points to orally compose.

Learning story 2: Lego construction

All of the Lego pieces were in small trays on top of the table of desks. Bem stood up and stared at the available pieces, touching a few. Jalen and Brad had already started building when Bem arrived. She looked carefully at their construction, and said, 'Who's this?' referring to a character Jalen built. 'It's Joe and he is part of the Jolesco team who plans to fight with a weapon,' Jalen replied. Bem continued, 'My story's about Rapunzel. You know that one? I see you have some faces. Can I use them?' Bem reached down and picked up three yellow Lego heads and reached for her base that she worked from yesterday. She announced, 'I'm adding a mom and a dad,' and sat down to build bodies out of Lego bricks and legs. Then, she pummeled through the trays to locate what she referred to as 'girl hair.' Once this task was complete, Bem started designing a witch by locating a black hat and broom. In talking to the group, she verbalized some of her building plans. 'Well, I can use food to trick Rapunzel into thinking the witch is good.' After meticulously building a tray using four Lego bricks and a small cup, plate and loaf of bread, Bem had set her trap. Bem was creative in her approach to constructing a storyline that matched the available Lego pieces (Figure 19.1).

Figure 19.1 The ugly witch setting her trap

Bem successfully used the digital camera to take a series of photographs of the trap scene. She turned the camera on, focused it, and clicked the button to take the photo. She was very conscious of perspective from studying the pictures in the Lego books. For this scene, Bem took four photos all from different angles. After viewing them on a computer screen, Bem selected this one to be inserted into her story, a close-up of the witch with the table of enticing food. While Bem did not follow the storyline exactly as featured in the movie Rapunzel, *she was able to demonstrate the ability to create a plausible plot with all the necessary characters. Each selection of material resources purposefully added details to the storyline. For example, the addition of the black, pointed hat to the black body made it highly likely that her peers would recognize this character as a witch. This showed that Bem had an awareness of the audience and manipulated her resources to serve her storytelling goal.*

Bem's material construction of story scenes remained independent of her peers for the most part. She worked quietly on her own, rarely asking for feedback. She was driven by the plot she already worked out in her head and through designing the scenes. For this particular story, Bem constructed six different story scenes, each building on the previous one in a logical way. Her use of material resources remained true to the Lego pieces. For example, she used a Lego tree to represent a tree in the forest. However, Bem's ingenuity came into play with the ways in which she placed each of the objects on the storyboard and the angles of her photographs. It was as if Bem was an artist performing her work through the use of Legos and digital photography, each adding another layer of complexity to the other. Her learning was distributed and mediated across the learning resources available in this context (Kervin *et al.*, 2019). Bem was in a state of becoming during this series of events (Kuby & Rucker, 2016).

Learning story 3: Digital book making

The digital version of Bem's story, Rapunzel and the Ugly Witch, was written in English which was the language Bem selected based on her audience of mainly English-only peers. The story was written using the series of photographs Bem took herself of story scenes built with Legos and the use of speech bubbles containing dialogue. Her technology skills flourished as she learned to upload her photographs to a Lego computer program called Story Visualizer and arranged the photos in the order she wanted them to appear in her book. This process was fluid as she made several changes along the way, showing how her story morphed as she began writing it. The story shifting was a result of her interactions with the digital photographs. In addition, Bem utilized backgrounds made available in the program to add depth to her story, with the last page using only words as a conclusion. Bem's story was logical and cohesive as it traced the adventure of Rapunzel and her parents. According to Bem, 'Well, there was a princess named Rapunzel, and she had a mom and dad. Then, this old witch stopped by their house, and the mom felt bad, and the witch came into their house to get food. Then, the trap was set. The witch offered food to Rapunzel but it had poison in it and the witch took her away. Then, her parents look for her, but she was in a jail and the witch put chains on her. There's a good ending because mom and dad save Rapunzel and put the witch in jail.' Bem's recounting of her story provides a great deal of depth about her storyline, characters and plot. She is clearly able to articulate this through oral language. This is told in a simpler version in the digital book where Bem creatively and effectively used speech bubbles to speak on behalf of the characters, a more sophisticated approach to storytelling. Her photographs are rich visual supplements for the actions and events occurring throughout the pages (Figure 19.2).

The digital book created by Bem was a result of the complex entanglements between humans and non-human objects including the use of technology (Toohey *et al.*, 2015). Bem was familiar with basic technology from her school experiences such as playing reading and math games or answering questions for Accelerated Reader quizzes, but she did not have more sophisticated skills. Sally scaffolded her understanding of uploading photos, reordering photos and adding speech bubbles along with her dialogue. At times, Bem's peers offered assistance which she willingly accepted. These took the form of quick, individualized mini-lessons. Bem

Figure 19.2 Selected pages from Bem's story: Rapunzel and the Ugly Witch

was a quick learner and eager to take what she learned and apply it independently. She used a trial-and-error approach until the book met her expectations. Each decision enhanced the overall quality of her story. The construction of her book took several weeks as each intentional and agentive move unfolded during the meaning-making process. Multiple modes were brought together to form a cohesive ensemble (Kress, 2010).

Concluding Thoughts

Bem's learning stories showcased her as an agentive learner who utilized the resources around her intentionally to tell her story. In addition to interacting and collaborating with her classmates, Bem was capable of manipulating the available Lego resources and the technology resources (e.g. the digital camera and the computer program) to compose her story. The richness of Lego resources including the Lego books, various building blocks, minifigure heads and multiple accessories on different topics further supported Bem's multimodal meaning-making/storytelling process.

These learning stories have the potential to inform how teachers may create their own learning stories about the students in their classrooms. Karlsdottir and Einarsdottir (2020) offer suggestions for the use of learning stories. First, creating a learning story requires one to understand children's competencies and their strengths as learners. This is counter to the deficit-based environments that perpetuate in many schools especially regarding students learning English as a new language. Second, learning stories are valuable for understanding the various pathways that children may decide to take in order to express themselves, particularly students who are not part of the mainstream culture. Last, these evidence-based narratives can be used in the profession to speak against the exclusive use of print-based practices for instructional and assessment purposes.

References

Baroutsis, A. (2020) Sociomaterial assemblages, entanglements and text production: Mapping pedagogic practices using time-lapse photography. *Journal of Early Childhood Literacy* 20 (4), 732–754.

Brown, S. (2020) Literacy in early childhood: Multimodal play and text production. In J. Mitchell and E. Vaughn (eds) *Participatory Literacy Practices for P-12 Classrooms in the Digital Age* (pp. 1–19). Hershey, PA: IGI Global.

Burnett, C. and Merchant, G. (2020) *Undoing the Digital: Sociomaterialism and Literacy Education*. London: Routledge.

Carr, M. and Lee, W. (2019) *Learning Stories in Practice*. Thousand Oaks, CA: Sage.

Fenwick, T. (2012) Matterings of knowing and doing: Sociomaterial approaches to understanding practice. In P. Hager, A. Lee and A. Reich (eds) *Practice, Learning and Change: Practice-Theory Perspectives on Professional Learning* (pp. 67–83). Dordrecht: Springer.

Karlsdottir, K. and Einarsdottir, J. (2020) Supporting democracy and agency for all children: The learning stories of two immigrant boys. *Contemporary Issues in Early Childhood* 21 (4), 325–339.

Kervin, L. and Comber, B. (2021) Digital writing from the start to the end: Creating a book for a friend. *Theory Into Practice* 60 (2), 137–147.

Kervin, L., Comber, B. and Baroutsis, A. (2019) Sociomaterial dimensions of early literacy learning spaces: Moving through classrooms with teacher and children. In H. Hughes, J. Franz and J. Willis (eds) *School Spaces for Student Wellbeing and Learning* (pp. 21–38). Cham: Springer.

Kress, G. (2005) *Before Writing: Rethinking the Paths to Literacy*. New York: Routledge.

Kress, G. (2010) *Multimodality: A Social Semiotic Approach to Contemporary Communication*. New York: Routledge.

Kuby, C.R. and Rucker, T.G. (2016) *Go Be A Writer!: Expanding the Curricular Boundaries of Literacy Learning with Children*. New York: Teachers College Press.

Lee, W. and Carr, M. (2002) Documentation of learning stories: A powerful assessment tool for early childhood. Paper presented at Dialogue and Documentation: Sharing our Understanding of Children's Learning and Developing a Rich Early Years Provision, Pen Green, Corby.

Stock, L. (2014) *LEGO Friends: Perfect Pet*. London: DK Childrens.

Toohey, K., Dagenais, D., Fodor, A., Hof, L., Nuñez, O., Singh, A. and Schulze, L. (2015) 'That sounds so cooool': Entanglements of children, digital tools, and literacy practices. *TESOL Quarterly* 49 (3), 461–485.

Wohlwend, K.E. (2013) *Literacy Playshop: New Literacies, Popular Media, and Play in the Early Childhood Classroom*. New York: Teachers College Press.

Part 4

Out-of-School Contexts

20 Multimodal Literacies at Home: A Survey Study of Chinese-Norwegian Bilingual Children

Junyi Yang and Joshua Lawrence

Introduction

I think the app is more effective than a language course.

One Chinese parent in Norway shared this sentiment when talking about children's literacy learning. In this regard, evolving technologies continuously offer new pathways for learning. Children today use technologies and multimodal literacies for learning and meaning-making (Jewitt & Kress, 2003). This shift toward multimodal literacies has been extensively studied in school settings (Brown & Allmond, 2021; Park *et al.*, 2013; Zheng *et al.*, 2015) and increasingly studied in home settings (for a review, see Kumpulainen & Gillen, 2020). Some bilingual studies have also shed light on these changes by examining technology's pedagogical opportunities in language learning (Little, 2019; Smith & Li, 2020; Zhao & Flewitt, 2019). For example, Zhao and Flewitt (2019) observed children's use of social media and discovered the multimodal nature of their language use, concluding that digital tools offer more opportunities for home language practices. Smith and Li (2020) studied immigrant children's reading activities in the digital environment and found a positive correlation with learning motivation. Nevertheless, compared with studies that address emergent bilingual children's use of print resources, less is known about their digital environment and how they connect with children's individual differences.

Moreover, there is an overrepresentation of studies that examine English as one of the pair of languages (Proctor & Zhang-Wu, 2019). Given that English has a unique place in the global marketplace of languages, it is not clear how findings from these studies may or may not generalize to families that navigate other language dyads and triads. In this chapter, we centered upon a less-studied population, Chinese-Norwegian emergent bilingual children. According to Statistics Norway (2020), over 13,000 Chinese people are living in Norway. Many of them are in Norway for career opportunities or to advance their education (Statistics Norway, 2008). Even if this population is not large, hundreds of bilingual children speak Chinese at home while learning Norwegian in kindergarten/school. In Norway, children have access to kindergarten when they are one year old. They enter school at the age of six and start learning English as a subject in Grade 1. In Norwegian kindergartens, free play is the foundation for learning, while digital practices serve as tools for enriching the learning environment (Norwegian Ministry of Education and Research, 2017). In primary and secondary schools, digital skills are identified as one of the five necessary skills for all children, along with oral skills, reading, writing and numeracy (Norwegian Directorate for Education and Training, 2006). Therefore, it would be of interest to determine how children experience the digital environment at home and transition from kindergarten to primary school.

In this chapter, we focused on Chinese-Norwegian emergent bilingual children from three to eight years old, and examined how they learned languages using multimodal literacies at home. Our expansive definition of literacy includes a broader range of sources than are usually examined, including books, audio-recordings, videos, games and other tools that are available at home. To understand the details of children's multimodal literacy resources, we adopted content analysis to study their favorite books and applications (hereafter, apps). Content analysis is a systematic way to examine and summarize texts of various formats (Cohen *et al.*, 2017), which matches the data and purpose of the study. The analysis highlighted the textual and visual structure of the resources through the language, genre and format of the books and the educational features of the apps. Furthermore, we sought to contrast their multimodal literacies experience across families and determine what individual differences connect with their use of multimodal literacies at home. The primary research questions of this study are: (1) What multimodal literacy resources and practices do Chinese-Norwegian emergent bilingual children have at home? and (2) Do their multimodal literacy resources and practices differ across age and language dominance?

Methods

Participants

The sample consists of 86 Chinese parents (71 mothers and 15 fathers) who have a three- to eight-year-old child (mean = 64 months, *SD* = 17 months). The families are scattered all over Norway, with around half living in the larger Oslo area. Eighty-five percent of the parents have been living in Norway for more than five years. Most children were born in

Norway, and their average age for attending kindergarten was 22 months (*SD* = 14 months). The sample represented a relatively highly educated group, with only 13% not having a university bachelor's degree.

Procedure and questionnaire

We approached targeted parents through social media and personal contact. Parents answered the self-administered questionnaire online in Chinese. For those parents who have more than one child, we asked them to consider the youngest child from three to eight years old. The survey asked parents about the children's print- and screen-based resources and practices at home and parental judgment of their children's language skills.

Print-based

Parents reported the number of children's books at home in three languages: Chinese, Norwegian and English. They also reported if their child likes to read. Parents who reported that their children like to read were then asked to list three of their child's favorite books, regardless of language.

Screen-based

Parents reflected on multimodal literacy resources their child could access at home, such as smartphones and tablets, PC, TV, ebooks and learning machines (a product designed for children with education purpose, which is used for language learning). They also reported in detail about the children's use of apps (i.e. types, languages, time spent, with or without parent participation).

Language dominance

We translated and altered items from the Alberta Language and Development Questionnaire (ALDeQ; Paradis *et al.*, 2010) to solicit information about children's language skills. Parents were asked to compare their child's speaking, listening, vocabulary, narratives and pragmatics in Chinese and Norwegian with same-age children in Norway. We summed the total score of parental judgment to differentiate children's language dominance. Children whose parents reported higher scores for them on Chinese language skills were coded as Chinese dominant ($n = 43$), and children whose parents reported higher scores for them on Norwegian skill dimensions were coded as Norwegian dominant ($n = 43$).

Analysis

We used both qualitative and quantitative approaches in the analyses. We conducted a content analysis with a qualitative approach to study children's favorite books and a language-learning app. In the analysis of books, we coded and analyzed language, genre and format dimensions.

The language code was established with reference to the reported book title. For example, if parents wrote *Peppa Pig*, then we assumed their children read it in English. As such, we labeled 小猪佩奇 (*Xiaozhu Peiqi*) as in Chinese, and *Peppa gris* as in Norwegian. We used an existing genre and format coding scheme (Anderson, 2013), which classified the books into early childhood books, fiction, traditional literature, autobiography and biography, informational books and poetry categories. We also coded format features related to the textual and non-textual supports available in each text. For instance, we identified books where the narrative was driven by illustrations or the text was adapted for young readers. Apps were coded according to the scheme developed by Callaghan and Reich (2018), which aimed at examining the educational features, including codes associated with the following dimensions: clarity and simplicity of goals; quality of feedback and rewards; the structure of challenge; and motion-based interactions. Our quantitative analysis included testing differences in children's experience with multimodal literacy across age group and language dominance. We explored Spearman correlation matrices to understand the relationships between and within children's print- and screen-based literacies at home. All quantitative analyses were conducted in Stata 16 (StataCorp, 2019).

Results

Print-based

Most families (85%) had more than 10 children's books at home, 55% of which had over 50 children's books. Figure 20.1 displays the average number of children's books at home. The left-hand bars indicate that families of Norwegian-dominant children had more Norwegian books ($M = 2.3$) than families of Chinese-dominant children ($M = 1.9$), but the difference was not significant, t (84) = 1.39, $p = 0.16$. The right-hand bars show that there were more Chinese books in Chinese-dominant homes ($M = 2.8$) than in Norwegian-dominant homes ($M = 1.9$), and the difference is significant, t (83) = 3.17, $p < 0.01$. Interestingly, Chinese-dominant children also had significantly more English books ($M = 1.2$), t (83) = 2.29, $p < 0.05$, and older children had more Norwegian books, t (84) = 2.44, $p < 0.05$.

Forty-nine parents reported that their child liked to read and noted the titles of their child's favorite books. We obtained 126 book title entries, of which 70 entries referenced unique books and 56 entries were duplicates of 16 popular books. Books such as *Detektivbyrå nr. 2* (Horst, 2019), *Peppa Pig* (Astley & Baker, 2018) and some classic fairy tales were popular among Chinese-Norwegian bilingual children. The favorite books were reported in different languages; the majority were in Chinese (67%), then in Norwegian (22%), and a smaller proportion in English (11%).

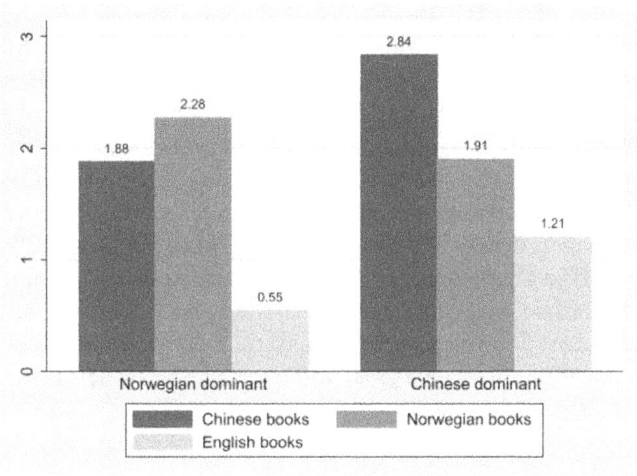

Figure 20.1 Norwegian- and Chinese-dominant children's books at home (on average)

Note: 0 = less than 5 books; 1 = 6–10 books; 2 = 11–20 books; 3 = 21–50 books; 4 = more than 50 books.

Our categorical analysis indicated that books covered various topics and some books spanned genres (as has being seen in previous studies, such as Andersen, 2013). Often the main characters were children or animals that personify humans, engage in everyday activities, tackle various tasks or embark on mysterious journeys. To separate early childhood books from fiction and informational books, we used word count as the criterion. Early childhood books are defined as books written for young children containing only short or no texts (Anderson, 2013). According to this criterion, the books fell into six genres: early childhood books (47%), fiction (33%), traditional literature (14%), informational books (4%), biography (1%) and poetry (1%).

The format evaluation was straightforward. The great majority of early childhood books (92%) are picture storybooks where the story is conveyed by pictures, some with a brief text. Meanwhile, a few books (8%) were from series such as 'I Can Read' and 'World of Reading' and were formatted as easy-to-read books. This type of book targets beginner readers and provides graded easy-to-read texts for their independent reading. We found most early childhood books, namely picture books and easy-to-read books, were in Chinese (77%) and favored by children aged three to five (81%).

On the other hand, fiction books were favored by older children. Fiction books in the sample had two discernable subgenres: fantasy and detective. The fiction books were all illustrated books where texts carry out the storyline while pictures serve as a visual aid. Compared with early childhood books, fiction books had longer texts, more characters and more complex plots. We also explored the relationship between the language of the books and children's age, and found that older children preferred to read in Norwegian (28%) and English (14%) than younger children (respectively, 15% and 8%).

We found many examples of traditional works of literature in our sample, including fairy tales, fables, folktales and myths. Over half of them (61%) had been commercialized and were well known and available across languages; others had Norwegian (17%) or Chinese (22%) heritage and were only available in one language. Interestingly, we found that traditional literature was represented in homes with children at every age band and across language groups. Lastly, a few children had informational books (4%), biography (1%) and poetry (1%) as their favorite books, which were all in Chinese.

Screen-based

Most children in our sample had access to smartphones and tablets (88%) and TV (81%). Figure 20.2 displays children's access to different literacy resources by language dominance. The left-hand bars indicate that households with Norwegian-dominant children tended to watch more TV (88%), but the difference was not significant, t (84) =1.67, $p = 0.10$. The right-hand bars indicate that more Chinese-dominant children used smartphones and tablets (95%) than their Norwegian-dominant counterparts (81%) did, t (84) = 2.04, $p < 0.05$. Other resources such as PC (17%), e-books (5%), learning machine (6%) and smart speaker (1%) were available in some families, but in general, they had less exposure to these bilingual children.

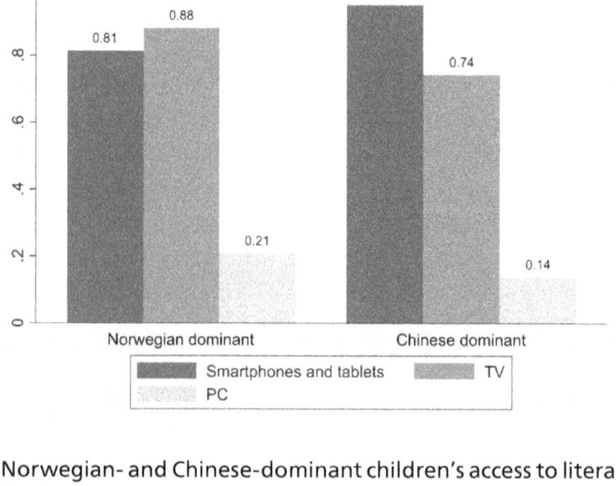

Figure 20.2 Norwegian- and Chinese-dominant children's access to literacy resources (as a proportion)

In the questionnaire, we focused on children's usage of smartphones and tablets. Parents reported on children's apps usage. The most frequent usage was for watching videos; most of these bilingual children (92%) spent some time watching videos but less than 7 hours per week. The following uses were playing games (44%), learning Chinese (24%), listening to audio (14%) and reading (7%). We summed up all the time spent in apps in different languages and presented it across children's language dominance. The majority used apps in one language (77%). A small group of children used apps in two languages (15%) and three languages (3%). Figure 20.3 depicts the children's total time spent in apps in different languages. For apps in Chinese (the dark bars), one can see that 31 Norwegian-dominant children spent no time whereas 27 Chinese-dominant children spent at least one hour per week. The *t*-test demonstrated that Chinese-dominant children spent significantly more time than Norwegian-dominant children did, $t\ (84) = 3.80$, $p < 0.001$. For apps in Norwegian (the light bars), 34 Chinese-dominant children spent no time whereas 20 Norwegian-dominant children spent at least one hour per week. The difference was also significant, $t\ (84) = 2.69$, $p < 0.001$. It is noteworthy that 33 children spent at least one hour in English apps, regardless of language dominance. Moreover, we found that older children tended to spend more time in Norwegian apps than younger children did, $t\ (84) = 3.05$, $p < 0.01$.

For app usage style, parental participation varied across different app types. With audio apps, 58% of parents used them with their children; this was followed by learning apps (43%), video apps (34%) and reading apps (33%). Game apps had the least parental participation, with only 21% of parents taking part. Overall, 62% of parents reported that their child played with smartphones and tablets by themselves, while 38% of parents used apps together with their child. Nonetheless, parental participation did not differ by children's age or language dominance.

To explore children's learning with screen-based literacy, we looked into a Chinese learning app that is popular among Chinese-Norwegian bilingual children, 洪恩识字 (*Hongen Shizi*) (iHuman-Chinese, 2020). The app targets children aged two to eight years, and develops Chinese characters reading and writing skills. It contains over 1200 Chinese characters. For each Chinese character, the learning consists of four sections:

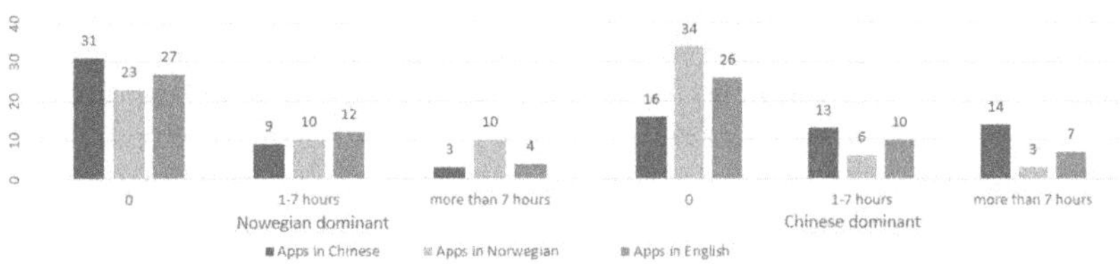

Figure 20.3 Norwegian- and Chinese-dominant children's language use and time spent on apps

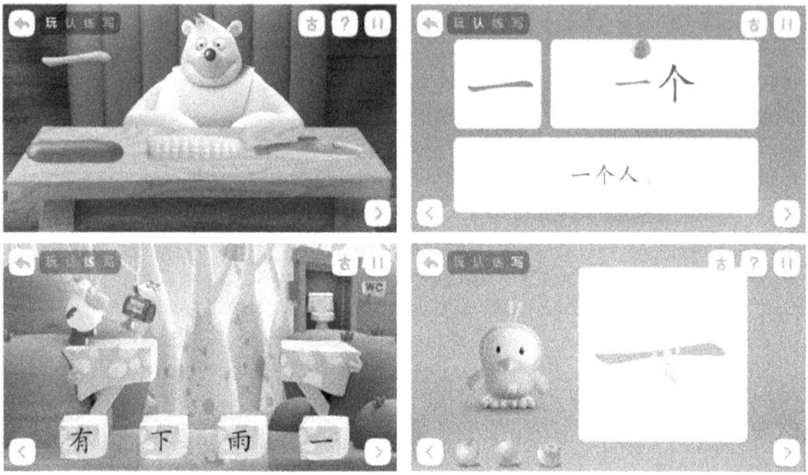

Figure 20.4 The four learning sections of character for 'one,' 一 (yi) in a Chinese learning app

play, recognize, practice and write (see Figure 20.4). First, users play a game while being exposed to the new character (see top left). The games, such as cooking, racing, bowling, jigsaw puzzle and dressing-up, are diverse but straightforward. Second, users learn to recognize the character using a word phrase and a sentence (see top right). They hear the sound while the ball jumps on the character accordingly. Then, users drill and practice recognizing the new character with a game-like exercise where they listen to the instruction and choose the right answer (see bottom left). Fourth, users practice writing by tracing the new character three times (see bottom right). After completing the four sections, users can move on to the next character.

The app learning surface defines clear goals. All instructions are verbal, taking into account that the users are beginner readers. Some sections provide modeling goals. For example, in the writing section (see Figure 20.4, bottom right), there is a hand demonstrating the tracing direction. In-play guidance is also available: when the user pauses for more than a specific time, the verbal prompts will repeat and there will be visual prompts. Positive feedback is in various forms: verbal (e.g. 'Very good!'), visual (e.g. fireworks) and sound effects (e.g. cheering music). It also has reward systems. By finishing the tasks in each section, users collect stars and character cards. For every five new characters, children need to take the assessment to unlock new characters. The characters are placed in order of complexity, guaranteeing the scaffolded challenge. Users mostly use dragging and tapping to interact with the touchscreen. The app also provides paid services, such as supplementary exercises and leveled reading. Overall, the app covers a variety of educational features.

Table 20.1 Zero-order spearman correlation between print-based and screen-based literacy at home

	Screen-based[b]	Apps in Chinese	Apps in Norwegian	Apps in English
Print-based[a]	−0.08	0.23	−0.01	0.03
Books in Chinese	−0.14	0.39***	−0.09	−0.06
Books in Norwegian	−0.04	−0.06	0.23*	−0.13
Books in English	0.02	0.14	−0.21	0.33**

Notes: *$p < 0.05$, **$p < 0.01$, ***$p < 0.001$. [a]Print-based refers to the total number of children's books at home. [b]Screen-based refers to the total number of types of screen-based resources (smartphone and tablet, TV, PC, etc.) children have access to at home.

Print-based versus screen-based

Using Spearman correlation (see Table 20.1), we explored the relationship between children's print-based and screen-based literacy at home. There is no connection between the total number of children's books and digital devices at home. Nevertheless, we found that children tend to use language consistently across print- and screen-based resources. Namely, children who have more Chinese books at home also spend more time in Chinese apps, $r = 0.39$, $p < 0.001$. The same pattern was observed with Norwegian, $r = 0.23$, $p < 0.001$, and English, $r = 0.33$, $p < 0.01$.

Discussion

This chapter explored how Chinese-Norwegian emergent bilingual children engage in meaning-making across multiple modalities to learn languages at home. We drew on a parent-reported survey and an analysis of books and apps referenced in those surveys to provide an overview of their home multimodal literacies. The results revealed robust connections between children's language dominance and their multimodal literacy experience. Namely, children with better Chinese skills are inclined to have more children's books in Chinese and spend more time with Chinese apps. Similarly, Norwegian-dominant children tend to have more Norwegian books and engage with more Norwegian apps. Books often serve as an indicator of a thriving home literacy environment in many studies (for example, Friedlander, 2020; Sénéchal & LeFevre, 2002), so it is not surprising that the books in the home link to children's language dominance. Additionally, we found a correlation between app use (i.e. watching videos and playing games) and children's language dominance, which is less documented in the literature but not unexpected (van Daal *et al.*, 2019).

Our results are consistent with previous studies that showed that bilingual children tend to shift to the majority language when they enter school (Lyutykh & Shumow, 2013; Zhang, 2010). This language shift is reflected in changes of literacy resources: more books in Norwegian, more favorite books in Norwegian, and more time spent in Norwegian apps. Furthermore, Norwegian-dominant children have more access to TV, whereas Chinese-dominant children use more smartphones and tablets. This finding underlines an important point. As TV programs in Norway (especially for children) are in Norwegian, parents who want to expose their children to more Chinese have to seek for resources. Therefore, they turn to smartphones and tablets. The same trend was observed for books at home. Norwegian books are accessible for all families, either in libraries or in bookstores. However, parents need to work harder to source Chinese books by bringing them from China or paying for international postage. Thus, Chinese literacy resources in some part also probably index parents' determination to support their child's Chinese development.

English as the third language plays a role in Chinese-Norwegian bilingual children's multimodal literacy environment. More than one-third of the children in our sample reported spending time using English apps and consuming English media. Several related explanations suggest themselves. First, English dominates our media landscape, from print to digital media; it is natural for children to be exposed to English. Second, English is a popular language in Norwegian society, and most Chinese parents can speak English. Exposure and familiarity could also contribute to children's consumption. Furthermore, we found that the Chinese-dominant children have more English books than their Norwegian-dominant counterparts do. This may indicate that our sample includes 'ambitious parents' (Curdt-Christiansen, 2009), who want their child to master Chinese and other languages, especially English.

This chapter used a parent-report questionnaire to learn about children's multimodal literacies practices and language dominance. This method has limitations. First, even though parents are intimate caregivers, they may not be up to date with their children's online activities all the time (Kumpulainen & Gillen, 2020). We assume parents' reports represented plausible estimates of online activity but they do not provide a nuanced and precise description of this activity. To learn more about children's attitudes and practices, observations and think aloud would be optimal. Second, conducting standardized measures for both Chinese and Norwegian language skills is practically demanding, so we used parental judgment. It is considered as a reliable source for children's language measure (Pua *et al.*, 2017; Schwartz & Moin, 2012). The instrument we referred to, ALDeQ, is found valid in multiple studies across languages (Hansen *et al.*, 2019; Sorenson Duncan & Paradis, 2020). We believe it is sufficient to determine a binary category of language dominance but our ongoing work makes greater use of standardized language assessments.

Implications

Technology is rapidly changing, affecting children's home literacy experience. Ten years ago, TV and PCs used to be the most popular resources at home (Hill, 2010), while now we find smartphones and tablets have replaced PCs to create opportunities for children's meaning-making. This chapter provides implications for understanding the challenges faced by Chinese bilingual families in Norway, and for understanding the kinds of support that language learners are turning to in an increasingly connected literacy and media landscape. The implications could be relevant for all kindergartens/schools and teachers. First, with the great majority of children having access to and being familiar with the digital environment at home, teachers can take advantage of digital literacy resources and activities to extend learning from school to home. Second, bilingual children tend to use their dominant language in reading books and using apps at home. Correspondingly, for improving a particular language, access to more books and apps in their favorite genre in the particular language would be of use. Third, children's preference for book genres varies across age: younger children prefer picture storybooks, older children prefer fantasy and detective fiction, and traditional literature has audiences across all ages. Kindergartens/schools can facilitate children with suitable books to promote language and literacy learning. In summary, by knowing children's preferences and parents' supports and behaviors at home, educators can better understand and further facilitate children's language and literacy learning.

References

Anderson, N.L. (2013) *Elementary Children's Literature: Infancy through Age 13* (4th edn). London: Pearson Education.

Astley, N. and Baker, M. (2018) *Peppa Pig* (S. Sheng, trans.). Anhui: Time Publishing and Media. (Original work published 2015.)

Brown, S. and Allmond, A. (2021) Constructing my world: A case study examining emergent bilingual multimodal composing practices. *Early Childhood Education Journal* 49 (2), 209–221. doi:10.1007/s10643-020-01062-4

Callaghan, M.N. and Reich, S.M. (2018) Are educational preschool apps designed to teach? An analysis of the app market. *Learning, Media and Technology* 43 (3), 280–293. doi:10.1080/17439884.2018.1498355

Cohen, L., Manion, L. and Morrison, K. (2017) *Research Methods in Education*. Abingdon: Taylor & Francis. See http://ebookcentral.proquest.com/lib/oslo/detail.action?docID=5103697.

Curdt-Christiansen, X. (2009) Invisible and visible language planning: Ideological factors in the family language policy of Chinese immigrant families in Quebec. *Language Policy* 8 (4), 351–375. doi:10.1007/s10993-009-9146-7

Friedlander, E.W. (2020) The home literacy environment in rural Rwanda and its relationship to early grade reading. *Scientific Studies of Reading* 24 (2), 123–140. doi:10.1080/10888438.2019.1642894

Hansen, P., Łuniewska, M., Simonsen, H.G., Haman, E., Mieszkowska, K., Kołak, J. and Wodniecka, Z. (2019) Picture-based vocabulary assessment versus parental questionnaires: A cross-linguistic study of bilingual assessment methods. *International Journal of Bilingualism* 23 (2), 437–456. doi:10.1177/1367006917733067

Hill, S. (2010) The millennium generation: Teacher-researchers exploring new forms of literacy. *Journal of Early Childhood Literacy* 10 (3), 314–340. doi:10.1177/1468798410372820

Horst, J.L. (2019) *Detektivbyrå nr. 2* (H.J. Sandnes, illus.). Oslo: Egmont Kids Media Nordic.

iHuman-Chinese (2020) *Chinese Literacy and Reading for Children*. See https://www.ihuman.com/website/pc/en/shizi/

Jewitt, C. and Kress, G. (2003) *Multimodal Literacy*. New York: Peter Lang. See https://www.peterlang.com/view/title/57553.

Kumpulainen, K. and Gillen, J. (2020) Young children's digital literacy practices in the home. In O. Erstad, R. Flewitt, B. Kümmerling-Meibauer and Í. Susana (eds) *The Routledge Handbook of Digital Literacies in Early Childhood* (pp. 95–108). New York: Routledge.

Little, S. (2019) Is there an app for that? Exploring games and apps among heritage language families. *Journal of Multilingual and Multicultural Development* 40 (3), 218–229.

Lyutykh, E. and Shumow, L. (2013) Family engagement in heritage language and literacy. In D.B. Hiatt-Michael, M. Caspe and H. Kreider (eds) *Promising Practices for Engaging Families in Literacy* (pp. 59–73). Charlotte, NC: Information Age.

Norwegian Directorate for Education and Training (2006) *National Curriculum for Knowledge Promotion in Primary and Secondary Education and Training – Framework for Basic Skills*. Oslo: Norwegian Directorate for Education and Training.

Norwegian Ministry of Education and Research (2017) *Framework Plan for Kindergartens*. Retrieved from https://www.udir.no/globalassets/filer/barnehage/rammeplan/framework-plan-for-kindergartens2-2017.pdf

Paradis, J., Emmerzael, K. and Duncan, T.S. (2010) Assessment of English language learners: Using parent report on first language development. *Journal of Communication Disorders* 43 (6), 474–497. doi:10.1016/j.jcomdis.2010.01.002

Park, Y., Zheng, B., Lawrence, J.F. and Warschauer, M. (2013) Technology-enhanced reading environments. In M. Thomas, H. Reinders and M. Warschauer (eds) *Contemporary Computer-Assisted Language Learning* (pp. 267–285). London: Bloomsbury Academic.

Proctor, C. and Zhang-Wu, Q. (2019) Cross-linguistic relations among bilingual and biliterate learners: Interdisciplinary perspective and convergences. In V. Grover, P. Uccelli, M. Rowe and E. Lieven (eds) *Learning through Language* (pp. 218–234). Cambridge: Cambridge University Press.

Pua, E.P.K., Lee, M.L.C. and Liow, S.J.R. (2017) Screening bilingual preschoolers for language difficulties: Utility of teacher and parent reports. *Journal of Speech, Language and Hearing Research (Online)* 60 (4), 950–968. doi:10.1044/2016_JSLHR-L-16-0122

Schwartz, M. and Moin, V. (2012) Parents' assessment of their preschool children's bilingual development in the context of family language policy. *Journal of Multilingual and Multicultural Development* 33 (1), 35–55. doi:10.1080/01434632.2011.638078

Sénéchal, M. and LeFevre, J.A. (2002) Parental involvement in the development of children's reading skill: A five-year longitudinal study. *Child Development* 73 (2), 445–460. doi:10.1111/1467-8624.00417

Smith, S.A. and Li, Z. (2020) Closing the enjoyment gap: Heritage language maintenance motivation and reading attitudes among Chinese-American children. *International Journal of Bilingual Education and Bilingualism*. doi:10.1080/13670050.2020.1742653

Sorenson Duncan, T. and Paradis, J. (2020) How does maternal education influence the linguistic environment supporting bilingual language development in child second language learners of English? *International Journal of Bilingualism* 24 (1), 46–61. doi:10.1177/1367006918768366

StataCorp (2019) *Stata Statistical Software: Release 16*. College Station, TX: StataCorp.
Statistics Norway (2008) *Kinesiske Innvandrere Studerer Eller jobber* [*Chinese Immigrants Study or Work*]. See https://www.ssb.no/befolkning/artikler-og-publikasjoner/kinesiske-innvandrere-studerer-eller-jobber.
Statistics Norway (2020) *Immigrants and Norwegian-born to Immigrant Parents*. See https://www.ssb.no/en/befolkning/statistikker/innvbef.
van Daal, V.H.P., Sandvik, J.M. and Adèr, H.J. (2019) A meta-analysis of multimedia applications: How effective are interventions with e-books, computer-assisted instruction and TV/video on literacy learning? In J.E. Kim and B. Hassinger-Das (eds) *Reading in the Digital Age: Young Children's Experiences with E-books: International Studies with E-books in Diverse Contexts* (pp. 259–296). Cham: Springer. doi:10.1007/978-3-030-20077-0_14
Zhang, D. (2010) Language maintenance and language shift among Chinese immigrant parents and their second-generation children in the U.S. *Bilingual Research Journal* 33 (1), 42–60. doi:10.1080/15235881003733258
Zhao, S. and Flewitt, R. (2019) Young Chinese immigrant children's language and literacy practices on social media: A translanguaging perspective. *Language and Education* 34 (3), 1–19. doi:10.1080/09500782.2019.1656738
Zheng, B., Lawrence, J., Warschauer, M. and Lin, C.H. (2015) Middle school students' writing and feedback in a cloud-based classroom environment. *Technology, Knowledge and Learning* 20 (2), 201–229. doi:10.1007/s10758-014-9239-z

21 How Young Emergent Bilinguals Rely on Multiple Modes to Make Meaning in Digital Multimodal Texts

Kyungjin Hwang

Introduction

Language is no longer considered the only channel for communication (Bezemer & Kress, 2008; New London Group, 1996; van Leeuwen, 2017). Literacy no longer refers only to the ability to read and write but also to the ability to understand and construct the diverse semantic possibilities available via different text formats associated with different domains (Cope & Kalantzis, 2009b; Jewitt *et al*., 2001; Kress, 2000; Kress & van Leeuwen, 1996). As the concepts of language and literacy change, scholars have been exploring multiple sign systems or modes to make sense of diverse texts, understand language and its use, and shape a new form of language learning and teaching (e.g. Bengochea *et al*., 2018; Jewitt, 2005; Kress, 2000). Multimodality is a study of how meaning is made in a specific context with multiple semiotic modes and how these modes are integrated into a multimodal text (van Leeuwen, 2017).

Multimodality has evolved along with technological development. The internet has blurred the boundary of written text, image and audio, as digital technology has been increasingly used as an educational tool. It has contributed to the shift in what counts as a text and what it means to be literate (Jewitt, 2005; Kress & van Leeuwen, 2001; Siegel, 2006). As a result, many language and literacy teachers capitalize on digital multimodal texts such as films, streaming media, animations and web pages in their classrooms (e.g. Dalton *et al*., 2015; Jocius, 2013; Rowe & Miller, 2016).

This current study explores how two young American children rely on multiple modes and what kinds of meaning they make when they learn Korean through digital multimodal texts. Drawing on multimodality as the theoretical lens (Cope & Kalantzis, 2020; Cope *et al*., 2017; Kress, 2010), this study qualitatively analyzes learners' journal entries, study notes, audio-recorded class conversations and retrospective interviews to closely demonstrate multimodal learning practices and discuss the pedagogical and theoretical significance.

Theoretical Framework

According to multimodality theory (see Jewitt *et al.*, 2001; Kress, 2000, 2010; Kress & van Leeuwen, 2001), meaning arises through multiple modes such as images, gestures, gazes, sounds or languages. Multimodality is based on Halliday's (1978) systemic-functional linguistics (see Kress & van Leeuwen, 1996), in which language conveys meanings formed within a social system. Likewise, modes are socially and culturally shaped resources that are neither fixed nor universal but fluid (Jewitt, 2009; Kress, 2003, 2010; Kress & van Leeuwen, 2001).

A sign is a physical vehicle through which meaning is constructed and expressed (Siegel, 2006). According to Kucer (2014), a sign system operates on the surface structure as a physical medium through which the underlying meaning in the deep structure is conveyed. The surface structure can be represented as multimodal elements that can be seen, touched or heard. In this sense, all *meaning-making* is by nature multimodal (Cope & Kalantzis, 2009a). Differing surface structures eventually aim to reveal the meaning in the deep structure. Cope and Kalantzis (2020) present multimodal meaning functions such as reference, agency, structure, context and interest.

Modes move across sign systems to generate new ideas. This is called *transmediation* (Siegel, 2006; Suhor, 1984), which is 'not simply translating a signifier into a signified, but by expanding the meaning of one sign, through another' (Siegel, 2006: 69). For instance, sign systems move from language to art, video to music, or image to language. In this process, transmediation helps learners' comprehension and supports their different learning styles. Modes also interact with each other. Kress (2003) refers to this as *synesthesia*. For example, 'gestures may come with sound; images and text sit side by side on pages' (Cope & Kalantzis, 2009a: 363). The meaning of integrated modes is greater than the sum of the respective verbal, visual, spatial and aural modes (Cope & Kalantzis, 2009a).

In this study, I analyze and discuss how two young emergent bilinguals are involved in multimodal practices to make meaning in digital multimodal texts. By employing a multimodal approach in the language learning of the emergent bilinguals, I highlight the potential, engagement, initiative, agency and creativity that learners gain from a richer modal affordance.

Literature Review

This review demonstrates how young emergent bilinguals engage in a meaning-making process through multimodality, expand their linguistic repertoires with the help of other modes, and express their identity and agency through active engagement in multimodal texts. This review includes only studies in which emergent bilinguals or second language learners are the primary research populations, language and literacy classrooms are the principal pedagogical focuses, and the theoretical framework is explicitly aligned with the overall field of multimodality.

Participating in a meaning-making process

Many studies (Ajayi, 2009; Brown & Allmond, 2021; Ho *et al.*, 2011) have explored how multimodal choices enhance meaning-making. For instance, Ajayi (2009) illustrates that multimodal pedagogy has the potential for meaning-making. Through multimodal texts, English as second language learners realized the different kinds of human expression and had opportunities to expand interpretation and engagement with the world. Bengochea *et al.* (2018) explored young emergent bilinguals' multimodal choices in sociodramatic play. The results demonstrate the importance of multimodal repertoire to make meaning and construct knowledge of social worlds.

A growing body of scholarship suggests the potential of digital tools to leverage the diverse meaning-making repertoires of emergent bilinguals (Dalton *et al.*, 2015; Jocius, 2013; Pacheco & Smith, 2015). Pacheco and Smith (2015) investigated how bilingual adolescents rely on and utilize multiple languages and modes in a digital multimodal writing activity. The learners meshed linguistic and other multiple modes, and expanded a range of meaning-making repertoires.

Taken together, multimodality affords opportunities for meaning-making, giving students a rich communicative palette and semiotics repertoire that they can strategically choose according to their own needs (García & Sylvan, 2011). Therefore, it is suggested that teachers leverage students' multimodal resources through dynamic pedagogy and instructional strategies.

Expanding linguistic repertoires through multiple modes

Previous studies show that multimodal texts promote students' academic and linguistic achievement (Ajayi, 2009; Cummins, 2008; Meskill & Mossop, 2000) because they help students better understand words and phrases in the target language (Verhallen & Bus, 2009). In Danzak's (2011) study, middle school English learners could discuss and practice the spelling, mechanics and syntax of English through graphic stories. Lenters and Winters (2013) indicated how a multimodal activity helped fifth-grade students who speak English as an additional language to understand important aspects of writing. The learners video-taped fairy tales, and this activity allowed them to set the context for the audience, introduce characters, make clear storylines, build dialogue, and convey meaning in various ways. Through this multimodal storytelling, the students could have more opportunities to understand language and literacy practices and strengthen their writing strategies.

Also, multimodal activities develop learners' pragmatic knowledge, such as how language is used in different settings and for various purposes. For example, English learners with limited literacy competency in Hepple *et al.* (2014) composed claymations, a stop-motion animation where clay figures are filmed. Through specific dialogic structures and language for the characters, the learners could develop a pragmatic understanding of English. Similarly, D'warte (2014) exhibited how emergent bilingual students deepened their metalinguistic awareness through visual mapping activities. They could also comprehend language registers such as 'how, when, where, and why their language changed in different contexts and for different audiences' (D'warte, 2014: 356).

Expressing identity and agency through multimodal practices

Multimodality provides learners with appropriate semiotic tools to express themselves (Kress & van Leeuwen, 1996). Notably, it motivates students to represent unique aspects about themselves in unique ways (Danzak, 2011; Johnson & Kendrick, 2017). Students can express their identities via a digital podcast project (Wilson *et al.*, 2012), a multimodal composition project (Smith *et al.*, 2021) and a collaborative multimodal project (Cummins *et al.*, 2015).

Multimodality also supports constructing a counter-discourse that disrupts a narrative that devalues one's identity (Ajayi, 2015; Walsh, 2009). Multiple modes and media offer increased tools for critical meaning-making that questions the inequitable practices of society and configures counter-discourse activities (Ajayi, 2015). For example, Walsh (2009) described how Chinese immigrant students articulated their identity by creating a multimodal website to showcase the discrimination experienced by their ancestors.

Besides, the freedom of choosing different modalities assists students in expressing their transnational identities. Maintaining transnational identities is crucial because they connect individuals, societies and countries. Skerrett's (2013) research demonstrated how an adolescent formed positive transnational identities when activating multiliterate and multilingual repertoires in writing practices. Vasudevan *et al.* (2010) also depicted how multimodal projects allowed an immigrant learner to utilize her experience and knowledge, such as cultural events and family life, in her English language arts class.

Research needs

Whereas previous studies have demonstrated young emergent bilinguals' capacity to utilize a range of modalities to make meaning, expand linguistic repertoires and express their identities, little is known about how they rely on multiple modes, move from one mode to another and integrate modes in multimodal language learning. To fill the gap, this current study investigates the emergent bilinguals' multimodal activities based on multimodal meaning functions (Cope & Kalantzis, 2020), transmediation (Siegel, 2006) and synesthesia (Kress, 2003). This study's multimodal framework focuses on the bilingual repertoires of learners using multimodal texts. It also focuses on learners' interest, agency and sociocultural awareness.

In this study, I first explore the meaning-making processes by analyzing two young children's journal entries, study notes, audio-recorded class conversations, and retrospective interviews in which the participants are asked to recall important events. I then take an in-depth look at their multimodal practices and discuss them. Finally, I conclude with the pedagogical and theoretical implications of leveraging the multimodal repertoires of emergent bilinguals. This study has two research questions to explore: (1) How do emergent bilinguals rely on multiple modes to understand and produce multimodal texts? and (2) What are the positive effects of digital multimodal learning on emergent bilinguals?

Context of the Study

This study has two participants, James and Emily (pseudonyms). They are siblings, and I met them for the first time at a local Korean language school in the United States in the spring of 2020. They are native English speakers born in the United States and enrolled in the school to learn Korean. At the time of the research, Emily was seven years old and in the second grade, and James was nine years old and in the fourth grade. I was their Korean teacher in the beginner class. The school is a non-profit Korean language school partially sponsored by the South Korean Consulate. It provides lessons in the language, traditions and current trends of South Korea for Koreans and non-Koreans of all ages who want to learn about Korean language and culture.

James and Emily's father is European-American, and their mother, Grace (pseudonym), was born in South Korea in 1985 and was adopted by American parents shortly after birth. She is biologically Korean but was raised in Alabama by European-American parents and did not have the opportunity to learn the Korean language, culture or history and to interact with Koreans as a child. Grace and her two children went to a local Korean festival in the fall of 2019, where they casually stopped by a kiosk introducing the Korean school. Grace knew that her children were interested in learning Korean, so she enrolled her children in a Korean school for the spring semester of 2020.

After the spring semester of the Korean language school was officially over, Grace emailed me to see if I was interested in tutoring her children in Korean during the summer. In the email, she clearly stated the purpose and direction of the tutoring. She wanted her children to not forget what they had learned during the school year, and she wanted me to teach them not only language but also Korean heritage, culture and traditions in a natural and conversational way. Grace said in an email, 'You can teach them culture, history, Korean mannerisms, Korean social cues, or signs of respect in Korea.' So, I planned to teach the children sociocultural elements that are associated with language through multiple modes across image, gesture, gaze, sound, writing, music, speech and so on. I also wanted the children to attend to a meaning-making process that would represent their agency and interest, relying on the modes that come to them most easily. Accordingly, I decided to teach Korean to the two children using a popular digital multimodal medium – YouTube videos.

Methodology

Emily and James joined in a 10-week project that involves learning Korean through the use of YouTube videos (see Table 21.1). I met with each of them separately for two hours once a week over the course of three months. The first criterion for selecting videos for the class was that they should have to do with Korean-based topics related to heritage, culture and tradition. Second, all videos had to be produced in Korean with Korean subtitles. I used those subtitles as reading material that could

Table 21.1 Weekly plan

Week	Video topic	Description
1	A Korean Folk Tale 1: 'Sister Sun and Brother Moon'	An animated tale about the origin of the sun and the moon
2	A Korean Folk Tale 2: 'The Magic Grindstone'	An animated tale about why sea water tastes salty
3	Korean Convenience Store Culture	A video blog about shopping at a Korean convenience store
4	Food: Kimchi	A video on the origin, types and recipes of Kimchi, a traditional Korean food
5	A Documentary TV Show	A documentary about three gifted young children learning English in Korea
6	Number Songs	A video that explains the two ways to count the numbers 1 to 10 in Korean
7	Aesop's Fables: 'The Country Mouse and the City Mouse'	An animated tale of a Korean version, 'The Country Mouse and Seoul Mouse'
8	A Song: 'Twinkle Little Star'	A song sung with Korean lyrics
9	History: The Division of Korea (North and South)	An animated cartoon of the division of Korea
10	Interviews	• Retrospective interview with children (each 35 mins) • Interview with mother (50 mins)

provide linguistic information. Third, the videos should be short, under five minutes, and include multiple modes in addition to language. I used these digital multimodal texts to help the children understand and interpret the meaning of the videos across multiple modes. I also required them to keep journal entries and take study notes.

Data sources

The data included audio-recorded class conversations, the researcher's ethnographic field notes and the children's journal entries and study notes. To triangulate the data, retrospective interviews were conducted with the children at the end of the project. I also interviewed their mother, Grace, to gain more insight into the children's learning process and outcomes, as well as to learn about the overall parental educational direction and to discover the impact and effectiveness of multimodal learning.

Data analysis

Guided by Kress and van Leeuwen's (1996, 2001) multimodal framework, I analyzed the students' multimodal learning and meaning-making process. First, the learners' journal entries and study notes were reviewed and analyzed to examine how they draw on multimodal resources and produce alternative meanings. Next, the audio-recorded class conversations were carefully listened to and reviewed to contextualize and enrich the understanding of their multimodal products. Lastly, retrospective interview transcripts and field notes were selected and triangulated with other data.

Findings

Juxtaposing meanings in multimodal forms

In Week 7, Emily and James watched an animated video, the Korean version of Aesop's Fable, 'The Country Mouse and the City Mouse.' After watching the video, Emily drew images that revealed the meaning of the newly learned vocabulary (see Figure 21.1). She transposed from one meaning form to another and juxtaposed meanings in a multimodal combination of Korean, English and images. The video facilitated her cognitive activity of linking the language and image relationship, which made her meaningfully recognize and comprehend words and phrases in the target language.

Reframing meanings from one mode to another

In Week 2, Emily and James watched a video entitled 'The Magic Grindstone.' It was an animated traditional fairy tale about why sea water

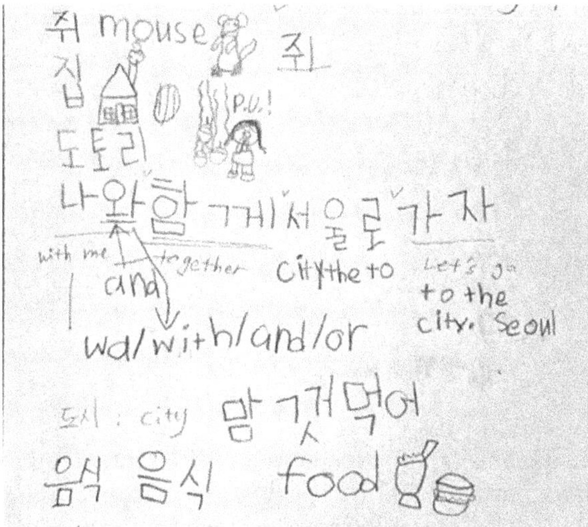

Figure 21.1 Emily's notes from Week 7

tastes salty. James' notes (see Figure 21.2) exhibited the process of switching from one mode to another in making meaning. In Example A, James converted the modes from the physical action of moving images to sentence-level linguistic structures such as the subject 착한 농부는 [the kind farmer], the object 할아버지를 [the old man], and the verbs 업고 [carried] and 달렸어요 [ran]. In Example B, James used the newly learned phrase 문 사이로 [through the open door] from a scene in the video. He created a new sentence, 오누이가 문 사이로 말했어요 [Brother and sister talked through the open door]. These examples reveal his cognitive process of switching from one mode to another and expanding the linguistic repertoire of the target language.

Integrating multiple modes

In Week 2, after watching the video 'The Magic Grindstone,' the two children were asked to write or draw the most memorable scenes or stories in their journals. As shown in Figure 21.3, they both drew pictures and added several Korean words – e.g. 해 [sun], 집 [house], 농부 [farmer], 소금 [salt] – to refer to things, people and spaces in their drawings. To expand meanings, Emily detailed the characters' facial expressions

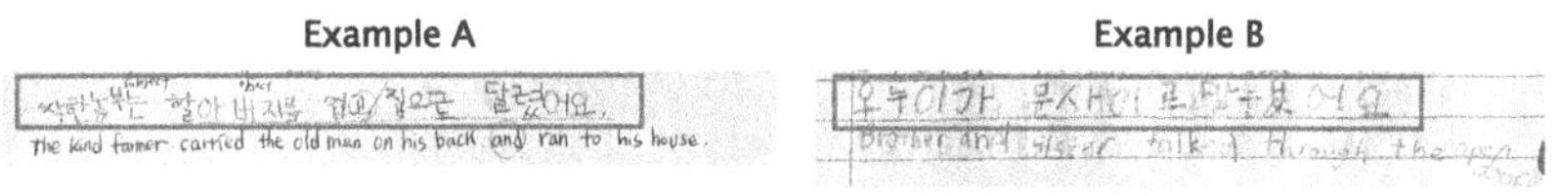

Figure 21.2 James' notes from Week 2

Emily **James**

Figure 21.3 Journal entries from Week 2

and movements, and James added one English sentence above the drawings: 'It is said that the grindstone is how the ocean became salty.' These examples show how the children combined pictures and languages to convey and expand meaning (see Figure 21.3).

Giving learners the power to tell their unique stories

In Week 5, Emily and James watched several documentary videos in which Korean children are learning English. The videos showed how much the Korean children love learning English, and how they actually study and use English in their everyday lives. After watching the videos, James paralleled himself with the characters and positioned himself in the language learning situation. He told his story, particularly about why he is learning a new language and what it is like to learn a new language:

> I already know two languages, English and Spanish. They both do letters, not characters, but this (Korean) is kind of new for me. I needed a new experience since I was already good at Spanish. And my mom was Korean, so I'm just like maybe I should learn some Korean. (Class conversation, James)

As shown in his journal entry (see Figure 21.4), James was fully involved in the topic, using the agentive subject 'I'. In particular, he wrote, 'the reason I learn Korean is because I am part Korean.' The multimodal text gave him an opportunity to tell his story, his reason and his identity.

Providing rich information on cultural and social elements

In Week 9, Emily and James watched a video on the Korean War. The video was about why Korea was divided into North and South. After watching the video, I asked them to record a journal entry (see Figure 21.5). Both of them drew pictures and added Korean words related to the context or acts of the image. Emily wrote the word 전쟁 [war] in the

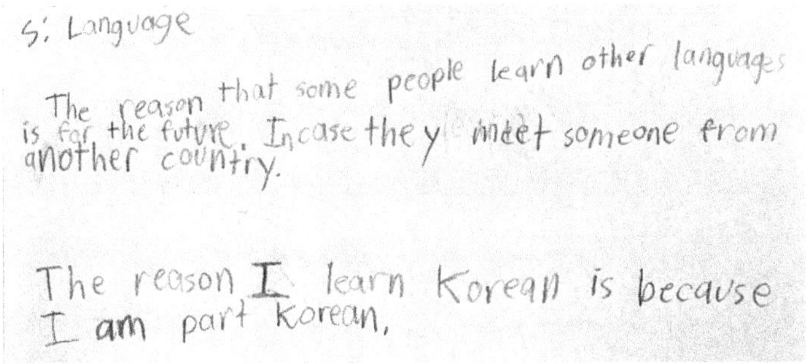

Figure 21.4 James' journal entry from Week 5

speech bubble of a man riding a horse and James added the words 휴전선 [truce line] and 군인 [soldier]. He additionally explained the picture with a sentence, 'Korean 군인 [soldier] standing at 휴전선 [truce line],' using both English and Korean. The actions of the characters and arrangements of the artifacts that appeared in the children's pictures organized meanings. In addition, the words or sentences added by the children made the meanings much clearer. The meanings formed by the multiple modes were situated culturally, socially, historically, politically and semiotically. This lesson led to a deeper conversation with their family after class:

> They've shown an interest. They talked to us about the last class that you had with them here at the house. They talked about North Korea and South Korea history and other stuff with me. They shared it with their dad too. (Interview with mother, Grace)

Motivating learners to continue their language learning

In Week 8, the two children learned a song in Korean, 반짝반짝 작은 별 [Twinkle Little Star]. Since they were already familiar with the 'Twinkle Little Star' melody, they sang along in Korean easily.

Figure 21.5 Journal entries from Week 9

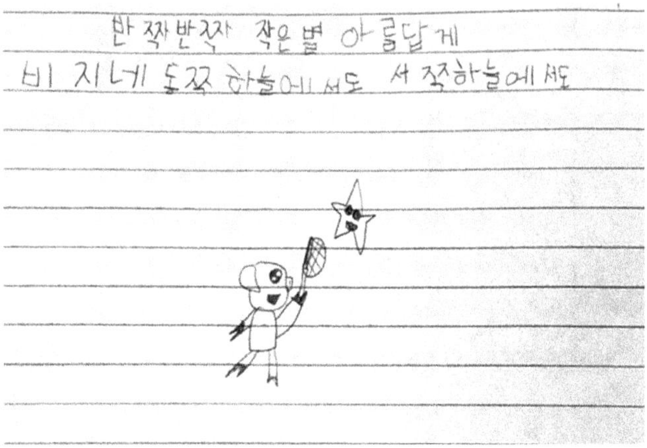

Figure 21.6 Emily's journal entry from Week 8

> In Week 8, I taught the children a song. I think it would be better to be familiar with the melody itself, so I chose a nursery rhyme called Twinkle Little Star. As expected, Emily sang along very happily. Just after reciting the lyrics of the Korean subtitles a few times, Emily fully memorized the song. I found she also recognized the lyrics linguistically. Emily wrote all the Korean lyrics in her journal entry and drew her favorite scenes. Emily asked me about the parts she didn't understand, such as what the east means and what the west means in Korean. (Researcher's field note, Week 8)

Emily memorized all the Korean lyrics of the song. Alongside this, she drew her favorite scene from the video and wrote some parts of the lyrics in Korean (see Figure 21.6). I found how she combined melodies with drawings and language, both spoken and written. Their mother, Grace, said that Emily sang the song over and over at home.

> I think the singing has been the cutest because she sings and hums the songs in Korean, even when she's playing with her dolls. She is doing it and even she is subconsciously doing it. (Interview with mother, Grace)

As the music mode became perceived by Emily as a fun play, it motivated her to continue singing in Korean.

Discussion

Multimodal learning practices

Focusing on how Emily and James rely on multiple modes to understand YouTube videos and make new meanings, this study achieved three key findings: juxtaposing meanings in multimodal forms; reframing meanings from one mode to another; and integrating multiple modes. In this section, I discuss these three findings in connection with previous studies.

First, it was clear that multimodal texts provided the two learners with opportunities for making meaning (Kress, 2000). The learners recognized meaning-making devices that YouTube videos offered and utilized those devices to understand the texts. They were able to fully comprehend through the videos what they could not fully understand in language alone. Also, when they recorded a journal entry after watching a video, they expressed their understanding through multiple modes. This finding is supported by Ajayi (2009), who found that multimodal texts provided students with opportunities to express themselves and engage with the world in diverse ways. Indeed, multimodal texts present a rich semiotic repertoire that individuals can strategically choose to make meaning (Bengochea *et al.*, 2018; García & Sylvan, 2011).

Second, I found that the learners actively attempted to move content from one sign system to another. This mode switching was an example of 'representational processes of reframing a meaning from one form to another' (Cope & Kalantzis, 2020: 34). For example, when Emily learned a song in Week 8, she memorized all the Korean lyrics of the song and then expressed comprehension of the lyrics in image and language. This was not a linear or simple translation but a developing transformation of modes. Also, when James converted the modes from the physical action of moving images to a sentence-level linguistic mode, he expanded his Korean repertoire to more abstract and specific language elements. These findings reflect those of Siegel (2006: 69), who also held the view that 'it involves transformation, not simply translating a signifier into a signified, but by expanding the meaning of one sign, through another.'

Third, this study highlighted the combination and orchestration of modes in multimodal ensembles. It was very common for the two children to combine drawings and language with additional modes. The videos helped their cognitive activities by linking the language and image relationship, which enabled them meaningfully to recognize and comprehend words and phrases in the target language. Through the multimodal combination, the learners interweaved available semiotic resources to engage in the meaning-making process. The interweaving modes created intersemiotic relations and generative messages that no single mode could express independently (Jewitt, 2009; Kress & van Leeuwen, 2001; Pacheco & Smith, 2015; Stein, 2008). It can therefore be assumed that the multimodal practices expand a range of communicative repertoires to convey meaning to audiences.

Pedagogical and theoretical implications of multimodal learning

The findings of this research demonstrate several positive educational and theoretical implications of multimodal learning activities. Notably, multimodality helps realize a learner-centered approach by allowing learners to participate in their learning as an active agent for the following three reasons.

First, multimodality lowers the barriers of entry so that emergent bilinguals can easily participate in learning. In a class where only the linguistic mode is privileged, their voices may be silenced because of their relatively limited linguistic proficiency in the target language. However, in multimodal learning, learners can have a multimodal choice and the autonomy to choose their favorite and familiar modes in their learning. For example, when the children in this study wrote multimodal journal entries in their preferred mode, they revealed ideas, feelings and understandings that it might be difficult to express in the linguistic mode alone. As the choice of modes increases, the children can play an active role in representing their voices.

Second, multimodal learning provides learners with the opportunity to articulate their experiences, identities, knowledge and interests related to people, events or places in their lives in distinctive ways. For example, James demonstrated his transnational identity when he paralleled himself with the characters in a video and positioned himself in the situation. He reflected on his second language learning, particularly about why he is learning a new language and what it is like to learn a new language. This finding aligns with previous studies, which reveal that multimodality supports students in expressing transnational identity with multiple points of entry for representing and keeping their identities (Canagarajah, 2012; Cummins *et al.*, 2015; Danzak, 2011; Johnson & Kendrick, 2017). In particular, Short *et al.* (2000: 163) revealed that when learners were allowed to express what a book they had read meant to them by drawing pictures, 'they [were] not drawing an illustration of the book's plot, but a quick sketch of the connections and images the book [raised] in their minds.'

Third, multimodal learning makes learning more fun and interesting and motivates learners to continue their language learning. Since everyone has inherently different strengths, having a choice of a particular sign can boost their interest (Kress, 2003). For example, Emily memorized all the Korean lyrics of the song she learned and sang it repeatedly, even at home. The multimodal learning was enjoyable to Emily, and it motivated her to continue learning.

In addition, multimodal practices have impacts on bilingual development and the expansion of learners' linguistic repertoires. Multimodality facilitates understanding of the linguistic concept and sentence structure. For example, when James transferred the meaning he understood in the video through an action mode into a linguistic mode, he was able to think of the sentence structure consisting of subject, verb and object, as well as their grammatical relationship. Emily also demonstrated her accurate comprehension of vocabulary by strengthening the relationship between language and images when she sang along repeatedly while watching the music video. Instead of learning vocabulary or grammar meaninglessly, they learned meaningfully depending on action, space and situation.

A digital multimodal text also allows children to understand the proper application of cohesive devices and to structure the relationship between vocabularies (D'warte, 2014). Understanding the grammatical elements helps them gain a deep understanding of how meaning is formed in texts, such as the relationships and actions of speakers and the sequence of events. This finding is echoed in previous research, which reveals that multimodal texts are supportive to bilingualism and biliteracy (Ajayi, 2009; Cummins, 2008; Meskill & Mossop, 2000). For example, the multimodal storytelling in Lenters and Winters (2013) provided learners with a chance to set the context for the audience, introduce characters, build dialogue and convey meaning in various ways. Through this process, students better understood language and literacy practices as well as strengthened their writing strategies.

The final implication of this study is that multimodality enhances the cultural and social understanding of emergent bilingual learners. Digital multimodal texts afford various cultural topics, authentic stories of people, places, history or food, which provide rich information to understand language, people and culture. These materials allow learners to comprehend and generate meaning across the historical, cultural and social uses of signs (Kress, 2010). In addition, multiple modes allow learners to bridge transnational identities (Kim, 2018) and share cultural histories and practices (Skerrett, 2012; Vasudevan *et al.*, 2010). As a result, learners can positively reinforce their cultural identity and self-esteem for their transnational background.

Conclusion

Although the two children in this study have quite limited linguistic proficiency as emergent bilinguals, they comprehend the multimodal texts and represent meaning across sign systems. This result illustrates that language is no longer privileged in representation and communication (Kress, 2000). Instead, this study supports the idea that multimodality affords opportunities to utilize an array of semiotic tools available to engage with authentic materials and represent unique aspects of children's lives in an empowering way. In other words, multimodality affords self-expression, something that children can do spontaneously rather than something they have to be taught (Kress & van Leeuwen, 1996).

Although this current study investigates the emergent bilinguals' multimodal activities, the children would not have learned as much from just watching the videos on their own. It is the teacher who coordinates the multiple modes for learning and provides appropriate materials that aid learning through multiple modes. This study clearly shows how a teacher can use multiple modes to guide children's language learning. Combined with the journal entries and notes, the learners in this study could have the opportunity to study and reinforce the language and meaning of the multimodal texts.

Multimodality is not a new phenomenon, but this research contributes to the theoretical understanding of multimodality and the pedagogical implication for leveraging learners' multimodal repertoires in language learning. Although limited, the analysis of the multimodal practices of the young emergent bilinguals provides a more comprehensive look into the complex meaning-making process and how they engage with the broader semiotic options in the multimodal texts, resulting in positive experiences of their agency and identity expression. This study suggests that the teacher's job should not only be to deliver knowledge according to an assigned curriculum but also to create a multimodal learning environment in which learners can have an optimal learning path for their needs.

Acknowledgments

The author would like to thank the two children and their mother who participated in this study.

References

Ajayi, L. (2009) English as a second language learners' exploration of multimodal texts in a junior high school. *Journal of Adolescent & Adult Literacy* 52 (7), 585–595.

Ajayi, L. (2015) Critical multimodal literacy: How Nigerian female students critique texts and reconstruct unequal social structures. *Journal of Literacy Research* 47 (2), 216–244.

Bengochea, A., Sembiante, S.F. and Gort, M. (2018) An emergent bilingual child's multimodal choices in sociodramatic play. *Journal of Early Childhood Literacy* 18 (1), 38–70.

Bezemer, J. and Kress, G. (2008) Writing in multimodal texts: A social semiotic account of designs for learning. *Written Communication* 25 (2), 166–195.

Brown, S. and Allmond, A. (2021) Constructing my world: A case study examining emergent bilingual multimodal composing practices. *Early Childhood Education Journal* 49 (2), 209–221. doi:10.1007/s10643-020-01062-4

Canagarajah, S. (2012) *Translingual Practice: Global Englishes and Cosmopolitan Relations*. New York: Routledge.

Cope, B. and Kalantzis, M. (2009a) A grammar of multimodality. *International Journal of Learning* 16 (2), 361–425.

Cope, B. and Kalantzis, M. (2009b) 'Multiliteracies': New literacies, new learning. *Pedagogies: An International Journal* 4 (3), 164–195.

Cope, B. and Kalantzis, M. (2020) *Making Sense: Reference, Agency, and Structure in a Grammar of Multimodal Meaning*. Cambridge: Cambridge University Press.

Cope, B., Kalantzis, M. and Abrams, S.S. (2017) Meaning-making and learning in the era of digital text. In F. Serafini and E. Gee (eds) *Remixing Multiliteracies: Theory and Practice from New London to New Times* (pp. 35–49). New York: Teachers College Press.

Cummins, J. (2008) Technology, literacy, and young second language learners: Designing educational futures. In L. Parker (ed.) *Technology-mediated Learning Environments*

for Young English Learners: Connections in and out of School (pp. 61–98). Mahwah, NJ: Lawrence Erlbaum.
Cummins, J., Hu, S., Markus, P. and Kristiina Montero, M. (2015) Identity texts and academic achievement: Connecting the dots in multilingual school contexts. *TESOL Quarterly* 49 (3), 555–581.
Dalton, B., Robinson, K., Lavvorn, J., Smith, B.E., Avey, T., Mo, E., Uccelli, P. and Proctor, C.P. (2015) Fifth-grade students' multimodal compositions: Modal use and design intentionality. *The Elementary School Journal* 115 (4), 548–569.
Danzak, R.L. (2011) Defining identities through multiliteracies: EL teens narrate their immigration experiences as graphic stories. *Journal of Adolescent & Adult Literacy* 55 (3), 187–196.
D'warte, J. (2014) Linguistic repertoires: Teachers and students explore their everyday language worlds. *Language Arts* 91 (5), 352–362.
García, O. and Sylvan, C.E. (2011) Pedagogies and practices in multilingual classrooms: Singularities in pluralities. *Modern Language Journal* 95 (3), 385–400.
Halliday, M.A.K. (1978) *Language as a Social Semiotic: The Social Interpretation of Language and Meaning*. Baltimore, MD: University Park Press.
Hepple, E., Sockhill, M., Tan, A. and Alford, J. (2014) Multiliteracies pedagogy: Creating claymations with adolescent, post-beginner English language learners. *Journal of Adolescent & Adult Literacy* 58 (3), 219–229.
Ho, C.M., Nelson, M.E. and Müeller-Wittig, W. (2011) Design and implementation of a student-generated virtual museum in a language curriculum to enhance collaborative multimodal meaning-making. *Computers & Education* 57 (1), 1083–1097.
Jewitt, C. (2005) Multimodality, 'reading', and 'writing' for the 21st century. *Discourse: Studies in the Cultural Politics of Education* 26 (3), 315–331.
Jewitt, C. (2009) *The Routledge Handbook of Multimodal Analysis*. New York: Routledge.
Jewitt, C., Kress, G., Ogborn, J. and Tsatsarelis, C. (2001) Exploring learning through visual, actional and linguistic communication: The multimodal environment of a science classroom. *Educational Review* 53 (1), 5–18.
Jocius, R. (2013) Exploring adolescents' multimodal responses to *The Kite Runner*: Understanding how students use digital media for academic purposes. *Journal of Media Literacy Education* 5 (1), 310–325.
Johnson, L. and Kendrick, M. (2017) 'Impossible is nothing': Expressing difficult knowledge through digital storytelling. *Journal of Adolescent & Adult Literacy* 60 (6), 667–675.
Kim, S. (2018) 'It was kind of a given that we were all multilingual': Transnational youth identity work in digital translanguaging. *Linguistics and Education* 43, 39–52.
Kress, G. (2000) Multimodality: Challenges to thinking about language. *TESOL Quarterly* 34 (2), 337–340.
Kress, G. (2003) *Literacy in the New Media Age*. New York: Routledge.
Kress, G. (2010) *Multimodality: A Social Semiotic Approach to Contemporary Communication*. Abingdon: Taylor & Francis.
Kress, G. and van Leeuwen, T. (1996) *Reading Images: The Grammar of Visual Design*. New York: Routledge.
Kress, G. and van Leeuwen, T. (2001) *Multimodal Discourse: The Modes and Media for Contemporary Communication*. London: Edward Arnold.
Kucer, S.B. (2014) *Dimensions of Literacy: A Conceptual Base for Teaching Reading and Writing in School Settings*. New York: Routledge.
Lenters, K. and Winters, K.L. (2013) Fracturing writing spaces: Multimodal storytelling ignites process writing. *The Reading Teacher* 67 (3), 227–237.
Meskill, C. and Mossop, J. (2000) Electronic texts in ESOL classrooms. *TESOL Quarterly* 34 (3), 585–592.

New London Group (1996) A pedagogy of multiliteracies: Designing social futures. *Harvard Educational Review* 66 (1), 60–93. doi:10.17763/haer.66.1.17370n67v22j160u

Pacheco, M.B. and Smith, B.E. (2015) Across languages, modes, and identities: Bilingual adolescents' multimodal codemeshing in the literacy classroom. *Bilingual Research Journal* 38 (3), 292–312.

Rowe, D.W. and Miller, M.E. (2016) Designing for diverse classrooms: Using iPads and digital cameras to compose eBooks with emergent bilingual/biliterate four-year-olds. *Journal of Early Childhood Literacy* 16 (4), 425–472.

Short, K.G., Kauffman, G. and Kahn, L.H. (2000) 'I just need to draw': Responding to literature across multiple sign systems. *The Reading Teacher* 54 (2), 160–171.

Siegel, M. (2006) Rereading the signs: Multimodal transformations in the field of literacy education. *Language Arts* 84 (1), 65–77.

Skerrett, A. (2012) Languages and literacies in translocation: Experiences and perspectives of a transnational youth. *Journal of Literacy Research* 44 (4), 364–395.

Skerrett, A. (2013) Building multiliterate and multilingual writing practices and identities. *English Education* 45 (4), 322–360.

Smith, B.E., Pacheco, M.B. and Khorosheva, M. (2021) Emergent bilingual students and digital multimodal composition: A systematic review of research in secondary classrooms. *Reading Research Quarterly* 56 (1), 33–52.

Stein, P. (2008) Multimodal instructional practices. In J. Coiro, M. Knobel, C. Lankshear and D.J. Leu (eds) *Handbook of Research on New Literacies* (pp. 871–898). Mahwah, NJ: Lawrence Erlbaum.

Suhor, C. (1984) Towards a semiotics-based curriculum. *Journal of Curriculum Studies* 16 (3), 247–257.

van Leeuwen, T. (2017) Multimodal literacy. *Viden Om Literacy* 21, 4–11.

Vasudevan, L., Schultz, K. and Bateman, J. (2010) Rethinking composing in a digital age: Authoring literate identities through multimodal storytelling. *Written Communication* 27 (4), 442–468.

Verhallen, M.J. and Bus, A.G. (2009) Video storybook reading as a remedy for vocabulary deficits: Outcomes and processes. *Journal for Educational Research Online/Journal Für Bildungsforschung Online* 1 (1), 172–196.

Walsh, C.S. (2009) The multi-modal redesign of school texts. *Journal of Research in Reading* 32 (1), 126–136.

Wilson, A.A., Chavez, K. and Anders, P.L. (2012) 'From the Koran and Family Guy': Expressions of identity in English learners' digital podcasts. *Journal of Adolescent & Adult Literacy* 55 (5), 374–384.

22 Emergent Bilingual Families' Involvement Strategies for Scientific Sense-Making in a Science Museum: A Multimodal Interaction Analysis

Min-Seok Choi

Introduction

As a Korean child living in the United States, Jun occupied a liminal space between worlds: home and school, Korean and English, present and future. Understanding this bind, Jun's mother regularly took him to a local science museum to take advantage of the opportunity to explore science concepts and discourse. Envisioning their migration back to Korea in the near future, Jun's family viewed the local science museum as a linguistic space wherein Jun could practice science literacy in both languages. The museum offered rich resources with which Jun's mother could help him move between these worlds as he engaged in scientific discourse. Jun's literacy practices were aligned with the recent research on bilingualism and biliteracy that has illuminated that each emergent bilingual (EB) differently develops their bilingual and biliterate competence in diverse contexts (Bauer & Gort, 2012; Durán, 2017; Kwon, 2019).

Such diversity in EBs' bilingual and biliterate development cannot be shaped only by their experience of formal instruction (e.g. Reyes, 2001), but also by home and community experiences where EBs have opportunities to practice their heritage language and engage in other literacy practices (e.g. Kwon, 2019). Along this line, family science learning research (Ellenbogen *et al.*, 2003) has examined the role played by family as an educational institution in EBs' out-of-school literacy, knowledge acquisition and identity construction (Dierking, 1989). Family is defined as a group of mixed-aged people who co-construct their knowledge and experience through their talk-in-interaction and have a shared system of acting and interacting (Ash, 2004; Crowley *et al.*, 2001). Ellenbogen *et al.* (2003) emphasize the importance of family culture in children's meaning-making around scientific exhibits.

A growing body of research on family science learning employs an ethnographic approach to capture diverse families' cultural practices in science museums (Ash, 2004) and their resources used in their meaning-making, such as embodied actions and artifacts (Rowe, 2012; Rowe & Kisiel, 2012). Building on this scholarship, as part of a larger ethnographic study on EB families in informal learning contexts, I conducted ethnographic fieldwork of heritage language families' visits to a science museum and their meaning-making with exhibits. I repeatedly observed a Korean EB child and his family, and found that the family often used signage text as a resource for their interactions as well as sense-making. Similarly, I saw many other EB families use signage text to help their children make sense of exhibits and learn scientific language and knowledge. Based on my observations of, and interviews with, diverse heritage language speaking families in the museum, I became interested in EB children and their families' use of exhibit objects and signage text in their meaning-making.

To date, little attention has been given to families' reading of signage text in science museums and its role in children's learning and family interaction. Given that signage text written only in English often produces linguistic barriers to EB families, EB family members may engage each other with diverse semiotic resources for their collaborative sense-making as they engage signage text. This study addresses the following question: as the family reads signage text, how do a Korean EB child and his family members make use of and make available to one another various types of resources for sense-making in a science museum?

Family Science Learning

Recent research on children's informal science learning has shown that families as an educational institution co-construct their shared meanings through participation and conversation in the science museum setting (Ash, 2004; Crowley *et al.*, 2001). Families bring their family culture and agenda into their talk-in-interaction through which they build a system of acting and interacting (Ellenbogen *et al.*, 2003). As they interact, family members use various types of semiotic resources to help children make sense of an exhibit and grasp scientific knowledge. Ellenbogen *et al.* (2003) emphasize the role of family culture in children's meaning-making around scientific exhibits, stressing that an ethnographic approach is useful for capturing how a family's particularity and uniqueness contribute to children's informal science learning.

In the field of informal science education (ISE), research on EB family science learning, especially how diverse resources are used in meaning-making and scientific sense-making, has been scarce. A few ISE studies have paid attention to diverse minoritized populations such as those from low-income, minority ethnic backgrounds (e.g. Dawson, 2014), Hispanic mothers (e.g. Weiland, 2015) and disenfranchised youth (e.g. Rahm & Ash, 2008). Yet relatively little attention has been paid to EBs and their literacy practices in science museums as part of family science learning (except for Ash, 2004). Ash (2004) analyzes how a bilingual family's dialogue engages their children in science practices (e.g. observing, questioning, interpreting, explaining). She demonstrates the way families use diverse mediational tools (e.g. questions) to cross boundaries between different contexts (e.g. between Spanish and English) and to engage children in scientific sense-making. Ash considers resources such as pictures, objects and languages in a broad sense, but does not take into account how family actions incorporate those resources into interaction and make visible embodiments as emergent resources for interaction.

Multimodal Literacy

In science museums, families use diverse forms of resources, including resources made available by the museum and resources produced and shared among themselves, to make sense of exhibits. Most museums provide multiple resources to 'help publics make sense of science and engage in dialogue with scientists and policy makers' (Rowe, 2012: 50). In a museum, children perform the role of 'scientist' through a series of sense-making actions (e.g. see, touch, smell): using scientific tools, observing the results of their input, reporting their observation and reprocessing the sequence. While emphasizing an ethnographic understanding of the family interaction in the museum, Rahm (2004) illustrates how individuals build meaning together with both linguistic and nonlinguistic resources; Rahm calls attention to diverse semiotic resources beyond the language used by a family as they co-construct meaning.

Rowe (2012) similarly attends not only to how multimodal interactions with exhibits can transmit information, but also to how these interactions support visitors in generating meaning or engaging each other in dialogue. Rowe's attention to the role of interaction in visitors' meaning-making and mutual engagement is aligned with the concept of literacy as a social practice (Street, 2006). New Literacy Studies (NLS) as a research orientation defines literacy not as a mental process, but as social and cultural processes, in which the ways people read and write text are 'determined by the values and practices of different social and cultural groups' (Gee, 2015: 36).

Children's sense-making in a science museum is not only an individual, cognitive process, but an interactive, social and cultural one. Taking this perspective, I focus on how an EB family used objects and signage text as resources in order to make sense of an exhibit and build a shared understanding of scientific concepts. Essential to the 'nature of interpersonal interaction for understanding all written as well as spoken texts' is involving interlocutors or interactants in their ongoing conversation (Tannen, 2007: 4). To illustrate the way in which an EB family builds 'an achievement in conversational interaction' as 'a joint production' (Tannen, 2007: 27) with diverse resources, I employ Tannen's notion of 'involvement strategies,' but extend it to include more diverse semiotic resources, as a family's talk-in-interaction at exhibits is a semiotic process in which multimodal resources are configured.

Methods

Drawn from a large ethnographic study of a Korean EB child (Jun, a pseudonym, aged seven) and his family at a local science museum in a midwestern state over approximately 18 months, this case study analyzed the conversational interactions between Jun and his mother. Data sources include field notes, video-tapes of observed family interaction (approximately 30 hours in total), interviews with Jun's mother (six occasions) and informal conversations with Jun. Acquainted through a local heritage language community with me, the family allowed me to observe their visits to the museum (11 occasions). On each visit to the museum, I followed their movement trajectory and video-taped the family's talk-in-interaction for the duration of their stay, which typically lasted approximately three hours. To illustrate the patterned way Jun's family members used resources in meaning-making in detail, I present a few excerpts from one event (21 December 2016) as an example.

The family in the museum

Jun's family in the museum usually consisted of Jun and his mother, but sometimes included extended group members such as friends. Minho (a pseudonym), Jun's best friend, often came with Jun to the museum. Jun's family had been in the US for 2.5 years at the time of my observation. They came to the US for Jun's father's employment as a senior researcher at a state university. They were likely to go back to Korea, but Jun's mother was not sure when that would be. This temporary immigration status created concern for Jun's parents about his transition from US schooling to Korean schooling, especially in terms of the change of language for instruction. In order to help Jun meet his academic needs in the US and to prepare him for his return to Korea, Jun's mother was teaching Jun math and science in both Korean and English at home, and regularly brought Jun to the science museum to support Jun's science learning in both languages. To engage Jun in scientific knowledge and reasoning, Jun's mother drew his attention to the signage text as an entrance point for the family to explore scientific discourses. In doing so, his mother not only accessed the knowledge and experience Jun mobilized from school, but also employed their talk-in-interaction as a linguistic space in which she taught scientific terms in Korean.

As both Jun and his mother mobilized their knowledge, they took epistemic stances and positioned one another. I also participated in Jun's exploration. Introduced by his mother as 선생님 [a teacher], I often asked Jun clarification questions about his engagement with exhibits or his interaction with his mother, which prompted him to explain his reasoning to me with honorifics in Korean. Based on my observations, I found that Jun's family centered their time on having Jun either (a) explore new scientific knowledge through talk-in-interaction or (b) develop his friendship through play. Although both ways of using the space are important to understanding how Jun's family makes meaning with semiotic resources, this study focuses on the way Jun's family engages in the scientific conversation through their examination of an exhibit.

The event

The event on which I will focus was selected as an example to illustrate the ways in which Jun and his mother employed diverse semiotic resources to make meaning together in their literacy activity. I chose this event because of both its uniqueness and its representativeness. The family generally traveled around the museum and determined what exhibit to examine together. However, in this event (21 December 2016), Jun's family (Jun, Jun's mother, and Minho) found an exhibit incidentally at the rest area near a restroom during their visit. This area included a set of sofas and a table. On the table was an exhibit with signage text underneath exhibit objects. Due to the arrangement of the seats, Jun's engagement with the exhibit began without his mother's access to the exhibit (see Figure 22.1). To engage his mother in his sense-making, Jun employed diverse resources as part of his communicative means. With the asymmetric visibility of and access to the exhibit and given resources (e.g. signage text) in mind, Jun and his mother collaboratively built their understanding on each other's embodied actions with diverse semiotic resources.

This event is also an example of the way Jun mobilized his knowledge and practices across borders (Ash, 2004). In the interview with his mother (20 January 2017), I learned that Jun often took an expert's stance in dialogue with his mother by using the knowledge and literacy practices he learned and used in school. His mother emphasized that the way he took an epistemic stance in dialogue about an exhibit in the museum helped her access his schooled literacy and science knowledge. Also, this was around the time when Jun started reading the signage text in response to his mother's stress on using signage text as a guide to making sense of science exhibits in the museum. In an informal conversation with her on that day,

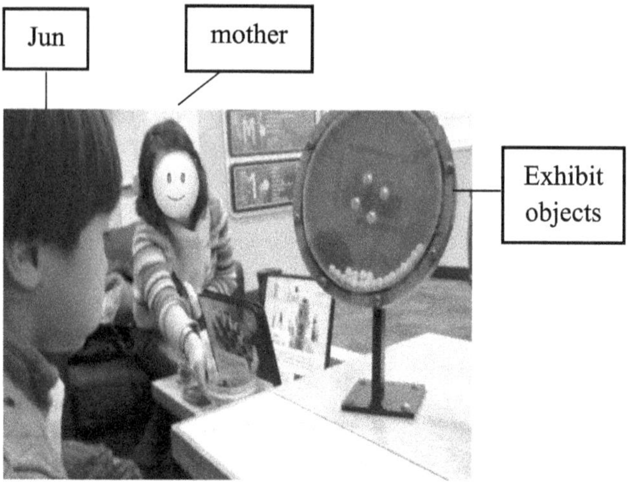

Figure 22.1 Organization of the semiotic ecology with participants

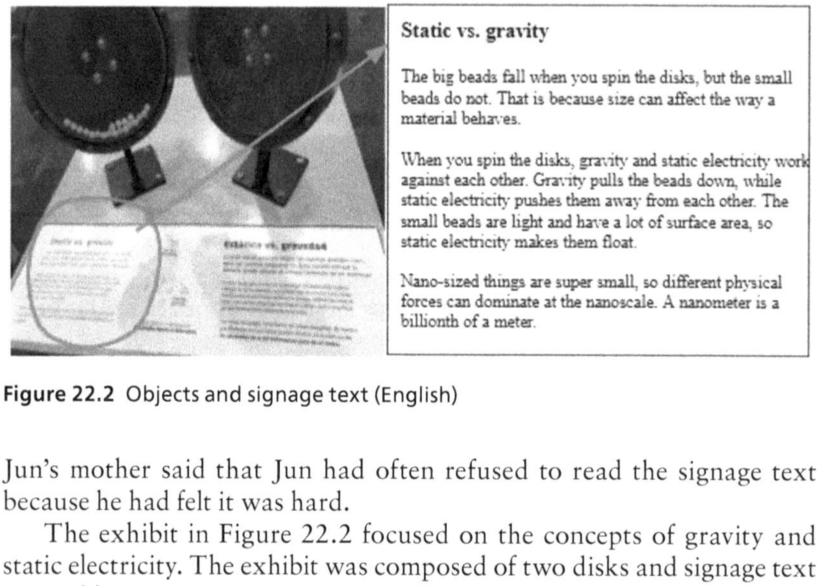

Figure 22.2 Objects and signage text (English)

Jun's mother said that Jun had often refused to read the signage text because he had felt it was hard.

The exhibit in Figure 22.2 focused on the concepts of gravity and static electricity. The exhibit was composed of two disks and signage text on a table. Visitors were expected to spin the two disks and compare the different sized beads' movement to learn how two forces, static electricity and gravity, worked together in each disk differently depending on the size of materials.

Analysis

To capture what resources were used for the family to make meaning together during their examination of an exhibit, I employed a multimodal interaction analysis (Goodwin, 2018; Mondada, 2011, 2014) and analyzed the family's multimodal conversational interaction with diverse resources including the signage text. I first created a multimodal transcript of their interaction by adopting Wortham and Reyes' (2014) transcription conventions and adding images of the interactions to the utterances of the selected moment. In representing the coordination of words and embodied actions through lines and arrows, I focused on how the embodied gestures and words elaborated on each other to deliver meanings.

Findings

To correspond to other chapters in this volume and speak to the role of multimodality in young EBs' literacy, I briefly report my observations about the family's use of heritage language in their meaning-making and then focus my attention on demonstrating how the family used nonlinguistic resources with words to make meaning together. I found three patterns of family interaction: (1) Jun and his mother communicated mostly in Korean but used some terms and words in English, particularly scientific words they picked up from signage text (e.g. gravity); (2) Jun and his mother used the signage text as a reference to make sense of exhibits; and (3) Jun constantly involved his mother in his sense-making. To describe ways in which Jun and his mother practiced their family literacies, I demonstrate how his mother engaged him in reading the signage text and how Jun used the text along with other semiotic resources to construct the meaning of the exhibit and to involve his mother. Central to the family's involvement strategies were two embodied practices, *pointing gestures and gazes* and *manipulating objects*.

As soon as Jun engaged with the exhibit his mother directed Jun's attention to the signage text. Jun read the text, spun the disks and said, 'Ah, this one is faster [translation].' However, his mother's follow-up question, 'what is it? [translation]' prompted him to read the text again. For 20 seconds, Jun read the text with his pointing finger following his eye movement (Table 22.1, Line 9). Jun made his reading visible to his mother through his gaze fixed on the text and his finger pointing moving along with it. This contributed to her assumption that he picked up the words he used in Lines 10 and 12, *floated* and *gravity*. Especially in Line 12, while holding his pointing finger at the beads in the right disk, Jun turned his gaze to his mother, saying '*grav*, there is *gravity* [translation].' This allowed her to access how he made sense of the phenomenon, although she was not able to see, from her location, what the materials were and what phenomenon Jun was observing.

Jun demonstrated to his mother his engagement with the exhibit and the text through sequentially organized actions. First, he drew her attention by calling out to her and articulated a particular phenomenon (*float*) only in English after reading the text (Line 10), which would make her

Table 22.1 Transcript excerpt

#	S	Original verbatim [English translation]	Description and images of gesture & use of objects
9	J		 J reads the text again for 20 seconds
10		엄마, 왜 float 했는지 알아? [mom, you know why they *floated*?]	
11	M	왜? [why?]	
12	J	gra-, grativity 가 있어 [*gra-*, there is *gravity*]	 J turns his gaze to his mother while holding his finger pointing at the beads in the right disk.

believe those English words were from the text. Next, he manipulated the objects and pointed at something among the objects, turning his gaze to his mother and using a technical term, *gravity*, only in English. Not only did Jun make sense of the objects, then, but manipulated them and used gazes and pointing gestures to involve his mother in his sense-making and reading of the text.

For the next few minutes, Jun made a series of actions with gestures and words together to involve his mother in his sense-making. For example, Jun spun the left disk and pointed at the floating beads while pointing at the word 'gravity' on the signage text. Later, Jun's mother moved next to Jun and read the signage text as she listened to Jun explain his sense-making. His mother used some words from the text to ask Jun another prompting question (Table 22.2, Line 30) to elaborate on his earlier statement. She asked, 'gravity is stronger, right? [translation],' but he did not respond. As a participant-observer, I jumped into the conversation and asked Jun another prompting question, 'which one has gravity, and which one doesn't? [translation],' assuming that Jun was considering the pairs (a pair of disks and a pair of words, gravity versus static electricity) as parallel.

Jun argued that only the right disk had gravity (Line 32), and this thought was guided by his reading of the title, *static vs. gravity* (Line 33).

Table 22.2 Transcript excerpt

#	S	Original verbatim [English translation]	Description and images of gesture and use of objects
30	M	구슬 크기에 따라 다른 거 아니야? 반응이? [is it different depending on the size of the beads? the reaction?]	
31	R	(8.0) 어떤 게 gravity 가 있고 어떤 게 gravity 가 없는거야? [(8.0) which one has gravity and which one doesn't?]	
32	J	이게 gravity 가 없고, 이게 gravity 가 있어요. [this has no gravity, and this has gravity]	J points at the left disk and shifts his finger pointing to the right disk.
33	R	왜? [why?]	
34	M	왜 그런데? [why so?]	
35	J	versus 하니까 [because it says 'versus']	 J finger-points at the title of the text with his gaze (static vs. gravity)

He might have thought that the competing relationship in the phrase, *static vs. gravity*, reflected the relationship between the disks because the pairs were placed side by side. Later, I learned in an interview with his mother that Jun did not know the meaning of the word *static* or what *static electricity* meant. Thus, although it is not clear how he interpreted the title and applied its meaning, as well as a textual organization into his sense-making of the objects at this moment, it is clear that Jun took the contrasting frame in the phrase, *vs.*, and used it to understand the relationship between the two disks. This conversation indicated that his interpretation was informed not only by the content of the signage text but also by its textual organization, specifically how words were presented in relation to other surrounding environments (the two disks, in this case). More importantly, Jun used pointing gestures and gaze to help me and his mother see what he considered as resources in understanding the exhibit.

To make sense of the exhibit in question, Jun used diverse semiotic resources including languages (Korean and English), scientific terms (e.g. gravity), gaze, pointing gestures and parallel environment (objects – text), making visible to his mother how he read the text and observed the phenomenon. A set of resources was configured as Jun demonstrated his engagement with the exhibit in a sequential organization of an event with a series of activities: Jun (1) engaged with the text (e.g. reading aloud, pointing at words, etc.); (2) transformed his interaction with the object materials (e.g. shifting gazes between the exhibit and the text, putting different inputs into the object); and (3) verbally explained what scientific knowledge the exhibit illustrated (e.g. using scientific words from the signage text). His mother's evaluation and questions followed, prompting Jun to elaborate on his explanation or re-engage with the text to demonstrate his understanding through reading. These sequentially organized activities allowed his mother to observe Jun's engagement with the exhibit, his uptake of scientific knowledge, and the role of signage text in his learning. It is also important to note that these activities involved a series of actions wherein multiple semiotic resources were used. For example, Jun's engagement with the text was made visible through his gaze fixed at the text and the movement of his pointing gesture as he read. Jun's mother also observed that Jun transformed his way of configuring the resources as he shifted his gaze from the text to the exhibit and repeated this action. That is, Jun made it visible to his mother through various actions that he was making a connection between the text and the exhibit.

Discussions and Conclusion

This study's attention to embodied actions employed to involve interlocutors in their sense-making is important because it demonstrates that reading signage text is not just a linguistic process, which extends Tannen's (2007) notion of involvement strategies. Tannen (2007: 26) argues that 'one cannot truly understand the meaning of a given utterance without having a broad grasp of conversational coherence: where utterance came from and where it is headed, how it fits into a recognizable schema in terms of the organization of the discourse and of the interaction'. In this sense, Jun and his mother's involving of each other in Jun's sense-making through the reading of the signage text is a linguistic process as Jun and his mother constantly textualized their knowledge and experience to be taken up by one another. However, without their embodied actions configured along with those linguistic practices, they would not be able to infer the meaning of each other's speech. Therefore, this study extends Tannen's idea of involvement by demonstrating how involvement is necessarily multimodal, especially children's meaning-making in science museums.

Paying attention to the nonlinguistic resources used to involve each other in their meaning-making is necessary to understand what learning opportunities were made for Jun. Bloome *et al.* (2009: 314) define a *learning opportunity* as 'a social event in which a person or people are positioned to adopt and adapt (take up) a set of social and cultural practices associated with academic domains.' As Jun's mother pointed at the signage text and asked him follow-up questions about the content, Jun mobilized the literacy practices used in school (e.g. finger-pointing while reading), utilizing it to take an expert's stance in relation to his mother, e.g. 'mom, you know why they floated? ... we all have gravity' (Interview with his mother, 10 January 2017). That is, as Jun and his mother involved each other in their meaning-making, they constantly created learning opportunities for Jun.

Although the text was not provided in the family's heritage language, reading signage text at exhibits helped Jun and his family not only to build their shared understanding of Jun's sense-making but also to cross boundaries (e.g. between English and Korean, between home and school; see also Ash, 2004). Jun drew upon his prior knowledge about gravity ('we all have gravity') from school, which gave his mother access to his school learning (Interview with his mother, 10 January 2017). Although it was not shown in this event, Jun's mother often translated signage text into Korean and came up with everyday expressions in Korean as an alternative to scientific jargon (e.g. 'fly away' or 'disappear' rather than 'evaporate'). In doing so, she aimed to expand Jun's ways of talking about science in Korean because she believed it would be helpful for Jun to talk about science with others in Korea (Interview with his mother, 10 January 2017).

In sum, this study sheds light on understanding EB families in multiple ways. EB families use their full communicative repertoires including named languages and multimodal resources (García & Li, 2014) to make sense of exhibits and to build meaning together. Given that both language and nonlinguistic resources are always used together, I suggest that future studies trace how EBs develop their communicative repertoires (Rymes, 2014), which emphasizes individuals' historically accumulated communicative resources and practices used in meaning-making, through family talk and interaction. As EB families are situated in their unique social and cultural contexts, it is important to investigate how they accommodate their needs as they make use of those communicative resources in their informal science learning.

Findings from this study provide insights for teachers and educators on how they can better support EBs in schools, which often aim to socialize EBs like Jun to be able to understand and use scientific discourses in English-medium instruction settings. As this study shows, Jun's family considered the museum as a space for learning the discourse in both languages, and their embodied actions played a key role in involving the interlocutors in their sense-making in both Korean and English. Paying attention to the family's embodied actions in meaning-making, teachers may imagine ways to create opportunities for learning content in English as well as developing their heritage language out of the meaning-making. This study calls for teachers to pay close attention to EBs' full communicative repertoires that go beyond their linguistic resources and include embodied practices and use of artifacts available in school-based practices. Also, one's communicative competence is often narrowly defined as individuals' linguistic proficiency, to be observed regardless of the contexts where communication occurs, and the resources being made available in other participants' actions. This study demonstrates that communication cannot be separated from its semiotic ecology in the context, complexly configured and reconfigured during meaning-making into which linguistic practices are embedded as a part. By taking the expanded notion of communicative competence, teachers may acknowledge ways in which EBs creatively tap into their linguistic and cultural backgrounds as resources and build their actions upon others' actions to communicate. This perspective will enable teachers to see their EBs as competent readers and to envision how their instructional conversations can allow EBs to draw on diverse resources or build on others' actions.

References

Ash, D. (2004) Reflective scientific sense-making dialogue in two languages: The science in the dialogue and the dialogue in the science. *Science Education* 88 (6), 855–884.

Bauer, E.B. and Gort, M. (2012) *Early Biliteracy Development: Exploring Young Learners' Use of Their Linguistic Resources*. Abingdon: Routledge.

Bloome, D., Beierle, M., Grigorenko, M. and Goldman, S. (2009) Learning over time: Uses of intercontextuality, collective memories and classroom chronotopes in the construction of learning opportunities in a ninth-grade language arts classroom. *Language and Education* 23 (4), 313–334.

Crowley, K., Callanan, M.A., Jipson, J., Galco, J., Topping, K. and Shrager, J. (2001) Shared scientific thinking in everyday parent-child activity. *Science Education* 85 (6), 712–732.

Dawson, E. (2014) 'Not designed for us': How science museums and science centers socially exclude low-income, minority ethnic groups. *Science Education* 98 (6), 981–1008.

Dierking, L.D. (1989) The family museum experience: Implications from research. *Journal of Museum Education* 14 (2), 9–11.

Durán, L. (2017) Audience and young bilingual writers: Building on strengths. *Journal of Literacy Research* 49 (1), 92–114.

Ellenbogen, K.M., Luke, J.J. and Dierking, L.D. (2003) Family learning research in museums: An emerging disciplinary matrix? *Science Education* 88 (1), 48–58.

García, O. and Li, W. (2014) *Translanguaging: Language, Bilingualism and Education*. New York: Palgrave Macmillan.

Gee, J. (2015) *Social Linguistics and Literacies: Ideology in Discourses*. New York: Routledge.

Goodwin, C. (2018) *Co-operative Action*. New York: Cambridge University Press.

Kwon, J. (2019) Parent–Child translanguaging among transnational immigrant families in museums. *International Journal of Bilingual Education and Bilingualism* 1–16. DOI: 10.1080/13670050.2019.1689918

de la Luz Reyes, M. (2001) Unleashing possibilities: Biliteracy in the primary grades. In M. de la Luz Reyes and J.J. Halcon (eds) *The Best for our Children: Critical Perspectives on Literacy for Latino Students* (pp. 96–121). New York: Teachers College Press.

Mondada, L. (2011) Understanding as an embodied, situated and sequential achievement in interaction. *Journal of Pragmatics* 43 (2), 542–552.

Mondada, L. (2014) The local constitution of multimodal resources for social interaction. *Journal of Pragmatics* 65, 137–156.

Rahm, J. (2004) Multiple modes of meaning-making in a science center. *Science Education* 88 (2), 223–247.

Rahm, J. and Ash, D. (2008) Learning environments at the margin: Case studies of disenfranchised youth doing science in an aquarium and an after-school program. *Learning Environments Research* 11 (1), 49–62.

Rowe, S. (2012) Scientific visualizations as discourse nexus. In S. Norris (ed.) *Multimodality in Practice: Investigating Theory-in-practice-through-methodology* (pp. 50–65). New York: Routledge.

Rowe, S. and Kisiel, J. (2012) Family engagement at aquarium touch tanks – Exploring interactions and the potential for learning. In E. Davidsson and A. Jakobsson (eds) *Understanding Interactions at Science Centers and Museums* (pp. 63–77). Boston, MA: Sense.

Rymes, B. (2014) *Communicating beyond Language: Everyday Encounters with Diversity*. New York: Routledge.

Street, B. (2006) Autonomous and ideological models of literacy: Approaches from new literacy studies. *Media Anthropology Network* 17, 1–15.

Tannen, D. (2007) *Talking Voices: Repetition, Dialogue and Imagery in Conversational Discourse*. New York: Cambridge University Press.

Weiland, I. (2015) An exploration of Hispanic mothers' culturally sustaining experiences at an informal science center. *Journal of Research in Science Teaching* 52 (1), 84–106.

Wortham, S. and Reyes, A. (2014) *Discourse Analysis beyond the Speech Event*. New York: Routledge.

23 New Directions

Sally Brown and Ling Hao

This volume expands our understandings of the complexities of literacy learning for young emergent bilinguals across the world. Each context offers unique insights into the challenges multilingual children face in both in- and out-of-school settings, especially when facing monolinguistic, monocultural and print-centric ideologies. Additionally, we hope that these chapters offer a sense of hope for pushing back against destructive policies and practices while deepening your understanding of new ways of thinking, seeing and valuing young emergent bilinguals.

How do we use the findings represented within these chapters to go in new directions in terms of research and classroom practices? First, we can broaden our definition of *text* so that it moves beyond linguistics and comprehensively involves a social semiotic perspective that values the everyday practices in the lives of people (Kress & van Leeuwen, 2001), thus becoming a place where 'multimodality is realized' (Stein, 2008: 11). Second, spend time closely reading the literature review in Chapter 1 which draws conclusions about the continued need for research in the area of multilingualism involving digital practices. Further areas for investigation are embedded within each of the chapters. We highlight some of these elements below.

For example, Wohlwend's Chapter 2 and her most recent work, *Literacies that Move and Matter* (Wohlwend, 2021), stretch modal categories to embodied and environmental modes. This perspective may be used to drive research in new directions where nonverbal forms of communication practices are intentionally used to open new spaces for meaning-making. New thinking about the environmental cues that classroom layouts and embodied expectations send to children as they engage in meaning-making activities are thought provoking. It may even be necessary to pay attention to modal density and intensity in determining participatory relationships arising from the interplay of modes. Choi's Chapter 22 showcases an application of embodied practices during museum visits. His work extends what we know about the role of actions within two languages – Korean and English – as well as the ways in which a family member supports the social processes around out-of-school outings. The uptake of scientific knowledge is facilitated by translanguaging practices and the use of gestures. This study guides future research into the role of material environments in communicative competence.

Overall, the chapters represent a wide range of learning contexts across the world, languages, and levels of English proficiency. Challenges can be intense for newcomers or children in the very beginning stages of learning a new language. A translanguaging pedagogy becomes even more critical. This is addressed in Chapter 21 where Hwang features two young boys beginning to learn Korean. She encourages us to push past linguistics and to use diverse modes as a way for newcomers to learn their new language. Given that there are limited studies examining newcomers' use of multimodal literacy practices, this is an area for future investigation.

We are also presented with evidence to rethink binary distinctions between two languages as presented in Chapters 3 and 5. Instead of seeing each language as a separate entity, a translanguaging perspective can help guide a deeper level of the rich complexities of the fluidity of languages (including dialects) and how they are enacted by young children. Additionally, translanguaging is not separate from multimodal literacies. Rather, translanguaging is multimodal and draws from all semiotic resources (García & Li, 2014). We can use this same framework to think differently about children's use of dialects, which include Black Language as in Chapters 4 and 16. Black Language is multifaceted and its use unfolds in dynamic, fluid ways, just like other languages. These authors push us forward in problematizing the exclusive use of White Mainstream English (WME) in classroom settings at all levels and the considering identity issues.

Several of the chapters critique a nonlinear view of text designing and instead encourage us to rethink our classroom composing routines. When applying multimodal composing practices in classrooms, one cannot expect students to mirror the traditional writing process where you begin by brainstorming and move to drafting, revising, editing and publishing. Instead, the multimodal process moves back and forth between various processes including a significant collaborative element. This means creating new spaces for learning where students are agentive designers. Further, choice is essential as we ponder new directions. Chapter 13 helps us understand the power of agency in the multimodal work of children – choices regarding seating, partnerships, drawing, writing, etc. and the implementation of authoring as a recursive process. The use of multimodal storytelling, as indicated in Chapters 12 and 18, helps us see the fluid and sometimes messy process for multilingual students. A reflective pedagogical stance (Cope & Kalantzis, 2015) has the potential to adapt instruction in the moment as the teacher reads student reactions to determine the next move. We must continue to ponder ways to best support various avenues for multimodal composing by our young emergent bilinguals.

We are continually reminded of the importance of the out-of-school literacies as rich resources for school-based literacies. Over several decades, the concept of funds of knowledge (González *et al.*, 2005) has helped many educators embrace and value home experiences and knowledge, as discussed in Chapter 11, to build bridges between school and home. The authors of Chapter 7 extend this concept in a unique way, to students' funds of perejivanie (experiences) (Megale & Liberali, 2020). This brings together traditional funds of knowledge with the concept of translanguaging. Value is placed on the woven nature of cognition and emotion within one's life experiences that may be materialized through language practices. Using this research framework has the potential to gain a deeper set of possibilities for constructing meaning.

The social practices surrounding digital literacy events are also worthy of a closer look. Several chapters show how digital drawings are an equally important composing component to written words and oral narratives. There are opportunities to apply translanguaging practices using digital venues as well as opportunities to build identities as authors or by performative accomplishments. The overlapping of the social aspects of digital work and the material aspects push us toward a sociomateriality framework as a way to better understand the role of affect in literacy practices.

Thinking not only about affect but also about the socioemotional lives of young emergent bilinguals brings forth new understandings about the challenges of spaces where English is forced upon students, and where their home experiences and cultures are not valued. A community of care and respect is needed for students to feel safe enough to develop socially and emotionally. Chapter 17 reminds us to use multimodal texts as a resource for the application of Theory of Mind (ToM) principles that afford students innovative opportunities for productive functioning within complexities of 21st-century global environments.

A clear case has also been made for the importance of listening in multimodal learning environments. Intentional listening to the voices of emergent bilingual children offers an avenue to cultivate mindful responses that are void of our own biases and ideologies. By listening and looking closely, it is possible to notice the use of imaginations and translanguaging in the remix of class content. This is a reflective process that continually requires rethinking our instructional practices and positioning of diverse students. Chapter 15 reminds us to listen to the voices of refugee children and their families, especially as school expectations revolve solely around linguistic practices as evidence of learning. More research is needed with our refugee populations as we look to support these children and families in their early learning experiences.

We would be remiss if we did not mention the role of technology and digital tools in the future of multimodality research and classroom practices. Whether emergent bilinguals are telling their own stories or retelling versions of children's literature, digital tools provide choices beyond the linguistic mode. Tablets and other digital devices provide numerous semiotic resources for meaning-making. The use of digital tools is closely interwoven with embodied practices where children move around the room while engaged in text designing. Chapter 14 introduces a STEERS model that uses sponsorship as a way to equalize technology capital (Selwyn, 2013), which is a critical consideration when using technology in the classroom with children in order to ensure equity for children with fewer opportunities for technological experiences.

After reporting on the multimodal literacies of Chinese-Norwegian (trilingual) children and families, Chapter 19 presents us with a better understanding of their usage, preferences and supports. This provides a foundation for future research in this area. For example, the results may inform ways to work with children and families when school is conducted in hybrid and/or virtual environments. There is also an opportunity to examine these factors across other language groups and in other contexts, especially when blending the perspectives of family members and children.

All of these aspects of teaching and learning taken together inform identity work. The languages used, the resources presented, and the planning of rich learning opportunities impact the identities that students construct for themselves or that are constructed for them. We must be particularly respectful of the ways in which learning environments position emergent bilinguals. Without paying attention, students may devalue their own languages and cultures while seeing themselves as incapable of academic work. The chapters in this book highlight the importance of building positive identities for and with emergent bilinguals and making moves to keep them from being marginalized by the English-only, monolingual, print-centric practices common in many classrooms around the world. Multimodal learning options provide opportunities for more comprehensive representations of knowledge and identities.

Change is not possible without the actions of informed educators who are willing to enact some of the practices presented in this volume. The ideas, concepts and activities are based in research and showcase not only ways to change one's mindset when working with young emergent bilinguals, but also subtle changes to the curriculum and learning spaces that allow all children to thrive. Multimodal literacy learning opportunities need to be facilitated with an open mind and a free acknowledgment of the assets of young learners, which means spending time getting to know students, their families, languages, cultures and other experiential assets they bring to the literacy events.

There is still a need to continue to push for changes in the early childhood curriculum that embrace play, leverage authentic language interactions and see multimodality as a foundational aspect of learning in real, lived experiences. Country, state and school policies drive instructional mandates. This requires advocacy from all of us. In order to change politically driven educational decisions, there must be a collaborative effort – university faculty, educators, parents and students. We must move beyond monolithic and monolingual ideologies if equality is the goal.

References

Cope, B. and Kalantzis, M. (2015) The thing you do to know. An introduction to the pedagogy of multiliteracies. In B. Cope and M. Kalantzis (eds) *A Pedagogy of Multiliteracies: Learning by Design* (pp. 1–36). New York: Macmillan.

García, O. and Li, W. (2014) *Translanguaging: Language, Bilingualism and Education*. New York: Palgrave McMillan.

González, N., Moll, L. and Amanti, C. (2005) Introduction: Theorizing practices. In N. González, L. Moll and C. Amanti (eds) *Funds of Knowledge: Theorizing Practices in Households, Communities and Classrooms* (pp. 1–24). Mahwah, NJ: Lawrence Erlbaum.

Kress, G. and van Leeuwen, T. (2001) *Multimodal Discourse: The Modes and Media of Contemporary Communication*. New York: Oxford University Press.

Megale, A.H. and Liberali, F.C. (2020) Implications of the concept of funds of perejivanie as an alternative for multilingual education. *Revista X* 15 (1), 55–74.

Selwyn, N. (2013) *Distrusting Educational Technology: Critical Questions for Changing Times*. New York: Routledge.

Stein, P. (2008) *Multimodal Pedagogies in Diverse Classrooms: Representation, Rights, and Resources*. New York: Routledge.

Wohlwend, K. (2021) *Literacies that Move and Matter: Nexus Analysis for Contemporary Childhoods*. New York: Routledge.

Index

Ingram Content Group UK Ltd.
Milton Keynes UK
UKHW022007100423
419677UK00021B/446

9 781800 412347